Software
Validation,
Verification,
Testing
and
Documentation

Software
Validation
Verification
Testing
and
Documentation

EDITED BY
STEPHEN J. ANDRIOLE

PETROCELLI BOOKS
Princeton, New Jersey

Composition by Eastern Graphics

Library of Congress Cataloging-in-Publication Data
Main entry under title:

The Sourcebook of Software validation, verification, testing, and documentation.
    "Edited from a number of government reports
produced by the U.S. Department of Commerce's National
Bureau of Standards (NBS)."
    Bibliography: p.
    Includes index.
    1.Computer software—Validation. 2. Computer
software—Verification. 3. Computer software—
Testing. 4. Electronic data processing documentation.
I. Andriole, Stephen J.
QA76.76.V47S68   1985   005.1′4   85-29750
ISBN 0-89433-269-4

Contents

Book Three
Software Testing

Book Four
Software Validation, Verification and Testing Technique and Tool Reference Guide

Book Five
Management Guide to Software Documentation

Book Six
Computer Model Documentation Guides

Editor's Introduction

This **Sourcebook on Software Validation, Verification, Testing, and Documentation** was edited from a number of government reports produced by the U.S. Department of Commerce's National Bureau of Standards (NBS). In its continuing march toward the identification and refinement of computing standards, NBS recently turned its attention to this important area. In fact, in the minds of many of those connected with information processing and computer-based problem-solving of all kinds, the areas of software validation, verification, testing, and documentation are an extremely neglected group, especially given their importance to successful computing.

There are a variety of reasons why neglect has been the rule rather than the exception. Software validation, verification, testing, and—perhaps especially— documentation are inherently unexciting, tedious, and usually expensive. Though this is not to suggest that the activities are not cost-effective; to the contrary, investments in software validation, verification, testing, and documentation tend to yield many applied dividends. The activities are also neglected because of where they typically occur in the interactive systems design and development process. Frequently, a great deal of project resources are spent long before software is developed to the stage where it can be meaningfully validated or tested. Documentation is even a poorer relation, often receiving only the crumbs of project resources.

The five books of this volume deal with these activities in sequence and in detail. The first book, **Planning for Software Validation, Verification, and Testing,** was edited by Patricia B. Powell of the Center for Programming Science and Technology, Institute for Computer Sciences and Technology, NBS. She begins with a look at the overall software development process and the role of software validation, verification, and testing in that process. She then develops a framework for integrated validation, verification, and testing followed by a discussion of how to plan software evaluation. Of particular interest is the section that contains a number of examples about how to apply several manual and automated verification, validation, and testing techniques. These examples suggest a number of ways one can evaluate software using a set of manual, partially automated, and fully automated

Software Validation, Verification, Testing, and Documentation

tools. This section concludes with a discussion of software maintenance, a valuable subject within the context of evaluation.

Book Two of this Sourcebook was written by W. Richards Adrion, Martha A. Branstad, and John C. Cheriavsky and deals with software validation, verification, and testing at a much more specific level. Instead of concentrating on planning and project management, Adrion, Branstad, and Cheriavsky focus on the role that software verification and evaluation should play in the software engineering process. Verification involves making sure that the algorithms do what they are supposed to do. Desk-checking, peer review, walk throughs and simulation are suggested by Adrion, Branstad, and Cheriavsky as "general verification techniques." Desk-checking ideally involves inviting a programmer who has not been part of the software development process to check the code for its integrity vis a vis known requirements. Peer review repeats the process with a panel of programmers, while walk throughs work backwards from test data generated from the software then used to determine (by a panel) if the software is doing what it is supposed to do. Simulations can be used to determine software integrity vis a vis a simulated model of ideal performance.

Adrion, Branstad, and Cheriavsky also discuss some functional verification techniques, including error guessing, cause-effect graphing, and design-based verification. Error guessing involves exploiting the intuitive talents of certain individuals. Cause-effect graphing requires one to analyze the effect of specific program inputs that are categorized according to common properties. This categorization permits the analysis of a limited but diagnostic number of (causal) input and (effectual) output types. Design-based verification involves the use of test data generated via a detailed functional analysis. The static analysis verification techniques—implemented without executing the computer program—described by Adrion, Branstad, and Cheriavsky include flow analysis and symbolic execution. Flow analysis involves the use of a flow diagram of the computer program to "analyze the program behavior, to locate instrumentation breakpoints, to identify paths, and other static analysis activities." It also facilitates the pinpointing of inconsistencies and anomolies. Symbolic execution involves developing symbolic expressions for the various paths in the computer program and then checking the expressions against the program and one another.

Some of these verification procedures are manual and some have been automated. Book Two looks at a variety of these techniques and describes them in some detail.

Book Three of this Sourcebook deals with structured testing using a specific methodology. Written by Thomas J. McCabe of McCabe and Associates, Inc., Book Three is entitled, **Structured Testing: A Software Testing Methodology Using the Cyclomatic Complexity Metric.** This book discusses a number of applications of a structured software testing methodology that enables one to avoid programs that are inherently untestable by first measuring and limiting program complexity. The first part of this book defines and develops a program complexity measure. The second part discusses the complexity measure, while the third illustrates how to apply the techniques.

The heart of Book Three lies with the development of the complexity measure itself. Using graph theory, McCabe derives a program complexity measure which contains a number of mathematical theorems and notations. This discussion, while complicated, sets up the following discussions about how to apply the technique to the programming process. More specifically, the last part deals with how to design, code, and implement a test with implications for software maintenance. Book Three concludes with a look at some of the empirical evidence that exists to support the use of McCabe's structured testing methodology.

Book Four, edited by Patricia B. Powell, describes thirty techniques and tools for software validation, verification, and testing. Each description includes the basic features of the technique or tool, the input, the output, an example, and assessment of the effectiveness and usability of the tool or technique, applicability, an estimate of the learning time and training required for tool use, and an estimate of the resources needed to implement the tool or technique. There are also references for each of the thirty techniques and tools. Obviously Book Four is extremely valuable, representing a great deal of research and analysis. In fact, it represents one of the very few surveys of existing software validation, verification, and testing tools and techniques, and is therefore of enormous value to someone who is currently searching for a tool or technique that might help them evaluate existing or newly developing software.

The fifth and final book in this volume deals with software documentation. In the world of interactive computers, it would be difficult to find a more controversial subject. Documentation is frequently done poorly or not at all. Like software validation, verification, and testing, it is expensive and time-comsuming. It is also far from glamourous, and many of those connected with the design and development of interactive software systems would much rather play with hardware than attend to sticky documentation issues. Nevertheless, research suggests conclusively that good documentation can catapult a system into routine use while the lack of documentation can relegate a system to obscurity. The discussions of documentation presented include one by Albrecht J. Neumann and one by the Federal Computer Performance Evaluation and Simulation Center. The first discussion by Neumann constitutes a **Management Guide for Software Documentation.** In this guide, Neumann discusses a variety of topics relevant to all aspects of documentation, including alternative definitions of documentation, the problems connected with the development of documentation and their causes, some solutions to the most common documentation problems, and the resources necessary for the successful development of documentation.

The second discussion of documentation by the Federal Computer Performance Evaluation Simulation Center deals with documentation from a much more specific perspective. The report itself on which the second half of Book Five is based was originally prepared for the U.S. Air Force in support of its software ac-

Software Validation, Verification, Testing, and Documentation

quisition activities. The version reprinted here is a more generic one and is therefore relevant to all kinds of software documentation problems. It is included in this sourcebook because documentation is a natural outgrowth of successful software validation, verification, and testing. In fact, one could easily argue that documentation should not be undertaken until a thorough software evaluation has been conducted. The specific sections of this discussion include guidelines for preparing a management summary manual, guidelines for preparing a user's manual, guidelines for preparing a programmer's manual, and guidelines for preparing an analyst's manual.

Both documentation discussions in Book Five are targeted at the development of three dimensional documentation packages consisting of accurate functional descriptions, diagnostic sytems specifications, and genuinely useful user manuals.

All of the reports published in this Sourcebook should help you design and develop software likely to be more responsive to your requirements. This Sourcebook is an extremely practical one, oriented toward the development of systems that are easy to use, maintain, and distribute. The excellent research and analysis published here but originally conducted under the auspices of the National Bureau of Standards we hope will result in a much wider distribution of the work than would otherwise be the case if distribution was limited to only NBS publications. Our experience has suggested that many truly extraordinary government publications never see the light of day because of very narrow distribution practices; the commercial publication of these NBS reports we hope will stimulate a discussion and debate about the problems presented by the need for software evaluation and documentation.

Stephen J. Andriole

Book One
Planning for Software Validation, Verification, and Testing

Abstract

Today, providing computer software involves greater cost and risk than providing computer equipment. One major reason is hardware is mass-produced by proven technology, while software is still produced primarily by the craft of individual computer programmers. The document is for those who direct and those who implement computer projects; it explains the selection and use of validation, verification, and testing (V,V&T) tools and techniques for software development. A primary benefit of practicing V,V&T is increasing confidence in the quality of the software. The document explains how to develop a plan to meet specific software V,V&T goals.

Key words: automated software tools; software lifecycle; software testing; software verification; test coverage; test data generation; validation; institute for computer science technology (ICST); and automatic data processing (ADP); validation, verification, & testing (V,V&T).

1. Introduction

The Institute for Computer Sciences and Technology (ICST) carries out the following responsibilities under P.L. 89-306 (Brooks Act) to improve the Federal Government's management and use of ADP:

- Develops Federal automatic data processing standards;
- Provides agencies with scientific and technological advisory services relating to ADP; and
- Undertakes necessary research in computer sciences and technology.

In partial fulfillment of Brooks Act responsibilities, ICST issues Special Publications (S.P.). This document describes an approach to validation, verification, and testing of computer software that pervades the entire development and maintenance process. The document consists of four additional chapters which can be grouped into two sections, described below.

Software development is an exercise in problem solving. The solution is embodied in the final product, the computer software. This product consists of the programs (computer instructions) and the manuals describing the software and its use. Executing the program with data on a computer provides the solution. During the development of the target software, there are several intermediate products produced by the project requestor and the developers. The methodology to enhance the overall correctness of the final product by working with the intermediate products is the subject of this document.

In problem solving, a key activity is to determine that the solution is correct. Validation, Verification, and Testing (V,V&T) is a process composed of the set of procedures, activities, techniques and tools used to ensure that a software product does solve the intended problem.

The chapters in Book One are grouped into two principal sections: V,V&T Background, and V,V&T Planning Guide.

V,V&T Background consists of two chapters. Chapter 2 describes a phased approach to software development and the fundamental concepts of V,V&T. Chapter 3 describes three classes of V,V&T techniques and tools, and a scheme for integrating them.

3

Software Validation, Verification, Testing, and Documentation

V,V&T Planning Guide consists of two chapters. Chapter 4 explains how the goals for V,V&T can be identified and how to develop a project V,V&T plan. Chapter 5 discusses the application of V,V&T principles through examples.

Audience

Book One is directed toward those (managers, customers, etc.) who influence *how* software development is done and to those (programmers, analysts, etc.) who *do* development. It assists a project manager working with the customer in establishing V,V&T goals. It further assists project managers in developing a plan for achieving the goals. Finally it guides in the judicious selection of the appropriate set of V,V&T practices, techniques, and tools.

To the software engineer who is responsible for performing the various V,V&T functions, Book One, in conjunction with the rest of this volume provides guidance to the actual use of the selected techniques and tools. For each technique or tool there is information including functions, inputs, outputs, resources required for use, and sources for more detailed information. In addition to aiding in the application of individual techniques and tools, information on their integrated use is presented.

Book One is also a resource to another group within the ADP environment in that it addresses certain needs of the ADP policy maker. It presents certain fundamental concepts, elements of a general V,V&T approach, and many of the specifics necessary to implement the approach. It provides information that may be helpful in forming a basis for policies relating to V,V&T practice. It also contains information relevant to the formulation and implementation of the software V,V&T functions in a typical ADP environment.

Philosophy

This section provides assistance in all aspects of V,V&T. It is not a total "project cookbook," wherein all the techniques and tools must be used on every project. Projects vary in size, scope, complexity, and other characteristics that influence the specific V,V&T approach. Each project must be evaluated to determine how V,V&T might be applied.

	V,V&T BACKGROUND	V,V&T PLANNING GUIDE	
Chapters		4	5
	− POLICY MAKER −	− − − − PLANNER − − − −	
		− − − − SELECTOR − − − −	

Figure 1.1.1
Reading Scenarios

Introduction

The use of V,V&T does not, of itself, guarantee success. It requires judge-ment, training, and experience. Like other methodologies, the application of V,V&T may be good or bad; but, it should never be blind.

User of this Material

For the reader who is encountering this material for the first time, reading Chapters 1 through 3 is recommended. Reading of subsequent chapters should be guided by intended use of the information. Suggested reading scenarios for three types of read-ers are presented in Figure 1.1.

2. An Overview of Software Development

Systematic approaches to problem solving, including software development, proceed through a sequence of steps or phases with probable looping back to previous phases. This type of approach yields several important benefits.

First, because the problem solving process is subdivided into separate phases, the problem solver is eased into a gradual process. The problem solver is able to approach separately the problem, the solution, and its implementation. The problem solver need not deliberate on all three at once. This allows larger, more complex problems to be resolved successfully.

Second, a phased process provides intermediate monitoring and control points. The existence of phases and intermediate products increases the visibility of the process. This encourages the involvement of the group for whom the problem is being solved and increases their control of the problem solving.

Third, the existence of a series of intermediate specifications, i.e. requirements, design, and code, of the solution facilitates early and continual evaluation of the solution as it moves toward implementation. In software development this process of continual review and evaluation is validation, verification, and testing (V,V&T).

This chapter discusses software development as a problem solving activity. It introduces the concepts of software V,V&T and a phased approach to software development. Specifically, it describes:

Software Validation, Verification, and Testing: Evaluation and Review Throughout the Problem Solving Process—The process of obtaining increasing levels of confidence in a solution through a series of checkpoints and reviews is discussed as it applies to software development and the analogies previously presented.

A Problem Solving Model for Software Development—A specific series of problem solving phases for software development is described, including the V,V&T activities associated with each.

Software Validation, Verification, and Testing:
Evaluation and Review Throughout the Problem Solving Process

Validation, Verification, and Testing (V,V&T), in general terms, is a process of review, analysis, and testing employed throughout the software development lifecycle. It is a methodology which helps ensure the production of quality software. *Validation* determines the correctness of the end product, e.g. code, with respect to the software requirements, i.e. does the output conform with what was required? *Verification* is performed at each phase and between each phase of the development lifecycle. It determines that each phase and subphase product is correct, complete, and consistent with itself and with its predecessor product. *Testing,* either automated or manual, examines program behavior by executing the program on sample data sets, e.g. passing data, automatically or manually, through a design to determine the correctness of the program is testing the design.

V,V&T is commonly used as a single expression; this is not to infer that the methodology is an all or nothing process. Project constraints, such as criticality, error tolerance or budget, should determine how much validation, verification, or testing is applied to that project. This document uses the general term V,V&T, referring to the total methodology; it is understood that the reader will extract those portions of V,V&T which are feasible and applicable to the specific situation. V,V&T may be performed by an independent V,V&T group (IV&V), by the person(s) producing the product or a combination of both. Again, the decision as to who performs the V,V&T is project dependent. The objective of V,V&T is to ensure the correctness, completeness, and consistency of the final product.

Software V,V&T focuses on the prevention and the detection of errors, i.e. deviation from intent. This is accomplished through the use of both manual and automated techniques. Errors include deficiencies such as unsatisfied requirements, or, the converse, the inclusion of extraneous functions. An error may be in the coding of the software, a specification of the software, (e.g., a design specification) or the documentation (e.g., a user's manual). The error might be related to the functional correctness or another property, such as performance, or a more subjective attribute such as product form.

To describe the role of V,V&T in error detection and prevention, three categories of V,V&T activities are described. These are illustrated in Figure 2.1.1.

The objective of integrity checking, the first category of V,V&T activities, is to verify the integrity of the products at each phase of development. Each product is analyzed for internal consistency and completeness. For example, a requirements specification can be analyzed to detect inconsistent or contradictory requirements such as the specification of an output report that requires data which is unavailable.

The objective of evolution checking, the second category, is to ensure the completeness and consistency between levels of specification, where the second is a refinement or elaboration of the first.

The objective of appropriateness/sufficiency checking, the third category, is to

7

Software Validation, Verification, Testing, and Documentation

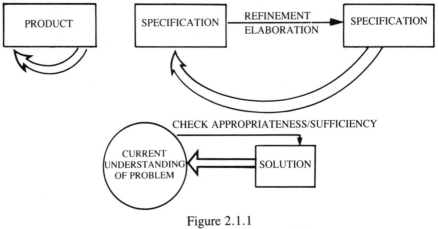

Figure 2.1.1
Three Categories of V,V&T Activities

compare this evolving solution against the problem as currently understood to ensure that it is a necessary and sufficient solution.

A Problem Solving Model for Software Development

The following discussion describes each phase/subphase by presenting the nature and purpose of each, the products produced, and the V,V&T activities which incrementally build confidence in the software product as it evolves. Figure 2.2.1 summarizes the V,V&T activities.

Initiation Phase

Description. The initiation phase begins with the recognition of a problem and concludes with a decision of whether or not to implement a software solution. The recognition of a problem may be sudden or gradual; the problem may be generally recognized or only perceived by a small group. The main activity of the initiation phase is a joint exploration of the problem by the group having the problem and the group responsible for solving it. The decision to pursue a solution must be based upon a clear understanding of the problem, a preliminary investigation of alternative solutions, and a comparison of the expected benefits versus the cost (design, construction and operation) of the solution.

Products. The primary result is a decision about the continuation of the project. To support this decision, there are often three products. These are:

8

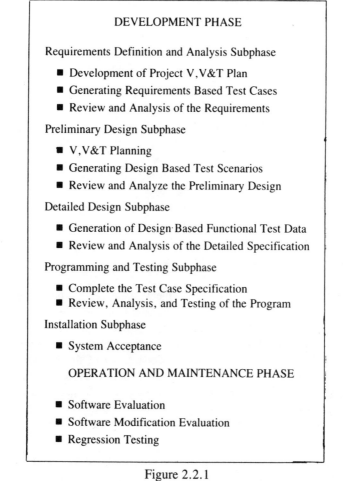

DEVELOPMENT PHASE

Requirements Definition and Analysis Subphase

- Development of Project V,V&T Plan
- Generating Requirements Based Test Cases
- Review and Analysis of the Requirements

Preliminary Design Subphase

- V,V&T Planning
- Generating Design Based Test Scenarios
- Review and Analyze the Preliminary Design

Detailed Design Subphase

- Generation of Design Based Functional Test Data
- Review and Analysis of the Detailed Specification

Programming and Testing Subphase

- Complete the Test Case Specification
- Review, Analysis, and Testing of the Program

Installation Subphase

- System Acceptance

OPERATION AND MAINTENANCE PHASE

- Software Evaluation
- Software Modification Evaluation
- Regression Testing

Figure 2.2.1
Summary of V,V&T Activities

The project request or proposal: defines the problem to be solved and the scope and objectives of the proposed solution.

The feasibility study: states the assumptions being made, defines alternative solutions and assesses technical and operational feasibility.

The cost/benefit analysis: estimates and compares the costs (construction and operation) and the expected benefits (both quantifiable and intangible).

V,V&T Activities. The three products are reviewed by the problem posers, the problem solvers, and the decision makers (e.g., higher level management in control of required resources). The following questions are generally answered in this review.

Has the scope, cost, impact, and urgency of the problem been adequately defined?

Has a technically feasible and operationally viable solution been identified?

Have alternative solutions been identified?

Have alternatives been adequately studied?

Have the costs of the solutions been analyzed and compared against the expected benefits? What are the probabilities of achieving these benefits? What are the risks involved?

Development Phase

As an example, this phase is divided into five subphases for the purpose of illustration. These are each separately described.

Requirements Definition and Analysis Subphase

Description. The goal of the requirements subphase is to put the problem into a rigorous form upon which a solution can be based i.e., a statement of the requirements which a software solution must satisfy. Requirements identification is iterative, involving the problem posers and the problem solvers. Requirements may be modified in later subphases as a better understanding of the problem is gained. These modifications are documented, creating a traceable record of the progress and evolution of the final product. Also during this subphase, two planning activities are performed. First, project plans, budgets, and schedules for the development phase and each subphase are developed. In addition, the V,V&T goals are identified and a plan for achieving these goals is developed.

Products. This subphase results in the preparation of four products. The first three are completed, while the fourth is finished during subsequent phases.

The software requirements document: Specifies what the system must do. This includes the requisite information flows and processing functions. Acceptance criteria for deciding that the requirements are satisfied as specified is an important part of this product.

The project plan: Specifies a strategy for managing the software development. It defines the goals and activities for all phases and subphases. It includes: resource estimates over time and intermediate milestones including management and technical reviews. It defines methods for design, documentation, problem reporting, and change control. It also specifies supporting techniques and tools.

The Validation, Verification, and Testing Plan: Specifies goals of the V,V&T activities including software testing. It is the design of a project specific

V,V&T process and identifies techniques and tools to assist in achieving the goals. It specifies plans (schedules, budgets, responsibilities, etc.) for performing the V,V&T activities.

The Software Test Case Specification: Describes the scenarios and cases for testing each requirement. The acceptance criteria are used to develop test cases. Expected results for each test case are included.

V,V&T Activities. There are three basic thrusts to these activities. These are: Development of the Project V,V&T Plan: Goals for V,V&T activities are determined; a V,V&T process is designed; techniques and tools are chosen, schedules and budgets are established.

Generating Requirements Based Test Cases: These form a basic set of test cases. They help clarify and determine the measurability of the software requirements and form a basis for acceptance testing.

Review and Analysis of the Requirements: The goal is to ensure that the requirements identified will result in a feasible and a usable solution to the entire problem. They are reviewed for clarity, completeness, correctness, consistency, testability, and traceability to the problem statement.

Preliminary Design Subphase

Description. During preliminary design, the problem solvers (the software developers) assisted by the problem posers (the customer/user) formulate and analyze alternative solutions. This may reveal flaws in the requirements and result in its modification. This iteration continues until all issues have been resolved.

This subphase results in a high level specification of the solution. The solution is conceptual in nature, defining information aggregates, information flows, and logical processing steps. It will describe all the major interfaces, and their inputs and outputs. Implementation details, e.g., actual programs and physical data structures are generally not addressed.

Project plans (schedules, budgets, deliverables, etc.) are reviewed and revised as appropriate for the scope and complexity of the solution formulated.

Products. There is one new product of this subphase—the preliminary design specification. In addition, each of the four products of the requirements subphase may undergo revision or be supplemented with new data.

The Preliminary Design Specification: Documents the high level solution developed during this phase. This may be packaged in two separate documents, i.e., a system/subsystem specification and a data/database specification.

A Revised Requirements Specification: Design activities may reveal inconsistent, infeasible, or ambiguous requirements and result in the revision of their specification.

An Updated Project Plan: Upon the completion of the preliminary design, the scope and complexity of the solution are well understood. As a result, the project plan (schedules, budgets, deliverables, etc.) is made more accurate and realistic.

An Updated V,V&T Plan: This plan may warrant revision based upon new or revised requirements.

Software Test Case Specification: Additional test scenarios and test cases are developed to exercise and test aspects of the design.

V,V&T Activities There are three areas of V,V&T activity:

V,V&T Planning: The V,V&T plan is reviewed and revised as deemed necessary.

Generating Design Based Test Scenarios: Complementing and expanding the requirements based test data generated focusing on the logical functions performed.

Review and Analyze the Preliminary Design: To assure internal consistency, completeness, correctness and clarity; to verify that the design is linked to and, when implemented, will satisfy the requirements.

Detailed Design Subphase

Description. The purpose of this subphase is to refine, resolve deficiencies, define additional details, and package the logical solution created in the previous subphase. Implementation details are addressed. Ambiguities are removed from the design specification. The detailed design specification describes the physical solution (algorithms and data structures) which is an elaboration of the logical solution specified in the preliminary design. The result is a solution specification that can be implemented in code with little or no need for additional analysis.

The detailed design team may discover processing operations that are impractical or impossible to implement, necessitating modification of the preliminary design and possibly the requirements as well.

The user and participants in the review are consulted in making major design decisions.

Products. There are two new products of this subphase and additional information added to an existing one:

The Detailed Design Specification: A fully detailed description of the software (algorithms and data) to be coded in the following subphase.

Software Test Case Specification: This is now a substantially complete description of test data and the expected results.

Problem Reports: Formal statements of observed problems. This may necessitate going back to a previous subphase.

V,V&T Activities. The two V,V&T activities of this phase are:
Generation of Design Based Functional Test Data: Formulated test data based on the physical structure of the system.

Review and Analysis of the Detailed Specification: To assure internal consistency, completeness, correctness, and clarity; to verify that the detailed design is linked to and is a correct refinement of the preliminary design; to validate that the design when implemented will satisfy the requirements.

Programming and Testing Subphase

Description. This subphase results in a program which is ready for installation. Programming is the process of implementing the detailed design specification into code. Only minor, if any, design issues are resolved during this subphase.

Completed code undergoes testing as described in the V,V&T plan. Generally, three types of testing are performed: unit, integration, and system. While unit testing is done by the programmer, the person(s) responsible for integration and system testing is project specific.

Unit testing checks for typographical, syntax, and logic errors. Each of the modules of code are checked individually by the programmers who wrote them to ensure that each correctly implements its design and satisfies the specified requirements.

Integration testing focuses on checking the intermodule communication links, and testing aggregate functions formed by groups of modules.

System testing examines the operation of the system as an entity. This type of testing ensures that the software requirements have been satisfied both singly and in combination.

The final activity of this subphase is planning the installation of the software.

Products. There are six new outputs produced during this subphase and one other which is completed.

Software Test Case Specification: Final revisions and additions to the test data are made.

Program Code: Fully documented and tested code, which is ready for installation.

Test Results and Test Evaluation Reports: The documentation of the comparison of actual and expected results.

User Documentation: Manuals describing the input and report formats, user commands, error messages, and instructions for operation by the user.

Maintenance Manual: Documentation to maintain the system.

Installation Plan: Specifies the approach to and details of the installation of the software.

Software Validation, Verification, Testing, and Documentation

Problem Reports: Formal statements of observed problems. This may necessitate going back to a previous subphase.

V,V&T Activities. The V,V&T activity of this phase focuses upon the program produced.

Complete the Test Case Specification: Final additions and modifications necessary due to design changes made during coding.

Review, analysis and testing of the program: Includes checking for adherence to coding standards, manual/automated analysis of the program, and the execution of the program on test data ensuring that it meets the acceptance criteria.

Installation Subphase

Description. The result of this subphase is a system incorporating the developed programs, other software components, the hardware, and production data. The activities of the subphase are guided by the installation plan developed. The first task is to integrate the system components. Integration consists of installing hardware, installing the program(s) onto the computer, reformatting/creating the data base(s), and verifying that all components have been included. Modification to program code may be necessary to obtain compatibility between hardware and software, or between different software modules.

The next task is to test the system. The test data from earlier subphases is enhanced and used here. The result is a system qualified and accepted for production use.

The third task is the start of system operation. The strategies for this include immediate cutover, phased cutovers, or parallel operation. This task also includes operator and user training.

Products. The new product of this subphase is the Installation Report, but previously completed products may be updated to incorporate findings of the installation activity.

Installation Report: Describes the results of the installation activities, including data conversion, installation testing/results, and software/system problems and modifications necessary.

V,V&T Activities. The primary V,V&T activity centers on acceptance of the system by the customer. This could be a simple statement signed by a customer representative. This marks the end of the development phase.

Operation and Maintenance Phase

Description. The final phase involves the actual use of the software and monitoring its operation to ensure that it succeeds in solving the user's problem.

Most often, some need for modifying the software arises during this phase.

An Overview of Software Development

The maintenance process involves determining the reason for each modification. The cause could be an error made in the original development, the recognition of a new requirement, or the desire for a design modification to improve performance, usability, etc. Once the cause is determined, the software (code and documentation) is 'redeveloped' from that point. For example, the redevelopment due to a change in requirements will result in modifications to the requirements specification, the design, the code, and user and operation manuals.

Problem reporting, change requests, and other change control mechanisms are used to facilitate the systematic correction and evolution of the software. In addition, performance measurement and evaluation activities are performed to ensure that the system continues to meet its requirements in the context of a changing system environment.

Products. To track and manage the evolution of the software in this post development phase, several new outputs are produced:

Problem reports: Formal statements of observed problems. The analyses of these may result in software change requests.

Change requests: Requests for specific modification to the software. These could be generated due to an error (i.e., problem report) or a modification of the requirements or design.

Revision to initial development products: As a result of change requests any one or all of the products of the initiation and development phases may require revision.

V,V&T Activities. The V,V&T activities of this phase can be separated into two categories: the monitoring and evaluation of the system, and the problem correction activities. The first is an on-going activity. The second is driven by the problem reports and change requests.

Software evaluation: Activities aimed at assessing the operation of the software and assuring continued satisfaction of user requirements.

Software modification evaluation: As needs for change are discovered and requests for modifications are made, the requested modifications are evaluated in the same manner as the original software is evaluated. After modifications are made, the changes are reviewed and tested to ensure that the expected changes in the software is achieved.

Regression testing: Rerunning test cases which a program has previously executed correctly in order to detect errors created during software correction/modification activities.

3. A Framework for Integrated Validation, Verification, and Testing

To do effective V,V&T, the development team needs to select a well-matched, compatible set of techniques and tools. The selection is based on the V,V&T goals of the project. These goals take into account the characteristics of problems and the constraints on the solution. From the user's perspective, the techniques and tools must ensure functional, efficient, reliable and low maintenance software. The developer is concerned with these issues as well as the integrity and composition of the software. This blend of concerns is the guiding force in selecting V,V&T techniques and tools. This chapter presents information which assists in the selection of a complementary set of techniques and tools and their application throughout development. Specifically, it will discuss the following:

Types of analyses that are performed—description of static, dynamic, and formal analyses,

An integrated approach to performing V,V&T—combining the three types of analysis in a complementary fashion to achieve a V,V&T technology, and

Application of the V,V&T approach—the use of the three types of analysis in applying V,V&T to requirements, design, and code.

Static Analysis

The static analysis detects errors through examination of the product, Figure 3.1.1. Some examples of the errors detected are: language syntax errors, misspellings, incorrect punctuation, improper sequencing of statements, and missing specification elements. Static analysis techniques may be manually or automatically applied, however, automated techniques require a machine readable product.

Manual static analysis techniques may be applied to all development products, e.g., requirements statement, program code, or a users manual. In general, they are straightforward and, when applied with discipline, are effective in preventing and detecting errors.

The application of certain manual techniques, such as desk checking, inspection, and walkthroughs, provide certain advantages over the use of specialized auto-

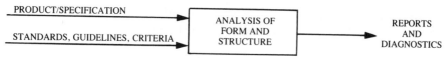

PRODUCT/SPECIFICATION

STANDARDS, GUIDELINES, CRITERIA

ANALYSIS OF
FORM AND
STRUCTURE

REPORTS
AND
DIAGNOSTICS

Figure 3.1.1
General Form of Static Analysis

mated techniques. One advantage is that different perspectives can be addressed simultaneously. A product may be examined for high level as well as detailed properties. Another advantage is that manual analysis provides an opportunity for the analyst to apply various heuristics, i.e. aids to discover errors, and subjective judgments. A general weakness of the manual techniques is that correct usage often involves tedious and repetitious activities. As the size of the application increases, the tendency is to compromise on the thorough application of the technique which results in an increasing chance of error.

Automated static analysis tools most often operate on program source code but can operate on requirements and design. Two kinds of static analyzers can be identified. The first gathers and reports information about a program. These kinds of analyzers generally do not search for any particular type of error in a program. A symbol cross reference generator is an example of this type.

The second kind of analyzer detects specific classes of errors or anomalies in a program. Examples of this type include: (1) parsers which determine the adherence of a program to the language syntax; they may include additional local programming conventions/standards such as program length; (2) techniques for analyzing the consistency of actual and formal parameter interfaces (see Figure 3.1.2); (3) techniques for comparing all variable references with their declarations to check for consistency; and (4) techniques for analyzing a program for erroneous sequences of events or operations, for example, attempting to read from a file before it is opened.

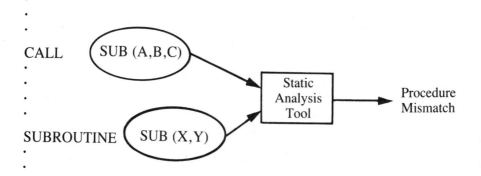

CALL SUB (A,B,C)

SUBROUTINE SUB (X,Y)

Static
Analysis
Tool

Procedure
Mismatch

Figure 3.1.2
Module Interface Consistency Checks

17

A much more detailed description of many specific techniques and tools can be found in the Technique and Tool Reference Guide[POWE].

Dynamic Analysis

Dynamic analysis is the process of detecting errors through the study of the response of a program to a set of input data. It is usually accomplished through an automated simulation or the execution of a program, but may be manually performed, e.g., a walkthrough. Dynamic analysis (see Figure 3.2.1). is the processes of:

preparing for test execution,

test execution, and

analysis of test results.

Preparing for test execution includes test data preparation and formulation of expected results.

Test data preparation involves the formulation of test scenarios, test cases and the data which are to be entered into the program. Test scenarios and test cases are chosen as the result of analyzing the requirements and design specifications and the code itself. The test data should demonstrate and exercise externally visible functions, program structures, data structures, and internal functions including impossible and improbable test cases. Each test case includes a set of input data and the expected results. The expected results may be expressed in terms of final values and as statements (assertions), embedded in the software, about intermediate states of program execution.

The development of assertions takes place during the design and programming subphases of the lifecycle. In general, assertions are statements that specify the intent of a program's behavioral properties and constraints. Assertions about inputs, outputs, and intermediate steps of each function may be generated. A special notation (an assertion language) often is used to specify the assertions. Assertions are developed and inserted into the actual design specification and program code, usually as specially formatted comments.

Currently, test preparation is accomplished primarily through manual methods. These include definition of specification based functional tests and cause-effect graphing, a test case design methodology. Specification based functional testing is a method of developing test scenarios, test data and expected results through the ex-

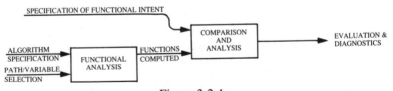

Figure 3.2.1
General Form of Dynamic Analysis

amination of the program specifications (in particular, the requirements, design and program code). Test scenarios based upon the requirements have the objective of demonstrating that the functions, performance and interface requirements and solution constraints are satisfied. Test cases are determined from the design to test functions, structures, algorithms and other elements of the design. Test data are determined from the program to exercise computational structures implemented in the program code.

Cause-effect graphing [MYER] is a technique to develop test cases based upon inputs and input conditions. For each case, the expected outputs are identified. This technique operates on the requirements and design specifications.

Test execution involves running a program with the prepared test cases and then collecting the results. Testing may be planned and performed in a top-down or bottom-up fashion or a combination of the two. Top-down testing is performed in parallel with top-down construction in that a module is developed and tested while submodules are left incomplete as stubs or dummy routines. Bottom-up testing consists of testing pieces of code, individual modules, and small collections of modules in that order, before they are integrated into the total program. Bottom-up testing may require the development of test driver routines.

Test execution may be performed manually. Design and code walkthroughs (i.e., a manual simulation) provide a straightforward dynamic analysis method used prior to execution and during debugging.

Instrumentation, the insertion of code into a program to measure program characteristics, may be required to assist in testing. It may be done to capture intermediate values of a computation, measure execution frequencies during testing, or to detect assertion violations. Instrumentation may be done manually, or automatically as with test coverage analyzers and dynamic assertion processors.

Four types of tools are commonly used to assist in test execution. They are:

Test coverage analyzers,

Execution monitors,

Dynamic assertion processors, and

Performance monitors.

Test coverage analyzers capture and report execution details (e.g., statement execution counts). Some test tools (often built into a compiler or runtime system) monitor execution and check for the adherence to certain language semantics (e.g., array subscripts must remain within declared bounds, divisors must be non-zero). Dynamic assertion processors monitor program execution and report violations of the assertions supplied by the analyst. Performance monitoring tools report execution data describing execution frequency and timing information.

The process of analyzing the outputs of testing involves comparing the actual to expected results. This analysis requires a specification of the expected results for each case. Comparison of actual and expected results may be performed manually, or if the data are machine readable, an automated comparator may be used. The detection of assertion violations is normally accomplished through analyzing the assertion results generated by the instrumented program.

Dynamic analysis also includes determining the thoroughness of the testing. Commonly used metrics are the numbers (or percentages) of executable statements, branches, and paths actually exercised by the tests. Each succeeding metric subsumes the others. Since the number of paths grows exponentially with the number of decision points, even small programs can have many thousands of paths. For this reason, attempting to ensure that a high percentage of paths, exclusive of loop iterations, is exercised can be very costly. The statement and branch coverage metrics, although less conclusive, are most frequently used because they are relatively easy and inexpensive to implement.

Formal Analysis

Formal analysis involves the use of rigorous mathematical techniques to analyze the algorithms of a solution. Algorithms are analyzed for numerical properties (e.g. accuracy, stability, convergence), efficiency, and correctness. At present, formal analysis is primarily a manual activity with limited automated assistance.

For more detailed information about techniques and tools for measurement of testing in the analysis of the numerical properties of algorithms, two types of analysis can be identified. The first type makes a conjecture about an algorithm's numerical properties and then proves a theorem to establish the conjecture. In the second type, an automated tool is used to analyze the numerical stability of a sequence of computations.

Complexity analysis first makes conjectures about the number of operations and/or the amount of space used on a problem of arbitrary but fixed size. The next step is to construct arguments which support the conjectures. There is considerable discussion as to how to measure or express software complexity. This technique has not reached maturity.

In another type of formal analysis, two basic approaches are used. One approach is to prove correctness of a whole program. The second approach is to prove correctness of particular program properties.

The basic strategy to both approaches is to construct a set of reasoning that shows that a solution specification satisfies its requirement(s). Typically, this is done by comparing the inferred transformations to the functional transformations dictated by the specifications of intent (see Figure 3.3.1).

To do the comparison, symbolic execution using selected control paths through the algorithmic specification is employed. For each path the values of each data object encountered are computed. Each value is not computed as a number but rather as a function or formula. Inputs are not assigned specific values but rather are treated as unquantified variables. As a result, at the end of tracing down the selected path, the functional relationships of outputs to inputs are determined. These func-

20

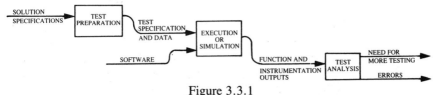

Figure 3.3.1
General Form of a Formal Function Analysis

tions or formulas are then compared to specifications of functional intent to see if the solution specification is correct as a value transformer.

The formal analysis of a specific path can ensure that the functions computed in traversing the path are correct, and thus that any input processed by traversal of that path will necessarily be transformed into correct output values.

Formal analysis has two major limitations: strict dependence on the validity of the assumptions on which the analysis is based, and the complexity of the pathwise analysis of even small programs. Formal analysis has not yet reached its full potential as a V,V&T technique for several reasons. For one, program specifications are rarely written with sufficient precision to permit a rigorous comparison of intent with the implemented program. Also accomplishing the analysis manually is extremely tedious and difficult (thus prone to error) and very few automated tools are currently available to facilitate effective application of formal techniques.

An Integrated Approach to V,V&T

Each of the three types of analysis—static, dynamic, and formal—provides the V,V&T analyst with different types of specific information about the solution being examined. Static analysis focuses on the form and structure of the solution, but not the functional or computational aspects. Dynamic analysis addresses the functional, structural, and computational aspects. It is used to detect errors relating to these, but in practice is not used to demonstrate the absence of errors and is limited in demonstrating correctness. Formal analysis can provide a strong statement regarding certain properties of a solution including correctness, but is limited by the difficulty of application and lack of automated support.

These three types of analysis can be integrated to not only achieve the benefits of each, but to be complementary and provide a powerful composite V,V&T technology.

This section briefly describes a strategy to achieve this integration (see Figure 3.4.1). The following three sections of this chapter describe how this strategy can be applied to software requirements and design specifications, and to the code itself.

The integration strategy is simple. First, static analysis techniques and tools are applied to analyze the form of the specification. These techniques and tools are straight forward to apply, applicable to all levels of specification, and identify flaws preventing the application of dynamic and formal techniques.

21

Software Validation, Verification, Testing, and Documentation

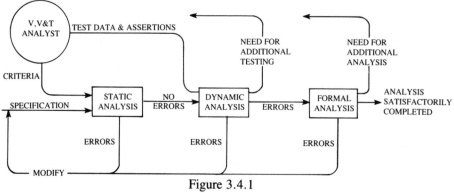

Figure 3.4.1
General V,V&T Integration Strategy

The second step is the application of dynamic analysis techniques and tools. These focus on the functional meaning of the solution and detect errors in their specification. These may be manually applied to the requirements and design specifications, with the code undergoing dynamic testing. This process, when applied with discipline, is effective, comprehensive and within the resource constraints of nearly all projects.

If additional assurances are required, the third step is the application of formal analysis techniques. These techniques can give strong assurances that the program design and code are fully traceable to the requirements and that they are a necessary and sufficient solution to the stated problem.

Requirements V,V&T

Figure 3.5.1 illustrates the integrated V,V&T approach for requirements specification. It involves the application of static analysis techniques and tools to inspect the form and structure of the requirements and dynamic analysis techniques and tools to examine their functional aspects. For requirements specification, the definition of dynamic analysis is extended to include all actions which examine behavioral and performance aspects of requirements. Static and dynamic analysis techniques and tools, whether strictly manual, automated, or a combination of both are generally applicable to the four types of requirements:

functional processing requirements,

performance requirements,

interface requirements, and

solution (design) constraints.

Static techniques and tools are most useful for analysis of product form and interface requirements and solution constraints, while dynamic analysis (such as simulation) is most useful for performance requirements.

22

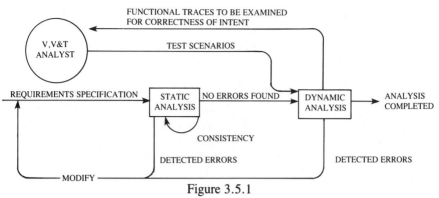

Figure 3.5.1
Integrated Approach to Requirements V,V&T

Static analysis normally focuses on checking adherence to specification conventions, completeness and language syntax. Dynamic analysis at this level normally focuses upon information flows and functional interrelationships. Manual methods such as inspections, peer reviews, and walkthroughs are effective in accomplishing both types of analyses if rigorously performed. An example of using a manual method and dynamic analysis is to include input data as part of a walkthrough.

The application of both types of analysis depends upon the method used to specify the requirements. If the constructs of the specification scheme are clearly defined and capable of being represented in a computer processable form, then automated tools to aid in performing both the static and dynamic analysis may be used. Several such specification methods with supporting tools are in existence, but not widely used or available.

The requirements specification methods commonly in use today support the representation of information aggregates and functional capabilities in a hierarchical form. This allows for two types of checks of the specification for internal consistency. The first examines the decompositions performed in creating the functional and information hierarchies. Each level of decomposition is checked to ensure that it is consistent with the previous. The second type of analysis examines the consistency between the functional and information views. Information aggregate specifications usually include indications of the functions which generate and utilize them. Conversely, function specifications usually include indications of the information aggregates which they generate and utilize. These two types of specifications are readily checked for consistency.

The dynamic analysis of a specification often involves the evaluation of the functional aspects of the solution with respect to the intent as documented in previous specifications. This is not possible because the requirements statement is the first formal specification. The only previous document to which it might be compared is the project request from the initiation phase. Normally, this is an insufficient basis for requirements analysis.

Consequently, the dynamic analysis of requirements is accomplished through the examination of expected functional behavior to determine if it will solve the problem. Exercising information transformations through plausible sequences of the required functions will provide insight to the expected behavior. This is usually guided by scenarios which describe expected use, including input values and expected results. (These scenarios form the basis for the software test data and are refined and complemented in the design and coding subphases.) This type of analysis aids in the recognition of errors, oversights, and contradictions in the requirements.

Design V,V&T

Figure 3.6.1 illustrates the integration strategy as applied to a design specification. Similar to the requirements analysis, static analysis techniques and tools are applied to analyze the form and structure of the design specification(s). Dynamic analysis techniques and tools are used to examine the functional aspects of the design. In addition, formal analysis may be applied to rigorous design specifications to gain additional assurances of correctness relating to certain functional properties.

The basis for design V,V&T is the design documentation. The mechanisms or design representation schemes used to specify the design determine the specific analysis techniques which can be employed. The degree of formality of the schemes used determines the need for and ability to perform static analysis. The content of the information captured by the scheme determines the dynamic and formal analysis techniques which may be applied. If the schemes can be translated into a computer processable form, then automated techniques may be used.

Syntactic and semantic errors can be detected by the static analysis of a design specification. The syntactic errors are errors in form rather than content. These are not the primary emphasis of static analysis. By assuring the correct form and struc-

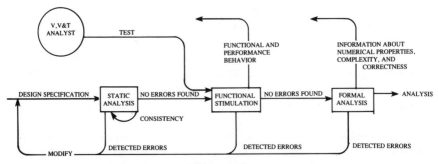

Figure 3.6.1
Integrated Approach to Design V,V&T

ture of the design specification, the way is cleared for more in depth analysis of the semantic content of a specification.

The semantic errors which can be detected in a design involve information or data decomposition, functional decomposition, control flow, and data flow. Selected examples of these are discussed below.

Design specification schemes generally provide mechanisms for specifying algorithms and their inputs and outputs in terms of modules. Various inconsistencies in specifying the flow of data objects through the modules are possible. For example, a module may need a particular data object which no other module creates. Conversely, a module may create a data object which is not input to any module. Static analysis can be applied to detect these types of data flow errors.

Certain errors made during the composition of a design can also be detected. Design specifications are usually created by iteratively supplying detail. Thus, most schemes facilitate the hierarchical expression of a design. Data aggregates and functional modules may be specified in terms of their gross overall characteristics and then specified in more detail. A hierarchical specification structure is regarded as an excellent vehicle for expressing and understanding a design. It does, however, leave open the possibility of inconsistencies between levels of detail. For example, the inputs and outputs specified for a high level module must be equivalent to the cumulative inputs and outputs of the submodules. Any inconsistencies indicate an error in the evolving solution. Static analysis can determine the presence or absence of such errors.

Dynamic analysis of a design is generally accomplished by some form of design simulation. This may be a manual walkthrough or simulation using a model of the design. A design walkthrough is similar to the analysis performed on the requirements except at a greater level of detail. It is guided by usage scenarios which are refined and expanded from those used in the requirements analysis. At the design stage, test cases are developed and used during the walkthrough to exercise all functions. During detailed design, test cases are developed and used to examine the software structure as well as its functions. (These test scenarios and test cases are used during the programming subphase for testing the code.) Manual walkthroughs, when rigorously performed and guided by documented test scenarios, are a cost effective technique for analyzing a software design.

For larger software designs and highly critical systems or components, an automated simulation may be appropriate. This requires the construction and execution of a solution model with the test scenarios. The model is validated as a faithful representation of the solution. The cost of simulation generally increases with the complexity of the model and the degree of model fidelity. Thus, model simulation is only used when it can be cost jutified.

Formal analysis techniques may be manually applied to a design specification This involves tracing paths through the design specification and formulating a composite function for each. This procedure is more feasible at higher levels of a hierarchical design specification because less detail is present, resulting in algorithm paths being relatively short and few in number. Thus, the evolved functions remain concise and manageable.

The purpose for deriving these composite functions for a given level of design is computed and compared to the functions of the previous level. This process assures that the design is continuing to specify the same functional solution as it is hierarchically elaborated.

The formal analysis of a design specification can be improved by using automated symbolic execution tools. Such tools can be expensive to create and operate. In return, however, they offer greater speed and capacity for manipulating detailed specifications. Thus, the functional effects of all levels of a design specification can be determined.

Unfortunately, such sophisticated tools are rarely applied in contemporary practice principally due to the novelty of such tools, the infrequent use of rigorous design formalisms, and expense. It is likely, as experience with these tools is gained and as better design representation schemes emerge, their use will increase.

Code V,V&T

The third and last application of the general V,V&T integration strategy is to program code. This is portrayed in Figure 3.7.1. The V,V&T procedure for code includes both static and dynamic analysis. It may also encompass formal analysis.

Because code is written to be compiled and executed, it is necessarily written in a computer language having defined syntax and semantics. Syntax rules are generally enforced through the use of a compiler. Unfortunately, most compilers do not carry out checking for many important semantic errors, e.g. array range subscript checking, type analysis or routine interface analysis.

Static analysis techniques and tools are used to ensure the proper form of programming products such as code and documentation. This can be accomplished by checking adherence to coding and documentation conventions, interface and type checking, etc. The checking can be done by manual techniques such as inspections and automated tools such as a code auditor.

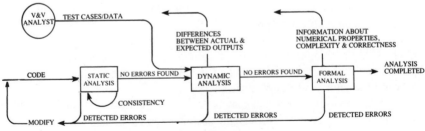

Figure 3.7.1
Integrated Approach to Code V,V&T

Next, dynamic analysis techniques are employed to study the functional and computational correctness of the code. Initially, manual techniques such as walk-throughs can be used as an effective forerunner to testing. These techniques can focus on modules to complement the role of testing.

Testing is accomplished by running the code on the test data sets which were developed during the requirements and design subphases. As emphasized earlier, the correctness of the test executions is determined more definitively when the expected results are specified. Testing for adherence to assertions is also highly advisable. The assertions, which are products of the design activity, provide additional information regarding expected behavior of the software.

In cases where software is being developed in an environment other than the production environment, testing is more problematical. Here the production environment can be simulated or taken into account informally. In any case, the validity of the test results depends upon the fidelity of the simulation or informal judgements. If there is a significant difference in the two environments, there will be an eventual need for some additional testing in the actual production environment. The balance between simulation testing and actual production environment testing must be determined for each individual project, based partially upon the availability and expensiveness of the production environment.

If assurances of correctness over and above those provided by dynamic analysis are required, then formal analysis should follow testing. For most projects, this simply takes the form of inspections to see that the various algorithms dictated by the design have been correctly implemented. Coming after a battery of successful tests, this activity needs to focus upon algorithms which are deemed crucial and yet inadequately tested (perhaps due to high cost of exercising them). Of course, some applications may be particularly critical in nature and demanding of very great assurance of correctness. Symbolic evaluation and other formal analysis methods can be effective in achieving such levels of confidence, but the cost is high, generally entailing development of special purpose evaluation tools.

Summary

It is reasonable to conclude that for any software project, the integration strategy for V,V&T activities will result in a better return on investment of costly resources and increased confidence in the desired qualities of the final product. Although the strategy is sound and is strongly endorsed, it does not address the problem of how to select and configure specific techniques and tools for a specific project. The problems in doing this appear to be of two major types:

Projects vary in many respects and this variation strongly affects the proper selection of techniques and tools, and

There are a multiplicity of techniques and tools but there is little guidance in their selection to meet specific project needs.

Software Validation, Verification, Testing, and Documentation

The first problem is addressed in Chapter 4. The second problem is addressed in succeeding chapters.

In time, a reasonable complement of proven V,V&T support techniques and tools will evolve. Then, with a judicious selection and systematic, integrated application during all lifecycle phases, it will be possible to effect significant reductions in the cost of software production as well as improvements in the quality of developed systems.

4. V,V&T Planning

An important part of problem solving is planning. This is certainly true in software development. Within this context, V,V&T planning is an integral part of the overall project development planning. It is started during the initiation of a project along with all other planning.

The objective is to establish a V,V&T plan to suit the needs of the project. Software development and maintenance projects vary with respect to many factors such as size, criticality, complexity, etc. These factors must be taken into account so that the plan is both feasible and effective.

This chapter describes the contents of a V,V&T plan and presents a process for developing one. First, it explains how V,V&T planning is part of the overall planning process. It briefly describes the outcome of a V,V&T plan and introduces a four step process to assist in developing part of the plan. The four steps are presented in detail.

Step I Identify V,V&T Goals   The result is a set of specific measurable goals of the validation, verification, and testing activities of the project.

Step II Determine Influences on V,V&T Activities   The result is a set of factors to be taken into account in the planning of the V,V&T activity.

Step III Select V,V&T Techniques and Tools   The outcome is a list of V,V&T practices, techniques and tools to satisfy the identified goals within the constraints of the environment.

Step IV Develop a Detailed V,V&T Plan   The result is a phase-by-phase V,V&T plan specifying V,V&T practices, as well as specific tasks, schedules, and budgets.

V,V&T Planning in the Total Project Context

Project planning is one of the major functions of project management. V,V&T planning is one part of project planning. Figure 4.1.1 illustrates this relationship and examples of planning products.

29

Software Validation, Verification, Testing, and Documentation

Figure 4.1.1
Software Project Planning

The objective of planning is to document a plan of action. It may include: objectives, approach, schedule, and allocated resources. A plan is used to initiate and control a project.

Figure 4.1.2 shows the evolution of a project plan. A project is formed to solve a problem. This first step in project formation is to define its mission or its objectives. Next, an approach is formulated. This is refined with additional details about the approach and documented in the project plan.

This chapter presents a V,V&T planning process which follows a similar set of steps. The interactions between the general and the V,V&T planning activities are important. The general planning activity will drive the V,V&T planning activity, which in turn will provide input and feedback to the first. Some of the important interactions are:

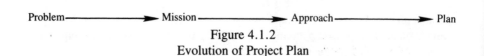

Figure 4.1.2
Evolution of Project Plan

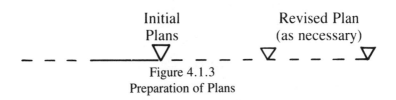

Figure 4.1.3
Preparation of Plans

V,V&T goals are established which complement the general project approach.

V,V&T techniques and tools will assist in achieving the V,V&T goals only if they are integrated with the project approach.

The details of the V,V&T plan, e.g., time and resource requirements, must be factored into the overall schedule and budgets.

Planning activities, including the preparation of the V,V&T plan, may begin in the initiation phase but are completed early in the development phase (Figure 4.1.3). Plans specifying tasks, budgets, schedules, etc. for the requirements and preliminary design subphases are completed early in the subphase. Plans specifying information for the subsequent subphases are also prepared to the level of detail possible. These, though, are likely to be revised as the technical scope, size and complexity of the solution are defined in the preliminary design activity. Special attention must be paid to activities that require long lead time, or need to begin early in the project, e.g., tool acquisition or development, personnel hiring or training.

The result of the V,V&T planning activity is a documented V,V&T plan. The complexity of the plan and the effort required to prepare it will depend upon the size and nature of the project. More effort and a greater level of detail may be required as the size, complexity, and critical nature of the project increases.

A V,V&T plan specifies goals of the project's V,V&T activities relating to the products of each phase. For these products, the activities and supporting techniques and tools are then described which make up the approach to achieve the goals. An abbreviated outline of a V,V&T plan is presented in Figure 4.1.4. A detailed outline is presented later.

The remainder of this chapter describes the four step approach to preparing a V,V&T plan. Each step and substep are presented in a standard format, including the following items as appropriate:

General Description

Outputs

Inputs

Interrelationships with Other Steps

Roles and Responsibilities

Software Validation, Verification, Testing, and Documentation

---

I. BACKGROUND AND INTRODUCTION

II. V,V&T GOALS

   1. Summary of V,V&T Goals and Measurement Criteria

   2. References and Related Documents

III. PHASE BY PHASE PLANS

For each phase, information including:
   1. V,V&T Goals for Each Product

   2. V,V&T Activities

   3. Techniques and Tools

   4. Assumptions and Other Information

   5. Roles and Responsibilities

   6. Schedules

   7. Budgets

   8. Personnel

Figure 4.1.4
Abbreviated Outline of a Project V,V&T Plan

Method and Supporting Techniques

Worksheet

Example

Comments

The worksheets are suggested as documentation aids. Examples are presented using these worksheets.

For small projects it may be sufficient to abbreviate the process, following it as necessary to achieve the ultimate objective, a V,V&T plan. For larger projects, the process provides a systematic method for developing a comprehensive V,V&T plan. In either case, the outcome should suit the goals of the project.

Step I: Identifying V,V&T Goals

General Description. V,V&T goals are formulated from software requirements, and, secondarily, software product standards. V,V&T goals address the functional structural, and computational correctness of the software, the correctness of the form, its performance, and other attributes such as reliability and portability. The achievement of these goals demonstrates that the software has the desired attributes. This is straightforward in some instances, e.g., demonstrating the correct operation of a tape sort/merge capability, while in others it may be a matter of de-

32

gree, e.g., clarity and understandability of documentation. The term *goal* describes a specific, measurable outcome. A complete definition of a goal includes the statement of the measurement criteria to determine that the goal has been reached.

Goals are established to define tangible results of the activity (e.g., a report) or a culminating event (e.g., a review). Measurement criteria specify how to determine that the result is satisfactory.

Goals relating to products (intermediate and final) are established which pertain to either their form or the content. The goal will precisely describe the desired product attributes. This distinction will be useful in selecting techniques and tools.

Goals relating to an activity or product should be examined as a set, and categorized as high, medium, or low in importance. This information will be used in Step III if trade-offs (because of time, budget, or resource constraints) are necessary. This examination also acts as a re-evaluation point, and may result in the revision, elimination, or combination of goals. The workwheet examples for Steps I and III are separate. To eliminate duplication, they can be combined into one worksheet.

Outputs of Step I

A set (one or more) of goals, measurement criteria, and importance of each V,V&T goal

Inputs to Step I

Project proposal

Statement of Problem/Needs

Statement of Software Requirements

Applicable Product Standards

Interrelationships with Other Steps

The list of goals from this step will be used in Step III

This step can be done parallel with Step II

Roles and Responsibilities

User/Customer—to identify the goals and measurement criteria to ensure that the product is acceptable

Development Staff and Management—to ensure that V,V&T goals and measurement criteria are both measurable and feasible and reflect existing standards and conventions concerning product quality

Methods and Supporting Techniques

Standards, guidelines and conventions that contribute to product quality

Requirement analysis and specification aids that support the identification and documentation of the software requirements

Checklists for identifying V,V&T goals based upon the software requirements

Software Validation, Verification, Testing, and Documentation

Inspection, walkthrough, review procedures that support the analysis and evaluation of the V,V&T goals

Example. Figure 4.2.1 identifies the goal, measurement criteria, and importance of testing critical modules.

Comments. A worksheet which assists in specifying goals and selecting the associated techniques and tools are described in the following sections. It can be used as an aid in documenting the results of this step.

V,V&T Goals Worksheet—used in Step I to define a specific set of goals and the measurement criteria

V,V&T Technique and Tool Selection Worksheet—used in Step 3 to select the techniques and tools to attain each goal

Step II: Determine Factors Influencing V,V&T Activities

General Description. This step involves collecting a mixture of both objective and subjective information (e.g., the attitudes of the technical staff concerning V,V&T). This information will, in some cases, lead to clear cut decisions regarding

Figure 4.2.1
Goals and Measurement Criteria

V, V&T GOALS WORKSHEET

PROJECT: _____

General Product: _____

Activity/ Product	Goal	Measurement Criteria	Importance
Product: Software	All critical modules will undergo thorough testing	Test data will be generated to: 1) Demonstrate the adherence to functional specification, including nominal values and extremes of the domain and range. 2) Exercise all module branches. 3) Traverse all recovery paths, i.e., an execution path where an error (e.g., illegal input data) is discovered and for which the system must continue to operate. (These paths must be identified in the program internal and external documentation.)	high

34

the implementation of a given technique or tool. In other instances, it may only indicate potential areas of difficulty or supply information to support a decision intuitively.

Four general areas in a suggested order of investigation are presented below.

Software V,V&T and development technology

Project groups and roles

Project constraints

Available computing resources

These areas of investigation are further described below.

Outputs of Step II

An assessment of available software engineering and V,V&T technology

The capabilities and expected involvement of various groups

The budget and schedule constraints upon the V,V&T activities

An inventory of computing resources.

Inputs to Step II

Software engineering standards, guidelines, procedures, development and maintenance methodologies, etc.

Information regarding technical personnel

Information regarding project budget and schedule

Information regarding computing resources

Interrelationships with Other Steps

This step can be performed in parallel with Step I—The Identification of V,V&T Goals

It provides inputs into Step III and Step IV.

Roles and Responsibilities
This activity is primarily the responsibility of the development organization.

Methods and Supporting Techniques
The following is a checklist of the four areas of investigation mentioned above:

Software V,V&T and Development Technology

Software V,V&T (see techniques and tools descriptions in [POWE])

techniques

tools

standards and guidelines

conventions and procedures

Software development

methodologies

specification techniques and design representation schemes

techniques and tools

documentation standards and guidelines

technical assistance

training

Project Groups and Roles

The following groups and their expected roles should be balanced against their knowledge, experience, attitudes, and expectations.

Customer

User

Technical staff

Management (e.g., project, or organizational, and support, e.g., legal)

Independent groups (e.g., quality assurance, independent V,V&T)

Project Constraints

Schedule of major project results

Budget information for:

analysis and review of each product

acquisition and/or development of support capabilities and tools

technical assistance and/or training in the use of selected techniques and tools

use of independent testing, V,V&T and quality assurance teams

Available Computing Resources

Available machines

Access methods and devices

Support utilities

Technical support

Step III: Select V,V&T Techniques and Tools

General Description. This step can be divided into two activities:

Establish a candidate list of techniques and tools to be used to reach each goal, and

Select and evaluate the techniques and tools from the candidate list to be used.

One input to the first activity is the list of V,V&T goals. Goals should have been established for: a) activities by phase/subphase, and b) the form and content of each product. The other input to this activity is information about each candidate technique or tool.

Candidate techniques and tools may be chosen from three sets: a) those commonly used on software development projects (information on these was collected during Step II); b) those used elsewhere which may be acquired; and c) those which can be developed by the project staff.

For each candidate technique or tool, some basic information is needed. This includes the availability of documentation, training, consulting support, and tool effectiveness. Also required are cost, time required for acquisition, and need for training project personnel.

Once the list of candidate techniques and tools has been created for a given goal, the selection activity begins. The feasibility of implementing each technique or tool is studied. The implementation requirements (e.g., personnel resources and level of expertise) are compared against the constraints identified in Step II (e.g., personnel experience). This identifies inappropriate candidates. The techniques and tools to be used are chosen from the remaining.

The assumptions made in the selection process need to be documented for use in Step IV. For example, assumptions regarding the acquisition, implication, application, and required training should be recorded.

Outputs of Step III

    A list of V,V&T techniques and tools

    Assumptions made in selection process

Inputs to Step III

    V,V&T goals

    Information on candidate tools and techniques

    Influences to be considered during selection (from Step II)

Interrelationships with Other Steps

    The list of V,V&T goals may be revised because one or more goals are determined to be infeasible

Roles and Responsibilities

The development staff have primary responsibility for this step. It should be performed by senior staff familiar with both the management and the technical aspects of the project. Generally, a representative of the groups who will use the techniques and tools should be involved in the selection process.

Methods and Supporting Techniques

The "Validation, Verification, and Testing Technique and Tool Reference Guide" [POWE] describes individual techniques and tools.

Worksheet and Example

Figure 4.4.1 shows the V,V&T Technique and Tool selection worksheet. Figure 4.4.2 shows a completed worksheet for a goal from the previous example.

Figure 4.4.1
V,V&T Technique and Tool Selection Worksheet

V, V&T TECHNIQUE AND TOOL SELECTION WORKSHEET

PROJECT: _____

Goals	Measurement Criteria	Candidate Techniques & Tools	Rationale for Choice/Elimination	Final Choice & Comments
The goals and criteria established during Step I.		Techniques or tools which may potentially be used in reaching each goal are listed in this column	Each technique or tool will be analyzed and either chosen or rejected. The decision is documented here.	The final choice(s) will be listed here. Also any information pertaining to the use or application should be stated here or reference to supplementary material given. It is important to note here any special information that should be taken into account in the detailed planning (Step IV) and/or implementation of the technique or tool.

Step IV: Develop a Detailed V,V&T Plan

General Description. The preceding three steps provide a definition and means of attaining V,V&T goals. The detailed V,V&T plan can now be formulated by defining each activity in terms of specific tasks and outcomes. The roles and responsibilities of the groups involved, (e.g., customer, user, technical, management) are defined; sign-off procedures at milestones are established. Underlying assumptions are stated, and interrelationships with other activities (preceding, parallel with, and succeeding) are defined. Budget allocations and schedules are established. Plans also include training and tool acquisition or development activities.

Outputs of Step IV:

A Detailed V,V&T Plan

Inputs to Step IV:

List of V,V&T techniques and tools

Project Schedule, budget, and personnel information

V,V&T goals

Technique and tool selection assumptions

Interrelationships with Other Steps

The plan is built on the outputs of prior steps

Figure 4.4.2
Completed V,V&T Technique and Tool Selection Worksheet

V, V&T TECHNIQUE & TOOL SELECTION WORKSHEET

PROJECT: _____

Goals	Measurement Criteria	Candidate Techniques & Tools	Rationale for Choice/Elimination	Final Choice & Comments
For critical functions: All critical modules will undergo thorough testing	The functions of these modules must be tested for extremal values of the domain and range, as well as on nominal test data: 1) All branches will be tested, including all 'recovery' paths, i.e. an execution path where an error (e.g., illegal input data) is discovered and for which the system must continue to operate (these paths must be identified in the program internal and external documentation).	–Data Flow Analyzer	Can be used to check out programs from the data flow perspective. Availability is uncertain.	Investigate availability
		–Assertion Generation and Assertion Processing	Assertion generation will aid in specification documentation and test generation. Assertion checking via an automatic processor will aid in testing and test coverage measurement. Availability is uncertain.	Investigate availability
		–Specification Based Functional Testing	This technique can be used in the requirements and design phases to incrementally build test sets.	Used in conjunction with test set documentation standards and test libraries to store data and results.
		–Test Coverage Analyzer	This tool can summarize test coverage to enable an accurate assessment of the thoroughness of the testing.	Will be used. Modifications to existing tool will be necessary.

Roles and Responsibilities

This involves both management and technical staff. Management approval is required for schedules and budgets. Customers/users approve their role.

Methods and Supporting Techniques

Presented below is an annotated outline of a general V,V&T plan. This can be used as a checklist.

An Outline of a Project V,V&T Plan

I. Background and Introduction

The purpose of this section is to establish the context for the document. It should be brief and introductory in nature. It should focus on those aspects of the problem and/or solution which are the sources of the goals for

V,V&T. Where additional information is necessary, it can be included or referenced.

A. Statement of Problem

B. Proposed Solution

C. Project Summary

D. References/Related Documents

II. V,V&T Goals and Measurement Criteria

This section presents the results of Step I. It presents the project V,V&T goals, measurement criteria, and importance. The exact format and content of this section may vary. If the worksheets are used, then they may be included. Alternatively goals could be summarized as presented below. A third alternative would be to state the project level information in this section and present all phase (and product) specific information in the next section.

A. V,V&T Requirements

A.1. Functional

A.2. Performance

A.3. Reliability

A.4. Other

B. V,V&T Goals and Measurement Criteria for each goal

B.1. General

B.2. Product specific

B.3. Phase specific

C. References/Related Documents

III. Phase by Phase V,V&T Plans

This section contains the description of project V,V&T practices. Section A defines the project approach: phases, their products, and the major reviews and check points. Where a practice is common to all phases it may be described here. Section B and later sections describe phase specific activities.

A. Project Background and Summary Information

A.1. Project Phases and Products

A.2. Major Reviews (both management and technical)

B. Requirements Subphase V,V&T Activities

B.1. Summary of V,V&T Goals

B.2. V,V&T Activities

B.3. V,V&T Techniques and Tools Selected

      a. Reviews

      b. Methods of Analysis

   B.4. Support Requirements and Assumptions

   B.5. Roles and Responsibilities

   B.6. Schedules

   B.7. Budgets

   B.8. Personnel

  C-F. Preliminary Design Through Installation respectively (same format as B).

Appendix A: Project and Environmental Considerations

   This section contains the information which was compiled during Step II.

  A. Technical Issues

  B. Organizational/Personnel Issues

  C. Project Budget and Schedule

  D. Computing Resources

Appendix B: Technique and Tool Selection Information

   This section contains the work sheets of Step III.

  A. Goals, and Related Techniques and Tools

  B. Worksheets

5. Example Applications of Validation and Verification Technology

This chapter presents a series of examples in which the concepts of software development, software V,V&T, and V,V&T planning are illustrated. The purpose is to show how these concepts may be applied in a variety of situations.

Four examples are presented, using an automobile insurance transaction processing system as the system being developed and maintained. The first three examples describe development activities in differing environments and the fourth describes selected maintenance activities.

The four examples are structured recognizing that programming environments present in government and industry settings vary significantly in resources available to support V,V&T. The transaction processing system is considered first in an environment where only manually applied techniques are employed. The progressive benefits of utilizing automated and more advanced techniques can then be seen by studying how V,V&T is done on the same application, first through adding a small number of automated tools to the set of manual techniques, and lastly through use of a full complement of modern automated tools.

Overview of Examples

Examples 2, 3, and 4 build upon Example 1. The tools introduced in Example 2 are to be used in addition to the manual techniques described in the first example. The discussion in each example centers on the additional capabilities introduced. Figure 5.1.1 presents an overview of the different V,V&T tools and techniques which are used in the four examples. The software development subphases for each example are:

Requirements,

Preliminary design,

Detailed design, and

Programming (includes testing).

Figure 5.1.2 shows the information flow and relationships among the four subphases of the software development lifecycle depicted in the examples. Each of the examples will be presented showing for each phase:

42

Figure 5.1.1
Overview of Examples

	Example (#1) Manual Techniques	Software Development (#2) Minimal — Tool Complements — (#3) Extensive		Maintenance (#4)
		Minimal	Extensive	
Supporting Technology	Graphical Requirements Representation	Requirements & Design Languages		Problem Reporting and Change Request Mechanisms
Static Analysis	Walkthroughs Formal Reviews	Cross-Referencer Requirements & Design Language Analyzers	Interface Checker Dataflow Analyzer Standards Checker	Ad Hoc
Dynamic Analysis	Functional Testing	Test Coverage Analyzers File Comparator	Assertion generation Assertion Checking	
Formal Analysis				

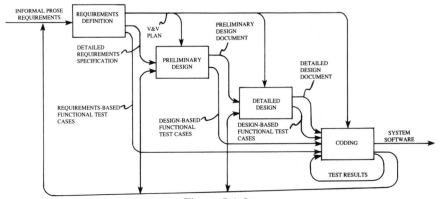

Figure 5.1.2
Example Software Development Lifecycle

Inputs to the phase,

Outputs from the phase,

Supporting technology used in the phase, and

Activities which comprise the phase.

Most activities will contain:

V,V&T purpose for the activity,

V,V&T technique(s) used by the activity, and

Example(s).

Tables 5.2.1, 5.3.1, 5.4.1, and 5.5.1 provide a summary of the development and V,V&T techniques and activities for the manual, minimal automation, full automation, and maintenance activities. These tables present a synopsis of the examples presented in this chapter.

The application area used in the examples is representative of a large number of government and commercial systems. Transaction processing systems are perhaps the most common of all commercial systems. Many banking, billing, payroll, inventory, and insurance applications are in this category. Thus, the four examples focus on this area.

The transaction processing system is set in the context of an auto insurance application. In order to limit the size of the presentations some simplifications have been made in the application area. An expert in the auto insurance field will surely detect omissions and simplifications in details of the system as described. The reader is encouraged, however, to not focus on the application area, but rather on the V,V&T principles applied. The details provided enable presentation of specific instances of the application of V,V&T techniques.

The Auto Insurance Management System (AIMS) described in the examples supports all the major activities of such a company: accounts payable (claims pro-

Table 5.2.1
Example 1 Summary
Software Development Using Manual V,V&T Techniques

Subphases	Requirements	Preliminary Design	Detailed Design	Programming
Input	■ Informal prose Requirements	■ Detailed Requirements Specifications – Revised Prose Description – Revised Graphical GR Representation ■ V,V&T Plan	■ Preliminary Design Document ■ V,V&T Plan ■ Test Cases	■ Detailed Design Document ■ V,V&T Plan ■ Test Cases
Output	■ Detailed Requirements Specifications ■ V,V&T Plan ■ Initial Test Cases	■ Preliminary Design Document – Further Refined GR System Representation – Detailed User Input/Output Specification – Basic Control Flow Design	■ Detailed Design Document ■ Additional Test Cases	■ System Software ■ Test Results

Table 5.2.1 (continued)

Subphases	Requirements	Preliminary Design	Detailed Design	Programming
Supporting Technology	■ Formal Requirements Reviews ■ A Graphical Requirements Representation Method ■ Requirements-based Functional Testing	– Basic System Information Specification ■ Additional Test Cases ■ Reviews ■ A Graphical Requirements Representation Method ■ Design-based Functional Testing	■ Reviews ■ Database Management System (DBMS) ■ Design-based Functional Testing	■ Compilers ■ Database Management System ■ Operating System ■ Reviews
Activities	■ Initial Requirements Review ■ Requirements Analysis ■ V,V&T Planning ■ Initial Test Case Generation ■ Interaction with customer ■ Sign-off by customer	■ Refinement of Graphical Representation ■ Specify Information Design ■ Design Program Architecture & Allocate Requirements ■ Design Basic Control Flow ■ Test Case Generation ■ Preliminary Design Review	■ Detailed Database Design ■ Detailed Module Design ■ Test Case Generation ■ Critical Design Review	■ Code Development ■ Module Testing ■ Function Testing ■ Acceptance Testing

Table 5.3.1
Example 2 Summary
Software Development Using a Minimally Automated V, V&T Tool Set

Subphases →	Requirements	Preliminary Design	Detailed Design	Programming
Input	■ (No Additional Input)	■ Detailed Requirements Specification Including Use of Requirements Specification Language	■ Preliminary Design Document Including Use of Requirement and Design Specification Languages	■ Detailed Design Document Including Use of Design Specification Language
Output	■ Detailed Requirements Specification Including Use of Requirements Specification Language	■ Preliminary Design Document Including Further Use of Requirements Specification Design Language	■ Detailed Design Document Including Use of Requirement and Design Specification Languages	■ (No New Outputs)
Supporting Technology	■ Requirements Specification Language ■ Requirements Specification Language Analyzer	■ Requirements Specification Language ■ Tool-Supported Design Language	■ Design Specification Language	■ Cross-Referencer ■ Test Coverage Analyzer ■ File Comparator
Activities	■ Requirements Analysis	■ Specify Information Design ■ Design Basic Control Flow	■ Detailed Module Design	■ Code Development ■ Module Testing ■ Function Testing

Table 5.4.1
Example 3 Summary
Software Development Using a Fully Automated V,V&T Tool Set

Subphases	Requirements	Preliminary Design	Detailed Design	Programming
Input	■ (No Additions to Minimal Tool Set)	■ (No Additional Inputs)	■ Preliminary Design Document Including Assertions	■ Detailed Design Document Including Assertions
Output	■ (No Additions to Minimal Tool Set)	■ Preliminary Design Document Including Assertions about the Design	■ Detailed Design Document Including Additional Assertions	■ (No Additional Outputs)
Supporting Technology	■ (No Additions to Minimal Tool Set)	■ Assertion Generation	■ Assertion Generation	■ Interface Checker ■ Data Flow Analyzer ■ Assertion Processor ■ Standards Analyzer
Activities	■ (No Additions to Minimal Tool Set)	■ Design Basic Control Flow	■ Detailed Module Design	■ Code Development ■ Module Testing

Table 5.5.1
Example 4 Summary
Software Maintenance

Subphases	Problem Reporting and Correction	Change Request Processing
Input	System Software System Documentation System Test Cases Problem Reports	System Software System Documentation System Test Cases Change Requests
Output	Updated System Software Updated System Documentation	Updated System Software Updated System Documentation
Supporting Technology	Fully Automated V,V&T Tool Set Configuration Control Procedures	Fully Automated V,V&T Tool Set Configuration Control Procedures
Activities	Problem Analysis Problem Correction	Requirements Analysis Redesign and Coding

cessing), accounts receivable (premium processing), management reports, and database management. AIMS must issue client premium due notices, checks to repair shops (or clients), recommend policies that should be cancelled, monitor the company's day-to-day financial health, and so forth. Further details of the system's requirements are included in the first example.

Example 1: Software Development Using Manual V,V&T Techniques

In this example the details of the AIMS are presented in addition to the actual manual V,V&T practices which are applied within each of the four phases of the software development lifecycle.

Requirements Subphase Activity Descriptions

Initial Requirements Review The informal prose requirements for the AIMS is given in Figure 5.2.1. Appropriate management and technical personnel from the software development group review these requirements for completeness, consistency, and correctness and prepares a list of questions which address particular aspects of the requirements. This list is then supplied to the customer and a Requirements Review meeting is scheduled and held with customer and user, e.g. clerks,

49

Software Validation, Verification, Testing, and Documentation

Figure 5.2.1
Informal Prose Requirements

AIMS Requirements

A system called the Auto Insurance Management System (AIMS) is to be developed which will provide an automated set of automobile insurance support capabilities integrated through the use of a common database. The basic capabilities to be provided include: accounts payable, accounts receivable, management report generation, and database management.

System Information: Information contained in the database includes client records, claims records and the payout account. There is one client record for each policy holder and contains:

- policy number;
- name and address of the client;
- agent number;
- policy effective date and expiration date;
- name, birth date, sex, marital status, driving record of each driver;
- vehicle information—make, model, style, year;
- Insurance coverage—comprehensive, medical, collision and deductable, premium rate classification, balance due, date due, credited amount (e.g., from prepaid premium), number of claims made on this policy and total amount paid out.

There is one claims record for each claim and contains:

- claim number and date of claim;
- associated accident report number;
- driver's name;
- payee (e.g., repair shop), name and address;
- agent number and policy number of client making claim.

There is one payout account record in the database and contains:

- account balance;
- date and time of the last change to the account balance;
- minimum allowed balance, date and time of last minimum change;
- maximum allowed balance, date and time of last maximum change;
- total year-to-date claims and premium total;

Accounts Payable: The accounts payable function processes claims transactions and issues payment checks to the payee which will either be the repair shop or the client. The transactions are input to the AIMS system from a file containing the day's claims. Having been input, a claims transaction is validated by checking the consistency of the client information contained in the transaction with that contained in the client record, by verifying that the claim number is valid for this agent, and by checking the "reasonableness" of the amount. Once validated, the new claims record is entered into the database, the amount of the claim is withdrawn from the payout account and the check is issued (i.e., printed). When the claims withdrawal is made from the payout account the account balance is updated and then compared to the minimum allowable balance. If the new balance is less, then a notice is issued (for management) indicating the situation. The date and time of last change to the account balance is also updated as well as the year-to-date claims total.

Accounts Receivable: The accounts receivable function issues policy notices and processes premium payments. Policy notices are issued by a batch program which runs once per day. The program reads all client records and checks each record to determine if a premium due notice or cancellation (i.e., past due) notice should be issued and if so, prints the appropriate notice. When a premium payment is received a transaction is entered into a file which is processed daily by the AIMS to update client records with the premium payment. The information included in the transaction includes the policy number, client's name, agent number, due date and amount paid. Once received, the transaction is validated by verifying that the input data is consistent with that in the client record and that the amount paid is sufficient. The client record is then credited with the payment and the amount is deposited in the payout account. The payout account balance, year-to-date premium total, and date and time of last change to the account balance are updated when the deposit is made. Note that the maximum allowable balance is not automatically checked. This is a manual function performed by management.

Management Reports: Four management reports are produced: claims report, new clients report, client profile report and client cancellation report. The claims report is produced on a monthly basis and gives the total number of claims and the total amount paid in claims for a given month. It also performs a trend analysis based on totals from prior months. The new clients report is produced on a monthly basis and lists new clients and their coverage for a given month. The clients are grouped by agent which allows mangement to view the sales progress of each agent. A company-wide sales trend analysis is also produced. The client profile report provides accident statistics based on driver's age, sex, marital status, etc. This report is produced semi-annually. The client cancellation report lists the clients which were cancelled during a given month and the reason for the cancellation.

Database Management: Database management activities provide for client and payout account management capabilities. Client records are entered, queried, modified and cancelled (i.e., mode inactive but not deleted). A log of all client transactions is also stored in the database (or possibly on tape). Payout account functions include query, modification of the balance limits, external deposits and external withdrawals. External deposits and withdrawals are made from/to other company financial resources whenever the account balance exceeds the allowable limits. A log of all deposits and withdrawals (including premiums and claims) is kept on the database.

Acceptance Criteria: The acceptance criteria for the AIMS is the successful execution of a set of acceptance tests. An execution is successful if it correctly performs the desired function within the required execution time. The acceptance tests are specified by an independent team and reviewed by management, user and development personnel.

agents. During the meeting the questions are discussed with the goal being a more specific and unambiguous set of requirements.

V,V&T Purpose. To produce a requirements specification providing the foundation from which more formal requirements specification, V,V&T planning, and test planning will be accomplished.

V,V&T Technique. The review itself is the V,V&T technique used in this activity. Some of the questions addressed during the review could be:

Shouldn't a claims record contain some kind of indication as to the nature of the claim? For example: if it is due to an accident, who was at fault?

How is the "reasonableness" of a claim amount determined?

How does one know what claim numbers are valid for which agents?

When is the premium rate computed? How is it computed?

Shouldn't the acceptance criteria include provisions for testing more than just the functional capabilities?

Requirements Analysis   The requirements analysis involves translation of the informal prose requirements into a formal representation. This will result in the identification of other aspects of the requirements which will need clarification or further definition. For this example, the graphical representation(GR) scheme used is a modification of the Systematic Activity Modeling Method [SAMM].

V,V&T Purpose. To identify inadequately specified requirements such as incomplete, ambiguous, or otherwise unclear requirements statements.

V,V&T Technique. Formal reviews serve as the V,V&T technique used to achieve the above purpose on this project. Problem issues which are identified during the requirements analysis are documented and distributed to the customer and a second Requirements Review is scheduled. This review again involves dialogue between the customer and the developers; it centers on the formal requirements statement and the identified issues. The result is a revised set of requirements in both formal and informal forms and a graphical representation(GR). Specific activities which are performed within this review are:

Verification that all requirements have been correctly represented using the formal scheme,

Identification of the problems encountered during the restatement elaboration of the requirements, and

Discussion and resolution of the problems.

Example:

The formal representation for the basic system and the accounts payable function are shown on the following pages (Figure 5.2.2). The graphical representation is interpreted as follows:

Master input files are at the top of the diagram and are represented by numbers.

Master output files are at the right of the diagram and are represented by numbers.

Files internal to a data flow diagram are labeled with a letter followed by a number.

The upperhalf of Figure 5.2.2 is the root which contains five modules, A-E. The data flow within the root and to and from master files are labeled according to their source. If the data are internal to the root, its identifier is preceded by the module letter.

The lower half of Figure 5.2.2 is an expansion of module A from the root. The lower left corner of each box contains the parent, i.e. A in the root. The lower right corner of each box is the letter designator for each module, i.e. A–E. Data created by the accounts payable activity is labeled according to its source, e.g. data B.1, a validated claims transaction, is created by module B, validate claims transaction, and used by modules C–E. Data B.2, invalid claims transaction notice, is created by B and put on master file 7, user/client notices.

Some of the problems which could be identified are:

What does the system do with an invalid claims transaction? Solution: Output a notice to the user identifying the errors.

The involved driver's record in the client's record needs to be updated to reflect a new claim due to an accident. There does not appear to be enough information in the client record for this. Solution: Add the necessary information to the claims transaction.

V,V&T Planning   V,V&T planning is one aspect of the overall planning process. It is accomplished in parallel with other planning activities and the requirements identification activity.

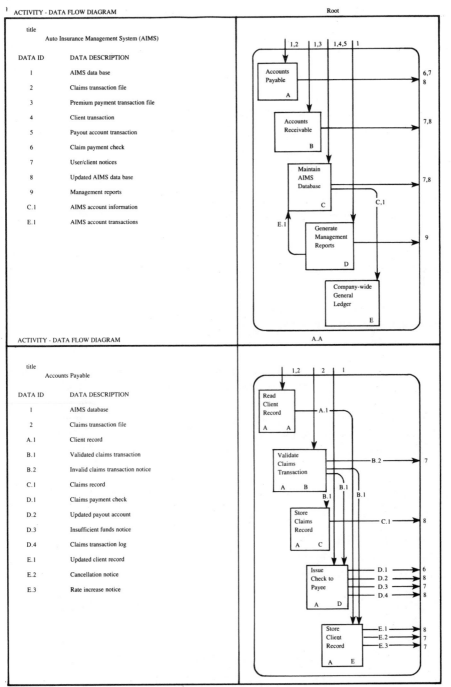

ACTIVITY - DATA FLOW DIAGRAM   Root

title
    Auto Insurance Management System (AIMS)

DATA ID   DATA DESCRIPTION

1   AIMS data base
2   Claims transaction file
3   Premium payment transaction file
4   Client transaction
5   Payout account transaction
6   Claim payment check
7   User/client notices
8   Updated AIMS data base
9   Management reports
C.1   AIMS account information
E.1   AIMS account transactions

ACTIVITY - DATA FLOW DIAGRAM   A.A

title
    Accounts Payable

DATA ID   DATA DESCRIPTION

1   AIMS database
2   Claims transaction file
A.1   Client record
B.1   Validated claims transaction
B.2   Invalid claims transaction notice
C.1   Claims record
D.1   Claims payment check
D.2   Updated payout account
D.3   Insufficient funds notice
D.4   Claims transaction log
E.1   Updated client record
E.2   Cancellation notice
E.3   Rate increase notice

Figure 5.2.2
Requirements Graphical Representation

53

Software Validation, Verification, Testing, and Documentation

V,V&T Purpose. To choose V,V&T practices which can be implemented to suit the project needs. The objectives are:

Identify the goals of the AIMS project's V,V&T activities,

Select supporting V,V&T techniques and tools, and

Develop plans for each phase's V,V&T activities. (Plans include tasks, e.g., acquiring or developing tools), schedules, responsibilities, and resources.)

V,V&T Technique. The process described in Chapter 4 is used to develop the V,V&T plans.

Initial Test Case Generation The AIMS requirements will be analyzed and test cases will be designed to test the functional capabilities of the system. These test cases will also form the basic set of acceptance tests.

V,V&T Purpose. To design test cases which, when used to test the AIMS software, will maximize the possibility of revealing the presence of errors in the software.

V,V&T Technique. Requirements-based functional testing is applied to generate this initial set of test cases.

Example:

In the accounts payable function a claims transaction is validated by checking (among other things) that the claim number is valid for the given agent. Each agent has a specified range in which claim numbers associated with claims issued by that agent must fall. Assuming an agent was assigned claim numbers in the range 801000 to 801999, test cases which are generated to test accounts payable should include claim numbers as follows.

Test Data Class	Test Claim Number	Expected Output	Comment
Non-extremal	801500	None	valid
Non-extremal	801317	None	valid
Extremal	801000	None	upper bound
Extremal	801999	None	lower bound
Extremal	800999	Invalid Claim Number	lower bound − 1
Extremal	802000	Invalid Claim Number	upper bound + 1
Special	80100A	Invalid Claim Number	
Special	80100Z	Invalid Claim Number	
Special	80150	Invalid Claim Number	
Special	−01500	Invalid Claim Number	
Special	80L500	Invalid Claim Number	

Preliminary Design Subphase Activity Descriptions

Refinement of Graphical Representation   The GR diagrams developed during requirements analysis will be decomposed to reflect the requirements for the system in more detail.

   V,V&T Purpose.   The completeness and consistency of the GR description of the requirements and preliminary design should be ensured.

   V,V&T Technique.   A review of the resulting diagrams will be performed to verify:
   that all of the basic activities necessary to perform a particular function have been identified,

   that all inputs and outputs required by each activity have been identified, and

   the consistency and completeness of the data flows.
   Example:

   Within the accounts payable function there is no indication as to the action which is to be taken when a claim transaction is processed for a claim which had been previously entered. This error would be discovered during the review of the GR activity for the accounts payable function.

Specify Information Design   The preliminary design of the information consists of a detailed user input/output specification and a description of the basic content and structure of the data used by the system. The detailed user input/output specification essentially amounts to preparing a user's manual for the system. The formats used to input claims and premium payment transactions are defined as well as the output responses. The printed report formats for the management reports are also defined. Specification of the basic data structures and content will consist of identification of variables and records needed by the system, and the relationships which exist among them.

   V,V&T Purpose.   The V,V&T purpose in this activity is twofold. First, the detailed user specifications need to be shown to be usable and that they satisfy the needs of the user. Second, the system data structures and content need to be verified and shown to be complete (i.e., that which is required to perform all system functions) and correct (i.e., the data types and relationships are consistent with the functions which need to be performed).

   V,V&T Technique
   A formal review will be held with the customer to review the detailed user input/output specifications. This will be preceded by informal dialogue between the user community and the developers to aid in the development of the specifications. Once satisfied, the customer will formally sign-off on the specification.

Software Validation, Verification, Testing, and Documentation

Formal inspections of the system data structures and content will be performed. Example:

Discovered by the customer participating in the formal review of the detailed input/output spec was that a client is not always the owner of the car, so that lienholder information needs to be included in the client record.

Design Program Architecture & Allocate Requirements   The program achitecture design gives a complete high-level description of the software. It refines and groups functions defining software components and interfaces.

V,V&T Purpose.   Requirements are cross-referenced by the design to ensure that all the requirements have been addressed.

V,V&T Technique.   Specification tracing.
Example:

A complete set of cross-references is defined and maintained. These show the evolution from the prose requirements to the requirements represented by the GR and finally to the components identified in the design.

Design Basic Control Flow   The GR represents the data flow within a system but only shows control flow in an implicit way. The system's control flow therefore needs to be explicitly designed. The activities identified in the GR will need to be mapped into modules. The control flow between modules must also be described. This is done using an informal design language. This defines the program architecture. The hierarchical structure of the modules comprising the system are developed.

V,V&T Purpose.   To produce a correct and understandable description of the basic control flow of the system.

V,V&T Technique.   An inspection of the control flow design will be performed to verify:
its consistency with the GR representation,

correctness of the high level logic, and

the quality of the modularization, i.e., are the functional boundaries natural?

Test Case Generation

V,V&T Purpose.   Generate test data that will exercise and test each function, and also demonstrate the code is consistent with the design.

V,V&T Technique.   Design-based functional testing.
Example:

56

Example Applications of Validation and Verification Technology

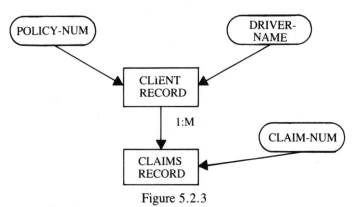

Figure 5.2.3
Sample Database Schema Showing Client-Claims Relation

Test cases for a function which adds the amount of the permium payment to the payout account would include: a negative (or zero) amount, an amount which is greater than zero but less than that which would leave the balance larger than the maximum allowed, and one which would leave the balance greater than the maximum allowed.

Preliminary Design Review   At the completion of the preliminary design activity, a formal review is held. This involves management and technical staff representing the developer and the customer/user. It covers all aspects of the design. Results of V,V&T activities are reviewed. Management of customer/user and developer sign-off of acceptance is required.

Detailed Design Subphase Activity Descriptions

Detailed Database Design   The format and structure of the data to be stored in the system database is designed. This includes description of data which are logically related in the form of records, and the relationships which exist between records. The logical structure of the database will be described using a graphical database design representation. Record descriptions will be specified in a Data Definition Language. Examples are shown in Figures 5.2.3 and 5.2.4.

In Figure 5.2.3, ovals represent record access (key) fields, boxes represent records, "1:M" means that for each client record there are potentially many (1 or more) claims records.

V,V&T Purpose.   The database design needs to be verified for consistency with the preliminary design. Moreover, the database structure will be verified to ensure that it is correct and is reasonable with respect to potential storage consumption and access time.

Figure 5.2.4
Sample CLAIMS Record Description

---

record name is CLAIMS
location mode is calc in CALC-KEY using POLICY-NUM

01	CLAIM-NUM	PIC 9 (6)
01	DATE-OF-CLAIM	PIC 9 (6)
01	ACC-REP-NUM	PIC 9 (9)
01	DRIVER	
	02 LAST	PIC X (15)
	02 FIRST	PIC X (15)
	02 MIDDLE-INTL	PIC X
01	PAYEE	
	02 NAME	PIC X (31)
	02 ADDRESS	
	03 STREET	PIC X (24)
	03 CITY	PIC X (15)
	03 STATE	PIC X (2)
	03 ZIP	PIC X (5)
01	POLICY-NUM	PIC 9 (8)
01	AGENT	PIC 9 (5)

V,V&T Technique. An inspection of the database design is performed to ensure that the above V,V&T purpose is met.

Example:

During the inspection of the database design an error is found in the claims record (Figure 5.2.4) where POLICY-NUM is identified as the key field where as the schema diagram (Figure 5.2.3) indicates CLAIM-NUM. The solution is to change the key field in the claims record description to CLAIM-NUM.

Detailed Module Design Detailed module design includes for each module a description of the function performed and descriptions of input and output data, as well as a high level description of how the function is to be done (i.e., the algorithm used).

V,V&T Purpose. To show that 1. all of the system's functional capabilities are addressed by one or more modules and 2. each module addresses one or more system functions. Moreover, relationships among and interfaces between all modules are identified and verified.

V,V&T Technique
Inspections of the system modules are held. Activities performed during the inspections include manual checking of the module interfaces to ensure that all

modules are used and that their inputs and outputs are consistent. Inspections are also used to verify informally the correctness of the algorithms used.

Requirements tracing is accomplished by identifying each module with the lowest level GR activity (from the preliminary design) in which the module is contained.

Example:

A module which updates the date and time of the last access to the payout account record has as one of its inputs the premium payment transaction. However, manual interface checking detects an inconsistency whereby the premium payment transaction is not supplied. As it turns out, the transaction is not used within the module and is deleted as an input.

Test Case Generation This involves refining and adding to test data previously developed.

V,V&T Purpose. Test cases are developed to exercise and test the internal structures and functions of modules.

V,V&T Technique
Branch testing
Path testing
Example:

The module which validates a claim number checks for six error conditions. Associated with these conditions are three actions. Test data is developed to exercise all combinations of error conditions and resulting actions, that is all branches and all paths through the modules.

Critical Design Review (CDR) At the completion of the detailed design a formal detailed design review is held. This primarily involves project management and technical personnel and covers all all aspects of the design (including the test cases). Management sign-off of their acceptance of the design is required.

Programming Subphase Activity Descriptions

Code Development The detailed design of a given component provides the information needed to write the code for that component in the host programming language, e.g., COBOL. Once written, the code is entered into the computer and all compilation errors are removed.

V,V&T Purpose. V,V&T of the compiled code is performed to:
Verify the consistency of the code with the detailed design,

DATA DECLARATION

   1. Are all variables declared?

   2. Are the correct attributes assigned?

   3. Are variables properly initialized?

   4. Are variable naming conventions followed?

   5. Is the proper explanatory comment included for each variable?

DATA REFERENCE

   1. Are there any unreferenced variables?

   2. Are there any references to unassigned variables?

   3. Are subscripts within range?

   4. Are there off-by-one errors in subscript computations?

          :
          :

Figure 5.2.5
Sample Portion of Code Inspection Checklist

Identify errors, and

Ensure adherence to programming standards.

V,V&T Technique.   Formal reviews of each system module.
Example:

During an inspection of "issue policy notices" module the section of code which is responsible for issuing a premium due notice is found to be in error. The error is that the premium due notice is printed without having the appropriate data moved into the printer buffer. A sample portion of the inspection checklist used is shown below in Figure 5.2.5. This particular error is discovered using question two under "data reference."

Module Testing An incremental, bottom-up testing strategy is used to test the AIMS modules. This involves individually testing the lowest level modules; then combining and testing those modules with the higher level modules which call them. The process continues until all modules are combined into the complete system. Test drivers are written to control the testing of the individual modules. The test data used is that created by design-based functional testing which were generated from analyses of the functional, structural and interface specifications of the individual modules during detailed design.

    V,V&T Purpose.   To reveal errors present in the individual modules.

Function Testing Function testing of AIMS uses the test cases developed from requirements-based functional testing during preliminary design to test the functional capabilities of the AIMS software.

V,V&T Purpose. To reveal errors where the software fails to perform a function as specified in the requirements.

Acceptance Testing Acceptance testing is similar to function testing in that it consists of a subset of the same test cases. But where the purpose of function testing is to reveal the presence of errors, acceptance testing is to demonstrate that the software performs according to its specification. Acceptance testing is a formal procedure and requires customer sign-off.

Example 2: Software Development Using a Minimally Automated V,V&T Tool Set

The minimally automated V,V&T tool set consists of a set of commonly available tools. These are used to supplement the manual techniques described earlier. The tools contained in the minimal set and the lifecycle phase in which they are applied are shown in Table 5.3.1.

Requirements

    Requirements representation language analyzer

Preliminary and Detailed Design

    Design representation language analyzer

Code

    Cross reference generator

    File comparator

    Test coverage analyzer

Requirements Subphase Activity Description

A tool-supported requirements statement language is used to formally specify the requirements. It is used in conjunction with the graphical represention technique which analyzes the gross requirements while the language representation is used to perform a more detailed analysis. It is used to directly support the V,V&T purpose to identify inadequately specified requirements in that a consistency analyzer is part of the tool. The reports generated by the tool are included with the other material for requirements reviews.

Example:

A Problem Statement Language (PSL) [TEIC] description of the accounts payable function is shown in Figure 5.3.1. In this example, the Problem Statement Analyzer (PSA) [TEIC] would identify an inconsistency with respect to the

```
/* Auto Insurance Management Systems (AIMS)
       Accounts payable */

INPUT: claims-transaction-file;
OUTPUT: claim-payment-check, client-notices;
SET: aims-data-base
INTERFACE: client;
       GENERATES: claims-transactions;
       RECEIVES: claim-payment-checks;
PROCESS: accounts-payable;
       UPDATES: aims-data-base;
       RECEIVES: claims-transactions;
       GENERATES: claim-payment-checks;
EOF
```

Figure 5.3.1
PSL Specification for Accounts Payable

accounts payable process. Accounts payable generates claim-payment-checks which have not been previously defined (it is misspelled in the OUTPUT definition).

Preliminary Design Subphase Activity Descriptions

Specify Information Design   A formal requirements specification language (such as PSL) can be used to specify a high-level system information design. Reports produced by the tool are included in the preliminary design document and are analyzed during the reviews.

Design Basic Control Flow   One of the difficulties encountered in the use of an informal design language is that of ensuring a consistent representation for all modules. The use of a tool-supported design language, such as Program Design Language (PDL) [CAIN], prevents this from happening.
    Example:

Figure 5.3.2 shows the PDL description for "Issue Policy Notices." The PDL for all modules is included in the reviews and walk-throughs.

Detailed Design Subphase Activity Description
As in the preliminary design described above, a formal, tool-supported design language is used to describe modules and their algorithms. The reports generated by the tool are included with the information used in the reviews and walkthroughs.

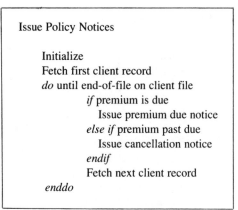

Figure 5.3.2
Preliminary Design PDL of "Issue Policy Notices" Function

During the inspection of this module two problems, an error and a standards violation, are identified. The error is that the program may very likely issue more than one premium notice. The problem occurs in line six. If current-date is greater than or equal to premium-due-date − 40 then current-date + 1 (when the program is next executed) will also be greater. One solution is to introduce an additional boolean variable in the client record, "issued," which is initially false but set to true when the notice is issued. Line six then becomes:

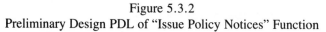

The standards violation is a result of the use of the integer literal constant "40" in line six, particularly since this value may be subject to change. A program constant called "response-interval" should be defined with the value 40 and referenced in line six.

Example:

Figure 5.3.3 shows the PDL of the detailed design for "Issue Policy Notices" from the preliminary design show in Figure 5.3.2.

Programming Subphase Activity Description

Code Development In addition to that described earlier, a cross-referencer is used to produce cross-reference lists of all identifiers used by a program. This list is included with the source code listings for module inspections.

Example:

63

```
Issue Policy Notices

 1        Get current-date
 2        Issue operator instructions
 3        Open data base
 4        Fetch first client record
 5        do until end-of-file on client file
 6                if current-date > = premium-due-date − 40
 7                        Issue premium notice
 8                else if current-date ≠ premium-due-date
 9                        Issue cancellation notice
10                endif
11                Fetch next client record
12        enddo
13        Close database

Issue operator instructions

14   Display program start message and data
15   Display prepare printer message
16   Wait until printer ready
```

Figure 5.3.3
Detailed Design PDL of "Issue Policy Notices" function

A careful examination of the cross-reference listing of module ISSUE-CHECK in ACCOUNTS-PAYABLE during the code inspection indicated that two variables, PAYOUT-ACCOUNT-BAL and PAYOUT-ACCT-BAL, were referenced. The error was that PAYOUT-ACCOUNT-BAL, should have been coded "PAYOUT-ACCT-BAL."

Module Testing   A test coverage analyzer is used to supplement module testing as described in Table 5.3.1. Each module to be tested is instrumented to collect execution frequency counts and then executed. The execution counts for each statement are then listed with the corresponding statement by a post-execution routine. Untested or poorly tested portions of the module can be identified and additional test cases can be generated to test those specific segments.

Example:

ACCOUNTS-PAYABLE processes claims transactions read from a file which contains a given day's claims. The module contains a check to verify that each record is indeed a claims transaction and, if not, invokes an error handling routine which logs the error. Use of a test coverage analyzer showed that this particular situation did not arise during testing of the module using the tests created during detailed design. As a result, those tests are supplemented with invalid claims transactions and the module retested. This, in turn, results in an error being revealed whereby the error handler responds with an incorrect output response.

Function Testing   Function testing is supplemented with the use of a file comparator. Associated with each of the requirements-based functional test cases is the expected output. This is stored on a file in the exact format expected to be produced. When the AIMS software is tested, the resulting output is stored on a separate file. A file comparator is used to detect automatically any discrepancies which may have occurred.

Example:

In preparing the test cases for the New Clients report, a form is used which formats the expected output data in accordance with the specification. Each report corresponding to a given test case is then stored on a file in the order in which the tests are to be executed. Testing is then performed and the actual output is compared to the expected output using a file comparator. The results show the presence of two errors, a format error and a data output error. The format error is a misalignment caused by incorrect spacing between output fields. The data output error is a missing agent name which is to be printed with the agent number.

Example 3: Software Development Using a Fully Automated V,V&T Tool Set

The fully automated V,V&T tool set is comprised of commonly used tools and techniques, and includes those tools contained in the minimal tool set described earlier as well as those described in this section. The additional tools and the applicable lifecycle phase are shown below.

Preliminary Design
  Assertion generation
Detailed Design
  Assertion generation
Code
  Interface checker
  Data flow analyzer
  Assertion processor
  Standards analyzer

65

Software Validation, Verification, Testing, and Documentation

Requirements Subphase Activity Description
(No additions to minimal tool set.)

Preliminary Design Subphase Activity Description

V,V&T Technique.   Assertion generation is used to specify the desired functional properties of the individual modules. This is done by including in the module specifications input and, to the extent possible, output assertions.
Example:

Policy numbers are stored in the database in blocks of arrays where each block contains a fixed number (n) of policy numbers (policy-num) and the address (policy-addr) of their associated client records. Policy numbers are stored in the policy-num array in ascending order. A procedure, find-policy, is called to search the policy-num array for a supplied policy number and return the address of its client record. If the supplied policy number is not found an address of zero is returned. The input and output assertions which capture the functional properties of find-policy are given below.

1) /* *assert input* policy-num (1)$<$ $=$ num$<$ $=$ policy-num (m) */ *and*
2) /* *assert input forall* i *in* 1 . . . n-1:policy-num (i)$<$ $=$ policy-num (i+1) */
3) /* *assert output* (*exists in* i *in* 1 . . . n : num $=$ policy-num (i)) */ *or*
4) /* *assert output* (addr$=$0 *and forall* i *in* 1 . . .n:num $=$ policy-num (i)) */

Detailed Design Subphase Activity Description

V,V&T Technique.   Assertions are generated to include algorithmic detail in addition to input and output specifications of the functional properties of the individual modules.
Example:

The example in the previous section describes the find-policy procedure and specifies the input and output assertions associated with it. Shown in figure 5.4.1 is the PDL for find-policy which is implemented using a binary search algorithm.
The input and output assertions capture the functional properties of the procedure independent of the algorithm used to implement the search. Assertions 1, 2 and 3, however, capture conditions which are very dependent upon the algorithm. Assertion 1 is always correct whenever num is in the policy-num array. If num is not in the array, assertion 1 is violated the last time through the loop (when high $=$ low). This is an acceptable result, however, in that num should be a valid policy number.

66

find-policy:

/* searches sorted global array policy-num for num (input argument) and, if found, returns the associated policy-addr in addr (output argument). If not found a zero is returned in addr */

/* *assert input* policy-num (1)< = num< = policy-num (n) */
/* *assert input forall* i *in* 1 . . .n − 1: policy-num (i)< = policy-num (i + 1) */

set addr *to* 0
set low *to* 1
set high *to* n

Programming Subphase Activity Descriptions

Code Development   The code development activities described in earlier sections are supplemented in a full tool set environment with an interface checker, data flow analyzer and standards analyzer. These tools can be separate but are often included as capabilities provided by a single tool. They are all static analysis techniques and are therefore applied prior to software testing. The output which results from each of the capabilities is included with the material for the formal code inspections.

V,V&T Techniques
Interface checking is used to check the consistency of the interfaces between modules.
Example:

An error is detected between the module which reads client records for premium payment processing and the "find-policy" module. It is an inconsistency in the type of the arguments for the policy numbers. "Find-Policy" is being called with a policy number of type character where it should be type integer.
Data flow analysis is used to identify variable reference/definition anomalies.
Example:

When data flow analysis is performed on the module which updates the payout account with a premium payment, a reference to an uninitialized variable is noted. The variable should contain the current date and time and is used to update the date and time of the last change to the payout account. A call to the routine which updates the time and date should be made prior to the reference.

Standards' analyzers are used to assure adherence to program coding and documentation standards. One of the primary capabilities provided by most commonly available standards' analyzers is the notification of the use of nonstandard language features.
Example:

```
    do until high < or num = policy-num (i)
(1) /* assert 1 < = low < = high < = n and policy-num (low) < = num < =
        policy-num (high) */
    set m to (low + high) /2
    if num < policy-num (i)
    set high to m - i
    else if num > policy-num (i)
    set low to m + i
    else goto successful
    enddo


/* unsuccessful */

(2) /* assert high = low - 1 and policy-num (high) < num < policy-num (low) */
    /* assert output addr = 0 and forall i in 1...n: num ≠ policy-num (i) */
    return

/* successful */

    set addr to policy-num (i)
(3) /* assert 1 < = low < = m < = high < = n and num = policy-num (m) */
    /* assert output exists i in 1...n: num = policy-num (i) */
    return

end find-policy;
```

Figure 5.4.1
Detailed PDL with ASSERTIONS

One of the requirements for the AIMS software is that it be portable. To assist in the development of portable code, a COBOL standards' analyzer is used. All places where a standards' violation occurs is either changed or justified. Even trivial nonstandard features such as the use of the abbreviation "DISP" for "DISPLAY" are detected. In addition, a variety of undesirable standard language constructs such as the "ALTER" statement and "NEXT SENTENCE" clause are detected with the tool.

Module Testing The module testing activities described in earlier sections are supplemented in a full tool set environment with a dynamic assertions processor. This processor is generally included as part of a broader dynamic analysis tool which includes, for example, statement execution counts.

V,V&T Technique. Assertions processor: A dynamic assertions processor translates assertions, usually specified as part of the source program, into source

```
                    .
                    .
                    .
13   100   CONTINUE
14 C*          ASSERT(1.LE.LOW.AND.LOW.LE.HIGH.AND.HIGH.LE.N
15 C*          .AND.POLNUM(LOW).LE.NUM.AND.NUM.LE.POLNUM(HIGH))
16             M = (LOW + HIGH)/2
17             IF ( NUM .LT. POLNUM(M) ) THEN
18                 HIGH = M + 1
19             ELSE IF ( NUM .GT. POLNUM(M) ) THEN
20                 LOW = M + 1
21             ELSE
22                 GO TO 200
23             ENDIF
24             IF(HIGH.LE.LOW.AND.NUM.NE.POLNUM(M) ) GO TO 100
                    .
                    .
                    .

*** ASSERTION VIOLATION AT LINE 14 OF SUBROUTINE FNDPOL:
    CURRENT EXECUTION COUNT = 2
    LOW = 1, HIGH = 65, N = 64, NUM = 22707,
    POLNUM(LOW) = 16747, POLNUM(HIGH) = 36757
```

Figure 5.4.2

Find-policy Subroutine and Corresponding Assertion Violation Message

language statements which check the validity of the assertion during program execution. Generally, when an assertion is violated, an informative message is output.
Example:

Figure 5.4.2 shows a portion of a FORTRAN implementation of the find-policy routine from Figure 5.4.1. Also shown is an example of an assertion violation message which was printed when the assertion in line 14 of the program was violated (i.e., false) during program execution. Subsequent analysis of the problem indicated that the error was an incorrect coding of line 18 from the PDL where HIGH should have been set to $M - 1$, not $M + 1$.

Example 4: Software Maintenance

System maintenance activities involve the processing of changes to the system software and documentation necessary to correct an error or to enhance or alter the system's functional capabilities. The maintenance activities described in this example are supported by the fully automated V,V&T tool set, described in earlier examples, augmented with software configuration control procedures.

Maintenance is generally divided into two classifications:

Problem reporting and correction, and

Change request processing.

Problem reporting and correction involves a formal notification (usually con-

69

sisting of a form which is filled out by a user) of an error in the software. The error is then verified and the offending module(s) identified and corrected. The effort required for the entire process is, in most cases, minimal in that any more than a very minimal redesign is seldom necessary.

Change request processing involves a formal notification (basically consisting of a requirements statement) of a desired enhancement, alteration or improvement (e.g., performance) in the system's functional capabilities. Change requests always require some software redesign and, as a result, involve a greater level of effort.

Each of these activities are illustrated in the following sections with some simple examples from the AIMS software.

Problem Reporting and Correction Activity Descriptions

Problem Analysis

When a problem report is received, the problem must be analyzed to determine the cause of the error. Often, the error needs to be recreated to obtain additional information pertaining to the source of the error. It may be that a user has made an error which was the result of a misunderstanding on his part. The misunderstanding could be the user's problem or it may be the user documentation that is incorrect.

If the problem is indeed an error in the software, then the offending code needs to be identified and possible solutions addressed. This is generally not an easy task. If the software has been developed using the lifecycle V,V&T techniques and tools described in the previous sections, the error has escaped very thorough attempts to uncover it. Although some V,V&T tools can provide assistance, they are generally not very helpful in locating the error. The best tool to use is one's brain. Tools are not meant to replace thinking but to assist in amplifying the thinking process.

Once the error has been located, possible solutions can be identified. These solutions vary from being very trivial code modifications to an extensive redesign. It is important to note that if good lifecycle V,V&T practices are utilized during software development, then the instances of redesign are significantly reduced.

Example:

An AIMS Problem Report is received describing an error in which a claims transaction is due to an invalid agent number although that particular agent number is listed in the user documentation as valid. Upon analysis of the problem, the cause of the error turns out to be that a new agent was added to the company with a new number assigned. The documentation was updated but the table of agent numbers in the AIMS software was not updated.

Problem Correction   When the source of an error is found to be in the software and the offending code is identified, the correction of the error needs to be made.

The code in the module which contains the error is modified. The V,V&T techniques and tools which are used during the code correction process will depend on the extent of the error. In the previous example, only a table addition is required. The compiler detects most errors and an inspection of the compiled table is generally all that is necessary before retesting. In a case where an entire algorithm is wrong, a formal review of the code is probably necessary, as well as use of the full automated V,V&T tool set to completely retest the module.

After the code has been modified and module testing completed, regression testing is performed. In cases where the module interfaces with another module(s), interface checking, hierarchy, module calling, etc. tools should be employed before regression checking. All system components which can potentially be affected by the change are retested using a standard set of system test cases augmented with tests aimed at revealing the original error (e.g., the actual input which caused the error should be included). When testing is complete, the actual output is compared with the expected (correct) output, possibly using a file comparator. If no errors are present, then the updated modules are incorporated into the production software and any pertinent documentation is updated.

Example:

An error was discovered where on midnight of December 30, 1980 the year-to-date premium total was reset so that premiums received on December 31 were counted in the 1981 total instead of the 1980 total. Upon examination, it was found that the end of year test was 365 days. 1980, however, being a leap year, contained 366 days and so the reset occurred a day early. In this case, the software correction is quite simple and is implemented with little difficulty. In fact, it is more difficult to correct the misinformation in the database than it is to correct the error.

Change Request Processing Activity Descriptions

Requirements Analysis The requirements analysis associated with system enhancements or alterations is essentially the same as described earlier in this chapter except for one fundamental difference. For all practical purposes, the feasibility of a particular enhanced or altered capability depends upon how well that capability can be implemented within the existing design. The more redesign that is necessary, the greater the magnitude of the cost to implement it. Redesign costs are not an issue during the requirements phase of the initial software development since there is no existing design. What this means is that the scope of what is or is not feasible is much narrower during the maintenance phase and therefore must be given consideration.

The V,V&T techniques applied during this requirements analysis are the same as before utilizing reviews, representation aids, etc. to assist in the analysis and specification.

Software Validation, Verification, Testing, and Documentation

Example:

High level company management issued a change request to enhance AIMS to interactively process claims and premium payment transactions. The current system batchs the transactions on a file which is then processed once a day. This results in a response time which is inconvenient for the agents as well as the customer. It is decided to enhance the system to process claims and premium payments interactively as they are received.

During requirements analysis, it is found that those system modules which are impacted by the redesign are those which control the input/output of the batch transactions. Replacement of those modules with ones which could perform interactive processing is relatively straightforward. Increased computer usage would, however, require additional hardware resources for normal production operation.

Management felt that the extra cost was worthwhile and thereby authorized the system change.

Redesign and Coding   The process followed for the implementation of a system enhancement or an alteration is no different than that followed for a complete software development as described earlier in this chapter. Therefore, no further discussion is required.

6. Summary

This document has presented information on lifecycle V,V&T and guidance on planning for V,V&T. It has covered:

Software development phases and accompanying V,V&T activities

A categorization of V,V&T techniques into static, dynamic, and formal analysis

Suggestions on how to integrate static, dynamic, and formal V,V&T analysis into a lifecycle

Guidance on steps and approaches to take when planning V,V&T activities

Recognition that V,V&T activities must be tailored to meet the needs of specific projects

A series of rather detailed examples of V,V&T approaches using increasing levels of automated support were also presented. A reference guide of techniques and tools [POWE] for V,V&T is a valuable companion for this document. A glossary of V,V&T terms is included as an appendix.

Glossary

BLACK BOX TESTING   see FUNCTIONAL TESTING

BOUNDARY VALUE ANALYSIS   a selection technique in which test data is chosen to lie along "boundaries" or extremes of input domain (or output range) classes, data structures, procedure parameters, etc. Choices often include maximum, minimum, and trivial values or parameters. This technique is often called stress testing.

BRANCH TESTING   a test method satisfying coverage criteria that require, for each decision point, each possible branch be executed at least once.

CAUSE EFFECT GRAPHING   test data selection technique. The inputs and outputs of the program are determined through analysis of the requirements. A minimal set of inputs is chosen avoiding the testing of multiple inputs which cause identical output.

COMPLETENESS   the property that all necessary parts of the entity in question are included. Completeness of a product is often used to express the fact that all requirements have been met by the product.

CONSISTENCY   the property of logical coherency among constituent parts. Consistency may also be expressed as adherence to a given set of rules.

CORRECTNESS   the extent to which software is free from design and coding defects, i.e. fault free. It is also the extent to which software meets its specified requirements and user objectives. (IEEE Software Engineering Terminology)

DEBUGGING   the process of correcting syntactic and logical errors detected during coding. With the primary goal of obtaining an executing piece of code, debugging shares with testing certain techniques and strategies but differs in its usual ad hoc application and local scope.

DESIGN BASED FUNCTIONAL TESTING   the application of test data derived through functional analysis (see FUNCTIONAL TESTING) extended to include design functions as well as requirement functions.

DRIVER   code which sets up an environment and calls a module for test.

DYNAMIC ANALYSIS   involves execution or simulation of a development phase product. It detects errors by analyzing the response of a product to sets of input data.

EXTREMAL TEST DATA   test data that is at the extremes, or boundaries, of the domain of an input variable or which produces results at the boundaries of an output domain.

Glossary

FORMAL ANALYSIS   uses rigorous mathematical techniques to analyze the algorithms of a solution. The algorithms may be analyzed for numerical properties, efficiency, and/or correctness.

FUNCTIONAL TESTING   application of test data derived from the specified functional requirements without regard to the final program structure.

INSPECTION   a manual analysis technique in which the program (requirements, design, or code) is examined in a very formal and disciplined manner to discover errors.

INSTRUMENTATION   the insertion of additional code into the program in order to collect information about program behavior during program execution.

INVALID INPUT (TEST DATA FOR INVALID INPUT DOMAIN)   test data that lies outside the domain of the program's function.

PATH TESTING   a test method satisfying coverage criteria that each logical path through the program be tested. Often paths through the program are grouped into a finite set of classes; one path from each class is then tested.

PROOF OF CORRECTNESS   the use of techniques of mathematical logic to infer that a relation between program variables assumed true at program entry implies that another relation between program variables holds at program exit.

REGRESSION TESTING   Rerunning test cases which a program has previously executed correctly in order to detect errors created during software correction or modification activities.

SIMULATION   use of an executable model to represent the behavior of an object. During testing the computational hardware, the external environment, and even code segments may be simulated.

SPECIAL TEST DATA   test data based on input values that are likely to require special handling by the program.

STATEMENT TESTING   a test method satisfying the criterion that each statement in a program be executed at least once during program testing.

STATIC ANALYSIS   direct analysis of the form and structure of a product without executing the product. It may be applied to the requirements, design or code.

STRESS TESTING   see BOUNDARY VALUE ANALYSIS.

TUB   special code segments that when invoked by a code segment under test will simulate the behavior of designed and specified modules not yet constructed.

SYMBOLIC EXECUTION   an analysis technique that derives a symbolic expression for each program path.

TEST DATA SET   set of input elements used in the testing process.

TEST DRIVER   a program which directs the execution of another program against a collection of test data sets. Usually, the test driver records and organizes the output generated as the tests are run.

TEST HARNESS   see TEST DRIVER.

TESTING   examination of the behavior of a program by executing the program on sample data sets.

VALID INPUT (TEST DATA FOR A VALID INPUT DOMAIN)   test data that lies within the domain of the function represented by the program.

Software Validation, Verification, Testing, and Documentation

VALIDATION   determination of the correctness of the final program or software produced from a development project with respect to the user needs and requirements.

VERIFICATION   in general, the demonstration of consistency, completeness, and correctness of the software at each stage and between each stage of the development lifecycle.

WALKTHROUGH   a manual analysis technique in which the module author describes the module's structure and logic to an audience of colleagues.

Bibliography

1. [ADRI] ADRION, W.R., BRANSTAD, M.A., CHERNIAVSKY, J.C., "Validation, Verification, and Testing of Computer Software," *NBS Special Publication 500-75*, February 1981.
2. [BRAN] BRANSTAD, M.A., CHERNIAVSKY, J.C. and ADRION, W.R., "Validation, Verification and Testing for the Individual Programmer," *NBS Special Publication 500-56*, Washington, D.C., October 1979.
3. [CAIN] CAINE, S.H. and GORDON, E.K., "PDL: A Tool for Software Design," *Proceedings of the National Computer Conference*, 1975.
4. [DARR] DARRINGER, J.C. King, "Applications of Symbolic Execution to Program Testing," *Computer*, April 1978.
5. [DEMI] DEMILLO, R.A., LIPTON, R.J. and SAYWARD, F.C., "Hints on Test Data Selection: Help for the Practicing Programmer," *Computer*, April 1978.
6. [DUKE] DUKE, M.O., "Testing in a Complex Systems Environment," *IBM Systems Journal*, Vol. 14, No. 4, 1975.
7. [ELSP] ELSPAS, B.K., LEVITT, N. and WALDINGER, R.J. "An Assessment of the Techniques for Proving Program Correctness," *ACM Computing Surveys*, Vol. 4, No. 2, June 1972, pp. 97-147.
8. [ELME] ELMENDORF, W.R. "Disciplined Software Testing," *Debugging Techniques in Large Systems*, R. Rustin, ed., Prentice Hall, 1971, pp. 137-140.
9. [FAIR] FAIRLEY, R.E., "Static Analysis and Dynamic Testing of Computer Software," *Computer*, April 1978.
10. [FIPS38] "Guidelines for Documentation of Computer Programs and Automated Data Systems," *NBS Federal Information Processing Standards Publication 38*, February 1976.
11. [FIPS64] "Guidelines for Documentation of Computer Programs and Automated Data Systems for the Initiation Phase," *NBS Federal Information Processing Standards Publication 64*, August 1979.
12. [FOSD] FOSDICK, L.D. and OSTERWEIL, L.J. "Data Flow Analysis in Software Reliability," *ACM Computing Surveys*, Vol. 8, No. 3, September 1976, pp. 305-330.
13. [GERH] GERHART, S.L. and YELOWITZ, L. "Observations of Fallibility in the Application of Modern Programming Methodologies," *IEEE Transactions on Software Engineering*, Vol. SE-2, No. 3, September 1976, pp. 195-207.
14. [GLAS] GLASS, R., "Software Reliability Guidebook," Englewood Cliffs, NJ, Prentice-Hall, 1979.
15. [GOOD] GOODENOUGH, J.B. and GERHART, S.L. "Toward a Theory of Test Data Selection," *IEEE Transactions on Software Engineering*, Vol. SE-1, No. 2, June 1975, pp. 156-173.
16. [HART] HARTWICK, R.D., "Test Planning," *AFIPS Conference Proceedings*, Vol. 46, 1977 NCC, pp. 285-294.
17. [HETZ] HETZEL, W.C., "Program Test Methods," Englewood Cliffs, NJ, Prentice-Hall, 1973.
18. [HOUGa] HOUGHTON, Raymond C., Jr., "Features of Software Development Tools," *NBS Special Publication 500-74*, Washington, D.C., February 1981.

Software Validation, Verification, Testing, and Documentation

19. [HOUGb] HOUGHTON, Raymond C., Jr., and OAKLEY, Karen A., eds., "NBS Software Tools Database," *NBSIR 80-2159,* October 1980.

20. [HOWDa] HOWDEN, W.E., "Reliability of the Path Analysis Testing Strategy," *IEEE Transactions on Software Engineering,* September 1976, pp. 208-214.

21. [HOWDb] HOWDEN, W.E., "Theoretical and Empirical Studies of Program Testing," *IEEE Transactions on Software Engineering,* Vol. SE-4, July 1976.

22. [HUAN] HUANG, J.C., "An Approach to Program Testing," *ACM Computer Surveys,* Vol. 7, No. 3, September 1975.

23. [MILLa] MILLER, E.F., Jr., "Program Testing: Art Meet Theory," *Computer,* July 1977.

24. [MILLb] MILLER, E.F. Jr., and HOWDEN, W.E., "Tutorial: Software Testing and Validation Techniques," Long Beach, CA, *IEEE Computer Society,* 1978.

25. [MULL] MULLIN, F.J., "Software Test Management," *COMPSAC 77 Proceedings,* Chicago, Illinois, November 1977.

26. [MYER] MYERS, G.J., "The Art of Software Testing," New York, Wiley, 1979.

27. [PANZ] PANZL, D.L., "Automatic Software Test Drivers," *Computer,* April 1978.

28. [POWE] POWELL, P.B., "Software Validation, Verification, and Testing Technique and Tool Reference Guide," *NBS Special Publication 500-93,* Washington, D.C., September 1982.

29. [SAMM] "SAMM (Systematic Activity Modeling Method) Primer," BCS 10167, October 1978.

30. [TEIC] TEICHROEW, D. and HERSHEY, E., "PSA/PSL: A Computer-Aided Technique for Structured Documentation of Information Processing Systems," *IEEE Transactions on Software Engineering,* Vol. SE-3, No. 1, 1977.

Book Two
Validation, Verification and Testing of Computer Software

Abstract

Programming is an exercise in problem solving. As with any problem solving activity, determination of the validity of the solution is part of the process. This survey discusses testing and analysis techniques that can be used to validate software and to instill confidence in the programming product. Verification throughout the development process is stressed. Specific tools and techniques are described.

Key words: Validation; software verification; software testing; test data generation; test coverage; automated software tools; software lifecycle.

7. Quality Assurance Through Verification

The National Bureau of Standards (NBS) has a mission under Public Law 89–306 (Brooks Act) to develop standards to enable the "economic and efficient purchase, lease, maintenance, operation, and utilization of automatic data processing equipment by Federal Departments and agencies." As part of its current standards initiative, NBS is studying methods to ensure the quality of software procured by the Government and software developed within the Government.

Testing is the traditional technique used to determine and assure the quality of products. For many items procured by the Government, the definition or description of a quality product and the testing methods used to ensure that quality are well established. These tests are usually physical tests based on both industry and Government standards (such as dimensions for fittings, strength for materials, power for motors, etc.). The success of these methods depends upon the definition of what constitutes a quality product, the determination of measurable properties that reflect the quality, the derivation of meaningful test criteria based on the measurable quantities, and the formulation of adequate tests to ensure the quality.

Unfortunately, software does not fit into the traditional framework of quality assessment. One reason is that software, in general, is a "one of a kind" product especially tailored for a particular application. There is often no standard product or specification to use as a model to measure against. Secondly, analogies to physical products with applicable dimensional, strength, etc. standards do not exist. Of greatest importance, the concept of what constitutes quality in software is not as well formulated. There is no universally accepted definition of software quality.

Attributes of Quality Software

There have been many studies directed toward the determination of appropriate factors for software quality [BOEH78], [MCCA77], [JONE76]. A number of attributes have been proposed; the set given by Figure 7.1 is representative. Most of these factors are qualitative rather than quantitative.

In Figure 7.1, the top level characteristics of quality software are reliability, testability, usability, efficiency, transportability, and maintainability. In practice,

81

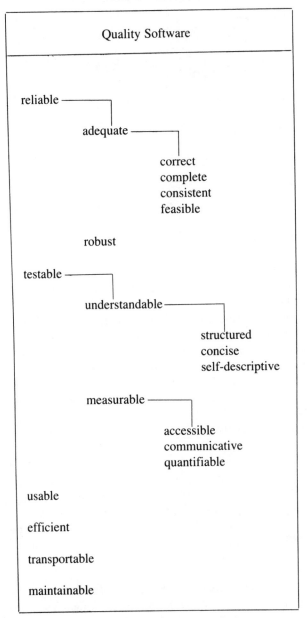

Figure 7.1
A Hierarchy of Software Quality Attributes

efficiency often turns out to be in conflict with other attributes, e.g. transportability, maintainability, and testability. As hardware costs decrease, efficiency of machine use becomes much less an issue and consequently a less important attribute of software quality. At present, a reasonable software development methodology will support the creation of software with all these qualities. While a piece of code may not be locally as efficient as a skilled programmer can write it disregarding all other factors, it must be designed to be as efficient as possible while still exhibiting the other desired qualities.

For our purposes in Book Two, two qualities stand out, reliability and testability. The others are equally important, but less related to testing and verification issues, and perhaps more qualitative than quantitative. Reliable software must be adequate, that is, it must be correct, complete, consistent, and feasible at each stage of the development lifecycle. An infeasible set of requirements will lead to an inadequate design and probably an incorrect implementation. Given that the software meets these adequacy requirements at each stage of the development process, to be reliable it must also be robust. Robustness is a quality which represents the ability of the software to survive a hostile environment. We cannot anticipate all possible events [ADRI80], and we must build our software to be as resilient as possible.

At all stages of the lifecycle, software should be testable. To accomplish this it must be understandable. The desired product (the requirements and design) and the actual product (the code) should be represented in a structured, concise, and self-descriptive manner so that they can be compared. The software must also be measurable, allowing means for actually instrumenting or inserting probes, testing, and evaluating the product of each stage.

Emphasis on particular quality factors will vary from project to project depending on application, environment, and other considerations. The specific definition of quality and the importance of given attributes should be specified during the requirements phase of the project.

Even if good quality is difficult to define and measure, poor quality is glaringly apparent. Software that is error prone or does not work is obviously poor quality software. Consequently, discovery of errors in the software has been the first step toward quality assurance. Program testing, executing the software using representative data samples and comparing the actual results with the expected results, has been the fundamental technique used to determine errors. However, testing is difficult, time consuming, and inadequate. Consequently, increased emphasis has been placed upon insuring quality through the development process.

The criticality of the problem determines the effort required to validate the solution. Software to control airplane landings or to direct substantial money transfers requires higher confidence in its proper functioning than does a carpool locator program since the consequences of malfunction are more severe. For each software project not only the product requirements but also the validation requirements should be determined and specified at the initiation of the project. Project size, uniqueness, criticality, the cost of malfunction, and project budget all influence the validation needs. With the validation requirements clearly stated, specific techniques for verification and testing can be chosen. Book Two surveys the field of verification and testing techniques. The emphasis is upon medium and large size projects but many of the individual techniques have broader applicability. Verification and testing for very small projects are discussed in [BRAN80].

Although a glossary is included as an appendix, the following terms are sufficiently important to warrant definition in the text. It should be noted that some of these terms may appear with slightly different meanings elsewhere in the literature.

VALIDATION   determination of the correctness of the final program or software produced from a development project with respect to the user needs and requirements. Validation is usually accomplished by verifying each stage of the software development lifecycle.

CERTIFICATION   acceptance of software by an authorized agent usually after the software has been validated by the agent, or after its validity has been demonstrated to the agent.

VERIFICATION   in general the demonstration of consistency, completeness, and correctness of the software at each stage and between each stage of the development lifecycle.

TESTING   examination of the behavior of a program by executing the program on sample data sets.

PROOF OF CORRECTNESS   use of techniques of logic to infer that an assertion assumed true at program entry implies that an assertion holds at program exit.

PROGRAM DEBUGGING   the process of correcting syntactic and logical errors detected during coding. With the primary goal of obtaining an executing piece of code, debugging shares with testing certain techniques and strategies, but differs in its usual ad hoc application and local scope.

Verification Throughout the Lifecycle

Figure 7.2 presents a traditional view of the development life cycle with testing contained in a stage immediately prior to operation and maintenance. All too often testing is the only verification technique used to determine the adequacy of the software. When verification is constrained to a single technique and confined to the latter stages of development, severe consequences can result. It is not usual to hear of testing consuming 50% of the development budget. All errors are costly but the later in the lifecycle that the error discovery is made, the more costly the error [INFO79]. Consequently, if lower cost and higher quality are the goal, verification should not be isolated to a single stage in the development process but should be incorporated into each phase of development. Barry Boehm [BOEH77] has stated that one of the most prevalent and costly mistakes made on software projects today is to defer the activity of detecting and correcting software problems until late in the project. The primary reason for early investment in verification activity is that expensive errors may already have been made before coding begins.

Figure 7.3 presents an amended life cycle chart which includes verification ac-

REQUIRE-MENTS	DESIGN	CODE	INTEGRATE	TEST	OPERATION & MAINTENANCE

Figure 7.2
The Software Development Life Cycle

Life Cycle Stage	Verification Activities
Requirements	Determine Verification Approach Determine Adequacy of Requirements Generate Functional Test Data
Design	Determine Consistency of Design with Requirements Determine Adequacy of Design Generate Structural and Functional Test Data
Construction	Determine Consistency with Design Determine Adequacy of Implementation Generate Structural and Functional Test Data Apply Test Data
Operation & Maintenance	Retest

Figure 7.3
Life Cycle Verification Activities

tivities. The success of phasing verification throughout the development cycle depends upon the existence of a clearly defined and stated product at each development stage. The more formal and precise the statement of the development product, the more amenable it is to the analysis required to support verification. Many of the new software development methodologies encourage a firm product from the early development stages.

We will examine each stage of the lifecycle and discuss the relevant activities. The following activities should be performed at each stage:

Analyze the structures produced at this stage for internal testability and adequacy.

Generate test sets based on the structures at this stage.

In addition, the following should be performed during design and construction:

Determine that the structures are consistent with structures produced during previous stages.

Refine or redefine test sets generated earlier.

Throughout the entire life cycle, neither development nor verification is a straightline activity. Modifications or corrections to structures at one stage will require modifications and reverification of structures produced during previous stages.

Requirements

The verification activities that accompany the problem definition and requirements analysis stage of software development are extremely significant. The adequacy of the requirements must be thoroughly analyzed and initial test cases generated with the expected (correct) responses. Developing scenarios of expected system use may help to determine the test data and anticipated results. These tests will form the core of the final test set. Generating these tests and the expected behavior of the system clarifies the requirements and helps guarantee that they are testable. Vague or untestable requirements will leave the validity of the delivered product in doubt. Late discovery of requirements inadequacy can be very costly. A determination of the criticality of software quality attributes and the importance of validation should be made at this stage. Both product requirements and validation requirements should be established.

Some automated tools to aid in the requirements definition exist. Examples include Information System Design and Optimization System (ISDOS) [TEIC77], The Software Requirements Engineering Program (SREP) [ALFO77], Structured Analysis and Design Technique (SADT) [ROSS77], and Systematic Activity Modeling Method (SAMM) [LAMB78]. All provide a disciplined frame work for expressing requirements and thus aid in the checking of consistency and completeness. Although these tools provide only rudimentary validation procedures, this capability is greatly needed and it is the subject of current research [TEIC78].

Design

Organization of the verification effort and test management activities should be closely integrated with preliminary design. The general testing strategy, including test methods and test evaluation criteria, if formulated; and a test plan is produced. If the project size or criticality warrants, an independent test team is organized. In addition, a test schedule with observable milestones is constructed. At this same time, the framework for quality assurance and test documentation should be established, such as [FIPS76], [BUCK79], or [IEEE79].

During detailed design, validation support tools should be acquired or developed and the test procedures themselves should be produced. Test data to exercise the functions introduced during the design process as well as test cases based upon the structure of the system should be generated. Thus as the software development proceeds, a more effective set of test cases is built up.

In addition to test organization and the generation of test cases to be used during construction, the design itself should be analyzed and examined for errors. Simulation can be used to verify properties of the system structures and subsystem interaction, design walk-throughs should be used by the developers to verify the flow and logical structure of the system while design inspection should be performed by the test team. Missing cases, faulty logic, module interface mismatches, data structure inconsistencies, erroneous I/O assumptions, and user interface inadequacies are items of concern. The detailed design must be shown internally consistent, complete, and consistent with the preliminary design and requirements.

Although much of the verification must be performed manually, the use of a formal design language can facilitate the analysis. Several different design methodologies are in current use. Top Down Design proposed by Harlan Mills of IBM [MILL70], Structured Design introduced by L. Constantine [YOUR79], and the Jackson Method [JACK75] are examples. These techniques are manual and facilitate verification by providing a clear statement of the design. The Design Expression and Configuration Aid (DECA) [CARP75], the Process Design Language [CAIN75], High Order Software [HAMI76], and SPECIAL [ROUB76] are examples of automated systems or languages which can also be used for analysis and consistency checking.

Construction

Actual testing occurs during the construction stage of development. Many testing tools and techniques exist for this stage of system development. Code walk-through and code inspection are effective manual techniques. Static analysis techniques detect errors by analyzing program characteristics such as data flow and language construct usage. For programs of significant size, automated tools are required to perform this analysis. Dynamic analysis, performed as the code actually executes, is used to determine test coverage through various instrumentation techniques. Formal verification or proof techniques are used to provide further quality assurance. These techniques are discussed in detail in Chapter 3.

During the entire test process, careful control and management of test information is critical. Test sets, test results, and test reports should be catalogued and stored in a data base. For all but very small systems, automated tools are required to do an adequate job, for the bookkeeping chores alone become too large to be handled manually. A test driver, test data generation aids, test coverage tools, test results management aids, and report generators are usually required.

Maintenance

Over 50% of the life cycle costs of a software system are spent on maintenance. As the system is used, it is modified either to correct errors or to augment the original system. After each modification the system must be retested. Such retesting activity is termed regression testing. The goal of regression testing is to minimize the cost of system revalidation. Usually only those portions of the system impacted by the modifications are retested. However, changes at any level may necessitate retesting, reverifying and updating documentation at all levels below it. For example, a design change requires design reverification, unit retesting and subsystem and system retesting. Test cases generated during system development are reused or used after appropriate modifications. The quality of the test documentation generated during system development and modified during maintenance will affect the cost of regression testing. If test data cases have been catalogued and preserved, duplication of effort will be minimized.

We will emphasize, in the following chapters, testing, verification, and validation during software development. The maintenance and operation stage is very important, but generally outside the scope of this report. The procedures described here for software development will, if followed correctly, make the task of maintaining, upgrading, evolving, and operating the software a much easier task.

8. An Overview of Testing

Concepts

The purpose of this chapter is to discuss the basic concepts and fundamental implications and limitations of testing as a part of software verification. There are many meanings attributed to the verb "to test" throughout the technical literature. Let us begin by looking at the Oxford English Dictionary definition:

Test: That by which the existence, quality, or genuineness of anything is, or may be, determined.

The objects that we test are the elements that arise during the development of software. These include modules of code, requirements and design specifications, data structures, and any other objects that are necessary for the correct development and implementation of our software. We will often use the term "program" in this document to refer to any object that may be conceptually or actually executed. A design or requirements specification can be conceptually executed, transforming input data to output data. Hence, remarks directed towards "programs" have broader application.

We view a program as a representation of a function. The function describes the relationship of an input (called a *domain element*) to an output (called a *range element*). The testing process is then used to ensure that the program faithfully realizes the function. For example, consider the function $1/x$. Its domain is the set of all floating point numbers excluding 0. Any program that realizes the function $1/x$ must, when given a floating point value r (r nonzero), return the value of $1/r$ (given the machine dependent precision). The testing problem is to ensure that the program does represent the function.

Elements of the function's domain are called *valid inputs*. Since programs are expected to operate reasonably on elements outside of a function's domain (called "robustness"), we must test the program on such elements. Thus any program that represents $1/x$ should be tested on the value 0 and perhaps also on meaningless data (such as strings) to ensure that the program does not fail catastrophically. These elements outside of the function's domain are called *invalid inputs*. How to choose these and other test input values is discussed in detail in Chapter nine.

Software Validation, Verification, Testing, and Documentation

The essential components of a program test are a description of the functional domain, the program in executable form, a description of the expected behavior, a way of observing program behavior, and a method of determining whether the observed behavior conforms with the expected behavior. The testing process consists of obtaining a valid value from the functional domain (or an invalid value from outside the functional domain to test for robustness), determining the expected behavior, executing the program and observing its behavior, and finally comparing that behavior with the expected behavior. If the expected and the actual behavior agree we say the test instance succeeds, otherwise we say the test instance fails.

Of the five necessary components in the testing process, the most difficult to obtain is a description of the expected behavior. Often ad hoc methods must be used to determine expected behavior. These methods include hand calculation, simulation, and other less efficient solutions to the same problem. What is needed is an *oracle*, a source which for any given input description can provide a complete description of the corresponding output behavior. We will discuss this process throughout Chapter 9.

Dynamic Testing

We can classify program test methods into *dynamic* and *static analysis* techniques. Dynamic analysis requires that the program be executed and, hence, involves the traditional notion of program testing, i.e. the program is run on some test cases and the results of the program's performance are examined to check whether the program operated as expected. Static analysis does not usually involve actual program execution. Common static analysis techniques include such compiler tasks as syntax and type checking. We will first consider some general aspects of dynamic analysis within a general discussion of program testing.

A complete verification of a program, at any stage in the life cycle, can be obtained by performing the test process for every element of the domain. If each instance succeeds, the program is verified, otherwise an error has been found. This testing method is known as *exhaustive testing* and is the only dynamic analysis technique that will guarantee the validity of a program. Unfortunately, this technique is not practical. Frequently functional domains are infinite, or if not infinite very large, so as to make the number of required test instances infeasible.

The solution is to reduce this potentially infinite exhaustive testing process to a finite testing process. This is accomplished by finding criteria for choosing representative elements from the functional domain. These criteria may reflect either the functional description or the program structure.

The subset of elements used in a testing process is called a *test data set* (test set for short). Thus the crux of the testing problem is to find an adequate test set, one that "covers" the domain and is small enough to perform the testing process for each element in the set. The paper of Goodenough and Gerhart [GOOD75] presents the first formal treatment for determining when a criterion for test set selection is adequate. In their paper, a criterion C is said to be *consistent* provided that test sets T1 and T2 chosen by C are such that all test instances of T1 are successful exactly when all test instances of T2 are successful. A criterion C is said to be complete provided that it produces test sets that uncover all errors. These definitions lead to the fundamental theorem of testing which states:

If there exists a consistent, complete criterion for test set selection for a program P and if a test set satisfying the criterion is such that all test instances succeed, then the program P is correct.

Unfortunately, it has been shown to be impossible to find consistent, complete test criteria except for the simplest cases [HOWD76]. The above just confirms that testing, especially complete testing, is a very difficult process. Examples of criteria that are used in practice for the selection of test sets include:

The elements of the test set reflect special domain properties such as extremal or ordering properties.

The elements of the test set exercise the program structure such as test instances insuring all branches or all statements are executed.

The elements of the test set reflect special properties of the functional description such as domain values leading to extremal function values.

Structural *vs* Functional Testing

The properties that the test set is to reflect are classified according to whether they are derived from a description of the program's function or from the program's internal structure. Test data generation based on *functional analysis* and on *structural analysis* is described in Chapter 9. Classifying the test data inclusion criteria given above, the first and the third are based on functional analysis criteria while the second is based on structural analysis criteria. Both structural and functional analysis should be performed to insure adequate testing. Structural analysis-based test sets tend to uncover errors that occur during "coding" of the program, while functional analysis-based test sets tend to uncover errors that occur in implementing requirements or design specifications.

Although the criterion for generating a structure-based test set is normally simple, the discovery of domain elements that satisfy the criterion is often quite difficult. Test data are usually derived by iteratively refining the data based on the information provided by the application of structural coverage metrics. Since functional analysis techniques often suffer from combinatorial problems, the generation of adequate functional test data is no easier. As a result, ad hoc methods are often employed to locate data which stress the program.

Static Testing

The application of test data and the analysis of the results are dynamic testing techniques. The class of static analysis techniques is divided into two types: techniques

Table 8.1
A Summary of Testing Techniques

Technique	Section	Manual/ Automatic	Static/ Dynamic	Structural/ Functional
Correctness proof	3.1	both	static	both
Walkthroughs	3.1	manual	dynamic	both
Inspections	3.1	manual	static	both
Design reviews and audits	3.1	manual	static	both
Simulation	3.1	automated	dynamic	functional
Desk checking	3.1	manual	both	structural
Peer review	3.1	manual	both	structural
Executable specs.	3.2	automated	dynamic	functional
Exhaustive testing	3.3	automated	dynamic	functional
Stress testing	3.3	manual	dynamic	functional
Error guessing	3.3	manual	dynamic	functional
Cause effect graphing	3.3	both	dynamic	functional
Design based functional testing	3.3	manual	dynamic	functional
Coverage based metric testing	3.4	automated	both	structural
Complexity based metric testing	3.4	automated	both	structural
Compiler based analysis	3.6	automated	static	structural
Data flow analysis	3.6	automated	static	structural
Control flow analysis	3.6	automated	static	structural
Symbolic execution	3.6	automated	static	structural
Instrumentation	3.7	automated	dynamic	structural
Combined techniques	3.8	automated	both	both

that analyze consistency and techniques that measure some program property. The consistency techniques are used to insure program properties such as correct syntax, correct parameter matching between procedures, correct typing, and correct requirements and specification translation. The measurement techniques measure properties such as error proneness, understandability, and well-structuredness.

The simplest of the consistency checking static analysis techniques is the syntax checking feature of compilers. In modern compilers, this feature is frequently augmented by type checking, parameter matching (for modules), cross reference tables, static array bounds checking, and aliasing. Two advanced static analysis techniques are symbolic execution and program proving. The latter proves the consistency of stated relations between program variables before and after program segments. Symbolic execution performs a "virtual" execution of all possible program paths. Since an actual execution does not occur, the method is considered a static analysis technique. Both are described in detail in Chapter 3.

Manual *vs* Automated Testing

A final classification of methods can be made upon the basis of whether the method is a *manual* method such as structured walkthrough or code inspection, or whether the method is *automated*.

In Table 8.1 we list the verification methods that will be discussed throughout the rest of the paper. We provide a classification according to whether the method is dynamic or static, structural or functional, manual or automated. We also provide a reference to where the method is discussed in the body of the report.

9. Verification Techniques

A description of verification, validation, and testing techniques can be arranged in several different ways. In keeping with the emphasis on verification throughout the lifecycle, we first present general techniques which span the stages of the lifecycle. The remaining sections of this chapter are organized along the lines of the usual testing plan, providing discussion of test data generation, test data evaluation, testing procedures and analysis, and the development of support tools. Each procedure will be briefly discussed, with emphasis given to its role in the validation process and its advantages and limitations.

General Verification Techniques

Techniques that can be used throughout the lifecycle are described here. The majority of the techniques involve static analysis and can be performed manually. They can be utilized without a large capital expenditure, although for analysis of large systems automated aids are advised. These include traditional informal methods of desk checking and review, disciplined techniques of structured walkthroughs and inspections, and formal methods of proof of correctness. In addition, the role simulation plays in validation and verification is described.

Desk Checking and Peer Review

Desk checking is the most traditional means for analyzing a program. It is the foundation for the more disciplined techniques of walkthroughs, inspections and reviews. In order to improve the effectiveness of desk checking, it is important that the programmer thoroughly review the problem definition and requirements, the design specification, the algorithms and the code listings. In most instances, desk checking is used more as a debugging technique than a testing technique. Since seeing one's own errors is difficult, it is better if another person does the desk checking. For example, two programmers can trade listings and read each others code. This approach still lacks the group dynamics present in formal walkthroughs, inspections, and reviews.

Another method, not directly involving testing, which tends to increase overall

94

quality of software production is peer review. There are a variety of implementations of peer review [MYER79], but all are based on a review of each programmer's code. A panel can be set up which reviews sample code on a regular basis for efficiency, style, adherence to standards, etc. and which provides feedback to the individual programmer. Another possibility is to maintain a notebook of required "fixes" and revisions to the software and indicate the original programmer or designer. In a "chief programmer team" [BAKE72] environment, the librarian can collect data on programmer runs, error reports, etc. and act as a review board or pass the information on to a peer review panel.

Walkthroughs, Inspections, and Reviews

Walkthroughs and inspections are formal manual techniques which are a natural evolution of desk checking. While both techniques share a common philosophy and similar organization, they are quite distinct in execution. Furthermore, while they both evolved from the simple desk check discipline of the single programmer, they use very disciplined procedures aimed at removing the major responsibility for verification from the developer.

Both procedures require a team, usually directed by a moderator. The team includes the developer, but the remaining 3-6 members and the moderator should not be directly involved in the development effort. Both techniques are based on a reading of the product (e.g. requirements, specifications, or code) in a formal meeting environment with specific rules for evaluation. The difference between inspection and walkthrough lies in the conduct of the meeting. Both methods require preparation and study by the team members, and scheduling and coordination by the team moderator.

Inspection involves a step-by-step reading of the product, with each step checked against a predetermined list of criteria. These criteria include checks for historically common errors. Guidance for developing the test criteria can be found in [MYER79], [FAGA76] and [WEIN71]. The developer is usually required to narrate the reading of the product. Many errors are found by the developer just by the simple act of reading aloud. Others, of course, are determined as a result of the discussion with team members and by applying the test criteria.

Walkthroughs differ from inspections in that the programmer does not narrate a reading of the product by the team, but provides test data and leads the team through a manual simulation of the system. The test data are walked through the system, with intermediate results kept on a blackboard or paper. The test data should be kept simple given the constraints of human simulation. The purpose of the walkthrough is to encourage discussion, not just to complete the system simulation on the test data. Most errors are discovered through questioning the developer's decisions at various stages, rather than through the application of the test data.

At the problem definition stage, walkthrough and inspection can be used to determine if the requirements satisfy the testability and adequacy measures as applicable to this stage in the development. If formal requirements are developed, formal methods, such as correctness techniques, may be applied to insure adherence with the quality factors.

Walkthroughs and inspections should again be performed at the preliminary and detailed design stages. Design walkthroughs and inspections will be performed for each module and module interface. Adequacy and testability of the module interfaces are very important. Any changes which result from these analyses will cause at least a partial repetition of the verification at both stages and between the stages. A reexamination of the problem definition and requirements may also be required.

Finally, the walkthrough and inspection procedures should be performed on the code produced during the construction stage. Each module should be analyzed separately and as integrated parts of the finished software.

Design reviews and audits are commonly performed as stages in software development. The Department of Defense has developed a standard audit and review procedure [MILS76] based on hardware procurement regulations. The process is representative of the use of formal review and includes:

System Requirements Review is an examination of the initial progress during the problem definition stage and of the convergence on a complete system configuration. Test planning and test documentation are begun at this review.

System Design Review occurs when the system definition has reached a point where major system modules can be identified and completely specified along with the corresponding test requirements. The requirements for each major subsystem are examined along with the preliminary test plans. Tools required for verification support are identified and specified at this stage.

The *Preliminary Design Review* is a formal technical review of the basic design approach for each major subsystem or module. The revised requirements and preliminary design specifications for each major subsystem and all test plans, procedures and documentation are reviewed at this stage. Development and verification tools are further identified at this stage. Changes in requirements will lead to an examination of the test requirements to maintain consistency.

The *Critical Design Review* occurs just prior to the beginning of the construction stage. The complete and detailed design specifications for each module and all draft test plans and documentation are examined. Again consistency with previous stages is reviewed, with particular attention given to determining if test plans and documentation reflect changes in the design specifications at all levels.

Two audits, the *Functional Configuration Audit* and the *Physical Configuration Audit* are performed. The former determines if the subsystem performance meets the requirements. The latter audit is an examination of the actual code. In both audits, detailed attention is given to the documentation, manuals and other supporting material.

Verification Techniques

A *Formal Qualification Review* is performed to determine through testing that the final coded subsystem conforms with the final system specifications and requirements. It is essentially the subsystem acceptance test.

Proof of Correctness Techniques

Proof techniques as methods of validation have been used since von Neumann's time. These techniques usually consist of an output "assertion" (specification) with respect to a program (or requirements or design specification) and an input assertion (specification). In the case of programs, the assertions are statements about the program's variables. The program is "proved" if whenever the input assertion is true for particular values of variables and the program executes, then it can be shown that the output assertion is true for the possibly changed values of the program's variables. The issue of termination is normally treated separately.

There are two approaches to proof of correctness: formal proof and informal proof. A formal proof consists of developing a mathematical logic consisting of axioms and inference rules and defining a proof to be either a proof tree in the natural deduction style [GENT35] or to be a finite sequence of axioms and inference rules in the Hilbert-Ackermann style [CHUR56]. The statement to be proved is at the root of the proof tree or is the last object in the proof sequence. Since the formal proof logic must also "talk about" the domain of the program and the operators that occur in the program, a second mathematical logic must be employed. This second mathematical logic is usually not decidable.

Most recent research in applying proof techniques to verification has concentrated on programs. The techniques apply, however, equally well to any level of the development lifecycle where a formal representation or description exists. The GYPSY [AMBL78] and HDM [ROBI79] methodologies use proof techniques throughout the development states. HDM, for example, has as a goal the formal proof of each level of development. Good summaries of program proving and correctness research are in [MANN74] and [ELSP72].

Heuristics for proving programs formally are essential but are not yet well enough developed to allow the formal verification of a large class of programs. In lieu of applying heuristics to the program, some approaches to verification require that the programmer provide information, interactively, to the verification system in order that the proof be completed. Examples include Gerhart's AFFIRM [GERH80] and Constable's PL/CV [CONS78]. Such information may include facts about the program's domain and operators or facts about the program's intended function.

A typical example of a program and its assertions is given below. The input assertion states that the program's inputs are respectively a non-negative integer and a positive integer. The output assertion states that the result of the computation is the smallest non-negative remainder of the division of the first input by the second. This example is due to Dijkstra and appears in [DIJK72].

Software Validation, Verification, Testing, and Documentation

Input Assertion $\{a>=0$ and $d>0$ and integer(a) and integer(b)$\}$
Program   integer r,dd;
            r := a; dd:=d
            while dd<=r do dd:=2*dd;
            while dd~=d do
                begin dd:=dd/2;
                        if dd<=r do r:=r−dd
                end

Output Assertion $\{0<=r<d$ and a congruent to r modulo d$\}$

    Informal proof techniques follow the logical reasoning behind the formal proof techniques but without the formal logical system. Often the less formal techniques are more palatable to the programmers. The complexity of informal proof ranges from simple checks such as array bounds not being exceeded, to complex logic chains showing non-interference of processes accessing common data. Informal proof techniques are always used implicitly by programmers. To make them explicit is similar to imposing disciplines, such as structured walkthrough, on the programmer.

Simulation

Simulation is most often employed in real-time systems development where the "real world" interface is critical and integration with the system hardware is central to the total design. There are, however, many nonreal-time applications in which simulation is a cost effective verification and test data generation technique.

    To use simulation as a verification tool several models must be developed. Verification is performed by determining if the model of the software behaves as expected on models of the computational and external environments using simulation. This technique also is a powerful way of deriving test data. Inputs are applied to the simulated model and the results recorded for later application to the actual code. This provides an "oracle" for testing. The models are often "seeded" with errors to derive test data which distinguish these errors. The data sets derived cause errors to be isolated and located as well as detected during the testing phase of the construction and integration stages.

    To develop a model of the software for a particular stage in the development lifecycle a formal representation compatible with the simulation system is developed. This may consist of the formal requirements specification, the design specification, or the actual code, as appropriate to the stage, or it may be a separate model of the program behavior. If a different model is used, then the developer will need to demonstrate and verify that the model is a complete, consistent, and accurate representation of the software at the stage of development being verified.

    The next steps are to develop a model of the computational environment in which the system will operate, a model of the hardware on which the system will be implemented, and a model of the external demands on the total system. These models can be largely derived from the requirements, with statistical representations developed for the external demand and the environmental interactions. The software behavior is then simulated with these models to determine if it is satisfactory.

Simulating the system at the early development stages is the only means of determining the system behavior in response to the eventual implementation environment. At the construction stage, since the code, is sometimes developed on a host machine quite different from the target machine, the code may be run on a simulation of the target machine under interpretive control.

Simulation also plays a useful role in determining the performance of algorithms. While this is often directed at analyzing competing algorithms for cost, resource, or performance tradeoffs, the simulation under real loads does provide error information.

Test Data Generation

Test data generation is the critical step in testing. Test data sets must contain not only input to exercise the software, but must also provide the corresponding correct output responses to the test data inputs. Thus the development of test data sets involves two aspects: the selection of data input and the determination of expected response. Often the second aspect is most difficult. As discussed previously, hand calculation and simulation are two techniques used to derive expected output response. For very large or complicated systems, manual techniques are unsatisfactory and insufficient.

One promising direction is the development of executable specification languages and specification language analyzers [SRS79], [TEIC77]. These can be used, as simulation is used, to act as an oracle providing the responses for the test data sets. Some analyzers such as the REVS system [BELL77] include a simulation capability. An executable specification language representation of a software system is an actual implementation of the design, but at a higher level than the final code. Usually interpreted rather than compiled, it is less efficient, omits certain details found in the final implementation, and is constructed with certain information "hidden." This implementation would be in Parnas' terms [PARN77] an "abstract program," representing in less detail the final implementation. The execution of the specification language "program" could be on a host machine quite different from the implementation target machine.

Test data can be generated randomly with specific distributions chosen to provide some statistical assurance that the system, when tested, is error free. This is a method often used in high density LSI testing. Unfortunately, while errors in LSI chips appear correlated and statistically predictable, this is not true of software. Until recently the domains of programs were far more intractable than those occurring in hardware. This gap is closing with the advance in VLSI.

There is another statistical testing procedure for hardware that applies to certain software applications. Often integrated circuits are tested against a standard "correct" chip using statistically derived test sets. Applications of this technique include testing mass produced firmware developed for microcomputers embedded in high volume production devices such as ovens, automobiles, etc. A second possibility is to use this concept to test "evolving" software. For the development of an upwardly compatible operating system, some of the test sets can be derived by using a current field tested system as an oracle. Compiler testing employs a similar test set for each different compiler tested. However, since most software is developed as a "one of a kind" item, this approach generally does not apply.

The apparent difficulty of applying statistical tests to software, test data are derived in two global ways, often called "black box" or functional analysis and "white box" or structural analysis. In functional analysis, the test data are derived from the external specification of the software behavior. No consideration is usually given to the internal organization, logic, control, or data flow in developing test data sets based on functional analysis. One technique, design-based functional analysis, includes examination and analysis of data structure and control flow requirements and specifications throughout the hierarchical decomposition of the system during the design. In a complementary fashion, tests derived from structural analysis depend almost completely on the internal logical organization of the software. Most structural analysis is supported by test coverage metrics such as path coverage, branch coverage, etc. These criteria provide a measure of completeness of the testing process.

Functional Testing Techniques

The most obvious and generally intractable functional testing procedure is exhaustive testing. As was described in Chapter 2, only a fraction of programs can be exhaustively tested since the domain of a program is usually infinite or infeasibly large and cannot be used as a test data set. To attack this problem, characteristics of the input domain are examined for ways of deriving a representataive test data set which provides confidence that the system will be fully tested.

As was stated in Chapter 8, test data must be derived from an analysis of the functional requirements and include representive elements from all the variable domains. These data should include both valid and invalid inputs. Generally, data in test data sets based on functional requirements analysis can be characterized as *extremal, non-extremal,* or *special* depending on the source of their derivation. The properties of these elements may be simple values, or for more complex data structures they may include such attributes as *type* and *dimension*.

Boundary Value Analysis

The problem of deriving test data sets is to partition the program domain in some meaningful way so that input data sets which span the partition can be determined. There is no direct, easily stated procedure for forming this partition. It depends on the requirements, the program domain, and the creativity and problem understanding of the programmer. This partitioning, however, should be performed throughout the development lifecycle.

At the requirements stage a coarse partitioning is obtained according to the overall functional requirements. At the design stage, additional functions are introduced which define the separate modules allowing for a refinement of the partition. Finally, at the coding stage, submodules implementing the design modules introduce further refinements. The use of a top down testing methodology allows each of these refinements to be used to construct functional test cases at the appropriate level. The following references [HOWD78] and [MYER79] give examples and further guidance.

Once the program domain is partitioned into input classes, functional analysis can be used to derive test data sets. Test data should be chosen which lie both inside each input class and at the boundary of each class. Output classes should also be covered by input which causes output at each class boundary and within each class. These data are the extremal and non-extremal test sets. Determination of these test sets is often called *boundary value analysis* or *stress testing*.

The boundary values chosen depend on the nature of the data structures and the input domains. Consider the following FORTRAN example:

```
INTEGER X
REAL A(100, 100)
```

If X is constrained, $a < X < b$, then X should be tested for valid inputs $a+1$, $b-1$, and invalid inputs a and b. The array should be tested as a single element array $A(1,1)$ and as a full 100×100 array. The array element values $A(I,J)$ should be chosen to exercise the corresponding boundary values for each element. Examples for more complex data structures can be found in [HOWD79], [MYER79].

Error Guessing and Special Value Analysis

Myers suggests that some people have a natural intuition for test data generation [MYER79]. While this ability cannot be completely described nor formalized, certain test data seem highly probable to catch errors. Some of these are in the category Howden [HOWD80] calls special, others are certainly boundary values. Zero input values and input values which cause zero outputs are examples. For more complicated data structures, the equivalent null data structure such as an empty list of stack or a null matrix should be tested. Often the single element data structure is a good choice. If numeric values are used in arithmetic computations, then the test data should include values which are numerically very close and values which are numerically quite different. Guessing carries no guarantee for success, but neither does it carry any penalty.

Cause Effect Graphing

Cause effect graphing [MYER79] is a technique for developing test cases for programs from the high level specifications. A high level specification of requirements states desired characteristics of behavior for the system. These characteristics can be used to derive test data. Problems arise, however, of a combinatorial nature. For example, a program that has specified responses to eight characteristic stimuli (called causes) given some input has potentially 256 "types" of input (i.e. those with characteristics 1 and 3, those with characteristics 5, 7, and 8, etc.). A naive approach to test case generation would be to try to generate all 256 types. A more methodical approach is to use the program specifications to analyze the program's effect on the various types of inputs.

The program's output domain can be partitioned into various classes called effects. For example, inputs with characteristic 2 might be subsumed by those with characteristics 3 and 4. Hence it would not be necessary to test inputs with just characteristic 2 and also inputs with characteristics 3 and 4, for they cause the same effect. This analysis results in a partitioning of the causes according to their corresponding effects.

A limited entry decision table is then constructed from the directed graph reflecting these dependencies (i.e. causes 2 and 3 result in effect 4, causes 2, 3, and 5 result in effect 6, etc.). The decision table is then reduced [METZ77] and test cases chosen to exercise each column of the table. Since many aspects of the cause effect graphing can be automated, it is an attractive tool for aiding in the generation of functional test cases.

Design Based Functional Testing

The techniques described above derive test data sets from analysis of functions specified in the requirements. Howden has extended functional analysis to functions used in the design process [HOWD80]. A distribution can be made between requirements functions and design functions. Requirements functions describe the overall functional capabilities of a program. In order to implement a requirements function it is usually necessary to invent other "smaller functions." These other functions are used to design the program. If one thinks of this relationship as a tree structure, then a requirements function would be represented as a root node. All functional capabilities represented by boxes at the second level in the tree correspond to design functions. The implementation of a design function may require the invention of other design functions. This successive refinement during top down design can then be represented as levels in the tree structure, where the $n + 1$st level nodes are refinements or subfunctions of the nth level functions.

To utilize design based functional testing, the functional design trees as described above are constructed. The trees document the functions used in the design of the program. The functions included in the design trees must be chosen carefully. The most important selection feature is that the function be accessible for independent testing. It must be possible to apply the appropriate input values to test the function, to derive the expected values for the function, and to observe the actual output computed by the code implementing the function.

Each of the functions in the functional design tree, if top down design techniques are followed, can be associated with the final code used to implement that function. This code may consist of one or more procedures, parts of a procedure, or even a single statement. Design-based functional testing requires that the input and output variables for each design function be completely specified. Given these multiple functions to analyze, test data generation proceeds as described in the boundary value analysis discussion above. Extremal, non-extremal, and special values test data should be selected for each input variable. Test data should also be selected which results in the generation of extremal, non-extremal, and special output values.

Structural Testing Techniques

Structural testing is concerned with ensuring sufficient testing of the implementation of a function. Although used primarily during the coding phase, structural analysis should be used in all phases of the lifecycle where the software is represented formally in some algorithmic, design or requirements language. The intent of structural testing is to stress the implementation by finding test data that will force sufficient coverage of the structures present in the formal representation. In order to determine whether the coverage is sufficient, it is necessary to have a structural coverage metric. Thus the process of generating tests for structural testing is sometimes known as *metric-based test data generation*.

Metric-based test data generation can be divided into two categories by the metric used: complexity-based testing or coverage-based testing. In the latter, a criterion is used which provides a measure of the number of structural units of the software which are fully exercised by the test data sets. In the former category, tests are derived in proportion to the software complexity.

Coverage-Based Testing

Most coverage metrics are based on the number of statements, branches, or paths in the program which are exercised by the test data. Such metrics can be used both to evaluate the test data and to aid in the generation of the test data.

Any program can be represented by a graph. The nodes represent statements or collections of sequential statements. The control flow is represented by directed lines or edges which connect the nodes. A node with a single exiting edge to another node represents a sequential code segment. A node with multiple exiting edges represents a branch predicate or a code segment containing a branch predicate as the last statement.

On a particular set of data, a program will execute along a particular *path*, where certain *branches* are taken or not taken depending on the evaluation of branch predicates. Any program path can be represented by a sequence, possibly with repeating subsequences (when the program has backward branches), of edges from the program graph. These sequences are called *path expressions*. Each path or each data set may vary depending on the number of *loop iterations* caused. A program

Software Validation, Verification, Testing, and Documentation

with variable loop control may have effectively an infinite number of paths. Hence, there are potentially an infinite number of path expressions.

To completely test the program structure, the test data chosen should cause the execution of all paths. Since this is not possible in general, metrics have been developed which give a measure of the quality of test data based on the proximity to this ideal coverage. Path coverage determination is further complicated by the existence of *infeasible paths*. Often a program has been inadvertently designed so that no data will cause the execution of certain paths. Automatic determination of infeasible paths is generally difficult if not impossible. A main theme in structured top down design [DIJK72] [JACK75] [YOUR79] is to construct modules which are simple and of low complexity so that all paths, excluding loop iteration, may be tested and that infeasible paths may be avoided.

All techniques for determining coverage metrics are based on graph representations of programs. A variety of metrics exist ranging from simple statement coverage to full path coverage. There have been several attempts to classify these metrics [MILL77]; however, new variations appear so often that such attempts are not always successful. We will discuss the major ideas without attempting to cover all the variations.

The simplest metric measures the percentage of statements executed by all the test data. Since coverage tools supply information about which statements have been executed (in addition to the percentage of coverage), the results can guide the selection of test data to insure complete coverage. To apply the metric, the program or module is instrumented by hand or by a preprocessor. A postprocessor or manual analysis of the results reveal the level of statement coverage. Determination of an efficient and complete test data set satisfying this metric is more difficult. Branch predicates that send control to omitted statements should be examined to help determine input data that will cause execution of omitted statements.

A slightly stronger metric measures the percentage of *segments* executed under the application of all test data. A segment in this sense corresponds to a *decision-to-decision path* (*dd-path*) [MILL77]. It is a portion of a program path beginning with the execution of a branch predicate and including all statements up to the evaluation (but not execution) of the next branch predicate. Segment coverage guarantees statement coverage. It also covers branches with no executable statements, e.g. an IF-THEN-ELSE with no ELSE statements still requires data causing the predicate to be evaluated as both true and false. Techniques similar to those used for statement coverage are used for applying the metric and deriving test data.

The next logical step is to strengthen the metric by requiring separate coverage for both the exterior and interior of loops. Segment coverage only requires that both branches from a branch predicate be taken. For loops, segment coverage can be satisfied by causing the loop to be executed one or more times (interior test) and then causing the loop to be exited (exterior test). Requiring that all combinations of predicate evaluations be covered requires that each loop be exited without interior execution for at least one data set. This metric requires more paths to be covered than segment coverage requires. Two successive predicates will require at least four sets of test data to provide full coverage. Segment coverage can be satisfied by two tests, while statement coverage may require only one test for two successive predicates.

Implementation of the above metric is again similar to that for statement and segment coverage. Variations on this metric include requiring at least "k" interior iterations per loop or requiring that all $2**n$ combinations of Boolean variables be applied for each n variable predicate expression. This latter variation has led to a new path testing technique called *finite-domain testing* [WHIT78].

Automated tools for instrumenting and analyzing the code have been available for a few years [MILL75] [LYON74] [RAMA74] [MAIT80]. These tools are generally applicable to most of the coverage metrics described above. Automation of test data generation is less advanced. Often test data are generated by interating the use of analyzers with manual methods for deriving tests. A promising but expensive way to generate test data for path testing is through the use of symbolic executors [BOYE75] and [HOWD77]. More on the use of these tools will be discussed in a later section.

Complexity-Based Testing.

Several complexity measures have been proposed recently. Among these are cyclomatic complexity [MCCA76], software science [HALS77], and Chapin's software complexity measure [CHAP79]. These and many other metrics are designed to analyze the complexity of software systems. Most, although valuable new approaches to the analysis of software, are not suitable, or have not been applied to the problem of testing. The McCabe metrics are the exception.

McCabe actually proposed three metrics: *cyclomatic, essential,* and *actual complexity*. All three are based on a graphical representation of the program being tested. The first two are calculated from the program graph, while the third is a runtime metric.

McCabe uses a property of graph theory in defining cyclomatic complexity. There are sets of linearly independent program paths through any program graph. A maximal set of these linearly independent paths, called a basis set, can always be found. Intuitively, since the program graph and any path through the graph can be constructed from the basis set, the size of this basis set should be related to the program complexity. From graph theory, the cyclomatic number of the graph, $V(G)$, is given by:

$$V(G) = e - n + p$$

for a graph G with number of nodes n, edges e, and connected components p. The number of linearly independent program paths though a program graph is $V(G) + p$, a number McCabe calls the cyclomatic complexity of the program. Cyclomatic complexity, $CV(G)$, where:

105

$$CV(G) = e - n + 2p$$

can be easily calculated from the program graph.

A proper subgraph of a graph, G, is a collection of nodes and edges such that if an edge is included in the subgraph, then both nodes it connects in the complete graph, C, must be in the subgraph. Any flow graph can be reduced by combining sequential single entry, single exit nodes into a single node. Structured constructs appear in a program graph as a proper subgraph with only one node which is single entry and whose entering edge is not in the subgraph, and with only one node which is single exit and whose exiting edge is not included in the subgraph. For all other nodes, all connecting edges are included in the subgraph. This single entry, single exit subgraph can then be reduced to a single node. Essential complexity is based on counting these single entry, single exit proper subgraphs of two nodes or greater. Let the number of these subgraphs be m, then essential complexity EV(G) is defined:

$$EV(G) = CV(G) - m$$

The program graph for a program built with structured constructs will obviously have all proper subgraphs as single exit, single entry. The number of proper subgraphs of a graph G of more than one node is $CV(G) - 1$. Hence the essential complexity of a structured program is one. Essential complexity is then a measure of the "unstructuredness" of a program.

Actual complexity, AV, is just the number of paths executed during a run. A testing strategy can be based on these metrics. If for a test data set, the actual complexity is less than the cyclomatic complexity and all edges have been executed, then either there are more paths to be tested or the complexity can be reduced by $CV(G) - AV$ by eliminating decision nodes and reducing portions of the program to in-line code. The cyclomatic complexity metric gives the number of linearly independent paths from analysis of the program graph. Some of these paths may be infeasible. If this is the case, then the actual complexity will never reach the cyclomatic complexity. Using a tool [MAIT80] which derives the three complexity metrics, both a testing and a programming style can be enforced.

Test Data Analysis

After the construction of a test data set it is necessary to determine the "goodness" of that set. Simple metrics like statement coverage may be required to be as high as 90% to 95%. It is much more difficult to find test data providing 90% coverage under the more complex coverage metrics. However, it has been noted [BROW73] that methodologies based on the more complex metrics with lower coverage requirements have uncovered as many as 90% of all program faults.

Verification Techniques

Statistical Analyses and Error Seeding

The most common type of test data analysis is statistical. An estimate of the number of errors in a program can be obtained from an analysis of the errors uncovered by the test data. In fact, as we shall see, this leads to a dynamic testing technique.

Let us assume that there are some number of errors, E, in the software being tested. There are two things we would like to know, a maximum liklihood estimate for the number of errors and a level of confidence measure on that estimate. The technique is to insert known errors in the code in some way that is statistically similar to the actual errors. The test data is then applied and the number of known seeded errors and the number of original errors uncovered is determined. In [MILL72] it is noted that, if one assumes that the statistical properties of the seeded and original errors is the same and that the testing and seeding are statistically unbiased, then

$$\text{estimate } E = IS/K$$

where S is the number of seeded errors, K is the number of discovered seeded errors, and I is the number of discovered unseeded errors. This estimate obviously assumes that the proportion of undetected errors is very likely to be the same for the seeded and original errors.

How good is this estimate? We would like to ascertain the confidence level for the various predicted error levels. Again from [MILL72], assuming that all seeded errors are detected ($K=S$), the confidence that number of errors is less than or equal to E is given by:

$$
\begin{array}{ll}
0 & ; I > E \\[2mm]
\dfrac{S}{S + E + 1} & ; I <= E
\end{array}
$$

More elaborate formulae for the case that all seeded errors are not found, and for cases where partial results are known are given in [MILL72] and [TAUS77].

Note that when $E = 0$ and no errors are detected other than seeded errors ($I <= E$) when testing, the confidence level is very high (for $S = 99$, confidence = 99%). Testing for the error free case can be accomplished with high confidence as long as no errors are uncovered. On the other hand, if nonseeded errors are discovered and the estimate for E is higher, our confidence in the estimate also decreases. If the $E = 10$, then with $S = 100$, our confidence drops to 90%. When the number of actual errors approaches or exceeds the number of seeded errors, then the confidence in our estimates decreases dramatically. For example, if $E = 10$ and $S = 9$, then the confidence is only 45%.

A strategy for using this statistical technique in dynamic testing is to monitor the maximum liklihood estimator, and perform the confidence level calculation as testing progresses. If the estimator gets high relative to the number of seeded errors, then it is unlikely that a desirable confidence level can be obtained. The errors should then be corrected and the testing resumed. If the number of real errors discovered remains small or preferably zero as the number of seeded errors uncovered approaches the total seeded, then our confidence level for an error free program increases.

Tausworthe [TAUS77] discusses a method for seeding errors which has some hope of being similar statistically to the actual errors. He suggests randomly choosing lines at which to insert the error, and then making various different modifications to the code introducing errors. The actual modifications of the code are similar to those used in mutation testing as described below.

Mutation Analysis

A relatively new metric developed by DeMillo, Lipton, and Sayward is called mutation analysis [DEMI78]. This method rests on the *competent programmer hypothesis* which states that a program written by a competent programmer will be, after debugging and testing, "almost correct." The basic idea of the method is to seed the program to be tested with errors, creating several mutants of the original program. The program and its mutants are then run interpretively on the test set. If the test set is adequate, it is argued, it should be able to distinguish between the program and its mutants.

The method of seeding is crucial to the success of the technique and consists of modifying single statements of the program in a finite number of "reasonable" ways. The developers conjecture a *coupling effect* which implies that these "first order mutants" cover the deeper, more subtle errors which might be represented by higher order mutants. The method has been subject to a small number of trials and so far has been successfully used interactively to develop adequate test data sets. It should be noted that the method derives both branch coverage and statement coverage metrics as special cases.

It must be stressed that mutation analysis, and its appropriateness, rests on the competent programmer and coupling effect theses. Since neither is provable, they must be empirically demonstrated to hold over a wide variety of programs before the method of mutations can itself be validated.

Static Analysis Techniques

As was described in Chapter 8, analytical techniques can be categorized as static or dynamic. The application and analysis of test data is usually described as a dynamic activity, since it involves the actual execution of code. Static analysis does not usually involve program execution. Many of the general techniques discussed such as formal proof techniques and inspections are static analysis techniques. In a true sense, static analysis is part of any testing technique. Any analysis to derive test data, calculate assertions, or determine instrumentation breakpoints must involve some form of static analysis, although the actual verification is achieved through dynamic testing. As was mentioned previously, the line between static and dynamic analysis is not always easily drawn. For example, proof of correctness and symbolic execution both "execute" code, but not in a real environment.

Most static analysis is performed by parsers and associated translators residing in compilers. Depending upon the sophistication of the parser, it uncovers errors ranging in complexity from ill-formed arithmetic expressions to complex type incompatibilities. In most compilers, the parser and translator are augmented with additional capabilities that allow activities such as code optimization, listing of variable names, and pretty printing, all such activities being useful in the production of quality software. Preprocessors are also frequently used in conjunction with the parser. These may perform activities such as allowing "structured programming" in an unstructured programming language, checking for errors such as mismatched common areas, and checking for module interface incompatibilities. The parser may also serve in a policing role. Thus software shop coding standards can be enforced, quality of code can be monitored, and adherence to programming standards (such as FORTRAN77 [ANSI78]) can be checked.

Flow Analysis

Data and control flow analysis are similar in many ways. Both are based upon graphical representation. In control flow analysis, the program graph has nodes which represent a statement or segment possibly ending in a branch predicate. The edges represent the allowed flow of control from one segment to another. The control flow graph is used to analyze the program behavior, to locate instrumentation breakpoints, to identify paths, and in other static analysis activities. In data flow analysis, graph nodes usually represent single statements, while the edges still represent the flow of control. Nodes are analyzed to determine the transformations made on program variables. Data flow analysis is used to discover program anomalies such as undefined or unreferenced variables. The technique was introduced by Cocke and Allen [ALLE74], [ALLE76] for global program optimization.

Data flow anomalies are more easily found than resolved. Consider the following FORTRAN code segment:

```
SUBROUTINE HYP(A,B,C)
U = 0.5
W = 1/V
Y = A ** W
Y = E ** W
Z = X + Y
C = Z ** (V)
```

There are several anomalies in this code segment. One variable, U, is defined and never used while three variables, X, V and E, are undefined when used. It is possible that U was meant to be V, E was meant to be B, and the first occurrence of Y on the left of an assignment was a typo for X. The problem is not in detecting these errors, but in resolving them. The possible solution suggested may not be the correct

Software Validation, Verification, Testing, and Documentation

one. There is no answer to this problem, but data flow analysis can help to detect the anomalies, including ones more subtle than those above.

In data flow analysis, we are interested in tracing the behavior of program variables as they are initialized and modified while the program executes. This behavior can be classified by when a particular variable is *referenced, defined*, or *undefined* in the program. A variable is referenced when its value must be obtained from memory during the evaluation of an expression in a statement. For example, a variable is referenced when it appears on the right hand side of an assignment statement, or when it appears as an array index anywhere in a statement. A variable is defined if a new value for that variable results from the execution of a statement, such as when a variable appears on the left hand side of an assignment. A variable is unreferenced when its value is no longer determinable from the program flow. Examples of unreferenced variables are local variables in a subroutine after exit and FORTRAN DO indices on loop exit.

Data flow analysis is performed by associating, at each node in the data flow graph, values for tokens (representing program variables) which indicate whether the corresponding variable is referenced, unreferenced, or defined with the execution of the statement represented by that node. If symbols, for instance u, d, r, and l (for null), are used to represent the values of a token, then *path expressions* for a variable (or token) can be generated beginning at, ending in, or for some particular node. A typical path expression might be drlllllrrlllllldllrllu, which can be reduced through eliminating nulls to drrrdru. Such a path expression contains no anomalies, but the presence of ...dd... in an expression, indicating a variable defined twice without being referenced, does identify a potential anomaly. Most anomalies, ..ur.., r..., etc. can be discovered through analysis of the path expressions.

To simplify the analysis of the flow graph, statements can be combined as in control flow analysis into segments of necessarily sequential statements represented by a single node. Often, however, statements must be represented by more than one node. Consider,

```
IF(X .GT. 1) X = X − 1
```

The variable X is certainly referenced in the statement, but it may be defined only if the predicate is true. In such a case, two nodes would be used, and the graph would actually represent code which looked like

```
        IF(X .GT. 1) 100 , 200
100     X = X − 1
200     CONTINUE
```

Another problem requiring node splitting arises at the last statement of a FORTRAN DO loop after which the index variable becomes undefined only if the loop is exited. Subroutine and function calls introduce further problems, but they too can be resolved. The use of data flow analysis for static analysis and testing is described in [OSTE76] and [FOSD76].

110

Verification Techniques

Symbolic Execution

Symbolic execution is a method of symbolically defining data that force program paths to be executed. Instead of executing the program with actual data values, the variable names that hold the input values are used. Thus all variable manipulations and decisions are made symbolically. As a consequence, all variables become string variables, all assignments become string assignments and all decision points are indeterminate. To illustrate, consider the following small pseudocode program:

```
IN a,b;
a :=a*a;
x := a + b;
IF x = 0 THEN x := 0 ELSE x := 1;
```

The symbolic execution of the program will result in the following expression:

$$\text{if } a^*a + b = 0 \text{ then } x := 0 \text{ else if } a^*a + b = 0 \text{ then } x := 1$$

Note that we are unable to determine the result of the equality test for we only have symbolic values available.

The result of a symbolic execution is a large, complex expression. The expression can be decomposed and viewed as a tree structure where each leaf represents a path through the program. The symbolic values of each variable are known at every point within the tree and the branch points of the tree represent the decision points of the program. Every program path is represented in the tree, and every branch path is effectively taken.

If the program has no loops, then the resultant tree structure is finite. The tree structure can then be used as an aid in generating test data that will cause every path in the program to be executed. The predicates at each branch point of the tree structure for a particular path are then collected into a conjunction. Data that causes a particular path to be executed can be found by determining which data will make the path conjunction true. If the predicates are equalities, inequalities and orderings, the problem of data selection becomes the classic problem of trying to solve a system of equalities and orderings.

There are two major difficulties with using symbolic execution as a test set construction mechanism. The first is the combinatorial explosion inherent in the tree structure construction. The number of paths in the symbolic execution tree structure may grow as an exponential in the length of the program leading to serious computational difficulties. If the program has loops, then the symbolic execution tree structure is necessarily infinite. Usually only a finite number of loop executions is required enabling a finite loop unwinding to be performed. The second difficulty is that the problem of determining whether the conjunct has values which satisfy it is undecidable even with restricted programming languages. For certain applications, however, the method has been successful.

Another use of symbolic execution techniques is in the construction of verification conditions from partially annotated programs. Typically, the program has attached to each of its loops an assertion, called an invariant, that is true at the first

111

statement of the loop and at the last statement of the loop (thus the assertion remains "invariant" over one execution of the loop). From this assertion, an assertion true before entrance to the loop and assertions true after exit of the loop can be constructed. The program can then be viewed as "free" of loops (i.e. each loop is considered as a single statement) and assertions extended to all statements of the program (so it is fully annotated) using techniques similar to the backward substitution method described above for symbolic execution. A good survey of these methods appears in [HANT76] and examples of their use in verifiers appear in [LUCK79] and [GERH80].

Dynamic Analysis Techniques

Dynamic analysis is usually a three step procedure involving static analysis and instrumentation of a program, execution of the instrumented program, and finally, analysis of the instrumentation data. Often this is accomplished interactively through automated tools.

The simplest instrumentation technique for dynamic analysis is the insertion of a turnstyle or a counter. Branch or segment coverage and other such metrics are evaluated in this manner. A preprocessor analyzes the program (usually by generating a program graph) and inserts counters at the appropriate places. Consider

```
      IF (X) 10,10,15
      .
      .
10    Statement i
      .
      .
15    Statement j
      .
      .
      DO 20 I = J,K,L
      .
      .
20    Statement k
```

A preprocessor might instrument the program segment as follows:

```
      IF (X) 100,101,15
      .
      .
100   N(100) = N(100) + 1
      GO TO 10
101   N(101) = N(101) + 1
10    Statement i
      .
      .
15    N(15) = N(15) + 1
      Statement j
```

```
          .
          .
          I = J
          IF (I.GT.K) THEN 201
20        N(20) = N(20) + 1
          .
          .
          Statement k
          I = I + L
          IF (I.LE.K) THEN 20
201       N(201) = N(201) + 1
```

For the IF statement, each possible branch was instrumented. Note that we used two counters N(100) and N(101) even though the original code branches to the same statement label. The original code had to be modified for the DO loop in order to get the necessary counters inserted. Note that two counters are used, N(20) for the interior execution count and N(201) for the exterior of the loop.

Simple statement coverage requires much less instrumentation than branch coverage or more extensive metrics. For complicated assignments and loop and branch predicates, more detailed instrumentation is employed. Besides simple counts, it is interesting to know the maximum and minimum values of variables (particularly useful for array subscripts), the initial and last value, and other constraints particular to the application.

Instrumentation does not have to rely on direct code insertion. Often calls to runtime routines are inserted rather than actual counters. Some instrumented code is passed through a preprocessor/compiler which inserts the instrumentation only if certain commands are set to enable it.

Stucki introduced the concept of instrumenting a program with *dynamic assertions*. A preprocessor generates instrumentation for dynamically checking conditions often as complicated as those used in program proof techniques [STUC77]. These assertions are entered as comments in program code and are meant to be permanent. They provide both documentation and means for maintenance testing. All or individual assertions are enabled using simple commands and the preprocessor.

There are assertions which can be employed globally, regionally, locally, or at entry and exit. The general form for a local assertion is:

ASSERT LOCAL(extended-logical-expression)[optional qualifier][control]

The optional qualifiers are ALL, SOME, etc. The control options include LEVEL, which controls the levels in a block structured program; CONDITIONS, which allows dynamic enabling of the instrumentation; and LIMIT, which allows a specific number of violations to occur. The logical expression is used to represent an expected condition to be dynamically verified. For example:

ASSERT LOCAL (A(2 : 6,2 : 10).NE.0) LIMIT 4

placed within a program will cause the values of array elements $A(2,2), A(2,3), \ldots, A(2,10), A(3,2), \ldots, A(6,10)$ to be checked against a zero value at that locality. After four violations during the execution of the program, the assertion will become false.

The global, regional, and entry-exit assertions are similar in structure. Note the similarity with verification conditions, especially if the entry-exit assertions are employed. Furthermore, symbolic execution can be employed to generate the assertions as it can be used with proof techniques. Some efforts are currently underway to integrate dynamic assertions, proof techniques, and symbolic evaluation. One of these is described below.

There are many other techniques for dynamic analysis. Most involve the dynamic (under execution) measurement of the behavior of a part of a program, where the features of interest have been isolated and instrumented based on a static analysis. Some typical techniques include expression analysis, flow analysis, and timing analysis.

Combined Methods

There are many ways in which the techniques described above can be used in concert to form a more powerful and efficient testing technique. One of the more common combinations today is the merger of standard testing techniques with formal verification. Our ability, through formal methods, to verify significant segments of code is improving [GERH78], and moreover there are certain modules, which for security or reliability reasons, justify the additional expense of formal verification.

Other possibilities include the use of symbolic execution or formal proof techniques to verify segments of code, which through coverage analysis have been shown to be most frequently executed. Mutation analysis, for some special cases like decision tables, can be used to fully verify programs [BUDD78b]. Formal proof techniques may be useful in one of the problem areas of mutation analysis, the determination of equivalent mutants.

Another example, combining dataflow analysis, symbolic execution, elementary theorem proving, dynamic assertions, and standard testing is suggested in [OSTE80]. Osterweil addresses the issue of how to combine efficiently these powerful techniques in one systematic method. As has been mentioned, symbolic evaluation can be used to generate dynamic assertions. Here, paths are executed symbolically so that each decision point and every loop has an assertion. The assertions are then checked for consistency using both dataflow and proof techniques. If all the assertions along a path are consistent, then they can be reduced to a single dynamic assertion for the path. Theorem proving techniques can be employed to "prove" the path assertion and termination, or the path can be tested and the dynamic assertions evaluated for the test data.

The technique allows for several tradeoffs between testing and formal methods. For instance, symbolically derived dynamic assertions are more reliable than manually derived assertions, but cost more to generate. Consistency analysis of the assertions using proof and dataflow techniques adds cost at the front end, but reduces the execution overhead. Finally there is the obvious tradeoff between theorem proving and testing to verify the dynamic assertions.

Test Support Tools

Testing, like program development, generates large amounts of information, necessitates numerous computer executions, and requires coordination and communication between workers. Support tools and techniques can ease the burden of test production, test execution, general information handling, and communication. General system utilities and text processing tools are invaluable for test preparation, organization, and modification. A well organized and structurable file system and a good text editor are a minimum support set. A more powerful support set includes data reduction and report generation tools. Library support systems consisting of a data base management system and a configuration control system are as useful during testing as during software development since data organization, access, and control are required for management of test files and reports. Documentation can be viewed as a support technique. In addition to the general purpose support tools and techniques, specific test support tools exist. Test drivers and test languages are in this category. The following paragraphs will discuss these test specific support tools and techniques.

Test Documentation

FIPS PUB 38 [FIPS76], the NBS guideline for software documentation during the development phase, recommends test documentation be prepared for all multipurpose or multiuser projects and for other software development projects costing over $5000. FIPS 38 recommends the preparation of a test plan and a test analysis report. The test plan should identify test milestones and provide the testing schedule and requirements. In addition, it should include specifications, descriptions, and procedures for all tests; and the test data reduction and evaluation criteria. The test analysis report should summarize and document the test results and findings. The analysis summary should present the software capabilities, deficiencies, and recommendations. As with all types of documentation, the extent, formality, and level of detail of the test documentation are functions of agency ADP management practice and will vary depending upon the size, complexity, and risk of the project.

Test Drivers

Unless the module being developed is a stand-alone program, considerable auxiliary software must be written in order to exercise and test it. Auxiliary code which sets up an appropriate environment and calls the module is termed a *driver* while code which simulates the results of a routine called by the module is a *stub*. For many modules both stubs and drivers must be written in order to execute a test.

When testing is performed incrementally, an untested module is combined with a tested one and the package is then tested. Such packaging can lessen the number of drivers and/or stubs which must be written. When the lowest level and modules, those which call no other modules, are tested first and then combined for further testing with the modules that call them, the need for writing stubs can be eliminated. This approach is called *bottom-up testing*. Bottom-up testing still requires that test drivers be constructed. Testing which starts with the executive module and incrementally adds modules which it calls, is termed *top-down testing*. Top-down testing requires that stubs be created to simulate the actions of called modules that have not yet been incorporated into the system. The testing order utilized should be coordinated with the development methodology used.

Automatic Test Systems and Test Languages

The actual performance of each test requires the execution of code with input data, an examination of the output, and a comparision of the output with the expected results. Since the testing operation is repetitive in nature, with the same code executed numerous times with different input values, an effort has been made to automate the process of test execution. Programs that perform this function of initiation are called *test drivers*, *test harnesses*, or *test systems*.

The simplest test drivers merely reinitiate the program with various input sets and save the output. The more sophisticated test systems accept data inputs, expected outputs, the names of routines to be executed, values to be returned by called routines, and other parameters. These test systems not only initiate the test runs but compare the actual output with the expected output and issue concise reports of the performance. TPL/2.0 [PANZ78] which uses a test language to describe test procedures is an example of such a system. In addition to executing the tests, verifying the results and producing reports, the system helps the user generate the expected results.

PRUFSTAND [SNEE78] is an example of a comprehensive test system. It is an interactive system in which data values are generated automatically or are requested from the user as they are needed. The system is comprised of a:

Preprocessor to instrument the code,

Translator to convert the source data descriptors into an internal symbolic test data description table,

Test driver to initialize and update the test environment,

Test stubs to simulate the execution of called modules,

Execution monitor to trace control flow through the test, object,

Result validator,

Test file manager, and

Post processor to manage reports,

A side benefit of a comprehensive test system is that it establishes a standard format for test materials, which is extremely important for regression testing. Currently automatic test driver systems are expensive to build and consequently are not in widespread use.

10. Summary

In the previous chapters we have surveyed many of the techniques used to validate software systems. Of the methods discussed, the most successful have been the disciplined manual techniques, such as walkthroughs, reviews, and inspections, applied to all stages in the lifecycle ([FAGA76]). Discovery of errors within the first stages of development (requirements and design) is particularly critical since the cost of these errors escalates significantly if they remain undiscovered until construction or later. Until the development products at the requirements and design stages become formalized and hence amenable to automated analysis, disciplined manual techniques will continue to be key verification techniques.

For the construction stage, automated techniques can be of great value. The ones in widest use are the simpler static analysis techniques (such as type checking), automated test coverage calculation, automated program instrumentation, and the use of simple test harnesses. These techniques are relatively straightforward to implement and all have had broad use. Combined with careful error documentation, they are effective validation methods.

Many of the techniques discussed in Chapter 9 have not seen wide use. The principal reasons for this include their specialization (simulation), the high cost of their use (symbolic execution), and their unproven applicability (formal proof of correctness). Many of these techniques represent the state of the art in program validation and are in areas where research is continuing.

The areas showing the most commercial interest and activity at present include automated test support systems and increased use of automated analysis. As more formal techniques are used during requirements and design, an increase in automatic analysis is possible. In addition, more sophisticated analysis techniques are being applied to the code during construction. More complete control and automation of the actual execution of tests, both in assistance in generating the test cases and in the management of the testing process and results, are also taking place.

We re-emphasize the importance of performing validation throughout the lifecycle. One of the reasons for the great success of disciplined manual techniques is their uniform applicability at requirements, design, and coding phases. These techniques can be used without massive capital expenditure. However, to be most effective they require a serious commitment and a disciplined application. Careful planning, clearly stated objectives, precisely defined techniques, good management, organized record keeping, and strong commitment are critical to successful validation. A disciplined approach must be followed during both planning and execution of the verification activities.

We view the integration of validation with software development as so important that we suggest that it be an integral part of the requirements statement. Validation requirements should specify the type of manual techniques, the tools, the form of project management and control, the development methodology, and acceptability criteria which are to be used during software development. These requirements are in addition to the functional requirements of the system ordinarily specified at this stage. Thus embedded within the project requirements would be a contract aimed at enhancing the quality of the completed software.

A major difficulty with a proposal such as the above is that we have neither the means of accurately measuring the effectiveness of validation methods nor the means of determining "how valid" the software should be. We assume that it is not possible to produce a "perfect" software system; the goal is to try to get as close as required to perfect. In addition, what constitutes perfect and how important it is for the software to be perfect may vary from project to project. Some software (such as reactor control systems) needs to approach perfection more closely than other software (such as an address labeling program). The definition of "perfect" (or quality attributes) and its importance should be part of the validation requirements. However, validation mechanisms written into the requirements do not guarantee high quality software, just as the use of a particular development methodology does not guarantee high quality software. The evaluation of competing validation mechanisms will be difficult.

A second difficulty with specifying a collection of validation methods in the requirements is that most validation tools do not exist in integrated packages. This means that the group performing the verification must learn several tools that may be difficult to use in combination. This is a problem that must receive careful thought. For unless the combination is chosen judiciously, their use can lead to additional costs and errors. The merits of the tool collection as a whole must be considered as well as the usefulness of any single tool.

Future work in validation should address the above issues. One possible course of action is to integrate the development and validation techniques into a "programming environment." Such an environment would encompass the entire software development effort and include verification capabilities to:

1. Analyze requirements and specifications
2. Analyze and test designs
3. Provide support during construction (e.g. test case generation, test harnesses)
4. Provide a data base sufficient to support regression testing

Summary

The use of such environments has the potential to improve greatly the quality of the completed software and also to provide a mechanism for establishing confidence in the quality of the software. At present the key to high quality remains the disciplined use of a development methodology accompanied by verification at each stage of the development. No single technique provides a magic solution.

Glossary

AUDIT   see DOD DEVELOPMENT REVIEWS

BLACK BOX TESTING   *see* FUNCTIONAL TESTING.

BOUNDARY VALUE ANALYSIS   a selection technique in which test data are chosen to lie along "boundaries" of input domain (or output range) classes, data structures, procedure parameters, etc. Choices often include maximum, minimum, and trivial values or parameters. This technique is often called stress testing.

BRANCH TESTING   a test method satisfying coverage criteria that require that for each decision point each possible branch be executed at least once.

CAUSE EFFECT GRAPHING   test data selection technique. The input and output domains are partitioned into classes and analysis is performed to determine which input classes cause which effect. A minimal set of inputs is chosen which will cover the entire effect set.

CERTIFICATION   acceptance of software by an authorized agent usually after the software has been validated by the agent, or after its validity has been demonstrated to the agent.

CRITICAL DESIGN REVIEW   *see* DOD DEVELOPMENT REVIEWS

COMPLETE TEST SET   a test set containing data that causes each element of a prespecified set of boolean conditions to be true. Additionally, each element of the test set causes at least one condition to be true.

CONSISTENT CONDITION SET   a set of boolean conditions such that complete test sets for the conditions uncover the same errors.

CYCLOMATIC COMPLEXITY   the cyclomatic complexity of a program is equivalent to the number of decision statements plus 1.

DD (decision to decision) PATH   a path of logical code sequence that begins at an entry or decision statement and ends at a decision statement or exit.

DEBUGGING   the process of correcting syntactic and logical errors detected during coding. With the primary goal of obtaining an executing piece of code, debugging shares with testing certain techniques and strategies, but differs in its usual ad hoc application and local scope.

DESIGN BASED FUNCTIONAL TESTING   the application of test data derived through functional analysis (see FUNCTIONAL TESTING) extended to include design functions as well as requirement functions.

DOD DEVELOPMENT REVIEWS   a series of reviews required by DOD directives. System requirements review, system design review, preliminary design review, critical design re-

Glossary

view, functional configuration audit, physical configuration audit, and formal qualification review comprise the set of required life cycle reviews.

DRIVER   code which sets up an environment and calls a module for test.

DYNAMIC ANALYSIS   analysis that is performed by executing the program code.

DYNAMIC ASSERTION   a dynamic analysis technique which inserts assertions about the relationship between program variables into the program code. The truth of the assertions is determined as the program executes.

ERROR GUESSING   test data selection technique. The selection criterion is to pick values that seem likely to cause errors.

EXHAUSTIVE TESTING   executing the program with all possible combinations of values for program variables.

EXTREMAL TEST DATA   test data that is at the extreme or boundary of the domain of an input variable or which produces results at the boundary of an output domain.

FORMAL QUALIFICATION REVIEW   *see* DOD DEVELOPMENT REVIEWS

FUNCTIONAL CONFIGURATION AUDIT   *see* DOD DEVELOPMENT REVIEWS

FUNCTIONAL TESTING   application of test data derived from the specified functional requirements without regard to the final program structure.

INFEASIBLE PATH   a sequence of program statements that can never be executed.

INSPECTION   a manual analysis technique in which the program (requirements, design, or code) is examined in a very formal and disciplined manner to discover errors.

INSTRUMENTATION   the insertion of additional code into the program in order to collect information about program behavior during program execution.

INVALID INPUT (TEST DATA FOR INVALID INPUT DOMAIN)   test data that lie outside the domain of the function the program represents.

LIFE CYCLE TESTING   the process of verifying the consistency, completeness, and correctness of the software entity at each stage in the development.

METRIC BASED TEST DATA GENERATION   the process of generating test sets for structural testing based upon use of complexity metrics or coverage metrics.

MUTATION ANALYSIS   a method to determine test set thoroughness by measuring the extent to which a test set can discriminate the program from slight variants (mutants) of the program.

ORACLE   a mechanism to produce the "correct" responses to compare with the actual responses of the software under test.

PATH EXPRESSIONS   a sequence of edges from the program graph which represents a path through the program.

PATH TESTING   a test method satisfying coverage criteria that each logical path through the program be tested. Often paths through the program are grouped into a finite set of classes; one path from each class is then tested.

PRELIMINARY DESIGN REVIEW   *see* DOD DEVELOPMENT REVIEWS

PROGRAM GRAPH   graphical representation of a program.

PROOF OF CORRECTNESS   the use of techniques of mathematical logic to infer that a relation between program variables assumed true at program entry implies that another relation between program variables holds at program exit.

Software Validation, Verification, Testing, and Documentation

REGRESSION TESTING testing of a previously verified program required following program modification for extension or correction.

SIMULATION use of an executable model to represent the behavior of an object. During testing the computional hardware, the external environment, and even code segments may be simulated.

SELF VALIDATING CODE code which makes an explicit attempt to determine its own correctness and to proceed accordingly.

SPECIAL TEST DATA test data based on input values that are likely to require special handling by the program.

STATEMENT TESTING a test method satisfying the coverage criterion that each statement in a program be executed at least once during program testing.

STATIC ANALYSIS analysis of an program that is performed without executing the program.

STRESS TESTING *see* BOUNDARY VALUE ANALYSIS

STRUCTURAL TESTING a testing method where the test data are derived solely from the program structure.

STUB special code segments that when invoked by a code segment under test will simulate the behavior of designed and specified modules not yet constructed.

SYMBOLIC EXECUTION a static analysis technique that derives a symbolic expression for each program path.

SYSTEM DESIGN REVIEW *see* DOD DEVELOPMENT REVIEWS

SYSTEM REQUIREMENTS REVIEW *see* DOD DEVELOPMENT REVIEWS

TEST DATA SET set of input elements used in the testing process.

TEST DRIVER a program which directs the execution of another program against a collection of test data sets. Usually the test driver also records and organizes the output generated as the tests are run.

TEST DRIVER a program which directs the execution of another program against a collection of test data sets. Usually the test driver also records and organizes the output generated as the tests are run.

TEST HARNESS *see* TEST DRIVER

TESTING examination of the behavior of a program by executing the program on sample data sets.

VALID INPUT (TEST DATA FOR A VALID INPUT DOMAIN) test data that lie within the domain of the function represented by the program.

VALIDATION determination of the correctness of the final program or software produced from a development project with respect to the user needs and requirements. Validation is usually accomplished by verifying each stage of the software development lifecycle.

VERIFICATION in general the demonstration of consistency, completeness, and correctness of the software at each stage and between each stage of the development lifecycle.

WALKTHROUGH a manual analysis technique in which the module author describes the module's structure and logic to an audience of colleagues.

WHITE BOX TESTING *see* STRUCTURAL TESTING

Bibliography

[ADRI80] W.R. Adrion and P.M. Melliar-Smith, "Designing for the Unexpected," *Computer* to appear (1980).

[ALFO77] M.W. Alford, "A Requirements Engineering Methodology for Real-Time Processing Requirements," *IEEE Transactions on Software Engineering*, vol. SE-2, no. 1, pp. 60–69 (1977).

[ALLE74] F.E. Allen, "Interprocedural Data Flow Analysis," *Proceedings IFIP congress 1974*, North-Holland Publishing Co., Amsterdam, pp. 398–402 (1974).

[ALLE76] F.E. Allen and J. Cocke, "A Program Data Flow Procedure," *Communications of the ACM*, vol. 19, no. 3, p. 137–147 (March 1976).

[AMBL78] A.L. Ambler, D.I. Good, J.C. Browne, W.F. Burger, R.M. Cohen, C.G. Hoch and R.E. Wells, "Gypsy: A Language for Specification and Implementation of Verifiable Programs," *Proceedings of an ACM Conference on Language Design for Reliable Software*, D.B. Wortman, ed., New York, pp. 1–10 (1978).

[ANSI78] ANSI FORTRAN X3.9-1978, American National Standards Institute, New York (1978).

[BAKE72] F.T. Baker, "Chief Programmer Team Management of Production Programming," *IBM Systems Journal*, vol. 11, no. 1, pp. 56–73 (1972).

[BELL77] T.E. Bell, D.C. Bixler and M.F. Dyer, "An Extendable Approach to Computer-Aided Software Requirements Engineering," *IEEE Transactions on Software Engineering*, vol. SE-3, no. 1, pp. 49–60- (1977).

[BOEH78] B.W. Boehm, J.R. Brown, H. Kaspar, M. Lipow, G.J. MacLeod and M.J. Merrit, *Characteristics of Software Quality*, North-Holland, Amsterdam-New York-Oxford, 1978.

[BOEH77] B.W. Boehm, "Seven Basic Principles of Software Engineering," *Software Engineering Techniques*, Infotech State of the Art Report, (1977).

[BOYE75] R.S. Boyer, B. Elspas and K.N. Levitt, "SELECT—A Formal System for Testing and Debugging Programs by Symbolic Execution," *Proceedings of 1975 International Conference on Reliable Software*, pp. 234–245 (1975).

[BRAN80] M.A. Branstad, J.C. Cherniavsky, and W.R. Adrion, "Validation, Verification, and Testing for the Individual Programmer," *Computer*, vol. 13, no. 12, (Dec. 1980).

[BROW73] J.R. Brown, et al., "Automated Software Quality Assurance," PROGRAM TEST METHODS, W. Hetzel, Ed., Prentice-Hall, Englewood Cliffs, Chapter 15 (1973).

[BUCK79] F. Buckley, "A Standard for Software Quality Assurance Plans," *Computer*, vol. 12, no. 8, pp. 43–50 (August 1979).

[BUDD78a] T. Budd, R.A. DeMillo, R.J. Lipton and F.G. Sayward, "The Design of a Prototype Mutation System for Program Testing," *AFIPS Conference Proceedings*, vol. 47, 1978, Computer Conference, pp. 623–627 (1978).

[BUDD78b] T.A. Budd and R.J. Lipton, "Mutation Analysis of Decision Table Programs," *Proceedings of the 1978 Conference on Information Science and Systems*, Johns Hopkins University, pp. 346–349 (1978).

[CAIN75] S.H. Caine and E.K. Gordon, "PDL: A Tool for Software Design," *Proceedings of the National Computer Conference*, AFIPS Press, Montdale, NJ, (1975).

[CARP75] L.C. Carpenter and L.L. Tripp, "Software Design Validation Tool," *1975 International Conference on Reliable Software*, April 1975.

Software Validation, Verification, Testing, and Documentation

[CHAP79] N. Chapin, "A Measure of Software Complexity," *Proceedings of the AFIPS National Computer Conference*, pp. 995–1002, June, 1979.

[CHUR56] A. Church, *Introduction to Mathematical Logic, Vol. 1*, Princeton University Press, Princeton, 1956.

[CONS78] R.L. Constable and M.J. O'Donnell, *A Programming Logic*, Winthrop Publishing Co., Cambridge (1978).

[DEMI78] R.A. DeMillo, R.J. Lipton and F.G. Sayward, "Hints on Test Data Selection: Help for the Practicing Programmer," *Computer*, vol. 11, no. 4, pp. 34–43 (1978).

[DIJK72] E.W. Dijkstra, "Notes on Structured Programming," in *Structured Programming*, O.J. Dahl, E.W. Dijkstra and C.A.R. Hoare, eds., Academic Press, London, 1972 (pp. 1–82).

[ELSP72] B. Elspas, K.N. Levitt, R.J. Waldinger and A. Waksman, "An Assessment of Techniques for Proving Program Correctness," *Computing Surveys*, vol. 4, no. 2, pp. 97–147 (1972).

[FAGA76] M.E. Fagan, "Design and Code Inspections to Reduce Errors in Program Development," *IBM Systems Journal*, vol. 15, no. 3, pp. 182–211 (1976).

[FIPS76] "Guidelines for Documentation of Computer Programs and Automated Data Systems," FIPS38, Federal Information Processing Standards Publications, U.S. Department of Commerce/National Bureau of Standards, Washington, D.C., February, 1976.

[FOSD76] L.D. Fosdick and L.J. Osterweil, "Data Flow Analysis in Software Reliability," *Computing Surveys*, vol. 8, no. 3, pp. 305–330 (September 1976).

[GENT35] G. Gentzen, "Investigations into Logical Deductions," in The Collected Works of Gerhard Gentzen, M.E. Szabo ed., North-Holland, Amsterdam, 1969 (pp. 68–128).

[GERH78] S.L. Gerhart, "Program Verification in the 1980's: Problems, Perspectives, and Opportunities," ISI/RR–78–71, Information Sciences Institute, Marina del Rey (August 1978).

[GERH80] S.L. Gerhart, D.R. Musser, D.H. Thompson, D.A. Baker, R.L. Bates, R.W. Erickson, R.L. London, D.G. Taylor, and D.S. Wile, "An Overview of AFFIRM; A Specification and Verification System, Proceedings IFIP *Congress 1980*, North-Holland Publishing Co., Amsterdam, to appear (1980).

[GOOD75] J.B. Goodenough and S.L. Gerhart, "Toward a Theory of Test Data Selection," *IEEE Transactions on Software Engineering*, vol. SE-1, no. 2, (1975).

[HALS77] M.H. Halstead, *Elements of Software Science*, Elsevier North-Holland, New York, 1977.

[HAMI76] N. Hamilton and S. Zeldin, "Higher Order Software—A Methodology for Defining Software," *IEEE Transactions on Software Engineering*, vol. SE-2, no. 1, pp. 9–32 (1976).

[HANT76] S.L. Hantler and J.C. King, "An Introduction to Proving the Correctness of Programs," *Computing Surveys*, vol. 8, no. 3, pp. 331–53 (1976).

[HOWD76] W.E. Howden, "Reliability of the Path Analysis Testing Strategy," *IEEE Transactions on Software Engineering*, vol. SE-2, no. 3, (1976).

[HOWD77] W.E. Howden, "Symbolic Testing and the DISSECT Symbolic Evaluation System," *IEEE Transactions on Software Engineering*, vol. SE-3, no. 4, pp. 266–278 (1977).

[HOWD78] W.E. Howden, "A Survey of Dynamic Analysis Methods," in *Tutorial: Software Testing and Validation Techniques*, E. Miller and W.E. Howden, ed., IEEE Computer Society, New York, 1978.

[HOWD80] W.E. Howden, "Functional Program Testing," *IEEE Transactions on Software Engineering*, vol. SE-6, no. 2, pp. 162–169 (1980).

[INFO79] *Software Testing, INFOTECH State of the Art Report*, Infotech, London (1979).

[IEEE79] IEEE Draft Test Documentation Standard, IEEE Computer Society Technical Committee on Software Engineering, Subcommittee on Software Standards, New York (1979).

[JACK75] M.A. Jackson, *Principles of Program Design*, Academic Press, New York, 1975.

[JONE76] C. Jones, "Program Quality and Programmer Productivity," IBM Technical Report, International Business Machines Corp., San Jose, (1976).

[KERN74] B.W. Kernighan, "RATFOR- A Preprocessor for a Rational FORTRAN," Bell Labs Internal Memorandum, Bell Laboratories, Murray Hill (1974).

[KOPP76] R. Koppang, "Process Design System—An Integrated Set of Software Development Tools," *Proceedings of the Second International Software Engineering Conference*, October 1976.

[LAMB78] S.S. Lamb, V.G. Leck, L.J. Peters and G.L. Smith, "SAMM: A Modeling Tool for Requirements and Design Specification," *Proceedings COMPSAC 78*, IEEE Computer Society, New York, 1978 (pp. 48–53).

[LIPT78] R.J. Lipton and F.G. Sayward, "The Status of Research on Program Mutation," *Proceedings*

Bibliography

of The Workshop on Software Testing and Test Documentation, IEEE Computer Society, New York, pp. 355–367, 1978.

[LUCK79] D. Luckham, S. German, F. von Henke, R. Karp, P. Milne, D. Oppen, W. Polak, and W. Schenlis, "Stanford Pascal Verifier User's Manual," AI Memorandum CS-79-731, Stanford University, Stanford (1979).

[LYON74] G. Lyon and R.B. Stillman, "A FORTRAN Analyzer," NBS Technical Note No. 849, National Bureau of Standards, Washington (1974).

[MAIT80] R. Maitland, "NODAL," in "NBS Software Tools Database," R. Houghton and K. Oakley, editors, NBSIR-xx, National Bureau of Standards, Washington (1980).

[MANN74] Z. Manna, *Mathematical Theory of Computation*, McGraw-Hill, New York, 1974.

[MCCA76] T.J. McCabe, "A Complexity Measure," *IEEE Transactions on Software Engineering*, vol. SE-2, no. 4, pp. 308–320 (1976).

[MCCA77] J. McCall, P. Richards, and G. Walters, "Factors in Software Quality," vols. 1–3, NTIS AD-A049-014,015,055 (1977).

[METZ77] J.R. Metzner and B.H. Barnes *Decision Table Languages and Systems*, Academic Press, New York (1977).

[MILL70] H.D. Mills, "Top Down Programming in Large Systems," in *Debugging Techniques in Large Systems*, R. Rustin ed., Prentice-Hall, 1970 (pp. 41–55).

[MILL72] H.D. Mills, "On statistical validation of computer programs," IBM Report FSC72-6015, Federal Systems Division, IBM, Gaithersburg, Md., 1972.

[MILL75] E.F. Miller, Jr., "RXVP—An Automated Verification System for FORTRAN," *Proceedings Workshop 4, Computer Science and Statistics: Eighth Annual Symposium on the Interface*, Los Angeles, California, February 1975.

[MILL77] E.F. Miller, Jr., "Program Testing: Art Meets Theory," *Computer*, vol. 10, no. 7, pp. 42–51 (1977).

[MILS76] "Technical Reviews and Audits for Systems, Equipment, and Computer Programs," MIL-STD-1521A (USAF), U.S.Department of the Air Force, Washington, D.C., (1976).

[MYER76] G.J. Myers, *Software Reliability—Principles and Practices*, John Wiley and Sons, New York (1976).

[MYER79] G.J. Myers, *The Art of Software Testing*, John Wiley and Sons, New York (1979).

[NEUM75] P.G. Neumann, L. Robinson, K. Levitt, R.S. Boyer, A.R. Saxema, "A Provably Secure Operating System," SRI Project 2581, SRI International, Menlo Park (1975).

[OSTE76] L.J. Osterweil and L.D. Fosdick, "DAVE—A Validation, Error Detection, and Documentation System for FORTRAN programs," *Software Practice and Experience*, vol. 6, pp. 473–486 (1976).

[OSTE80] L.J. Osterweil, "A Strategy for Effective Integration of Verification and Testing Techniques," Technical Report CU- CS-181–80, University of Colorado, Boulder (1980).

[PANZ78] D.J. Panzl, "Automatic Revision of Formal Test Procedures," *Third International Conference on Software Engineering*, May 1978.

[PARN77] D.L. Parnas, "The Use of Precise Specifications in the Development of Software," *Information Processing 77*, B. Gilchrist, editor, North-Holland, (1977).

[RAMA74] C.V. Ramamoorthy and S.F. Ho, Fortran Automated Code Evaluation System, ERL-M466, University of California, Berkeley, California, 1974.

[ROBI79] L. Robinson, "The HDM Handbook, Volumes I–III," SRI Project 4828, SRI International, Menlo Park (1979).

[ROSS77] D.T. Ross and K.E. Schoman, Jr., "Structured Analysis for Requirements Definition," *IEEE Transactions on Software Engineering*, vol. SE-3, no. 1, pp. 6–15 (1977).

[ROUB76] O. Roubine and L. Robinson, Special Reference Manual, Stanford Research Institute Technical Report CSG-45, Menlo Park, Calif., 1976.

[TAUS77] Robert C. Tausworthe, *Standardized Development of Computer Software*, Prentice-Hall, Englewood Cliffs, NJ, 1977.

[SNEE78] H. Sneed and K. Kirchoff, "Prufstand—A Testbed for Systematic Software Components," in *Proceedings INFOTECH State of the Art Conference on Software Testing*, Infotech, London (1978).

[SRS79] *Proceedings of the Specifications of Reliable Software Conference* IEEE Catalog No. CH1401-9C, IEEE, New York (1979).

[STUC77] L.G. Stucki, "New Directions in Automated Tools for Improving Software Quality," in *Cur-*

Software Validation, Verification, Testing, and Documentation

rent Trends in Programming Methodology, Volume II-Program Validation, R. Yeh, editor, Prentice-Hall, Englewood Cliffs, pp. 80–111 (1977).

[TAUS77] R.C. Tausworthe, *Standardized Development of Computer Software*, Jet Propulsion Laboratory, Pasadena, (1978).

[TEIC77] D. Teichroew and F.A. Hershey,III, "PSL/PSA: A Computer-Aided Technique for Structured Documentation and Analysis of Information Processing Systems," *IEEE Transactions on Software Engineering*, vol. SE-3, no. 1, pp. 41–48 (1977).

[TEIC78] D. Teichroew personal communication.

[WEIN71] G.M. Weinberg, *The Psychology of Computer Programming*, Van Nostrand Reinhold, New York, 1971.

[WHIT78] L.J. White and E.I. Cohen, "A Domain Strategy for Computer Program Testing," *Digest for the Workshop on Software Testing and Test Documentation*, Ft. Lauderdale, pp. 35–354 (1978).

[YOUR79] E. Yourdon and L.L. Constantine, *Structured Design*, Prentice-Hall, Englewood Cliffs, NJ, 1979.

Book Three
Structured Testing: A Software Testing Methodology Using the Cyclomatic Complexity Metric

Abstract

Various applications of the Structured Testing methodology are presented. The philosophy of the technique is to avoid programs that are inherently untestable by first measuring and limiting program complexity. Part 1 defines and develops a program complexity measure. Part 2 discusses the complexity measure in the second phase of the methodology which is used to quantify and proceduralize the testing process. Part 3 illustrates how to apply the techniques during maintenance to identify the code that must be retested after making a modification.

Keywords: measures; metric; program complexity; software testing; structured testing.

Preface

How To Read This Document

The main advice to the reader is "Don't become discouraged with Chapter 12." Chapter 12 deals with the derivation of a program complexity measure from graph theory; it contains mathematical theorems and notations. While it is critical to include this material to establish a mathematical basis for program complexity, it is possible that it may frustrate some readers. Those readers whose interests lie solely in the application of the theory (as opposed to the development of the theory) may safely skip Chapter 12. The rest of the paper contains the operational procedures which are directly applicable to the programming process.

The diagram on the following page shows the dependencies between the various sections in the paper.

If you are a *Programmer*, and your interest at this time is mainly how to limit and control complexity and not so much the testing process, then the chapters to concentrate on are 11–14. Start with Chapter 11, read as much of Chapter 12 as you want to. If you get frustrated, instead of filing the document, skip to Chapter 13 where many examples are presented; then digest Chapter 14 which explains how to compute the complexity in programming terms.

If your primary concern is the *testing* process, then the Chapters directly applicable are 15 through 18. They contain both the criteria and procedures to carry out the structured testing process. If the project's design is not complete and you have some control over the modularization process, then also read Chapters 11–14. If you are having trouble with an existing design, concentrate on Chapters 15, 16, and 18.

If your job is software *maintenance* you should concentrate on Chapters 19 and 20. They contain the operational steps for evaluating modifications and producing modification test data. It will be necessary, however, to understand Chapters 15, 16, and 18 to carry out this testing.

If you are a *Project Leader* or *Manager*, and your concern is wth development methodology, test plans, and quality assurance, you need to understand the complete approach. The document will give you the essence of the overall methodology; the discrete operational steps in the methodology are summarized in Chaper 21.

Software Validation, Verification, Testing, and Documentation

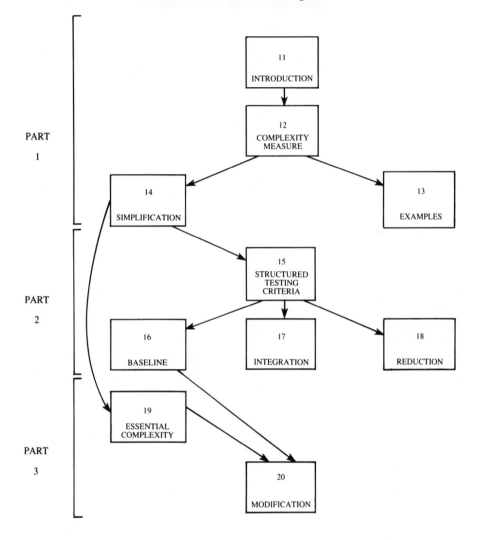

There is a lot of substance here for quality assurance and project planning—don't let the theoretics in Chapter 12 abort your journey.

If your concern is *Quality Assurance* and *Methodology Standards*, Appendix A, which presents live, real world data, may be of interest. Presented are a number of studies that independently validated various aspects of the complexity measure. This validation was performed by extracting empirical data from real projects.

For readers already familiar with and practicing the structured testing methodology, we recommend Chapter 21. The Summary lists the operational steps which can be incorporated into an overall project plan.

Part One
Measuring and Limiting
Program Complexity

11. Introduction

The chapters in Book Three discuss a software quality metric, the cyclomatic complexity metric, and how it may be applied to software testing. Discussions of other metrics and methodologies may be found in [PAIG], [HALS], [KOLE], [CHAP], [CHEN], [GILB], [JELI], [MCAL], and [MOHA].

The testing method described is performed in two phases. The first phase is to quantify and to limit the complexity of a program to permit thorough testing. This quantification is accomplished using a complexity measure that suggests a minimum on the number of distinct paths that must be tested. The second phase is the actual testing where the number of test paths is forced to meet the complexity measure.

Attention is first given to limiting the complexity of a program to assure testability. This viewpoint, however, is an oversimplification of the problem. A "program" of any reasonable size is typically developed and represented as the interaction of several procedures, subroutines, or paragraphs. In designing a "program," the design stage typically results in a hierarchy chart as shown in Figure 11.1, that explicitly shows the decomposition of a program's functions into distinct modules. If the programming language used is FORTRAN, the top module typically is the mainline code and each of the other modules are usually subroutines, functions, or externally-called programs. If COBOL is the programming language, the top is mainline code and the other modules are typically paragraphs.

The design modularization is critical to the quality of the end product. Each of the modules should have the following properties:

Testability—the testing effort to validate each module should be manageable.

Comprehensibility—each of the modules should be readable and understandable.

Reusability—if the modules are well-defined, they may re reusable in a different system.

Maintainability—the job of modifying and retesting each of the modules in the operational phase should be manageable.

This design modularization process is governed by two principles:

Introduction

The functional decomposition represented by the design hierarchy should result in several independent, cohesive modules which provide a natural decomposition of the problem.

The modularization must also be governed by "size" or "testability" of each of the modules. That is, the modularization should avoid modules that are inherently so complex that they are untestable.

The process of evaluating a module's cohesiveness and relative independence is largely a heuristic and creative process. Currently, it is virtually impossible to measure these attributes of a design. It is important to emphasize the second principle (testability of modules) so, in fact, the design can be reliably implemented. Whereas a module's cohesiveness or independence is not measurable, we will in this document, present techniques that quantify the testability attributes of the modules. This quantification of the testing effort can then be incorporated into test plans and a quality assurance phase that the product would have to satisfy before being accepted.

The structured testing principles presented here will constrain a program's complexity by limiting the complexity of each of its internal modules to the point that they can each be tested rigorously. If it is found that a particular module exceeds the complexity threshold, a further design refinement would be required. For example, if module 11 in Figure 11.1 is found to be too complex, the creation of several testable modules below 11 would be required. So, in short, a program's testability is assured by limiting the complexity of each of the modules within the program.

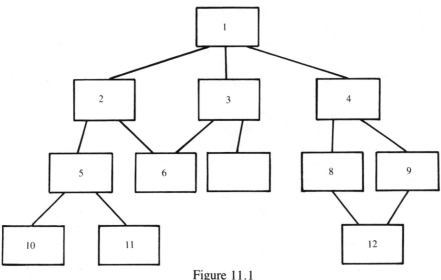

Figure 11.1
Hierarchy Chart

12. The Complexity Measure

The complexity measure will limit the number of independent paths in a program at the design and coding stages so the testing will be manageable during later stages. One of the reasons for limiting independent paths, instead of a limitation based on the length of a program, is the following dilemma: a relatively short program can have an overwhelming number of paths. For example, a 50-line FORTRAN program consisting of 25 IF statements in sequence, will have 33.5 million potential control paths. The approach taken here is to limit the number of basis (or independent) paths that will generate all paths when taken in combination.

One definition and one theorem from graph theory are needed to develop these concepts. In this section we will treat graphs with only one connected component—Chapter 17 will deal with the more general case. See [BERG] for graph theory concepts and a more formal treatment of connected components.

Definition 1   The cyclomatic number $v(G)$ of a graph G with n vertices, e edges, and 1 connected component is:

$$v(G) = e - n + 1.$$

Theorem 1   In a strongly connected graph G, the cyclomatic number is equal to the maximum number of linearly independent paths.

The application to computer programs will be made as follows: given a program module, associate with it a graph that has unique entry and exit nodes; each node in the graph corresponds to a block of statements where the flow is sequential and the edges represent the program's branches taken between blocks. This graph is classically known as the control graph [LEGA75]; and it is assumed that each node can be reached by the entry node and each node can reach the exit.

For example, the control graph in Figure 12.1 has seven blocks ((a) through (g)), entry and exit nodes (a) and (g), and ten edges.

To apply Theorem 1, the graph must be strongly connected which means that given two nodes (a) and (b), there exists a path from (a) to (b) and a path from (b) to

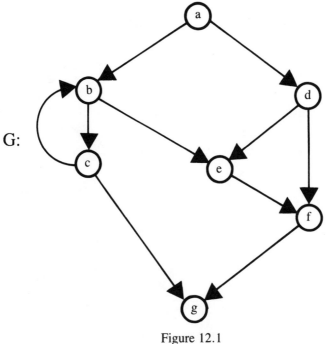

Figure 12.1
Control Graph G

(a). To satisfy this, we associate an additional edge with the graph which branches from the exit node (g) to the entry node (a) as shown in Figure 12.2.

Theorem 1 now applies, and it states that the maximal number of independent paths in G′ is $11 - 7 + 1$. (G has only one connected component so we set $p = 1$.). The generalized case where $p > 1$ is used for design complexity, see Chapter 17. The implication, therefore, is that there is a basis set of five independent paths that when taken in combination, will generate all paths. For example, the set of five paths shown below form a basis.

b1: abcg
b2: a(bc)*2g
b3: abefg
b4: adefg
b5: adfg

Note: The notation (bc)*2 means iterate the (bc) loop twice.

If any arbitrary path is chosen, it should be equal to a linear combination of the basis paths b1 − b5. For example, the path abcbefg is equal to b2 + b3 − b1, and path a(bc)*3g equals 2 * b2 − b1. To see this, it is necessary to number the edges in G Figure 12.3 and show the basis as edge vectors Figure 12.4.

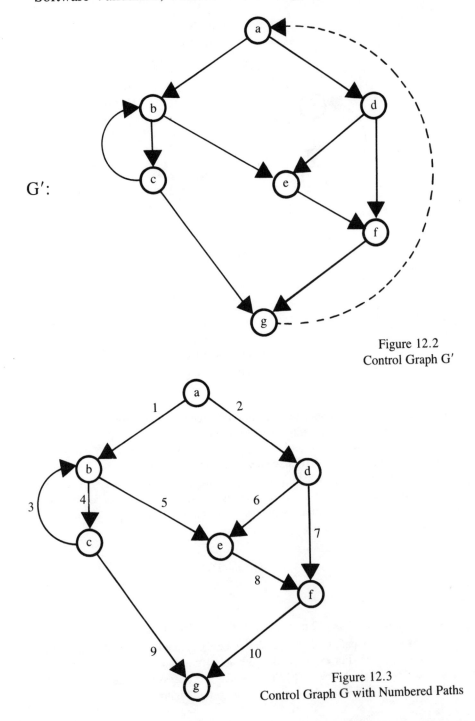

Figure 12.2
Control Graph G′

Figure 12.3
Control Graph G with Numbered Paths

G′:

136

The Complexity Measure

The path abcbefg is represented as the edge vector shown in Figure 12.4, and it is equal to b2 + b3 − b1 where the addition and subtraction are done component-wise. In similar fashion the path a(bc)*3g shown in Figure 12.4 is equal to 2 * b2 − b1.

It is important to notice that Theorem 1 states that G has a basis set of size five but it does not tell us which particular set of five paths to choose. For example, the following set will also form a basis.

adfg
abefg
adefg
a(bc)*3befg
a(bc)*4g

When this is applied to testing, the actual set of five paths used will be dictated by the data conditions at the various decisions in the program. The Theorem, however, guarantees that we will always be able to find a set of five that form a basis.

It should be emphasized that the process of adding the extra edge to G was performed only to make the graph strongly connected so Theorem 1 would apply. When calculating the complexity of a program or testing the program, the extra edge is not an issue, but rather it is reflected by adding 1 to the number of edges. The complexity v, therefore is defined as:

$$v = (e + 1) - n + 1$$

or more simply

$$v = e - n + 2.$$

	1	2	3	4	5	6	7	8	9	10
b1	1	0	0	1	0	0	0	0	1	0
b2	1	0	1	2	0	0	0	0	1	0
b3	1	0	0	0	1	0	0	1	0	1
b4	0	1	0	0	0	1	0	1	0	1
b5	0	1	0	0	0	0	1	0	0	1
abcbefg	1	0	1	1	1	0	0	1	0	1
a (bc) *3g	1	0	2	3	0	0	0	0	1	0

Figure 12.4
Basis for Control Graph G

13. Examples

Several actual control graphs and their complexity measures are presented in Figures 13.1 through 13.12, to illustrate these concepts. These graphs are from FORTRAN programs on a PDP-10. The programs were analyzed by an automated system, called FLOW, that recognizes the blocks and transitions in a FORTRAN program, computes the complexity, and draws the control graphs on a DATA DISK CRT. The straight edges represent downward flow (e.g., in Figure 13.2 below, the line between (2) and (3) means that (2) branches to (3)). The curved arcs represent backward branches (e.g., in Figure 13.2 (5) branches back to (2)).

The graphs in Figures 13.1 through 13.12 are presented in the order of increasing complexity to suggest the relationship between the complexity numbers and our intuitive notion of the complexity of the graphs.

One essential ingredient in any testing methodology is to limit the program logic during development in order that, first, the program can be understood, and second, the amount of testing required to verify the logic is not overwhelming.

In practice, often large programs have low complexity and small programs have very high complexity. Because of this, the common practice of attempting to limit complexity by controlling only how many pages a routine will occupy is entirely inadequate. This complexity measure has been used in production environments by *limiting the complexity of every module to 10*. Programmers have been required to calculate the complexity as they develop routines, and if it exceeded 10, they were required to recognize and modularize subfunctions or redesign the software. The only situation where the limit of 10 seemed unreasonable and an exception allowed, is in a large CASE statement where a number of independent blocks follow a selection function. (Reference Figure 13.8 for an example of a CASE statement graph.)

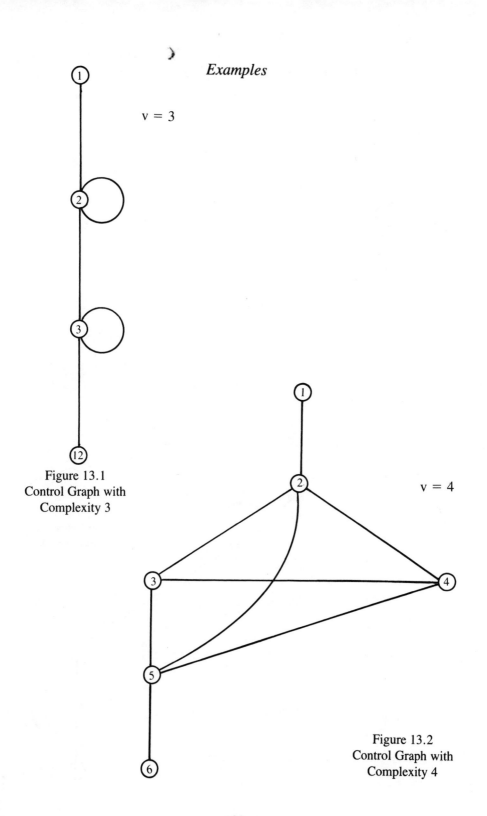

Examples

v = 3

Figure 13.1
Control Graph with
Complexity 3

v = 4

Figure 13.2
Control Graph with
Complexity 4

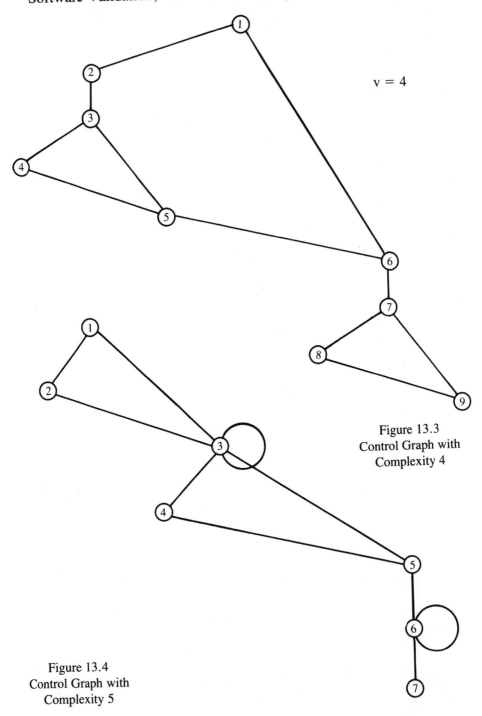

$v = 4$

Figure 13.3
Control Graph with
Complexity 4

Figure 13.4
Control Graph with
Complexity 5

Examples

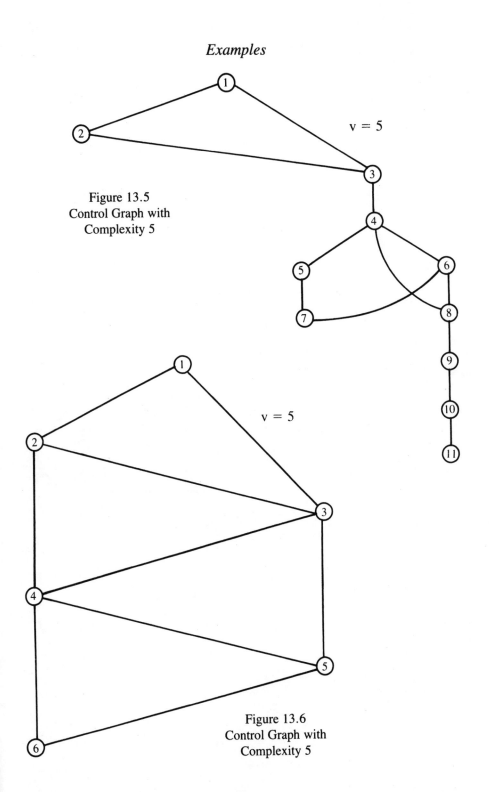

v = 5

Figure 13.5
Control Graph with
Complexity 5

v = 5

Figure 13.6
Control Graph with
Complexity 5

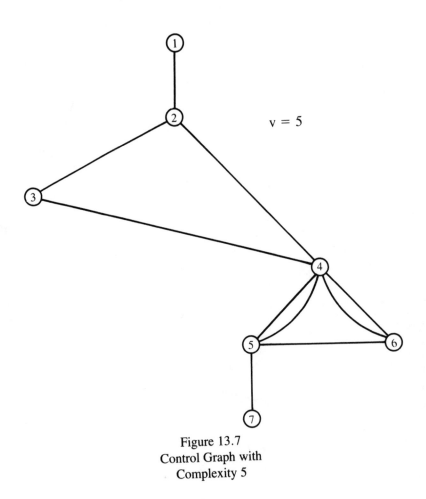

v = 5

Figure 13.7
Control Graph with
Complexity 5

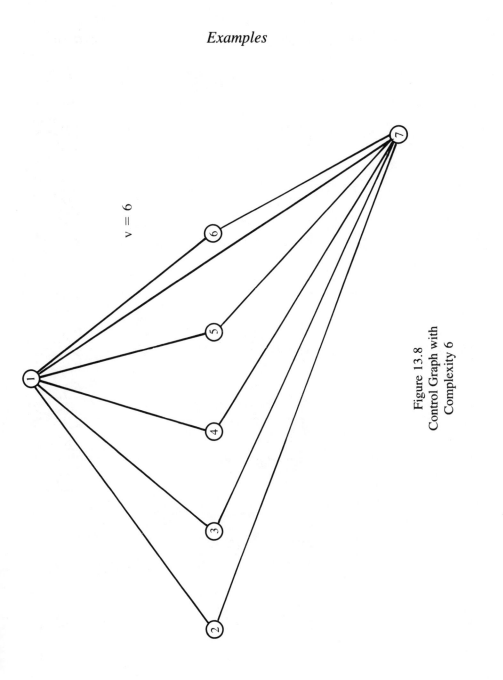

Figure 13.8
Control Graph with
Complexity 6

v = 6

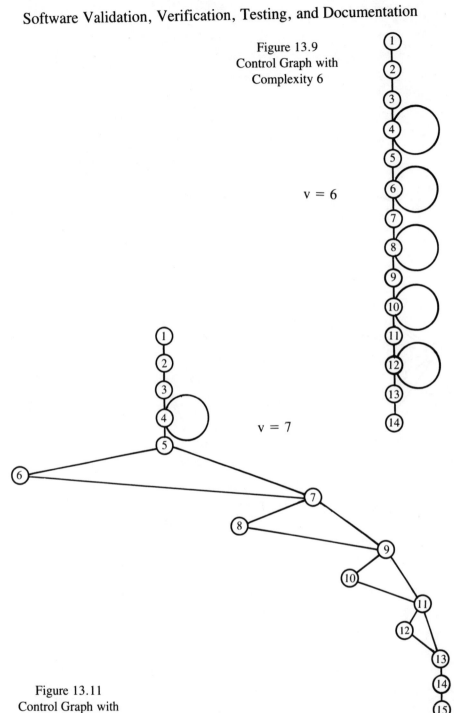

Figure 13.9
Control Graph with
Complexity 6

v = 6

v = 7

Figure 13.11
Control Graph with
Complexity 9

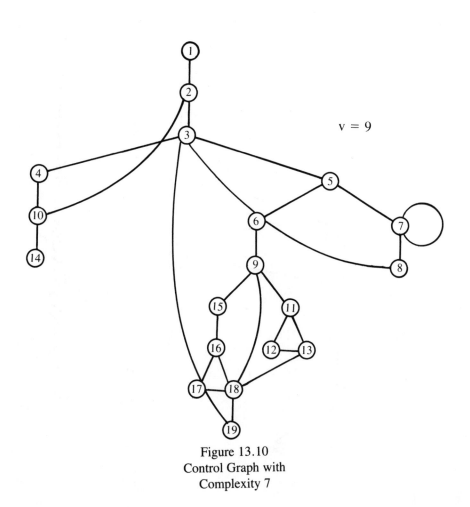

Figure 13.10
Control Graph with
Complexity 7

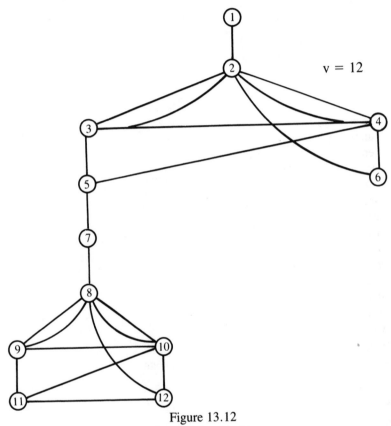

v = 12

Figure 13.12
Control Graph with
Complexity 12

14. Simplification

Since the calculation of $e - n + 2$ is error-prone and tedious, alternative methods of calculating complexity are presented. The results are presented without proof. The interested reader is referred to [MCCA] for proofs.

The first simplification allows the calculation of v by counting "splitting nodes" in the graph. A splitting node has more than one outcome and is associated with some conditional in the source program. A splitting node in the control graph is illustrated in Figure 14.1.

In FORTRAN a splitting node would be associated with an IF, conditional GOTO, computed GOTO, or DO statement. If S is the number of splitting nodes in a graph, then $v = S + 1$. For example, in Figure 14.2 the splitting nodes are (a), (b), (c), and (d), so $v = 4 + 1$.

Since each one of the splitting nodes in the graph is associated with some predicate or condition in the program, the expression $v = S + 1$ can be calculated by simply counting conditions in the source program. In fact, the number of conditions is a better complexity indicator than the number of predicates since a compound predicate can have more than one condition, e.g.:

IF c1 OR c2 THEN b1 ELSE b2

Since there are at least two ways the predicate can be true, the statement is modeled in Figure 14.3.

Notice that the complexity of the graph and the statement are both three. Notice, also, that the following statement is equivalent and also has complexity three.

IF c1 THEN b1
ELSE IF c2 THEN b1
ELSE b2

If a program contains an *n*-way predicate, such as a CASE statement with n cases, the *n*-way predicate contributes $n - 1$ to the count of S. For example, in Figure 14.4 the CASE predicate (a) has three outcomes so that it contributes two to S. This gives us $v = 2 + 1$. Notice that a CASE statement, with *n* cases can be simu-

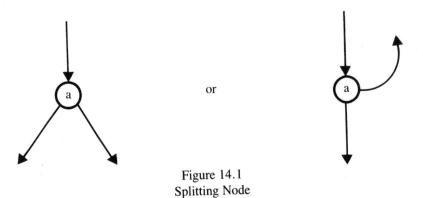

Figure 14.1
Splitting Node

lated with $n - 1$ nested IF-THEN-ELSE statements, which again produce the same complexity.

A second simplification allows the calculation of $e - n + 2$ by counting regions in the control graph. It uses Euler's formula:

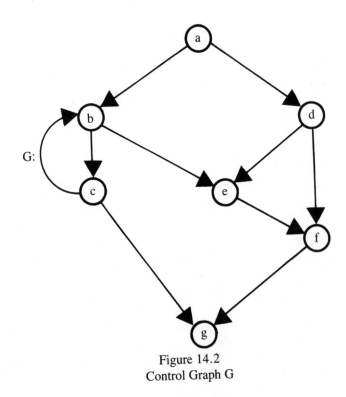

Figure 14.2
Control Graph G

148

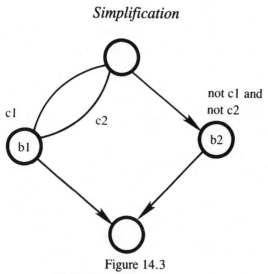

Figure 14.3
IF-THEN-ELSE Control Graph

If G is a connected plane graph (a graph with no edges crossing) with n vertices, e edges, and r regions, then $n - e + r = 2$.

By changing the order of the terms, we get $r = e - n + 2$. So if the graph is planar, the calculation of complexity reduces to counting regions as illustrated in Figure 14.5.

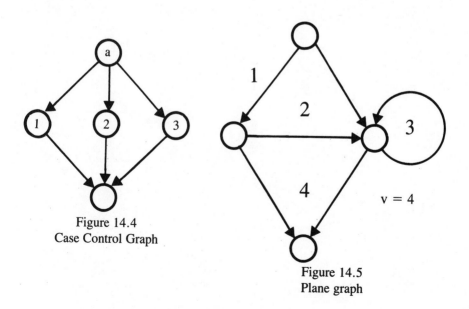

Figure 14.4
Case Control Graph

Figure 14.5
Plane graph

149

Part Two
Testing Methodology

15. The Structured Testing Criteria

The criteria that must be satisfied to complete the structured testing technique for a program with complexity v is:

Every outcome of each decision must be executed at least once.

At least v distinct paths must be executed.

It is important to understand that this is purely a criterion that measures the quality of the testing and *not* a procedure to identify test cases. In other words, the criteria above are a measure of the completeness of the testing that a programmer must satisfy. The criteria do not indicate how to arrive at the test data—we will discuss such a procedure in Chapter 16.

For example, a program of complexity five has the property that no set of four test paths will suffice (even if there are, for example, 39 distinct tests that concentrate on only these four paths). The Theorem in Chapter 12 establishes that in the case where only four paths have been tested, there must be, independent of the programming language or the data within the program, at least one additional test path that can be executed. On the other hand, the Theorem in Chapter 12 also establishes for a program of complexity five, that a 6th, 7th, 8th . . . path in a fundamental sense is redundant. That is, a combination of five basis paths will generate the additional paths.

Notice that most programs with a loop will have an arbitrarily high number of possible control paths, the testing of which is unrealizable. The power of the theorem in Chapter 12 is that it establishes a complexity number of v test paths that have two critical properties:

A test set of v paths can be realized (when this is violated, Chapter 18 will demonstrate that a program with lesser complexity will satisfy the same requirement).

Testing beyond v independent paths is redundantly exercising linear combinations of basis paths.

Several studies have shown that the distribution of run time over the statements in the program has a peculiar shape. Typically, 50% of the run time within a program is concentrated within only 4% of the code [KNUT]. When the test data is derived from only a requirements point of view and is *not* sensitive to the internal structure of the program, it likewise will spend most of the run time testing a few statements over and over again. The testing criteria in this paper establishes a level of testing that is inherently related to the internal complexity of a program's logic. One of the effects of this is to distribute the test data over a larger number of basis paths. Often the experience with the technique is that a lesser volume of testing is found to be more effective because it forces spreading the test data over more basis paths.

Operationally, the following experience with this technique has been observed. If a program's complexity is small (range 1-5), then conventional testing techniques usually satisfy the structured testing criteria. However, as complexity increases, the experience is that conventional testing techniques will typically *not* execute a complete set of basis paths. Explicitly satisfying the structured testing criteria will in these cases yield a more rigorous set of test data.

The criteria is illustrated with an example. The FORTRAN program in Figure 15.1 is designed to recognize strings of the form:

(i) A(B/C)*X

A string satisfying (i) has an 'A' followed by zero or more occurrences of 'B' or 'C' followed by an 'X'. If the string satisfies (i), the program is supposed to return the parameter BOOL 'true' and set the parameter COUNT to the total number of occurrences of 'B' and 'C'. If the string does not satisfy (i), the program is to return the parameter BOOL as 'false'.

Notice that in the program, statements have been numbered to facilitate drawing the flowgraph. The style used in producing the graph is a matter of individual taste—the reader may have to try drawing a few graphs to be comfortable with this technique.

There are several techniques, such as numbering statements and highlighting labels that help. Many of the nodes in the graph in Figure 15.1 have one entry and one exit and, therefore, can be deleted. Also, it helps to label edges coming out of a decision according to the conditions they represent. The flowgraph in Figure 15.2 employs both these techniques and it is generally easier to work with than the original.

The error in the program in Figure 15.1 is that BCOUNT should be added to COUNT after recognizing a *B*. We will examine some testing schemes and see how effective they are in detecting this bug.

A methodology often used [MILL] requires that
all statements must be executed

each decision must be executed both ways
A typical set of test data that fulfills these criteria is:

t1: #   (# denotes any character except A)
t2: ABC^ (^denotes any character except X)
t3: ABCX

Software Validation, Verification, Testing, and Documentation

The program SEARCH executes correctly in each test t1 through t3 so the test data fails to detect the error.

Applying the testing criterion discussed in Chapter 15, we need at least five distinct paths that cover all the edges in order to test SEARCH. The following set of five will do.

b1: ABCX
b2: #
b3: ACX
b4: ABX
b5: ABC^

Test b4 results in BOOL = 'true' and COUNT = 0, so it shows that the program does not meet the specification.

A few comments about practical experience using this technique may be in order. One misconception the reader may get is that it is necessary to have an automated system in order to use this method. Although an automated system can help, particularly in seeing the control graphs on a CRT, the main application of this technique has been by hand. Control graphs are drawn by hand, and the graph, the complexity v, and the data for the v distinct paths that are tested are all included as part of the standard documentation. Experience has shown that having the graphs and the actual test data proves invaluable later in modification and maintenance phases because the programmers know exactly which cases worked previously and they do

```
          SUBROUTINE SEARCH (STRING,PTR,BOOL,COUNT)
          INTEGER A,B,C,X
          INTEGER STRING (80), COUNT, PTR
          LOGICAL BOOL
          DATA A,B,C,X/"101,"102,"103,"130/
          BOOL = .FALSE.
          BCOUNT = 0
          COUNT = 0
  1       IF (STRING(PTR) .NE. A) GO TO 40
  2    10 CONTINUE
  3       PTR = PTR + 1
  4       IF (STRING(PTR) .NE. B) GO TO 20
  5       BCOUNT = BCOUNT + 1
  6       GO TO 10
  7    20 CONTINUE
  8       IF (STRING(PTR) .NE. C) GO TO 30
  9       COUNT = COUNT + BCOUNT + 1
 10       BCOUNT = 0
 11       GO TO 10
 12    30 CONTINUE
 13, 14   IF (STRING(PTR) .EQ. X) BOOL = .TRUE.
 15    40 RETURN
 16       END
```

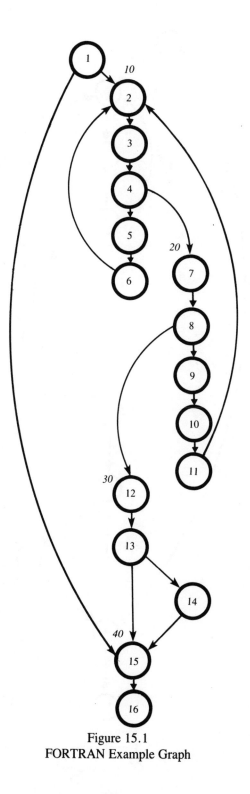

Figure 15.1
FORTRAN Example Graph

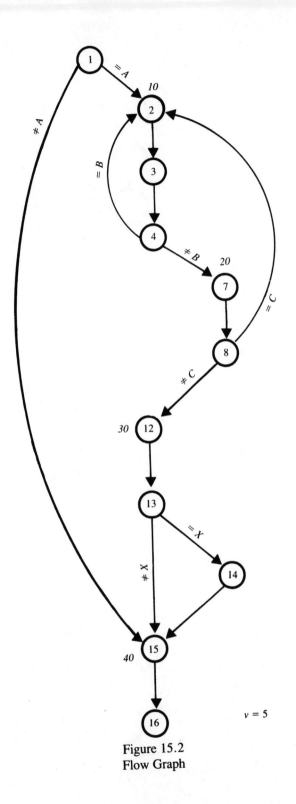

Figure 15.2
Flow Graph

156

not have to guess or take it on faith. Chapters 19 and 20 elaborate on the use of the test data in maintenance.

Often more than one test is performed on a path. The validation process for a particular path often consists of more than just exercising it once; all the functional requirements the path implements should be tested. Also, the programmer should explicitly look for data values that could produce errors along the path. This process may result in a large number of distinct test cases; however, it is critical that within this set of test cases, there are v distinct paths that cover every edge.

16. Identifying Test Paths: The Baseline Method

The technique described here gives a specific methodology to identify a set of control paths and test data to satsify the structured testing criteria. The technique, when applied, results in a set of test data and control paths equal in number to the cyclomatic complexity of a program. The technique is currently called the baseline method; it strengthens the structured testing method because it gives a specific technique to identify actual test data and test paths.

The Method

The first step is to pick up a functional "baseline" path through the program which represents a legitimate function and not just an error exit. The selection of this first baseline path is somewhat arbitrary. The key, however, is to pick a representative function provided in the program as opposed to an error path that results in an error message or recovery procedure. To test the baseline, exercise all the functional requirements implemented on the baseline. Also look for data that would produce errors on the baseline.

It is to be realized that this functional baseline path represents a sequence of decisions taken in a particular way.

The second step is to identify the second path by locating the first decision in the baseline path and flipping its result while simultaneously holding the maximum number of the original baseline decisions the same as on the baseline path. This is likely to produce a second path which is minimally different from the baseline path. Apply the same testing process described above to this path.

The third step is to set back the first decision to the value it had on the baseline path and identify and flip the second decision in the baseline path while holding all other decisions to their baseline values. This, likewise, should produce a third path which is minimally different than the baseline path. Test this path.

This procedure continues until one has gone through every decision and has flipped it from the baseline value while holding the other decisions to their original baseline values.

Since $v = S + 1$ if, for example, $v = 7$, there are 6 such decisions which one flips resulting in 6 paths that differ from the baseline path; all of which adds up to 7 distinct paths.

Since the selection of the baseline path is somewhat arbitrary, there is not necessarily "the" right set of test data for a program. That is, there may be several sets of test data that satisfy the structured testing criteria. The application of this baseline method will, however, generate a set of test data with the right properties:

> *v* distinct independent paths will be generated
> every edge in the program graph will be traversed.

An Example

The graph G, Figure 16.1, discussed in Chapter 12 is used to illustrate the method. The reader will have to trace through G to follow the discussion.

Step 1: Choose a Baseline path, path 1. As shown in G by dark lines, the path A–B–C–B–E–F–G is chosen as the baseline. It is assumed that this path represents one of the main functions in the program as opposed to an error path. This initial choice is somewhat arbitrary; keep in mind that the baseline path ideally performs the major full function provided in the program. Try to pick a baseline path that intersects a maximal number of decisions in the graph.

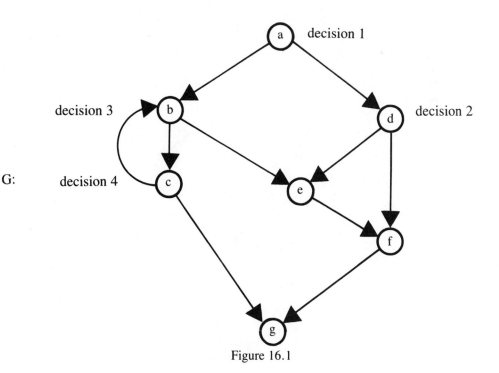

Figure 16.1

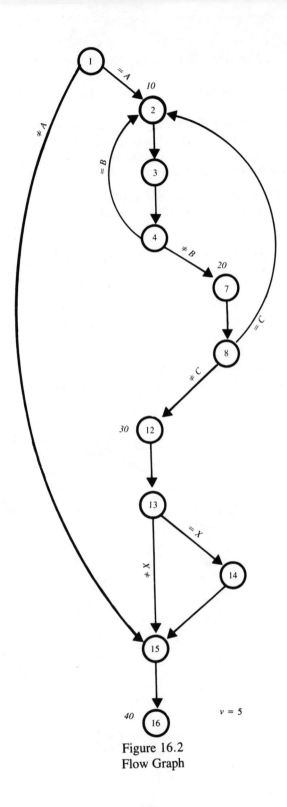

Figure 16.2
Flow Graph

160

Identifying Test Paths: The Baseline Method

Step 2: The first decision to be flipped is A. Path 2 should be chosen to differ minimally from the baseline—this yields the path A–D–E–F–G to be tested.

Step 3: Now flip the decision D in path 2 yielding the third path: A–D–F–G.

Step 4: Since A has been flipped from the baseline, the next decision to flip is B. This results in the path 4, A–B–E–F–G.

Step 5: The nodes E, F, and G in the baseline path A–B–C–D–E–F–G are not decisions. Since A and B have been flipped, the only decision remaining to reverse is C. This yields the fifth and last path: A–B–C–G.

Since we have flipped every decision once, this completes the procedure. Notice that the baseline procedure satisfied the structured testing criteria. The complexity of G is 5 ($v(G) = 11 - 7 + 1$); we have generated 5 independent paths that have traversed each edge.

Refer back to the sample FORTRAN program in Chapter 15. Figure 15.1 and its graph which is repeated as Figure 16.2. It is interesting to apply the baseline method to this program.

Assume the path 1–2–3–4–2–3–4–7–8–2–3–4–7–8–12–13–14–15–16, as shown by dark lines, representing the test data ABCX, is chosen as the baseline. The baseline procedure then yields paths with the following test data.

```
b1:  ABCX
b2:  #   (# denotes any character except A)
b3:  ACX
b4:  ABX
b5:  ABC^   (^ denotes any character except X)
```

This is the same test data presented in Chapter 15—here we have shown how to derive it.

17. Integration Testing

In Chapter 12, the notion of complexity was derived from the cyclomatic number of a graph. The discussion, however, was limited to graphs with only one component. In this section we will generalize the approach to cover graphs that have several components. The application will be to measure design complexity; specifically, we will quantify the effort required to perform integration testing of several modules within a design structure.

Our focus up to this point has been on one module at a time and the testing application has been at the unit level. A module will typically be represented in a FORTRAN, PL1, or PASCAL program as a procedure, function, or the main line code. In COBOL, a module is typically expressed as a paragraph which is referenced from several distinct places within the program.

Figure 17.1 is a standard representation of a design where M is the top level and calls module A and module B. The design in Figure 17.1 implies the following: M, A, and B are all distinct modules. They have their own internal specifications and will have their own unique test data. Modules A and B are called from M. They, however, may also be called in a different context by other modules and could be on a program library. Notice that this is quite different from a situation where A's code and B's code would be embedded within M.

Figure 17.2 is a graph which shows the algorithm we might find "inside" mod-

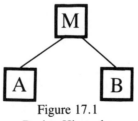

Figure 17.1
Design Hierarchy

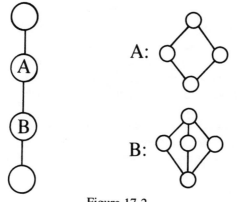

Figure 17.2
Graph of Design Hierarchy

ules M, A, and B. The graph in Figure 17.2 has three components, M, A, and B—each of the graphs we have previously discussed had only one component.

We have to add an extra edge to each component in a graph to satisfy the strong connectivity condition of Theorem 1. Therefore, the more general expression is $v = e - n + 2p$; this expresses the system complexity of a design with several component graphs as opposed to the more specific $v = e - n + 2$, which applies to a single component.

When the number of components is 3 ($P = 3$), the complexity calculation yields $v = 13 - 13 + 2* 3$. This design complexity of 6 represents the testing effort required to perform a top down integration of the three modules M, A, and B. For example, using a top down strategy, the following tests occur:

One test is required to verify the code within M. Stubs that simulate the actions of A & B are called to allow this testing of M.

Two tests are required to verify A's logic. Each of these calls on A are driven through M in order to invoke A. During A's testing, the stub for B is still in place.

Three tests are likewise required to verify B's logic. As above, each of the three calls on B would be driven "top down" through M.

As the complexity quantification indicated, it is indeed the case as shown above that six tests are required to integrate the three modules.

Notice that the design complexity in a graph with several components is equal to the summation of the unit level complexity. With the example above, the complexity can be computed as $v = v(M) + v(A) + v(B) = + 1 + 2 + 3$. For a formal proof of this, see [MCCA].

The application of the design level complexity is different in nature than the application of unit level complexity. Design level complexity is not limited in the sense that the unit level complexity is controlled. The main application of the design complexity is to quantify the integration effort of a collection of the modules.

There are occasions, however, when the design level complexity can be used to make a comparison of the relative complexity of subsystems within an overall design. This quantitative view of the subsystems complexity will give a more stable predictor of several project attributes than the more customarily used lines of code. For example, if the design level complexity of one subsystem is 2000, and a second subsystem complexity is 30, there are several implications—for example, the subsystem testing and integration are more closely correlated with this design complexity quantification than the subsystems' physical size in terms of lines of code.

18. The Reduction Technique

When this methodology is applied to an ongoing project or when an existing testing practice is analyzed, the usual outcome is that the actual number of paths tested is less than the cyclomatic complexity. The concept behind this methodology is to quantify and to limit the complexity of a program and then to require the testing to be at least as thorough as the quantification.

The idea in this section is that if the actual testing does not meet the cyclomatic complexity, then either the testing can be improved or the program logic can be simplified.

Let use assume that a program has been written. Its complexity v has been calculated. The number of distinct paths traversed during the test phase is ac (actual complexity). If ac is less than v, one of the following conditions holds:

The program contains additional paths that can be tested.

The complexity of v can be reduced by $v - ac$ ($v - ac$ decisions can be removed from the program).

Portions of the program can be reduced to in-line code (constant length loops have been used in order to conserve space).

The actual paths that are tested in a program are determined by the data flow and data conditions at the various decisions. Because of the data flow, a number of paths may not be realizable in a given program. The point of this section is that when the data flow and data conditions are considered, there must be at least v distinct paths or else the program can indeed be reduced.

Several examples are shown to illustrate case 2, the reduction technique; it should be noted that, in practice, the most frequent outcome is case 1 and the existing testing can, in fact, be improved.

Consider the following program:

```
J = 1;
IF I ≤ 3 THEN I = 2
        ELSE J = 14;
IF (I + J) ≤ 6 THEN OUTPUT (I, J);
```

The complexity is 3 and the control graph is shown in Figure 18.1.

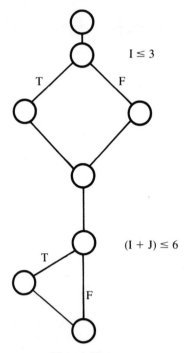

Figure 18.1
Program Control Graph

It is clear that ac = 2 since the only realizable paths on the graph are TT, FF. That is, one path where I ≤ 3 is true and (I + J) ≤ 6 is also true, and a second path where both conditions are false.

Since there are no additional paths to test, and there are no constant length loops, the program can be reduced to complexity 2:

```
J = 1
IF I ≤ 3 THEN
    BEGIN
    I = 2
    OUTPUT (I, J);
    END
ELSE
    J = 14;
```

As a second example, we will use the FORTRAN program in Chapter 15. Let us assume that the tests used are:

```
#    (# denotes any character except A)
A^   (^ denotes any character except X)
ABCBCX
```

```
       SUBROUTINE SEARCH (STRING, PTR, BOOL, COUNT)
       INTEGER, A, B, C, X
       INTEGER STRING (80), COUNT, PTR
       LOGICAL BOOL
       DATA A, B, C, X /"101", "102", "103", "130"/
       BOOL = .FALSE.
       COUNT = 0
       IF (STRING(PTR) .NE. A) GO TO 40
       PTR = PTR + 1
       IF (STRING(PTR) .NE. B) GO TO 40
       COUNT = 4
       BOOL = .TRUE.
  40   RETURN
       END
```

Figure 18.2 FORTRAN Program

Recall that these tests satisfy the C2 testing criterion that each decision outcome is executed at least once, but we have ac = 3 whereas v = 5. Now, if we believe that the tester really cannot find any additional tests, then the program can be reduced to complexity 3. In fact, if the tester insists that no more paths exist, a programmer must admit that the program in Figure 18.2 containing these three paths will suffice.

The point here is not that the program in Figure 18.2 is the desired one, but rather that the testing process can, and should, be improved.

A frequent error in testing strategy is to test only the expected data and overlook testing the error conditions. The third example illustrates this with the program SEARCH, in a case where test data checks only the expected conditions.

```
                    ABCBBCBBX
                    AX
                    ACCX
```

Once again, if the programmer claims that these are the only paths, the program can be reduced to the following complexity 3 code:

```
       SUBROUTINE SEARCH (STRING, PTR, BOOL, COUNT)
       INTEGER A, B, C, X
       INTEGER STRING (80), COUNT, PTR
       LOGICAL BOOL
       DATA A, B, C, X /"101", "102", "103", "130" /
       BOOL = .TRUE.
       COUNT = -1
  20   PTR = PTR+ 1
       COUNT = COUNT + 1
       IF ( (STRING(PTR) .EQ. B) OR (STRING (PTR) . EQ. C)) GO TO 20
       RETURN
       END
```

Figure 18.3 FORTRAN Program Revised

Software Validation, Verification, Testing, and Documentation

The one case where it may in fact be impossible to find v distinct paths is the situation where the programmer increases complexity to conserve space. For example, if the program contains a fixed-length loop, where the increment and limits are constant and are not modified by the body, then a loop that iterates n times is equivalent to n in-line copies of the body. For instance, the following code:

```
      DO 10 I = 1,3
10 A(I) = I
```

is equivalent to
```
      A(1) = 1
      A(2) = 2
      A(3) = 3
```

which has a complexity 1.

In summary, the cyclomatic complexity v of a program can be thought of as specification for testing the paths. If a given program does not have at least v distinct tested paths, then either the testing is incomplete or there is excessive logic that can be removed. The guideline is: if there is any logic that is untestable, then that logic is removable.

For large systems and certain applications, it is recognized that this objective may be very difficult and not practical to attain. Some cases in which reduction may not be possible are:

defensive programming

hardware mistrust

fault tolerant programming

Nonetheless, every effort should be made to accomplish this goal.

Part Three
Maintenance Methodology

19. Essential Complexity

An interesting question associated with a program's complexity is quantifying how well-structured a program is. That is, how do we quantify the degree to which a program has been written using only the standard structured control flow constructs in Figure 19.1.

This is an important concern since one of the basic ways to reduce the complexity of a program where v exceeds 10 is to recognize and to remove subfunctions from the main control flow so they become separate subroutines or functions. It turns out that if a program is structured (i.e., it uses only the constructs SEQUENCE, UNTIL, WHILE, IF, CASE), its complexity can be reduced in a straightforward manner. For example, in the graphs in Figures 19.2 and 19.3, the original structured program can be reduced to a program of complexity 1 by making the one-entry-one-exit subgraphs into functions.

The reduction process, more formally, is the process of replacing proper subgraphs with single-entry and exit nodes. Essential complexity is defined below in order to reflect how well a program is structured.

Let G' denote the reduced graph that results from removing all proper, single-entry, single-exit subgraphs. Also, leading edges and trailing edges should be removed so the first node is a decision node and the last node is a collection node. The essential complexity of a graph G is defined as $ev = v(G')$.

Although G1 through G3 has $v = 5$, Figures 19.3 through 19.5, each of the subgraphs of G1 could be removed whereas G3 cannot be reduced at all. If the graphs were highly complex, this would be crucial since G1 could be reduced into subroutines, each with complexity less than 10, but G3 could not be reduced. Therefore, a further modularization would require that the G3 program be thrown out and a new program be designed.

An example of reducing complexity by adhering to standard structured control flow constructs is Figure 19.6. This is a rewrite of Figure 15.1, the string recognition problem. The complexity of the original program is 6 while the complexity of the rewrite is 4. The essential complexity of the original program is 3 while the essential complexity of the rewrite is 2.

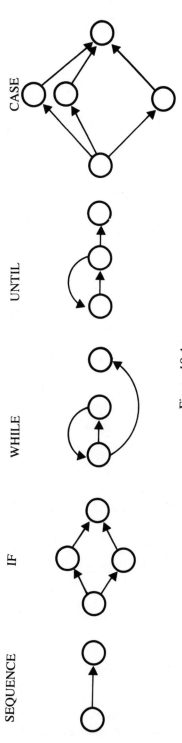

Figure 19.1
Structured Control Constructs

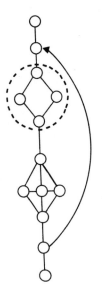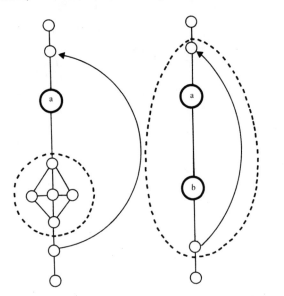

Figure 19.2
Reducing Complexity, Example 1

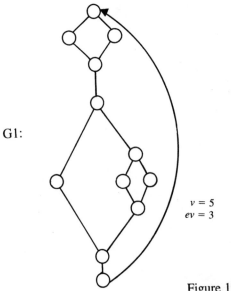

G1:

$v = 5$
$ev = 3$

G1':

$v = 1$

Figure 19.3
Reducing complexity, Example 2

Essential Complexity

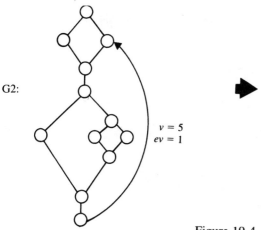

G2:

$v = 5$
$ev = 1$

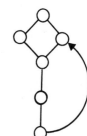

G2':

Figure 19.4
Reducing Complexity, Example 3

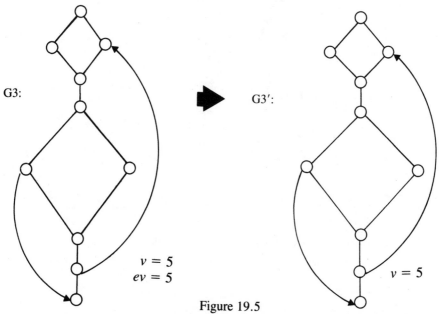

G3:

$v = 5$
$ev = 5$

G3':

$v = 5$

Figure 19.5
Non-Reducible Control Graph

```
               SUBROUTINE SEARCH (STRING,PTR,BOOL,COUNT)
               INTEGER A,B,C,X
               INTEGER STRING(80), COUNT, PTR
               LOGICAL BOOL
               DATA A,B,C,X/"101","102","103","130/
               COUNT = 0
               BOOL = .FALSE.
1              IF STR(PTR) .EQ. A
2                  THEN PTR = PTR + 1
3                  WHILE STR(PTR) .EQ. B .OR. STR(PTR) .EQ. C DO
4                      COUNT = COUNT + 1
5                      PTR = PTR + 1
6                  END
7                  IF (STR(PTR) .EQ. X) ) BOOL = .TRUE.
9              ENDIF
10         40  RETURN
```

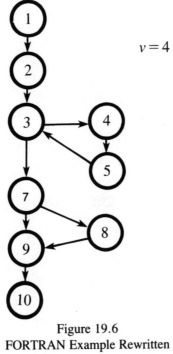

$v = 4$

Figure 19.6
FORTRAN Example Rewritten

20. Program Modification

The Problem

Several studies have indicated that software maintenance and modification often take as much as 70% of the total life-cycle cost. Much of this maintenance activity involves the modification and retesting of existing programs, for which very little methodology exists. This section introduces procedures for performing modifications and their tests in a more orderly manner.

Modifying Functional Statements

If a patch or modification to a program does not change the control flow structure, the change is typically confined to a functional node (a node with not more than one output edge). In programming terms, this type of change involves modifying functional statements such as: input, ouput, and statements that perform calculations. In contrast to this, a control flow change involves the modification or insertions of statements such as GOTO's, IF's, and DO-LOOPS which affect program control.

The method of verifying a functional statement change follows:

Identify all structured test paths that contain the changed node—these test paths should be contained in the Unit Development Folder or other suitable documentation

Re-execute all such paths that contain the changed node

The example in Figure 20.1 illustrates the procedure.

Notice that the retention of such unit test data forms a local test bed that can be used to regressively establish that the change does not destroy the original functions provided.

Modifying Control Flow

Example of Catastrophic Change

Assume the program in Figure 20.2 is being modified. Assume also that at the node X the programmer wants to have the code (b) and (c) execute.

175

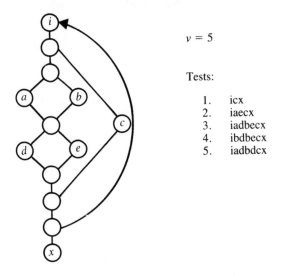

$v = 5$

Tests:

1.   icx
2.   iaecx
3.   iadbecx
4.   ibdbecx
5.   iadbdcx

If, for example, node e is changed, then the minimal amount of retesting is the subset of test paths that contain e:

2.   iaecx
3.   iadbecx
4.   ibdbecx

Figure 20.1
Program Modification

A common way to achieve this is to patch in the conditional GOTO's shown as dotted lines that branch to a point before (b) and then return after node C. This may seem innocent and, in fact, desirable, since the size of the blocks (b) and (c) could be large and the programmer may be enthusiastic about the space being saved. The point usually missed, however, is the structural change in the program. The two patches only had a modest effect on the cyclomatic complexity, which changed from 6 to 8. And, in general, cyclomatic complexity changes slowly with patches to control nodes (v goes up to 1 per conditional GOTO, and v is insensitive to the deletion or addition of functional nodes like (a)).

The essential complexity has, on the other hand, changed substantially with the patches: from 1 in the original to 8. The original program could be decomposed into several independent functions whereas the modified program could not, and the functions that were independent are now coupled. The main point here is that our common maintenance practices often have the effect of changing a well-structured program into a completely unstructured program. This can happen by changing only one source statement without being aware of the dramatic structural change.

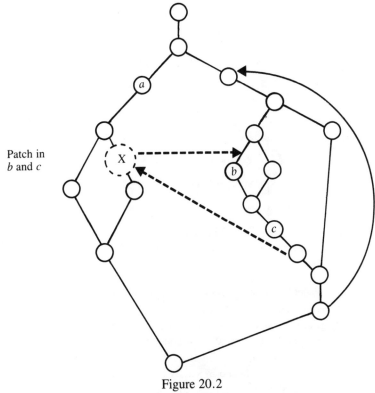

Patch in
b and *c*

Figure 20.2
Program Patch

Re-Test Methodology

The next two sections give the operational steps in performing maintenance testing. The first step identifies changes that are virtually untestable; it precludes such changes from being introduced. The second step actually quantifies the number of tests to be run given a structural change.

Evaluate Essential Complexity The previous example of catastrophic change illustrates the first step of the maintenance discipline:

> "Evaluate the effect of a control flow change on *essential complexity*; do not allow a well-structured program to severely degrade."

Re-test Quantification This leads to the central procedure for maintenance testing. This procedure quantifies the number of tests required to validate such a change.

177

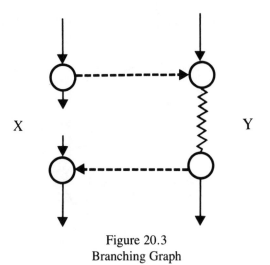

Figure 20.3
Branching Graph

Figure 20.3 depicts a situation where Y is the name of the code being branched into and X is the code being branched from.

The three particular cases arising in practice are shown in Figure 20.4.

In cases where Y is a subgraph with unique entry and exit nodes, we can compute the cyclomatic complexity $v(Y)$. In such cases, the number of paths to verify the patch is $2*v(Y) + 1$. Cases 1) and 2) satisfy this since code Y that was branched into has a single entry and exit.

For example, in Case 2, $v(Y) = 3$, so 7 tests are required to test the patch. Three paths should be tested through the normal entry of Y to demonstrate that the branch back into X is not taken. Three more paths that take the new branch into Y, traverse Y in three different ways and then return to X. And finally, one last test has to be made of the path that does not take the new path but falls into X instead.

In case 3 the block Y does not have a single entry and exit, so the expression $2*v(Y) + 1$ does not apply. This type of modification should be avoided since it will have a disastrous effect on the program's structure; the evaluation of essential complexity cited above would have precluded such a change.

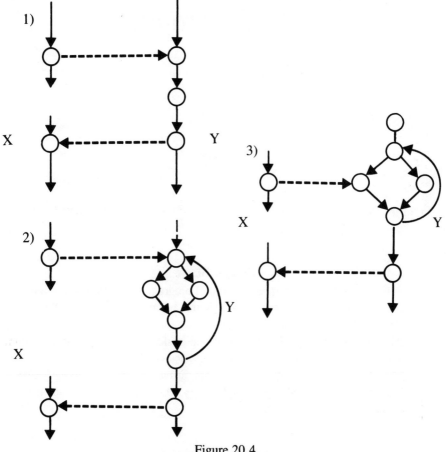

Figure 20.4
Branching Graph Amplified

21. Summary

In this section the operational steps of structured testing are consolidated and listed below.

Design Stage

If the algorithm is written in a high level program design language, limit complexity to seven. Experience has shown that when the coding takes place, complexity will approach 10.

If the internal specifications of software modules include the number of conditions that must be tested internally, limit such conditions to six.

If the above information is not available at the design phase, break modules you intuitively feel will exceed complexity 10 into submodules with complexity less than or equal to 10.

Coding Phase

Make an explicit flow graph organic to the programming process.

Calculate the cyclomatic complexity v with any of the three methods described in Chapter 14.

When complexity exceeds 10 go back to the design phase and refine the logic into modules, each with complexity 10 or less (the exceptions are the CASE statement or project specific contraints).

Unit Testing Phase

Use the baseline method to identify test paths and data until the number of such paths satisfies the following criteria:

v independent paths are represented.

Every edge in the flowgraph is covered at least one time.

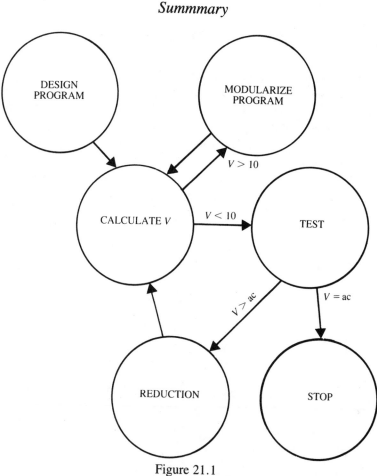

Figure 21.1
Structured Testing Technique

If the above criteria are not satisfied, then either:
　　More test paths exist that can be exercised or
　　The program contains redundant logic that can be removed.
Keep documentation on the paths tested available for the maintenance phase; typically in a unit development folder.

Maintenance Phase

Classify a proposed change to the code as a *functional* statement change or a *control* statement change.

In the case of *functional* statement change, regressively retest all original test paths in the unit development folder that intersect with changed functional statements.

In the case of a *control* statement change:

> If the essential complexity will substantially increase, do not make the change; the program will become unmaintainable. Take a different approach to the modification.
>
> Where the essential complexity will not increase, quantify and retest by the $2*v(T)+1$ rule.

Figure 21.1 illustrates the main steps in the structured testing technique.

Appendix A:
Empirical Evidence

We have been introducing this subject by graph theory, example, and intuition. Independent empirical data that validates this approach in the real world would be useful. In software, empirical evidence typically takes years to collect; data on the use of v, the cyclomatic complexity, is at this time sparce. However, the results are encouraging.

In a series of controlled experiments conducted at General Electric [CURTa] and [CURTb], v was found to predict the performance of programers on comprehension, modification, and debugging tasks. For example, on the debugging task, programmers were asked to locate and correct a single error in each of three programs. A statistically significant correlation was found between the complexity of the programs, as measured by v, and the time required to locate and correct the bugs. V, in fact, was a considerably better predictor of debugging time than was the number of lines of code.

A comparison of the program [BASI] produced by disciplined teams, conventional teams, and individuals was done in 1979. The participants in this experiment consisted of advanced undergraduate and graduate students at the University of Maryland. Their task was to design and implement a relatively simple compiler. The entire project required approximately two staff-months of effort and resulted in systems averaging about 1200 lines of code. The disciplined teams were required to use a set of state-of-the-art techniques such as top down design, walkthroughs, and chief programmer team organization. The conventional teams and individuals were given no such requirement and, in fact, had received no formal training in these techniques. The software produced by the disciplined teams was completed with less effort and with fewer errors than that produced by the conventional teams and individuals; the program modules were less complex as measured by v. Thus, the disciplined methodology in this study led to more reliable, less complex software.

Henry, Kafura, and Harris [HENR] reported empirical error data collected on the UNIX operating system. The authors obtained a list of errors from the UNIX User's Group and performed correlations on three metrics. The cyclomatic complexity v was the most closely related to errors of the three—the correlation between v and number of errors was .96.

Software Validation, Verification, Testing, and Documentation

Walsh [WALS] collected data on the number of software errors detected during the development phase of the AEGIS Naval Weapon System. The system contained a total of 276 modules, approximately half of which had a v of less than 10 and half a v of 10 or greater. The average error rate for modules with a complexity of less than 10 was 4.6 per 100 source statements while the corresponding error rate for the more complex modules was 5.6. As Walsh pointed out, one would expect a similar pattern for undetected errors as well. It would be expected that fewer errors should appear for the less complex modules during the maintenance phase.

Myers [MYER] calculated v for the programs contained in the classic text by Kernigan and Plauger [KERN]. For every case in which an improved program was suggested, this improvement resulted in a lower value of v. Myers describes one interesting case in which Kernigan and Plauger suggested two simplified versions of a program which has a v of 16. The two improvements were done and Myers found that both had a v of 10.

In a recently-completed study [SHEP], the performance of programmers in constructing programs from various specification formats was examined. An automated data collection system recorded the complete sequence of events involved in constructing and debugging each program. An analysis of the error data revealed that the major source of difficulty was related to the control flow and not to such factors as the sheer number of statements or variables. The most difficult program had the most complex decision structure while a considerably easier program performed extremely complex arithmetic calculations but had a simpler decision structure. Thus, v can be used to measure a truly difficult aspect of programming. A similar result was also reported by Curtis, Sheppard, and Milliman [CURTa].

Not only does v have a solid foundation in mathematics, but the studies cited illustrate that it predicts the difficulty experienced by programmers in working with software, the number of errors detected in program modules, and it conforms to subjective judgements of complexity.

Bibliography

1. [BASI] Basli, V.R. and Reiter, R.W. "Evaluating Automatable Measures of Software Development," *Workshop on Quantitative Software Models*, New York: IEEE, 1979.

2. [BERG] Berge, C. *Graphs and Hypergraphs*. Amsterdam, The Netherlands: North-Holland, 1973.

3. [CHAP] Chapin, N., "A Measure of Software Complexity," *AFIPS Conference Proceedings, NCC*, Vol. 48, 1979, pp. 995-1002.

4. [CHEN] Chen, E.T., "Program Complexity and Programmer Productivity," *Proceedings of Computer Software and Applications Conference*, 1977, pp. 142-148.

5. [CURTa] Curtis, B., Sheppard, S.B., & Milliman, P. "Third Time Charm: Stronger Prediction of Programmer Performance by Software Complexity Metrics," *Proceedings of the Fourth International Conference on Software Engineering*, New York: IEEE, 1979.

6. [CURTb] Curtis, B., Sheppard, S.B., Milliman, P., Borst, M.A., & Love, T. "Predicting Performance on Software Maintenance Tasks with the Halstead and McCabe metrics," *IEEE Transactions on Software Engineering*, 1979, 5, pp. 95-104.

7. [GILB] Gilb, T., *Software Metrics*, Winthrop Publishers, Inc., Cambridge, MA, 1977.

8. [HALS] Halstead, M.H., *Elements of Software Science*, Elsevier North-Holland, New York, 1977.

9. [HENR] Henry, S., Kafura, D., & Harris, K. "On the Relationships Among Three Software Metrics," *1981 ACM Workshop/Symposium on Measurement and Evaluation of Software Quality*, March 1981.

10. [JELI] Jelinski, Z., & Moranda, P.B., *Metrics of Software Quality*, McDonnell Douglas Astronautics Co., Report MDC-G7517, Ad-A077896, August 1979.

11. [KOLE] Kolence, K.W., "Software Physics and Computer Performance Measurement," *Proceedings of the ACM 1972 Annual Conference*, pp. 1024-1040.

12. [KERN] Kernighan, B.W., & Plauger, P.J., *The Elements of Programming Style*, New Jersey: Bell Telephone Laboratories, 1974.

13. [KNUT] Knuth, D.E. "An Empirical Study of FORTRAN Programs," *Software Practice and Experience*, April-June 1971, pp. 105-133.

14. [LEGA] Legard, H. & Marcotty, M. "A Genealogy of Control Structures," *CACM*, 18, pp. 629-639, Nov. 1975.

15. [MCAL] McCall, J.A., et al., *Factors in Software Quality*, RADC-TR-77-369, Vol. I, II, III (AD-A049-014, -015, -055), General Electric Co., Sunnyvale, CA, July 1977.

16. [MCCA] McCabe, T.J. "A Complexity Measure," *IEEE Trans. on Software Engineering*, SE-2 No. 4, pp. 308-320, Dec. 1976.

17. [MILL] Miller, E.F. "Program Testing: Art Meets Theory", *Computer*, 10, No. 7, pp. 42-51, July 1977.

18. [MOHA] Mohanty, S.N. & Adamowicz, "Proposed Measures for the Evaluation of Software", *Proceedings of Symposium on Computer Software Engineering*, N.Y., April 1976, pp. 485-497.

Software Validation, Verification, Testing, and Documentation

19. [MYER] Myers, G.J. "An Extension to the Cyclomatic Measure of Program Complexity," *SIGPLAN Notices*, 1977.
20. [PAIG] Paige, M. "An Analytical Approach to Software Testing", *Proceedings COMPSAC 78*, Chicago, 1978, IEEE Computer Society, New York, p. 527-532.
21. [SHEP] Sheppard, S.B. and Kruesi, E. "The Effects of the Symbology and Spatial Arrangement of Software Specifications in a Coding Task," *Technical Report TR-81-388200-3*, Arlington, VA: General Electric Company, 1981.
22. [WALS] Walsh, T.J. "A Software Reliability Study Using a Complexity Measure," In *Proceedings of the National Computer Conference*, New York: AFIPS, 1979.

Book Four
Software Validation, Verification, and Testing Technique and Tool Reference Guide

Abstract

Thirty techniques and tools for validation, vertification, and testing (V, V&T) are described. Each description includes the basic features of the technique or tool, the input, the output, an example, an assessment of the effectiveness and usability, applicability, an estimate of the learning time and training, an estimate of needed resources, and references.

Keywords: automated software tools; dynamic analysis; formal analysis; software testing; software verification; static analysis; test coverage; validation; V,V&T techniques, V,V&T tools.

22. Introduction

The Institute for Computer Sciences and Technology (ICST) carries out the following responsibilities under P.L. 89-306 (Brooks Act) to improve the Federal Government's management and use of ADP:

Develops Federal automatic data processing standards;

Provides agencies with scientific and technological advisory services relating to ADP; and

Undertakes necessary research in computer sciences and technology.

In partial fulfillment of Brooks Act responsibilities, ICST issues Special Publications (S.P.). Book Four is a reference guide for techniques and tools which may be used in conjunction with a validation, verification, and testing (V,V&T) methodology.

Book Four consists of three major sections in two chapters:

A suggested methodology for the selection of V,V&T techniques and tools;

Summary matrices by development phase usage; a table of techniques and tools with associated keywords; and an alphabetized table of keywords with associated techniques and tools; and

Descriptions of 30 V,V&T techniques and tools.

A glossary, included as Appendix A, defines terminology used in Book Four.

A Suggested Methodology for the Selection of V,V&T Techniques and Tools

Selecting techniques and tools begins with the determination of a goal—a specific, measurable outcome. For example, 90 percent statement execution is a goal. Once a goal is determined, the selection matrices are utilized to see if a technique or tool is applicable to the selected goal. For the example above, statement coverage is checked during code execution. Referencing the code selection matrix, one finds statement coverage. Next, the alphabetized keyword table is searched for the appropriate keyword(s). For the example, the tool for statement coverage is found to be test coverage analyzers. The last step is to reference the technique and tool descriptions (section 4) and confirm that the technique or tool does accomplish the desired goal. For the example under test coverage analyzers, the statement "Completeness is measured in terms of the branches, statements or other elementary constructs which are used during the execution of the program over the tests", confirms that a statement coverage analyzer measures the completeness of statement excution.

Selection Aids

Tables 22.1, 22.2, and 22.3 separate techniques and tools into the broadly defined software development phases: requirements, design, and code.

The purpose of a selection matrix is to suggest possible techniques or tools for a goal in a development phase. The goal is stated (directly or indirectly) in terms of the form or content of a development product (requirements, design, code). The matrices list V,V&T techniques and tools applicable to analyzing the form or content of a product. Specifically, manual and automated static analysis techniques and tools aid in analyzing the form of each of the three products. Dynamic and formal techniques and tools aid in analyzing the semantic content of each of the products.

Table 22.4 lists, alphabetically, the keywords and the associated technique or tool. It may be used to identify characteristics of the technique or tool from one of the three matrices in Tables 22.1, 22.2, or 22.3.

Table 22.5 lists each technique or tool described in section 4 with applicable keywords. It may also be used to identify the characteristics of a technique or tool.

The reader with sufficient knowledge may skip Tables 22.1 through 22.5 and go directly to the technique and tools section.

Selected Matrices and Keyword Tables

The pages that follow contain three selection matrices:

Table 22.1 Requirement Specifications

Table 22.2 Design Specifications

Table 22.3 Code

and

Table 22.4 V,V&T Techniques and Tool Keywords

Table 22.5 V,V&T Techniques and Tool with Keywords

Table 22.1
Selection Matrix I Requirement Specification

Analysis Type	Automated Tools	Manual Techniques	Reviews
Static	Requirements tracing aids (Note 1) Cross-reference Data flow analyzer	Requirements tracing aids (Notes 1&2) Inspections – Selected manual application of techniques listed in column one (Note 3)	Inspections Peer review Formal reviews
Dynamic	Requirements analysis Cause-effect graphing Assertion generation Data flow analyzer	Assertion generation (Note 4) Specification-based functional testing (Note 5) Cause-effect graphing (Note 5) Walkthroughs	Walkthroughs Formal reviews
Formal	Assertion generation	Formal verification (Note 6)	

NOTES

1) The requirements indexing and cross-referencing schemes are established and documented as part of the requirements specification.
2) Requirements tracing may be performed through a totally manual process.
3) Certain techniques may be manually applied to small applications or on selected portions of a given specification. This requires planning and preparation. The larger the amount of information being analyzed, the greater the probability of error.
4) Assertion generation is performed either for later analysis using an assertion processing tool, or for manual analysis as an adjunct to testing.
5) This is a test data generation technique/tool.
6) Axiomatic specification is necessary to support analysis.

Software Validation, Verification, Testing, and Documentation

Table 22.2
Selection Matrix II Design Specifications

Analysis Type	Automated Tools	Manual Techniques	Reviews
Static	Requirements tracing aids Cross-reference Data flow analyzer	Requirements tracing (Note 1) Inspections – Selected manual application of techniques listed in column one (Note 2)	Inspections Peer review Formal reviews
Dynamic	Cause-effect graphing	Assertion generation (Note 3) Specification-based ·functional testing (Note 4) Cause-effect graphing (Note 4) Walkthroughs	Walkthroughs Formal reviews
Formal	Analytic modeling of software designs (Note 6) Global roundoff analysis of algebraic processes (Note 5) Formal verification (Note 8)	Algorithm analysis Formal verification (Notes 7&8)	

NOTES
1) Requirements tracing may be performed through a totally manual process.
2) Certain techniques may be manually applied to small applications or on selected portions of a given specification. This requires planning and preparation. The larger the amount of information being analyzed, the greater the probability of error.
3) Assertion generation is performed either for later analysis using an assertion processing tool, or for manual analysis as an adjunct to testing.
4) This is a test data generation technique/tool.
5) Analyzes an algebraic algorithm, independent of a given level of specification and therefore is applicable to a design or code level specification.
6) Requires the manual development of a model, which is then run.
7) Axiomatic specification is necessary to support analysis.
8) Formal verification is a primarily manual exercise though supporting tools have been developed.

Table 22.3
Selection Matrix III Code

Analysis Type	Automated Tools	Manual Techniques	Reviews

Static	Requirements
	  tracing
		Requirements
		  tracing aids (Note 1)
			Inspections
			Peer review

	Cross-reference	Inspections	Formal reviews
	Data flow analyzer	– Selected manual	
	Control structure analyzer	application of techniques listed in	
	Interface checker	column one	
	Physical units checking	(Note 2)	
	Code auditor		
	Comparator		
	Test data generator		
Dynamic	Assertion processing	Assertion generation	Walkthroughs
	Test data generators	(Note 3)	Formal reviews

	Test support
	  facilities
		Regression testing
		  (Note 6)	

	Test coverage analysis	Walkthroughs	
	Mutation analysis (Note 4)		
	Interactive test aids		
	Execution time estimator/analyzer (Note 5)		
	Software montior (Note 5)		
	Statement coverage		
	Symbolic evaluation		

Formal	Formal verification
	  (Note 7)
		Formal verification
		  (Note 7)	

NOTES
1) Requirements tracing may be performed through a totally manual process.
2) Certain techniques may be manually applied to small applications or on selected portions of a given specification. This requires planning and preparation. The larger the amount of information being analyzed, the greater the probability of error.
3) Assertion generation is performed either for later analysis using an assertion processing tool, or for manual analysis as an adjunct to testing.
4) The objective of mutation analysis is to help assess the sufficiency of the test data.
5) Assist in testing the satisfaction of performance related requirements.
6) Testing after modification of tested software, i.e., retesting.
7) Formal verification is a primarily manual exercise though supporting tools have been developed.

Software Validation, Verification, Testing, and Documentation

Table 22.4
V,V&T Technique and Tool Keywords

Keywords	Technique/Tool
accuracy analysis	algorithm analysis
algorithm efficiency	algorithm analysis
amount of space (memory, disk, etc.) used	algorithm analysis
amount of work (CPU operations) done	algorithm analysis
assertion violations	assertion processing
bottle necks	analytic modeling of software designs
boundary test cases	specification-based functional testing
branch and path identification	control structure analyzer
branch testing	test coverage analyzer
call graph	control structure analyzer
check list	inspections
code reading	peer review
completeness of test data	mutation analysis
computational upper bound, how fast	algorithm analysis
consistency in computations	physical units testing
correspondence between actual and formal parameters	interface checker
data characteristics	assertion generation
dynamic testing of assertions	assertion processing
environment simulation	test support facilities
evaluation along program paths	symbolic execution
execution monitoring	software monitors
execution sampling	software monitors
execution support	test support facilities
expected inputs, outputs, and intermediate results	assertion generation
expected versus actual results	comparator
file (or other event) sequence errors	data flow analyzer
formal specifications	assertion generation
functional interrelationships	requirements analyzer
global information flow	interface checker
go/no go decisions	formal reviews
hierarchical interrelationships of modules	control structure analyzer
information flow consistency	requirements analyzer

194

Introduction

Keywords	Technique/Tool
inspections	peer review
inter-module structure	cross-reference generators
loop invariants	assertion generation
manual simulation	walkthroughs
module invocation	control structure analyzer
numerical stability	global roundoff analysis of algebraic processes
path testing	test coverage analyzers
performance analysis	requirements analyzer
physical units	assertion generation
portability analyzer	code auditor
program execution characteristics	execution time estimator/ analyzer
	software monitors
proof of correctness	formal verification
regression testing	comparator
requirements indexing	requirements tracing
requirements specification analysis	cause-effect graphing
requirements to design correlation	requirements tracing
requirements walkthrough	requirements analyzer
retesting after changes	regressing testing
round-robin reviews	peer reviews
rounding error propagation	global roundoff analysis of algebraic processes
selective program execution	interactive test aids
standards checker	code auditor
statement coverage	test coverage analyzers
statement testing	test coverage analyzers
status reviews	formal reviews
system performance prediction	analytic modeling of software designs
technical review	peer review
test case preparation (definition and specification)	test data generators
test data generation	mutation analysis
	specification-based functional testing
test harness	test support facilities

Software Validation, Verification, Testing, and Documentation

Table 22.4 (continued)

Keywords	Technique/Tool
testing thoroughness	test coverage analyzers
type checking	interface checker
uninitialized variables	data flow analyzer
unused variables	data flow analyzer
variable references	cross-reference generators
variable snapshots/tracing	interactive test aids
verification of algebraic computation	symbolic execution
walkthroughs	peer reviews

Table 22.5
V,V&T Technique/Tool With Keywords

Technique/Tool	Keywords
Algorithm Analysis	algorithm efficiency
	amount of work (CPU operations) done
	computational upper bound, how fast
	amount of space (memory, disk, etc.) used
	accuracy analysis
Analytic Modeling of	system performance prediction
Software Designs	bottlenecks
Assertion Generation	formal specifications
	data characteristics
	physical units
	loop invariants
	expected inputs,
	outputs and intermediate results
Assertion Processing	assertion violations
	dynamic testing of assertions
Cause-Effect Graphing	test case design using formal specification
	requirements specification analysis
Code Auditor	standards checker
	portability analyzer
Comparator	regression testing
	expected versus actual results

Introduction

Technique/Tool	Keywords
Control Structure Analyzer	call graph
	hierarchical interrelationships of modules
	module invocation
	branch and path identification
Cross-Reference Generators	inter-module structure
	variable references
Data Flow Analyzer	uninitialized variables
	unused variables
	file (or other event) sequence errors
Execution Time Estimator/Analyzer	program execution characteristics
Formal Reviews	go/no go decisions
	status reviews
Formal Verification	proof of correctness
Global Roundoff Analysis of Algebraic Processes	numerical stability
	rounding error propagation
Inspections	check list
Interactive Test Aids	selective program execution
	variable snapshots/tracing
Interface Checker	correspondence between actual and formal parameters
	type checking
	global information flow
Mutation Analysis	test data generation
	completeness of test data
Peer Review	technical review
	code reading
	round-robin reviews
	walkthroughs
	inspections
Physical Units Testing	consistency in computations
Regression Testing	retesting after changes
Requirements Analyzer	functional interrelationships
	information flow consistency
	performance analysis
	requirements walkthrough
Requirements Tracing	requirements indexing
	requirements to design correlation

Table 22.5 (continued)

Technique/Tool	Keywords
Software Monitors	execution sampling
	execution monitoring
	program execution characteristics
Specification-based Functional Testing	test data generation
	boundary test cases
Symbolic Execution	evaluation along program paths
	verification of algebraic computation
Test Support Facilities	test harness
	execution support
	environment simulation
Test Coverage Analyzers	branch testing
	statement testing
	statement coverage
	path testing
	testing thoroughness
Test Data Generators	test case preparation (definition and specification)
Walkthroughs	manual simulation

23. Introduction to Technique and Tool Descriptions

Each technique and tool description in this chapter is alphabetically presented in a standard format. The following list describes the entries and the order in which they appear:

Name

Basic Features

Information Input

Information Output

Outline of Method

Example

Effectiveness

Applicability

Learning

Cost

References

Algorithm Analysis

Basic Features

Two phases of algorithm analysis can be distinguished: "a priori analysis" and "a posteriori testing." In a priori analysis a function (of some relevant parameters) is devised which bounds the algorithm's use of time and space to compute an acceptable solution. The analysis assumes a model of computation such as: a Turing machine, RAM (random access machine), general purpose machine, etc. Two general kinds of problems are usually treated: (1) analysis of a particular algorithm; and (2) analysis of a class of algorithms. In a posteriori testing actual statistics are collected about the algorithm's consumption of time and space while it is executing.

Software Validation, Verification, Testing, and Documentation

Information input
   a. Specification of algorithm
   b. Program representing the algorithm

Information output
   a. *A priori* analysis
      Confidence of algorithms' validity
      Upper and lower computational bounds
      Prediction of space usage
      Assessment of optimality
   b. *A posteriqri* testing
      Performance profile

Outline of method

A *priori* analysis   Algorithms are analyzed with the intention of improving them, if possible, and for choosing among several available for a problem. The following criteria may be used: Correctness; Amount of work done; Amount of space used; Simplicity; Optimality; and Accuracy analysis.

Correctness.   There are three major steps involved in establishing the correctness of an algorithm:
   1. Understand that an algorithm is correct if, when given a valid input, it computes for a finite amount of time and produces the right answer.
   2. Verify that the mathematical properties of the method and/or formulas used by the algorithm are correct.
   3. Verify by mathematical argument that the instructions of the algorithm do produce the right answer and do terminate.

Amount of work done.   A priori analysis ignores all of the factors which are machine or programming language dependent and concentrates on determining the order of magnitude of the frequency of execution of statements. For denoting the upper bound on an algorithm, the O-notation is used. The following notational symbols are used in the following description: $**$ = exponentiation; [ ] = subscription.

Definition: $f(n) = O(g(n))$ if and only if there exist two positive constants C and $n[o]$ such that $f(n) \leq C\ g(n)$ for all $n \geq n[o]$.

The most common computing times for algorithms are:
$O(1) < O(\log n) < O(n) < O(n\log n) < O(n**2) < O(n**3)$ and $O(2**n)$, $O(1)$ means that the number of executions of basic operations is fixed and hence the total time is bounded by a constant. The first six orders of magnitude are bounded by a polynomial. However, there is no integer such that $n**m$ bounds $2**n$. An algorithm whose computing time has this property is said to require exponential time. There

are notations for lower bounds and asymptotic bounds (see reference (4) for details). The term "complexity" is the formal term for the amount of work done, measured by some complexity (or cost) measure.

In general the amount of work done by an algorithm depends on the size of input. In some cases, the number of operations may depend on the particular input. Some examples of size are:

Problem	Size of input
1. Find X in a list of names	The number of names in the list
2. Multiply two matrices	The dimensions of the matrices
3. Solve a system of linear equations	The number of equations and solution vectors

To handle the situation of the input affecting the performance of an algorithm, two approaches (average and worst-case analysis) are used. The *average* approach assumes a distribution of inputs and then calculates the number of operations performed for each type of input in the distribution and then computes a weighted average. The *worst-case* approach calculates the maximum number of basic operations performed on any input of a fixed size.

Amount of Space Used. The number of memory cells used by a program, like the number of seconds required to execute a program, depends on the particular implementation. However, some conclusions about space usage can be made by examining the algorithm. A program will require storage space for the instructions, the constants, and variables used by the program, and the input data. It may also use some work space for manipulating the data and storing information needed to carry out its computations. The input data itself may be representable in several forms, some of which require more space than others. If the input data has one natural form—for example, an array of numbers or a matrix—then we analyze the extra space used from the program and the input. If the amount of extra space is constant with respect to the input size, the algorithm is said to work "in place."

Simplicity. It is often, though not always, the case that the simplest and most straightforward way of solving a problem is not the most efficient. Yet simplicity in an algorithm is a desirable feature. It may make verifying the correctness of the algorithm easier, and it makes writing, debugging and modifying a program for the algorithm easier. The time needed to produce a debugged program should be considered when choosing an algorithm, but, if the program is to be used very often, its efficiency will probably be the determining factor in the choice.

Optimality. Two tasks must be carried out to determine how much work is necessary and sufficient to solve a problem:

(1) Devise what seems to be an efficient algorithm; call it A. Analyze A and

Software Validation, Verification, Testing, and Documentation

find a function such that, for inputs of size n, A does at most $g(n)$ basic operations.

(2) For some function f, prove a theorem that for any algorithm in the class under consideration there is some input of size n for which the algorithm must perform at least $f(n)$ basic operations.

If the functions g and f are equal, then the algorithm A is optimal.

Accuracy analysis. The computational stability of an algorithm is verified by determining that the integrity of round off accuracy is maintained. It is done manually at the requirements or specification level.

A *posteriori* testing   Once an algorithm has been analyzed, the next step is usually the confirmation of the analysis. The confirmation process consists first of devising a program for the algorithm on a particular computer. After the program is operational, the next step is producing a "performance profile"; that is, determining the precise amounts of time and storage the program will consume. To determine time consumption, the computer clock is used. Several data sets of varying size are executed and a performance profile is developed and compared with the predicted curve.

A second way to use the computer's timing capability is to take two programs which perform the same task whose orders of magnitude are identical and compare them as they process data. The resulting times will show which, if either, program is faster. Changes to a program which do not alter the order of magnitude but which purport to speed up the program also can be tested in this way.

Example

QUICKSORT is a recursive sorting algorithm (5). Roughly speaking, it rearranges the keys and splits the file into two subsections, or subfiles, such that all keys in the first section are smaller than all keys in the second section. Then QUICKSORT sorts the two subfiles recursively (i.e., by the same method), with the result that the entire file is sorted.

Let A be the array of keys and let m and n be the indices of the first and last entries, respectively, in the subfile which QUICKSORT is currently sorting. Initially, $m = 1$ and $n = k$. The PARTITION algorithm chooses a key K from the subfile and rearranges the entries, finding an integer j such that for $m \leq i < j$, $A(i) \leq K$; $A(j) = K$; and for $j < i \leq n$, $A(i) \geq K$. K is then in its correct position and is ignored in the subsequent sorting.

QUICKSORT can be described by the following recursive algorithm:

```
QUICKSORT (A,m,n)
if m < n then do          PARTITION (A,m,n,i,j)
                              QUICKSORT (A,m,j)
                              QUICKSORT (A,i,n)
                              end
```

Introduction to Technique and Tool Descriptions

The PARTITION routine may choose as K any key in the file between $A(m)$ and $A(n)$; for simplicity, let $K = A(m)$. An efficient partitioning algorithm uses two pointers, i and j, initialized to m and $n+1$, respectively, and begins by copying K elsewhere so that the position $A(i)$ is available for some other entry. The location $A(i)$ is filled by decrementing j until $A(j) \leq K$, and then copying $A(j)$ into $A(i)$. Now $A(j)$ is filled by incrementing i until $A(i) \geq K$, and then copying $A(i)$ into $A(j)$. This procedure continues until the values of i and j meet; then K is put in the last place. Observe that PARTITION compares each key except the original in $A(m)$ to K, so it does $n - m$ comparisons. See (5) for further details.

Worst Case Analysis If when PARTITION is executed $A(m)$ is the largest key in the current subfile (that is, $A(m) \geq A(i)$ for $m \leq i \leq n$), then PARTITION will move it to the bottom position $A(n)$ and partition the file into one section with $n - m$ entries (all but the bottom one) and one section with no entries. All that has been accomplished is moving the maximum entry to the bottom. Similarly, if the smallest entry in the file is in position $A(m)$, PARTITION will simply separate it from the rest of the list, leaving $n - m$ items still to be sorted. Thus if the input is arranged so that each time PARTITION is executed, $A(m)$ is the largest (or the smallest) entry in the section being sorted, then let $p = n - m + 1$, the number of keys in the unsorted section, then the number of comparisons done is

$$\sum_{p=2}^{k} (p-1) = \frac{k(k-1)}{2}.$$

Average Behavior Analysis If a sorting algorithm removes at most one inversion from the permutation of the keys after each comparison, then it must do at least $(n^{**}2 - n)/4$ comparisons on the average. QUICKSORT, however, does not have this restriction. The PARTITION algorithm can move keys across a large section of the entire file, eliminating up to $n - 2$ inversions at one time. QUICKSORT deserves its name because of its average behavior.

Consider a situation in which QUICKSORT works quite well. Suppose that each time PARTITION is executed, it splits the file into two roughly equal subfiles. To simplify the computation, assume that $n = 2^{**}p - 1$ for some p. The number of comparisons done by QUICKSORT on a file with n entries under these assumptions is described by the recurrence relation

$$R(p) = (2^{**}p) - 2 + 2R(p - 1)$$
$$R(1) = 0$$

The first two terms in $R(p)$, $(2^{**}p) - 2$, are $n - 1$, the number of comparisons done by PARTITION the first time. The second term is the number of comparisons

Software Validation, Verification, Testing, and Documentation

done by QUICKSORT to sort the two subfiles, each of which has $(n-1)/2$, or $(2^{**}(p-1))-1$, entries. Expand the recurrence relation to get

$$R(p) = (2^{**}p) - 2 + 2R(p-1) = (2^{**}p) - 2 + 2(2^{**}(p-1)-2) + 4R(p-2)$$
$$= (2^{**}p) - 2 + (2^{**}p) - 4 + (2^{**}p) - 8 + 8R(p-3)$$

thus

$$R(p) = \sum_{i=1}^{p-1}(2^{**}p) - (2^{**}i) = (p-1)(2^{**}p) - \sum_{i=1}^{p-1} 2^{**}i$$
$$= ((p-1)2^{**}p) - ((2^{**}p) - 2) = \log n\,(n+1) - n + 1$$

Thus if $A(m)$ were close to the median each time the file is split, the number of comparisons done by QUICKSORT would be of the order $(n\log n)$. If all permutations of the input data are assumed equally likely, then QUICKSORT does approximately $2n\log n$ comparisons.

Space Usage At first glance, it may seem that QUICKSORT is an in-place sort. It is not. While the algorithm is working on one subfile, the beginning and ending indices (call them the borders) of all the other subfiles yet to be sorted must be saved on a stack, and the size of the stack depends on the number of sublists into which the file will be split. This, of course, depends on n. In the worst case, PARTITION may split off one entry at a time in such a way that n pairs of borders are stored on the stack. Thus, the amount of space used by the stack is proportional to n.

n	1000	2000	3000	4000	5000
MERGESORT	500	1050	1650	2250	2900
QUICKSORT	400	850	1300	1800	2300

(Time is in milliseconds)

Testing. The results of comparing QUICKSORT and MERGESORT are reported in reference (4) and are summarized on page 000.

Effectiveness
Algorithm analysis has become an important part of computer science. The only issue that limits its effectiveness is that a particular analysis depends on a particular model of computation. If the assumptions of the model are inappropriate then the analysis suffers.

Applicability
An analysis of an algorithm can be limited by the current state of the art and the ingenuity of the analyst.

Learning
Algorithm analysis requires significant training in mathematics and computer science. Generally, it will be done by a specialist.

Introduction to Technique and Tool Descriptions

Costs

The cost to analyze an algorithm is dependent on the complexity of the algorithm and the amount of understanding about algorithms of the same class.

References

(1) BENTLY, L., "An Introduction to Algorithm Design," *Computer*, Feb. 1979.

(2) WEIDE, B., "A Survey of Analysis Techniques for Discrete Algorithms," *Computing Surveys*, Vol. 9, No. 4, Dec. 1977.

(3) AHO, A.V., HOPCROFT, J.E., and ULLMAN, J.D., "The Design and Analysis of Computer Algorithms," Addison-Wesley, Reading, Mass., 1974.

(4) HOROWITZ, E., and SAHNI, S., "Fundamentals of Computer Algorithms," Computer Science Press, Potomac, Maryland, 1978.

(5) HOARE, C.A.R., "Partition (Algorithm 63) and QUICKSORT (Algorithm 64)," *Communications of the ACM*, Vol. 4, No. 7, p. 321, July 1961.

(6) HOARE, C.A.R., "QUICKSORT," *Computer Journal*, Vol. 5, No. 1, 1963.

Analytic Modeling of System Designs

Basic features

The purpose is to provide performance evaluation and capacity planning information on a system design. The process follows the top down approach to design through hierarchical levels of resolution. It can be applied at early design stages when functional modules are relatively large and where knowledge of their execution behavior may be imprecise. As the design proceeds and the modules are further resolved, the estimates of their behavior and execution resource characterization become more precise. The approach is predicted on two representational bases: on extended execution graph models of programs and systems and on extended queueing network models of computer system hardware resources and workloads.

Information input

The information which is needed for this technique consists of functional design and performance specifications as follows:

a. Identification of the functional components of the software design to be modeled.

b. Identification of the execution characteristics (primarily, execution time estimate) of each functional component.

c. An execution flow graph which gives the definition of the order of execution of the various functional components.

d. Execution environment specifications which can include information such as operating system overhead and the workload on the system that could potentially impact the particular software under development.

e. System execution scenarios which provide the definitions of the external inputs to the model needed for each simulation of the model.

    f. Performance goals for the total system and components (an example is an upper bound for the mean and variance of the response time for a specified execution environment and scenario).

Information output
Output from the technique will consist of the following:
    a. A lower bound on the performance of the system.
    b. A comparison of the performance goals with the performance results.
    c. Identification of the functional components which had the greatest effect on system performance.

Outline of method
Much of the effort in using this technique comes in the preparation of the necessary input information. Once this has been done, it is generally submitted to a computer which performs the simulation of the execution of the model and reports the results, which are then analyzed and the model revised as necessary. The specific steps in the technique are as follows:

    a. The structure of the software design is characterized in terms of its functional components. In that software designs are generally hierarchical in structure, a model may be modified to represent the system at different levels of detail, each being analyzed at different stages in the process.

    b. The order of execution of the components is determined and the execution graph is constructed.

    c. Resource requirements (e.g., hardware or operating system resources) of the functional components are identified and a possible environment is studied with the specific resource workloads being determined. These workloads consist of the average wait and usage times for the resources controlled by the environment and used by the software (such as average disk access time).

    d. The workloads are then mapped into the model (as represented by the execution graph) based upon the identified environment resource requirements of the individual functional components.

    e. Next, the system execution scenarios are constructed. The external inputs comprising each scenario may be formulated, for example, in terms of the number of disk accesses required to find a needed data item within a particular component.

    f. Upon completion of the above steps, the model is driven, producing system and component performance results. (The "driving" of the model is usually done using a system simulation tool such as GPSS, General Purpose Systems Simulator, on a coded specification of the model.)

    g. The performance results are now compared with the performance goals of the system. If the goals are not met, performance critical components are then analyzed in order to determine where improvements can be made. The design is modified and the technique repeated. This process continues until the performance is acceptable or until it can be determined that the goals are unreasonable.

Example

Finite element analysis is a technique for determining characteristics such as deflections and stresses in a structure (i.e., building, airplane, etc.) otherwise too complex for closed form mathematical analysis. The structure is broken into a network of simple elements (beams, shells, or cubes depending on the geometry of the structure), each of which has stress and deflection characteristics defined by classical theory.

Determining the behavior of the entire structure then becomes a task of solving the resulting set of simultaneous equations for all elements.

The example developed below is a portion of a system which does a finite element analysis. Consider the software execution graph in Figure 23.1. Only the top level of the processing is illustrated here. The CPU time and I/O requirements for each component are shown in Table 23.1

The elapsed time to complete an I/O operation is assumed to be 30 ms. Other specifications are unimportant in this example.

The average response rate for this scenario is 3326 seconds (55.4 minutes). This is clearly unacceptable for an interactive transaction. The bottleneck analysis indicates that the CPU is the critical resource since it has a higher ratio to the elapsed time than the I/O ratio. Furthermore, the "find node location" component is the critical component.

The processing details of this collapsed model are not shown; however, close examination of the details indicates that a "find" data base command is invoked for each of the three search keys, and then takes the intersection of the records that qualify. Also, it is found that the result of the "find" for the problem number search key is invariant throughout the loop and need not be repeated. A knowledge of the nature of the problem leads to the observation that most of the time (85%) the "find" on the *node 1 key* yields the same result as the "find" on the *node 2 key* from the previous pass through the loop, and need not be repeated. The results of this analysis indicate changes which optimize the process.

These optimizations are reflected in the execution graph in Figure 23.2. This graph is more complex; however, the total processing requirements are reduced, as shown in Table 23.2.

The response time has been *reduced* by 3023 seconds, a substantial savings! The response time (303 seconds) is still unacceptable for most on-line applications. Another optimization, storing the "beam def" data in beam number sequence, precludes the sort. The resulting response time is 269 seconds. This optimization process continues until a resulting response time of 82 seconds is obtained.

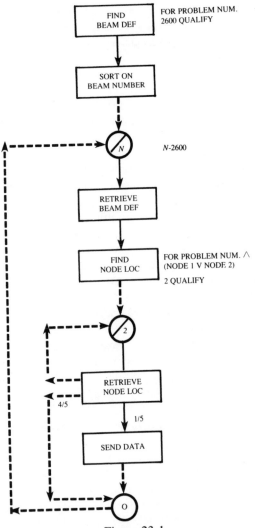

Figure 23.1

Optimization Example (reference (1))

The performance is still only marginally acceptable, but it is a dramatic improvement over the original design. The bottlenecks are detected and corrected prior to actual coding and, therefore, the modifications require minimal effort.

Effectiveness
The accuracy of the performance prediction is only as good as the quality of the performance specifications. The quality of the specifications usually improves during

Table 23.1
Resource Requirements for Optimization Example

Function	Disk Accesses	CPU Time(ms)
Find beam definition	7	111
Sort on beam number	72	32,644
Retrieve beam definition	72	88,832
Find node locations	21	3,018,726
Retrieve node locations	36	177,016
Send data	0	2,600
Total	208	3,319,929 ms.

the design process. A simplified approach is used to analyze queueing network models. This results in approximation of the relationships between contending resources. Several compensating features are used to offset the approximations used.

Applicability
The technique is generally applicable to nondistributed systems.

Learning.
The user of this approach needs to be familiar with the intricacies of the modeling techniques used.

Table 23.2
Resource Requirements for Revised Optimization Example

Function	Disk Accesses	CPU Time(ms)
Find beam definition	7	111
Sort beam number	72	32,644
Find node location	4	1,075
Retrieve beam definition	72	88,832
Find node location:		
B-tree I/O	17	102
Find 2 nodes	—	44,000
Retrieve 2 nodes	—	27,200
Find 1 node	—	26,000
Retrieve 1 node	—	71,800
Record I/O	36	216
Send data	0	2,600
Total	208	297,580 ms.

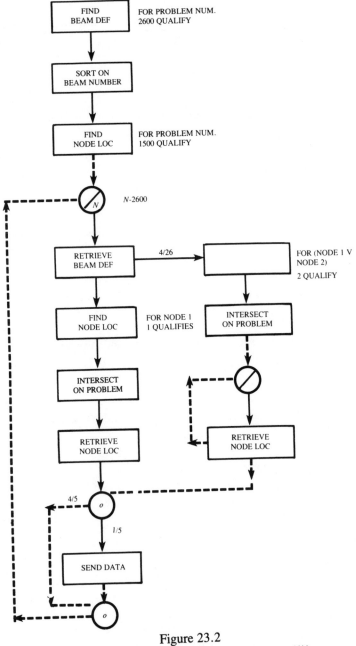

Figure 23.2
Revised Optimization Example (reference (1))

Costs

The preparation, analysis, and solution of the model costs approximately 5% to 15% of the total design costs.

References

(1) SMITH, C.U., "The Prediction and Evaluation of the Performance of Software From Extended Design Specification," Ph.D. Dissertation, University of Texas at Austin, August 1980.

(2) SMITH, C.U., and BROWNE, J.C., "Performance Specifications and Analysis of Software Designs," *Proceedings of the Conference on Simulation, Measurement, and Modeling of Computer Systems*, Boulder, CO, August 1979.

Assertion Generation

Basic features

Assertion generation is not so much a verification technique itself as it is foundational to a variety of other techniques. Assertion generation is the process of capturing the intended functional properties of a program in a special notation (called the assertion language) for insertion into the various levels of program specification, including the program source code. Other verification techniques utilize the embedded assertions in the process of comparing the actual functional properties of the program with the intended properties.

Information input

A specification of the desired functional properties of the program is the input required for assertion generation. For individual modules, this breaks down, at a minimum, to a specification of the conditions which are "assumed" true on a module entry and a specification of the conditions desired on module exit. If the specifications from which the assertions are to be derived include algorithmic detail, the specifications will indicate conditions which are to hold at intermediate points within the module as well. Additionally, assertions can state data characteristics, e.g. loop invariants, physical units or a variable, as input only (can not be set).

Information output

The assertions which are created from the functional or algorithmic specifications are expressed in a notation called the assertion language. This notation commonly includes higher level expressive constructs that are found, for example, in the programming language. An example of such a construct is a set. Most commonly, the assertion language is equivalent in expressive power to the first order predicate calculus. Thus, expressions such as "*forall i in* set S, $A[i]$ $A[i+1]$" or "*there exists* x such that $f(x) = 0$" are possible. The assertions which are generated, expressing the functional properties of the program, can then be used as input to a dynamic asser-

211

tion processor, a formal verification tool, walkthroughs, specification simulators, and inspections, among other V&V techniques.

Outline of method

Assertion generation proceeds hand-in-hand with the heirarchical elaboration of program functions. When, during development, a function is identified as being needed, it is usually first specified by what input it is expected to take and what the characteristics of the output are (outputs are often in terms of the input quantitites). For such a function it is possible to generate input and ouput assertions without any knowledge of how the function performs its task. The input assertion expresses the requirements on the data the function is to use during its processing. The output assertion expresses what is to be true on function termination.

Later, as the function is elaborated, the designer or coder will identify the necessary steps to be taken in order to accomplish what is required of the function. After each step it can be said that a "part" of the task has been accomplished. That part is necessary for the proper operation of the next step, and so on, until the entire function has been realized. The character of each part can be captured by an assertion in the same way as the description of the entire function. The output assertion for one step represents (at least part of) the input assertion for the following step. Such assertions are called intermediate assertions.

Each assertion, input, output, and intermediate is expressed using the assertion langauge and is placed into the specification of the function being implemented at the appropriate points. Thus, the program source text will include in it all the assertions developed during the requirements, design, and coding phases.

Some programming languages include facilities for expressing assertions in the source code but most do not. In such cases it is customary to include the assertions within comments, for indeed they are documentation expressing the desired functional characteristics of the program. Subsequent V&V tools, such as dynamic assertion processors, are constructed to utilize these special comments during their processing. Dynamic assertion processors are able to check the validity of the source assertions during program execution. Thus a method for dynamically verifying that the program is behaving according to its intended specification is possible.

For programs which contain loops (which is just about all programs), it is often important to formulate assertions which are always true at specific points within the loops. Such assertions are termed *invariant* or *inductive* assertions.

Example

Since assertion generation is so closely entwined with program development only a brief example is presented here. For more thorough examples see references (1-5).

During program development the requirement arises for sorting the elements of an array or table. In order to support flexible processing in the rest of the system, the array is declared with a large, fixed length. However, only a portion of the array has elements in it. The number of elements currently in the array, when passed to the sort routine, is contained in the first element of the array. The array is always to be sorted in ascending order. The sorted array is returned to the calling program through the same formal parameter.

The first specification of the sort routine may appear as:

```
      SUBROUTINE SORT (A, DIM)
C
C     A is the array to be sorted
C     DIM is the dimension of A
C
C     sort array
C
      RETURN
      END
```

Sort Specification

The characteristics of the subroutine may be partially captured by the following assertions. Notationally, v = "or" and & = "and."

$$\text{ASSERT INPUT } (0 \leq A(1) \leq DIM), (DIM \geq 2)$$
$$\text{ASSERT OUTPUT } (A(1) = 0 \lor A(1) = 1 \ \& \ true) \lor$$
$$(A(1) > 1 \ \& \ \text{FORALL I IN } [2 .. A(1)] \ A(I) \ A(I+1))$$

The input assertion notes the required characteristics of $A(1)$ and DIM. The ouput assertion indicates that if there were 0 or 1 elements in the array, the array is sorted by default. If there are at least 2 elements in the array, then the array is in ascending order.

The next level of the program may have the following appearance. An intermediate assertion is now shown.

```
      SUBROUTINE SORT (A, DIM)
C
C     A is the array to be sorted
C     DIM is the dimension of A
C
      ASSERT INPUT (0≤A(1) DIM), (DIM>2)
      IF (A(1) .LE. 1) GOTO 100
      ASSERT (2≤A(1)≤DIM)
C     Sort non-trivial array
C
C
100   ASSERT OUTPUT (A(1) = 0 v A(1) = 1 & true) v
      (A)(1)>1 & FORALL I IN [2 .. A(1)] A(I)≤A(I+1))
      RETURN
      END
```

Sort Routine with Assertions

Suppose a straight selection sort algorithm is chosen for the non-trivial case (i.e., find the smallest element and place it in $A(2)$, find the next smallest and place it in A(3), and so forth, where the original contents of A(I) is exchanged with the element that belongs in the Ith position in the sorted array). An appropriate intermediate assertion is included within the sorting loop.

```
C       PERFORM STRAIGHT SELECTION SORT
        DO 50 JJ = 2, A(1)
C
C           find smallest element in A(J) .. A(A(1)+2)
C           let that element be A(K)
C           exchange A(J) and A(K)
C
        ASSERT (2≤J≤A(1))
        (FORALL I IN [2 .. A(1)] A(I)≤A(I+1))
50      CONTINUE
                Sort Routine with an Intermediate Assertion
```

A significant issue which we have not dealt with yet is asserting, on termination, that the sorted array is a permutation of the orginial array. In other words, we wish to assert that in the process of sorting, no elements were lost. To do this at the highest level, our first attempt at the program requires advanced assertion language facilities. The interested reader is referred to references (1) and (5).

Effectiveness

Assertion generation, particularly when used in conjunction with allied techiques like dynamic assertion processing or functional testing, can be extremely effective in aiding V&V. Such effectiveness is only possible, however, when the assertions are used to capture the important functional properties of the program. Assertions such as the following are of no use at all:

```
I = 0
I = I + 1
ASSERT I>0
```

Capturing the important properties can be a difficult process and is prone to error. Such effort is well rewarded, though, by increased understanding of the problem to be solved. Indeed, assertion generation is effective because the assertions are to be parallel to the program specifications. This parallelism enables the detection of errors, but effort is required.

A cost-effective procedure, therefore, is to develop intermediate assertions only for particularly important parts of the computation. Input assertions should always be employed, and output assertions whenever possible.

Applicability

The technique is generally applicable, in all development phases and for all programming languages.

Introduction to Technique and Tool Descriptions

Learning

Training and experience in writing assertions is the key to their effective use. Thoughtful consideration of the material contained in the references should enable a programmer to begin with useful assertions. Experience will sharpen the ability, especially if a dynamic assertion processor or other allied technique is also used.

Costs

Assertion generation is generally a manual technique, i.e., no machine resources are required. Effective use requires thoughtful problem and solution consideration, but no more than is normally required in profesional task performance. Tools do exist that use symbolic execution to automatically generate loop invariant assertions. The cost then becomes that of symbolic execution.

References

(1) TAYLOR, R.N., "Assertions in Programming Languages," *SIGPLAN Notices*, Vol. 15, 1, January 1980, pp. 105-114.

(2) MANNA, Z; WALDING, R., "The Logic of Computer Programming," *IEEE-TSE*, *SE-4*, 3, May 1978, pp. 199-229 (especially pages 199-204).

(3) HOARE, C.A.R., "Proof of a Program: FIND," *CACM*,V. 14, 1, January 1971, pp. 39-45.

(4) HETZEL, W.D. ed., "Program TEST Methods," 1973, Articles on pages 7-10, 17-28, 57-72.

(5) CHOW, T.S., "A Generalized Assertion Language," *Proceedings of the Second International Conference on Software Engineering*, San Francisco, California, pp. 392-399.

(6) STUCKI, L.G., and FOSHEE, G.L., "New Assertion Concepts for Self-Metric Software," *Proceedings of the 1975 Conference on Reliable Software*, pp. 59-71.

Assertion Processing

Basic Features

Assertion processing is the process whereby the program's assertions (containing user specified assertions as described in the previous section) are checked during program execution. As such, the techniques serve as a bridge between the more formal program correctness proof approaches and the more common "black box" testing approaches.

Information Input

Information input to this technique consists of a program which contains the assertions to be processed. The program can be written in any language but may be restricted to a particular language if an automatic tool is used to perform the dynamic assertion processing. Moreover, if a tool is used, the format for specifying the assertions will be that defined by the particular tool. Generally, assertions are specified as comments in the source program.

Software Validation, Verification, Testing, and Documentation

Information Output

Output from a dynamic assertion process normally consists of a list of the assertion checks which were performed and a list of exception conditions with trace information for determining the nature and location of the violations.

Outline of Method

The assertions are generated by the developer as described in the "Assertion Generation" technique in the previous section. The assertions are then translated into host language program statements which actually perform the assertion checking at program execution time. The translation can be done manually or through the use of an automated dynamic assertion processor.

The translation process is shown in the following illustration. An assertion of the form:

```
(*ASSERT condition*)
is translated into:
IF NOT (condition) THEN
        Process assertion violation;
```

The processing of the assertion violation will, minimally, keep track of the total number of violations for each assertion, print a message indicating that a violation of the assertion has occurred, and print the values of the variables referenced in the assertion. In addition, the location, i.e. statement number, and the number of times the assertion is checked may be kept and printed when a violation occurs.

Sufficient information should be reported upon violation of an assertion to assist the programmer of the specific nature of the error.

An automated dynamic assertion processor can be of great assistance by alleviating for the programmer the burden of hand generating the source code necessary to perform the assertion checking. Not only will this save time but it will also perform the translation more reliably.

Specifying assertions within comments is a valuable form of documentation and also ensures that the source program is kept free of non-portable, tool specific directives.

It is important to note that dynamic assertion processing for non-real time programs must not alter the functional behavior of a program. Use of a good automated tool will ensure this. Execution time, however, will be increased; the amount of which will depend on the number of assertions which are processed. It is important to note that dynamic assertion processing can alter the functional behavior of a program by altering the execution timing.

In order to effectively utilize assertion processing, test data should be generated which will cause the execution of each assertion.

Example

The source program segment with untranslated assertion, below, is taken from a Pascal program which calls on routine 'sort' to sort array 'A,' consisting of 'N' integer elements, in ascending order. The assertion following the call to sort asserts that the elements are indeed in ascending order upon return from the sort procedure. The numbers to the left are the line numbers from the original source.

Source Program with Untranslated Assertion

```
12    Var
13              N : integer;
14              A : array [1..MAXN] of integer;


26    begin


56              sort (N,A);
57    (*assert forall i in [1..N − 1]:A[i] < = A[i + 1]*);
```

The source segment with translated assertion, that follows, is that which results after all of the assertions have been translated into Pascal. Note that a rather large number of statements were used to implement the assertion. This is due to the rather involved checking required to implement an "*assert forall. . . .*" Simpler assertions will require fewer statements. The spec could be reduced through the use of a common assertion violation procedure.

Source Program with Translated Assertion

```
12    Var
13              N : integer;
14              A : array[1..MAXN] of integer;
15              AssertVioCount : array [1..NumofAsserts] of integer;
16              AssertXqtCount : array [1..NumofAsserts] of integer;
17              assert : boolean;


29    begin


77              sort (N,A);
78    (*assert forall: in [1..N − 1] : A[i] = A[i + 1]*);
79                  AssertXqtCount[3]: = AssertXqtCount[3] + 1;
80                  assert : = true;
81                  i : = 1 ;
82              while(i < = N) and(assert) do (*check assertion*)
83                  if A[i] > A[l + 1] then
84                      assert : = false
85                  else
86                      i : = i + 1;
```

Software Validation, Verification, Testing, and Documentation

```
87              if not assert then begin(*assertion violation*)
88                    AssertVioCount[3] : = AssertVioCount[3] = 1;
89                    Writeln ('violation of assertion 3 at statement 57 '):
90                    Writeln ('on execution:', AssertXqtCount[3]);
91                    Writeln ('arrayA = ', A)
92              end (*assertion violation*);
```

During the testing the following values of A were used in successive executions of the sort routine:

execution	array A									
1	0	3	12	27	53	171	201	251	390	501
2	0	12	3	53	27	201	171	390	251	501
3	501	390	251	201	171	53	27	12	3	0
4	0	0	0	0	0	0	0	0	0	0
5	0	0	0	100	100	100	999	999	999	1000

The resulting execution produced the following assertion violation:

> violation of assertion 3 at statement 57 on execution: 3
> array A = 3 12 27 53 171 201 251 340 501 0

This was the only violation which occured.

Subsequent analysis of the sort procedure indicated that the error was due to an "add-by-one" error on a loop limit.

Effectiveness

The effectiveness of dynamic assertion processing will depend upon the quality of the assertions included in the program being analyzed. Moreover, if the translation is being done by hand, the amount of time required to translate, coupled with the unreliability associated with the process will reduce its effectiveness. Nevertheless, the technique can be of significant value in revealing the presence of program errors.

Applicability

The technique is generally applicable.

Learning

A functional understanding of assertions is all that is necessary in order to manually use this technique. If a tool is used, then an hour or so should be sufficient to learn the specification syntax for asssertions acceptable to that tool. Of course, the generation of useful assertions (see "Assertion Generation" writeup) is necessary in order for this technique to be truly valuable.

Costs

The costs associated with this technique are almost entirely comprised of the amount of time required to translate the assertions into source code. If done manually, this could amount to significant cost. If done automatically, the cost will be on the order of compilation (Assertion Processors are usually implemented as source language preprocessors). If a tool is not available, it may well be worth the cost to develop one in-house.

References

(1) STUCKI, L.G., and FOSHEE, G.L., "New Assertion Concepts for Self-Metric Software," *Proceedings, 1975 Conference on Reliable Software*, pp.59-71.

(2) ANDREWS, D.M.,"Using Executable Assertions for Testing," *13th Annual Asilomar Conference on Circuits, Systems, and Devices*, Nov. 1979.

Cause-Effect Graphing

Basic Features

Cause-effect graphing is a test case design methodology. It is used to select in a systematic manner a set of test cases which have a high probability of detecting errors that exist in a program. This technique explores the inputs and combinations of input conditions of a program in developing test cases. It is totally unconcerned with the internal behavior or structure of a program. In addition, for each test case derived, the technique identifies the expected outputs. The inputs and outputs of the program are determined through analysis of the requirement specifications. These specifications are then translated into a Boolean logic network or graph. The network is used to derive test cases for the software under analysis.

Information input

The information that is required as input to carry out this technique is a natural language specification of the program that is to be tested. The specification should include all expected inputs and combinations of expected inputs to the program, as well as expected outputs.

Information output

The information output by the process of cause-effect graphing consists of the following:

    a. An identification of incomplete or inconsistent statements in the requirement specifications.

    b. A set of input conditions on the software (causes).

    c. A set of output conditions on the software (effects).

d. A Boolean graph that links the input conditions to the output conditions.

e. A limited entry decision table that determines which input conditions will result in each identified output condition.

f. A set of test cases.

g. The expected program results for each derived test case.

The above outputs represent the result of performing the various steps recommended in cause-effect graphing.

Outline of method

A cause-effect graph is a formal language translated from a natural language specification. The graph itself is represented as a combinatorial logic network. The process of creating a cause-effect graph to derive test cases is described briefly below.

a. Identify all requirements of the system and divide them into separate identifiable entities.

b. Carefully analyze the requirements to identify all the causes and effects in the specification. A cause is a distinct input condition; an effect is an output condition or system transformation (an effect that an input has on the state of the program or system).

c. Assign each cause and effect a unique number.

d. Analyze the semantic content of the specification and transform it into a Boolean graph linking the causes and effects; this is the cause-effect graph.

Represent each cause and effect by a node identified by its unique number.

List all the cause nodes vertically on the left side of a sheet of paper; list the effect nodes on the right side.

Interconnect the cause and effect nodes by analyzing the semantic content of the specification. Each cause and effect can be in one of two states: true or false. Using Boolean logic, set the possible states of the causes and determine under what conditions each effect will be present.

Annotate the graph with constraints describing combinations of causes and/or effects that are impossible because of syntactical or environmental constraints.

e. By methodically tracing state conditions in the graph, convert the graph into a limited entry decision table as follows. For each effect, trace back through the graph to find all combinations of causes that will set the effect to be true. Each such combination is represented as a column in the decision table. The state of all other effects should also be determined for each such combination. Each column in the table represents a test case.

f. Convert the columns in the decision table into test cases.

This technique to create test cases has not yet been totally automated. However, conversion of the graph to the decision table, the most difficult aspect of the technique, is an algorithmic process which could be automated by a computer program.

Example

A database management system requires that each file in the database have its name listed in a master index which identifies the location of each file. The index is divided into ten sections. A small system is being developed which will allow the user to interactively enter a command to display any section of the index at his terminal. Cause-effect graphing is used to develop a set of test cases for the system.

    a. The specification for this system is as follows: To display one of the ten possible index sections, a command must be entered consisting of a letter and a digit. The first character entered must be a D (for display) or an L (for List) and it must be in column 1. The second character entered must be a digit (0-9) in column 2. If this command occurs, the index section identified by the digit is displayed on the terminal. If the first character is incorrect, error message A is printed. If the second character is incorrect, error message B is printed. The error messages are:

      A: INVALID COMMAND

      B: INVALID INDEX NUMBER

    b. The causes and effects have been identified as follows. Each has been assigned a unique number.

      Causes

      1.   Character in column 1 is D.

      2.   Character in column 1 is L.

      3.   Character in column 2 is a digit.

      Effects

      50. Index section is displayed.

      51. Error message A is displayed.

      52. Error message B is displayed.

    c. Figure 23.3, a Boolean graph, is constructed through analysis of the semantic content of the specification.

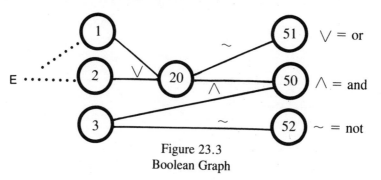

Figure 23.3
Boolean Graph

Node 20 is an intermediate node representing the Boolean state of node 1 or node 2. The state of node 50 is true if the state of nodes 20 and 3 are both true. The state of node 20 is true if the state of node 1 or node 2 is true. The state of node 51 is true if the state of node 20 is *not* true. The state of node 52 is true if the state of node 3 is *not* true.

Nodes 1 and 2 are also annotated with a constraint that states that causes 1 and 2 cannot be true simultaneously (the Exclusive constraint).

d. The graph is converted into a decision table, figure 23.4. For each test case, the bottom of the table indicates which effect will be present (indicated by a 1). For each effect, all combinations of causes that will result in the presence of the effect is represented by the entries in the columns of the table. Blanks in the table mean that the state of the cause is irrelevant.

e. Each column in the decision table is converting into test cases, figure 23.5.

Effectiveness

Cause-effect graphing is a technique used to produce a useful set of test cases. It also has the added capability of pointing out incompleteness and ambiguities in the

Figure 23.4
Decision Table

		Test Cases			
Causes		1	2	3	4
1		1	0	0	
2		0	1	0	
3		1	1		0
Effects					
50		1	1	0	0
51		0	0	1	0
52		0	0	0	1

Figure 23.5
Test Cases

Test Case #	Inputs	Expected Results
1	D5	Index section 5 is displayed
2	L4	Index section 4 is displayed
3	B2	INVALID COMMAND
4	DA	INVALID INDEX NUMBER

requirement specification. However, this technique does not produce all the useful test cases that can be identified. It also does not adequately explore boundary conditions.

Applicability

Cause-effect graphing can be applied to generate test cases in any type of computing application where the specification is clearly stated and combinations of input conditions can be identified. Manual application of this technique is a somewhat tedious, long, and moderately complex process. However, the technique could be applied to selected modules where complex conditional logic must be tested.

Learning

Cause-effect graphing is a mathematically-based technique that requires some knowledge of Boolean logic. The requirement specification of the system must also be clearly understood in order to successfully carry out the process.

Costs

Manual application of this technique will be highly labor intensive.

References

(1) ELMENDORF, W.R., "Cause-Effect Graphs in Functional Testing," IBM Systems Development Division, *TR-00.2487*, Poughkeepsie, New York, 1973.
(2) MYERS, GLENFORD, "The Art of Software Testing," Wiley-Interscience, New York, 1975.
(3) MYERS, GLENFORD, "Software Reliability: Principles and Practices," Wiley-Interscience, New York, 1976.

Code Auditor

Basic features

A code auditor is a computer program which is used to examine source code and automatically determines whether prescribed programming standards and practices have been followed.

Information input

The information input to a code auditor is the source code to be analyzed and the commands necessary for the code auditor's operation.

Information output

The information that is output by a code auditor is a determination of whether the code being analyzed adheres to prescribed programming standards. If errors exist, information is generated detailing which standards have been violated and where the violations occur. This information can appear as error messages included with a source listing or as a separate report. Other diagnostic information, such as a cross-reference listing, may also be output as an aid in making the needed corrections.

Outline of method

Code auditors are fully automated tools which provide an objective, reliable means of verifying that a program complies with a specified set of coding standards. Some common programming conventions that code auditors can check for are given below.

Correct syntax—Do all program statements conform to the specifications of the language definition?

Portability—Is the code written so that it can easily operate on different computer configurations?

Use of structured programming constructs—Does the code make proper use of a specified set of coding constructs such as IF-THEN-ELSE or DO-WHILE?

Size—Is the length of any program unit not more than a specified number of statements?

Commentary—Is each proagram unit appropriately documented; e.g., is each unit preceded by a block of comments which indicates the function of the unit and the function of each variable used?

Naming conventions—Do the names of all variables, routines, and other symbolic entities follow prescribed naming conventions?

Statement labeling—Does the numeric labeling of statements follow an ascending sequence throughout each program unit?

Statement ordering—Do all statements appear in a prescribed order; e.g., in a Fortran program, do all FORMAT statements appear at the end and DATA statements before the first executable statement of a routine?

Statement format—Do all statements follow a prescribed set of formatting rules which improve program clarity; e.g., are all DO-WHILE loops appropriately indented?

As demonstrated by this list, code auditors vary in sophistication according to their function. Each auditor, however, requires some form of syntax analysis to be performed. Code must be parsed by the auditor and given an internal representation suitable for analysis. Because this type of processing is found in many static analysis tools, many code auditors are part of a more general tool having many capabilities. For example, a compiler is a form of code auditor that checks for adherence to the specifications of a language definition. PFORT, a tool used to check Fortran programs for adherence to a portable subset of American National Standard Institute (ANSI) Fortran 66, also has the capability of generating a cross-reference listing.

Code auditors are useful to programmers as a means of self-checking their routines prior to turnover for integration testing. These tools are also of value to software product assurance personnel during integration testing, prior to formal validation testing, and again prior to customer delivery.

Example

Application   A flight control program is to be coded entirely in PFORT, a portable subset of ANSI Fortran 66. The program is to be delivered to a military government agency, which will install the software on various computer installations. In addition, the customer requires that each routine in the program be clearly documented in a prescribed format. All internal program comments are to be later compiled as a separate source of documentation for the program.

Error   A named common block occurs in several routines in the program. In one routine, the definition of a variable in that block has been omitted because the variable is not referenced in that routine. This is, however, a violation of a rule defined in PFORT, which requires that the total length of a named common block agree in all occurrences of that block.

Error discovery   A code auditor which checks Fortran for adherence to PFORT detects this error immediately. The programmer of this routine is informed that the routine is to be appropriately modified and that any confusion over the use of the variable is to be clarified in the block of comments that describe the function of each defined variable in the routine. A code auditor that checks for the presence of appropriate comments in each routine is used to verify that the use of the variable is appropriately documented. At the end of code construction, all such internal program documentation will be collated and summarized by another code auditor which processes machine readable documentation imbedded in source code.

Effectiveness
Code auditors are very effective tools in certifying that software routines have been coded in accordance with prescribed standards. They are much more reliable than manually performed code audits and are highly cost effective as they are less time consuming than manual audits.

Applicability
Code auditors can be generally applied to any type of source code. However, each specific tool will be language dependent (i.e., will operate correctly only for specified source languages), and will only accept input that appears in a prescribed format.

Learning
No special training is required to use code auditors. As code auditors may be used by a wide variety of people (programmers, managers, quality assurance personnel,

customers), ease in their use is an important attribute. In order to use code auditors effectively, however, some learning is required to gain familiarity with the standards upon which the auditor is based.

Costs
Code auditors are generally very inexpensive to use as their overhead is usually no more than the cost of a compilation.

References
1. BROWN, J.R. and FISCHER, K., "A Graph Theoretic Approach to the Verification of Program Structures," *Proceedings of the 3rd International Conference on Software Engineering*, May 1978.
2. RYDER, B.G., and HALL, A.D., "The PFORT Verifier," *Computing Science Technical Report* #12, Bell Laboratories, Murry Hill, New Jersey, March 1975.
3. FISCHER, K.F., "User's Manual for Code Auditor, Code Optimizer Advisor, Unit Consistency Analyses," TRW Systems Group, Redondo Beach, California, July 1974.
4. HOPKINS, T.R., "PBASIC—A Verifier for BASIC," *Software Practice and Experience*, Vol 10, pp. 175–181, 1980.

Comparators

Basic features
A comparator is a computer program used to compare two versions of source data to establish that the two versions are identical or to specifically identify where any differences in the versions occur.

Information input
Input to comparators consists of two versions of source data to be compared and those commands necessary for the comparator to operate. The source data may be:
    a. Source programs
    b. Sets of program test cases or test results
    c. Databases
    d. Arbitrary data files
    Many comparators provide various user options, such as whether blank lines are to be included in compare processing, to control comparison operation.

Information output
The output from a comparator is a listing of the differences, if any, between the two versions of input. Various report writing options are usually supplied by the comparator to designate the desired format of the output, e.g., whether each difference found should be preceded by line numbers. Many general comparator utility pro-

226

grams installed in large text-editing systems can also create a file of text-editor directives that can be used to convert one input file into the other.

Outline of method

Comparators are fully automated tools which serve to eliminate the tedious, time-consuming task of performing large numbers of comparisions. They are most useful during program development and maintenance. During program development, they provide a means of ensuring that only the intended portions of a program are changed when modifications are to be made to the latest version. When regression testing must be performed following software corrections or updates, comparators provide an efficient means of comparing current test cases and test results with past ones.

Comparators are widely available and are often provided as general utilities in operating systems. Other comparators may be more specialized and require input files to be of a prescribed format in order for the tool to operate correctly.

Comparators are invaluable tools in assisting configuration management and change control as the software takes different forms during development.

Example

Application A large command and control flight software system is being developed. During system testing, the generation of many different databases is required as a source of input data for each associated test case. Strict control of the databases, including identification of their similarities and differences, must constantly be maintained in order to properly verify test results.

Error A bug in the software causes the execution of Test Case 3 to generate test results which are totally incompatible with the results of Test Case 1, though the input in both test cases is almost identical.

Error discovery A comparator was used to compare the databases used in Test Case 1 and 3. The location of specific differences in the two files determined exactly which input data should be examined more closely and when traced through the program the error was found.

Effectiveness

Comparators are most effective during software testing and maintenance when periodic modifications to the software are anticipated. Their overall effectiveness is dependent upon the quality of their use.

Applicability

This method is generally applicable.

227

Software Validation, Verification, Testing, and Documentation

Learning

A minimal amount of effort is required to learn how to use comparators effectively. The tool's user documentation should provide sufficient information for its proper utilization.

Costs

Comparators are generally inexpensive to use. Their cost is similar to that of performing two passes of read operations on one file.

References

1. HETZEL, William, "Program Test Methods," Prentice-Hall, Inc., 1973.
2. DEC IAS/RSX-11 "Utilities Procedure Manual," *Digital Equipment Corporation*, 1978.

Control Structure Analyzer

Basic features

Application of an automated structure analyzer to either code or design allows detection of some types of improper subprogram usage and violation of control flow standards. It also identifies control branches and paths used by test coverage analyzers. A structure analyzer is also useful in providing required input to data flow analyzers and is related in principle to code auditors.

Information input

Two input items are required by a structure analyzer. The first is the text of the program or design to be analyzed. Typically the text is to be provided to the analyzer in an intermediate form, i.e., after scanning and parsing, but not as object code. Often structure analyzers are incorporated within compilers.

The second input item is a specification of the control flow standards to be checked. These standards are often completely implicit in that they may be part of the rules for programming in the given language or design notation. An example of such a rule is that subprograms may not be called recursively in FORTRAN. Individual projects may, however, establish additional rules for internal use. Many such rules, for instance limiting the number of lines allowed in a subprogram, can be checked by a code auditor. Others, however, can require a slightly more sophisticated analysis and are therefore performed by a structural analyzer. Two examples in this category are "All control structures must be well nested" and "Backward jumps out of control structures are not allowed."

Typically this second input item is not directly supplied to a structure analyzer, but is incorporated directly in the tool's construction. Therefore, substantial inflexibility is common.

Information output

Error reports and a program call graph are the most common output items of a structure analyzer. Error reports indicate violations of the standards that were input to the tool. Call graphs indicate the structure of the graph with respect to the use of subprograms; associated with each subprogram is information indicating all routines which call the subprogram and all routines which are called by it. The presence of cycles in the graph (A calls B calls A) indicate possible recursion. Routines which are never called are evident, as well as attempts to call nonexistent routines.

In checking adherence to control flow standards, the structure analyzer may also output a flow graph for each program unit. The flow graph represents the structure of the program with each control path in the program represented by an edge in the graph. Additionally, structurally "dead" code within each module is detectable.

The flow graph and the call graph are items required as input by data flow analyzers, and it is common for the two analysis capabilities to be combined in a single automated tool.

Outline of method

Since structure analysis is an automated static analysis technique, little user action is required. Aside from providing the input information, the user is only required to peruse the output reports and determine if program changes are required. Some simple manifestations of the tool may not provide detailed analysis reports; therefore, more responsibility is placed on the user to examine, for example, the call graph for the presence of cycles.

Example

a. An online management information system program, figure 23.6, calls a routine MAX to report the largest stock transaction of the day for a given issue. If MAX does not have the necessary information already available, RINPUT is called to read the required data. Since RINPUT reads many transactions for many issues, a sort routine is utilized to aid in organizing the information before returning it to the calling routine. Due to a keypunch error the sort routine calls routine MAX (instead of the proper routine MAXI) to aid in the sorting process. This error will show up as a cycle in the call graph and will be reported through use of a structure analyzer.

b. As part of the programming standards formulated for a project, the following rule is adopted:

"All jumps from within a control structure must be to locations after the end of the structure."

Figure 23.7 a segment of Pascal code, contains a violation of this rule which would be reported by a suitably constructed structure analyzer.

229

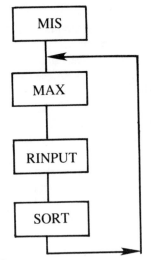

Figure 23.6
MIS Flow Chart

```
100   :     X: = 100;
while X > 70 do

        begin
          .
          .
          .
        if Z = 5 then goto 100;
          .
          .
          .
        end;
```

Figure 23.7 Goto Violation

Effectiveness
The technique is completely reliable for detecting violations of the standards specified as input. The standards, however, only cover a small range of programming
standards and possibly error situations. Thus, the technique is useful only in verifying very coarse program properties. The technique's prime utility, therefore, is in
the early stages of debugging a design or code specification.

Applicability
The technique is generally applicable and may be applied in design and coding

phases. Particular applicability is indicated in systems involving large numbers of subprograms and/or complex program control flow.

Learning
Minimal training is required for use of the technique. See "Outline of Method."

Cost
Little human cost is involved as there is no significant time spent in preparing the input or interpreting the output. For an average program, computer resources are small; the processing required can be done very efficiently and only a single run is required for analysis. For large or complex programs, the cost can be quite high. A plotter, which produces the most readable structure diagrams, drives the cost up.

References
1. FAIRLEY, Richard E., "Tutorial: Static Analysis and Dynamic Testing of Computer Software," *Computer*, Vol. 11, No. 4, pp. 14–23, April, 1978.
2. HOWDEN, W.E., "Reliability of the Path Analysis Testing Strategy," *IEEE Transactions on Software Engineering*, vol. SE-2, no. 3, 1976.

Cross-Reference Generators

Basic features
Cross-reference generators produce lists of data names and labels showing all of the places they are used in a program.

Information input
Input to cross-reference generators consists of a computer program in either source or object format.

Information output
Output from a cross-reference generator is an alphabetized list of variable names, procedure names and statement labels showing the locations in the program where they are defined and referenced. Other information, which is sometimes included, is data type, attributes, and usage information.

Outline of Method
Cross-reference generators provide useful information which can aid both program development and maintenance. They aid program development by helping identify errors such as misspelled identifiers and improperly typed variables. Program maintenance is aided by helping to locate, by variable or statement label, those portions which may be affected by a program change (e.g., a variable name needs to be changed).

Cross-reference generators are widely available and are usually provided with program source text analyzers such as compilers, standards checkers and data flow analyzers.

Cross-reference listings should be checked in detail after a program change has been made to check for misspelled identifiers and incorrect usage, etc.

Example

Application A communication network controller manages the control of a network of high-speed communication lines connecting a large number of CRT terminals to an airline reservation system computer.

Error A variable used to store message addresses is assigned an address which erroneously points to a location storing highly critical queue control information. A subsequent call to the device handler causes data to be read into the critical storage area causing a system crash.

Error discovery A quick study of software's cross-reference listing showed all the locations where the offending variable was used, one of which clearly showed that the error was due to improper use of a pointer variable.

Figure 23.8 shows a sample program listing and corresponding cross-reference list. The program is a utility routine used by a large aerodynamic analysis program. The tool which generated the report is called PFORT (2) which performs various FORTRAN source analyses. The list shows for each identifier its type (e.g., integer or real), usage (e.g., variable or function), attributes (e.g., argument, whether the variable has been set, scalar or array) and the line numbers where it is referenced.

Effectiveness

Cross-reference generators are most effective during the software maintenance phase to help determine where software errors are occurring, as seen in the previous example. Cross-reference generators are tools whose utility can often be taken for granted or even considered bothersome (e.g., "it produces too much paper"). Its lack of availability, however, will painfully demonstrate how necessary this seemingly basic capability is. Nevertheless, its true effectiveness is totally dependent upon the quality of its use.

Applicability

This method is generally applicable.

Learning

Minimal effort is required to learn how to effectively utilize cross reference generators.

Figure 23.8
Sample Cross-Reference Examples

PFORT VERIFIER 3/15/75 VERSION

```
        C
        C DRIVER PROGRAM TO TEST EUCLIDEAN NORM FUNCTION
        C
1               INTEGER X(100)
2               LOGICAL ERR
3               COMMON/ERROR/ERR
4       1       READ(5,10) I
5      10       FORMAT(I2,I5)
        C       END OF DATA CHECK
6               IF(I.GT.100) STOP
7               READ(5,10) (X(J), J = 1,I)
8               ERR = .FALSE.
9               ANS = ENORM(I, X)
10              IF (.NOT.ERR) GOTO 2)
11              WRITE (6,20)
12     20       FORMAT (15H BAD VALUE OF N)
13              GOTO 1
14      2       WRITE (6,30) ANS
15     30       FORMAT (6H NORM = ,E15.7)
16              GOTO 1
17              END
```

PROGRAM UNIT   *MAIN

NAME	TYPE	USE	ATTRIBUTES		REFERENCES			
ANS	R	V		SS	9	14		
ENORM	R	FN			9			
ERR	EL	V	C	SS	2	3	8	10
I	I	V		SS	4	6	7	9
J	I	V		SS	7			
X	EI	V		SA1	1	7	9	
10					4	5	7	
1					4	13	16	
20					11	12		
2					10	14		
30					14	15		

COMMON BLOCKS
ERROR ERR

Key to Figure 23.8

Type Key	*Use Key*
column 1:	columns 1, 2:
E explicitly typed	FA arithmetic-statement function argument

233

column 2:

I	INTEGER
R	REAL
D	DOUBLE PRECISION
C	COMPLEX
L	LOGICAL
H	HOLLERITH

FN	function name
E	external (function or subroutine)
GT	assigned goto variable
IF	intrinsic function
SF	arithmetic statement function
SN	subroutine name
V	variable

Attribute Key

column 1:
C   in COMMON

column 2:
E   in an EQUIVALENCE statement

column 3:
A   dummy argument

column 4:
S   value set by program unit

column 5, 6:
S   scalar
An   array with n dimensions

Costs

Cross-reference programs are widely available, usually as a function provided by a larger system (e.g., a compiler) and add only an incremental amount to the total cost.

References

1. RYDER, B.G. and HALL A.D., "The PFORT Verifier," *Computing Science Technical Report*, No. 12, Bell Labs, March, 1975.

Data Flow Analyzers

Basic features

Data flow analyzers are tools which can determine the presence or absence of data flow errors; that is, errors that are represented as particular sequences of events in a program's execution. The following description is limited to sequential analyzers although efforts are under way to include synchronous and concurrent events.

Information input

Data flow analysis algorithms operate on annotated graph structures which represent the program events and the order in which they can occur. Specifically, two types of graph structures are required: a set of annotated flowgraphs and a program invocation (or call) graph. There must be one flowgraph for each procedure. A flowgraph is a digraph whose nodes represent the execution units (usually statements) of the procedures, and whose edges are used to indicate the progression of execution units. Each node is annotated with indications of which program events occurred as a consequence of its execution. The program invocation (call) graph is also a digraph whose purpose is to indicate which procedures can invoke which others. Its nodes represent the procedures of the program and its edges represent the invocation relation.

Information output

The output of data flow analysis is a report on the presence of any specified event sequences in the program. If any such sequences are present, then the identity of each sequence is specified and a sample path along which the illegal sequence can occur is used. The absence of any diagnostic message concerning the presence of a particular event sequence is a reliable indicator of the absence of that sequence.

Outline of method

Data flow analyzers rely basically upon algorithms from program optimization to determine whether any two particular specified events can occur in sequence. Taking as input a flowgraph annotated with all events of interest, these algorithms focus upon two events and determine: 1) whether there exists some program path along which the two occur in sequence, and 2) whether on all program paths the two must occur in sequence. If one wishes to determine illegal event sequences of length three or more, these basic algorithms can be applied in succession.

A major difficulty arises in the analysis of programs having more than one procedure, because the procedure flowgraphs often cannot be completely annotated prior to data flow analysis. Flowgraph nodes representing procedure invocations must be left either partially or completely unannotated until the flowgraphs of the procedures which they represent have been analyzed. Hence, the order of analysis of the program's procedures is critical. This order is determined by a postorder traversal of the invocation graph in which the bottom level procedures are visited first, then those which invoke them, and so forth until the main level procedure is reached. For each procedure, the data flow analysis algorithms must determine the events which can possibly occur both first and last and then make this information available for annotation of all nodes representing invocations of this procedure.

Only in this way can it be assured that any possible illegal event sequence will be determined.

Example

The standard example of the application of data flow analysis is to the discovery of references to uninitialized program variables. In this case, the program events of interest are the definition of a variable, the reference to a variable, and the omission of a definition of a variable. Hence, all procedure flowgraphs are annotated to indicate which specific variables are defined, referenced, and undefined at which nodes. Data flow analysis algorithms are then applied to determine whether the definition omission event can be followed by the reference event for any specific variable without any intervening definition event for that variable. If so, a message is produced indicating the possibility of a reference to an uninitialized variable and a sample program path along which this will occur. A different algorithm is also used to determine if a specific variable definition omission must, along all paths, be followed by reference without intervening definition. For invoked procedures, these algorithms are also used to identify which parameters and global variables are sometimes used and always used as inputs and outputs. This information is used to annotate all nodes representing the invocation of this procedure, to enable analysis of these higher level procedures.

Data flow analysis might also be applied to the detection of illegal sequences of file operations in programs written in languages such as COBOL. Here the operations of interest would be opening, closing, defining (i.e., writing), and referencing (i.e., reading) a file. Errors whose presence or absence could be determined would include: attempting to use an unopened file, attempting to use a closed file, and reading an empty file.

Effectiveness

As noted, this technique is capable of determining the absence of event sequence errors from a program, or their presence in a program. When an event sequence error is detected, it is always detected along some specific path. Because these techniques do not study the executability of paths, the error may be detected on an unexecutable path and hence give rise to a spurious message. Another difficulty is that this technique is unreliable in distinguishing individual elements of an array. Hence, arrays are usually treated as if they were simple variables. As a consequence, illegal sequences of operations on specific array elements may be overlooked.

Applicability

Data flow analyzers can be applied to any annotated graph. Therefore, the availability of this technique is only limited and restricted by the availability of the (considerable) tools and techniques needed to construct such flowgraphs and call graphs.

Learning

This technique requires only a familiarity with and understanding of the output messages. No input data or user interaction is required.

Costs

This technique requires computer time, but the algorithms employed are highly efficient, generally executing in time which is linearly proportional to program size. Experience has shown that the construction of the necessary graphs can be a considerable cost factor, however. Potential users are warned that prototype tools exploiting this technique have proven quite costly to operate.

As noted above, no human input or interaction is required, resulting in only the relatively low human cost for interpretation of results.

References

1. OSTERWEIL, L.J. and FOSDICK, L.D., "DAVE—A Validation, Error Detection, and Documentation System for Fortran Programs," *Software—Practice and Experience*, 6, pp. 473–486, September 1976.
2. FOSDICK, L.D., and OSTERWEIL, L.J., "Data Flow Analysis in Software Reliability," *ACM Computing Surveys*, 8, pp. 305–330, September 1976.
3. HUANG, J.C., "Detection of Data Flow Anomaly Through Program Instrumentation," *IEEE Transactions on Software Engineering*, Vol. SE-5, No. 3, May 1979.

Execution Time Estimators/Analyzers

Basic features

Execution time estimators/analyzers are tools which provide information about the execution characteristics of a program. They can be considered as validation tools in that they can be used to validate performance requirements and are part of the programming phase of the lifecycle.

Information input

The programs which are to have their execution performance monitored are, essentially, the input needed by the tool. Depending on the sophistication of the particular tool being used, the programs may be processed by a processor which automatically inserts probes to measure performance or probes may need to be manually inserted. The probes usually consist of calls to a monitor which records execution information such as CPU and I/O time, and statement execution counts.

Information outputs

The output produced by execution time estimators/analyzers are reports which show either by statement and/or module the execution time distribution characteristics.

For example, a tool will provide information showing per module the number of entries to the module, cumulative execution time, mean execution time per entry and the percent execution time of the module with respect to the total program execution time.

Outline of method

Execution time estimators and execution time analyzers both perform similar functions but in different ways. Execution time estimators (1) function much in the same way as test coverage analyzers. A source program is instrumented with probes which collect statement execution counts when executed. Associated with each statement is a machine dependent estimate of the time required to execute the statement. The execution time estimate is multiplied by the statement execution count to give an estimate of the total time spent executing the statement. This is done for all statements in a program. Reports showing execution time breakdowns by statement, module, statement type, etc. can be produced.

Execution time analyzers are not usually as sophisticated as execution time estimators. Probes to measure the actual execution time of modules or program segments are inserted (usually by hand) into the source program. When the program has completed its execution, but just before it terminates, a routine is called which prints a report showing the execution characteristics of the monitored portions of the program.

The value of the tool lies primarily in its use as a performance requirements validation tool. In order to be used to formally validate performance requirements, however, it is necessary for the performance requirements to have been clearly stated and associated with specific functional requirements. Moreover, the system should have been designed so that the functional requirements can be traced to specific system modules.

Assuming that the above conditions are met, the tool could be used in the following way. The program to be analyzed would be monitored by the execution time estimator/analyzer during testing. The execution times for the modules corresponding to specific functional requirements would be compared with the performance requirement for that function. Those modules which fail to satisfy their performance requirements would be studied in more detail for possible efficiency improvements. The tool results can also help to identify execution time critical sections of code. Once the necessary optimitions have been made, the program should be again tested using the tool to validate the performance requirements.

Example

Application A particular module in a real time, embedded computer system is required to perform its function within a specific time period. If not, a critical time dependent activity cannot be performed, resulting in the loss of the entire system.

Error   The module in question contained an error which involved performing unnecessary comparisons during a table look-up function although the proper table entry was always found.

Error detection   The problem was discovered during system testing using an execution time analyzer which clearly indicated that the offending module was not able to meet its performance requirements. The specific error was discovered on further examination of the module.

Effectiveness

The use of execution time estimators/analyzers (as well as test coverage analyzers) has uncovered an interesting property of many programs. The majority of the execution time spent by a program is spent executing a very small percentage of the code. Knowledge gained of where this execution time critical code is located through the use of an execution time estimator/analyzer can be extremely helpful in optimizing a program in order to satisfy performance requirements and/or reduce costs.

Applicability

Execution time estimators/analyzers can be used in any application.

Learning

The learning required is simply that which is necessary to execute the tool.

Costs

The tool is automated and therefore does involve some cost. The amount will depend on the tool's sophistication, but generally will not be excessive.

References

1. "PPE Users Guide," Boole and Babbage, No. U-D503-0.
2. "Poseidon MK 88 Fire Control System Computer Program Verification and Validation Techniques Study," Vol. III, Ultrasystems, Inc., 500 Newport Center Dr., Newport Beach, CA, Nov. 1973.

Formal Reviews

Basic features

Formal reviews constitute a series of reviews of a system, usually conducted at major milestones in the system development lifecycle. They are used to improve development visibility and product quality and provide the basic means of communication between the project team, company management, and user representatives. They must provide judgmental decisions made by a team of blue ribbon specialists with a proven knowledge of current system operations. Formal reviews are most often implemented for medium to large size development projects, although small projects often employ a less rigorous form of the technique.

The most common types of formal reviews are held at the completion of the Requirements, Preliminary Design, Detailed (Critical) Design, Coding, and Installation phases. Whereas names of these reviews may vary by company, some generally recognized names are: Requirements Review, Preliminary Design Review (PDR), Critical Design Review (CDR), Code Construction Review, and Acceptance Test Review.

Information input
The input to a particular formal review will vary slightly depending on the stage of the lifecycle just completed. In general, each formal review will require that some sort of review package be assembled and then distributed at a review meeting. This package commonly contains a summary of the requirements which are the basis for the product being reviewed. These and other common inputs to formal reviews fall into three main categories, described below.

Project documents   These are documents produced by the development team to describe the system. The specific documents required are dependent upon the lifecycle phase just completed. For example: a review conducted at the conclusion of the requirements phase would necessitate availability of Functional Specifications or System/Subsystem Specifications.

Backup documentation   This type of input is documentation which is not usually contractually required, yet preparation of which is necessary to support systems development or otherwise record project progress. Specific types of backup documentation vary by the phase for which the review is performed. Rough drafts of user and maintenance manuals are examples of backup documentation examined during a design review to plan for continuation of the project. Program listings are an example of backup documentation utilized during a code construction review.

Other inputs   All other inputs are primarily used to clarify or expand upon the project documents and backup documents. They may include viewfoils and slides prepared by project management for the formal review meeting, the minutes of the previous phase review meeting, or preliminary evaluations of the project documents under review.

Information output
The information output associated with a formal review generally falls into the following categories.

Introduction to Technique and Tool Descriptions

Management reports   These are written reports from the project manager to upper management describing the results of the review, problems revealed, proposed solutions, and any upper management assistance required.

Outside reviewer reports   These are written reports to the project manager from participants of the review who have not worked on the project. These reports provide outside reviewers an opportunity to express their appraisal of the project status and the likelihood of meeting project objectives. It also allows them to make suggestions for correcting any deficiencies noted.

Action items   This is a list of all required post-review action items to be completed before a review can be satisfactorily closed out. With each item is an indication of whether customer or contractor action is required for resolution.

Review minutes   This is a written record of the review meeting proceedings which are recorded by a designee of the leader of the review team. The minutes of the review are distributed to each review team member after the completion of the review meeting.

Decision to authorize next phase   A decision must be reached at any formal review to authorize initiation of the next lifecycle phase.

Understanding of project status   At the conclusion of any formal review there should be a common understanding of project status among the project personnel present at the review.

Outline of method

Participants   The participants in a formal review are often selected from the following group of people:

Project manager

Project technical lead

Other project team members—analysts, designers, programmers

Client

User representataive(s)

Line management of project manager

Outside reviewers—quality assurance personnel, experienced people on other projects

Functional support personnel—finance, technology personnel

Subcontractor management, if applicable

Others—configuration management representative, maintenance representative

The process Formal reviews should be scheduled and organized by project management. Each review must be scheduled at a meaningful point during system development. The review effectively serves as the phase milestone for any particular phase.

There are five basic steps involved in every formal review.

- Preparation   All documentation that serves as source material for the review must be prepared prior to the meeting. These materials may be distributed to each participant before the meeting in order to allow sufficient time to review and make appraisals of the materials. The location and time of the meeting must be established, participants must be identified, and an agenda planned.

- Overview presentation   At the review meeting, all applicable Product and Backup Documentation is distributed and a high-level summary of the product is presented. Objectives are also given.

- Detailed presentation   A detailed description of the project status and progress achieved during the review period is presented. Problems are identified and openly discussed by the team members.

- Summary   A summary of the results of the review is given. A decision about the status of the product is made and a list of new action items is constructed and responsibility for completion of each item is assigned.

- Follow-up   The completion of all action items is verified. All reports are completed and distributed.

Example

By contract agreement, two weeks prior to completion of the requirements document, the producer of a program receives notification from his client that a requirements review meeting is desired. The client notifies a preselected chairperson to conduct the meeting. For participatnts the chairperson has selected the project manager, project technical lead, a member of the requirements definition team, and a member of the requirements analysis team. The client also has indicated that he would like to include the following people in the review: a representative from the user shop, a reviewer from an independent computing organization, and a representative from his own organization.

The chairperson informs all review participants of the date, time, and location of the review. Ten days prior to the meeting, the chairperson distributes all documents produced by the requirements definition and analysis teams (requirements document, preliminary plans, other review material) to each participant. In preparation of the meeting, each reviewer critically inspects the documents. The user representative is puzzled over the inclusion of a requirement concerning the use of a proposed database. The reviewer from the outside computing organization notes that the version of the operating system to be used in developing the system is very outdated. A representative of the client organization has a question concerning the use of a subcontractor in one phase of the project. Each reviewer submits his comments to the chairperson before the scheduled review meeting. The chairperson receives the comments and directs each to the appropriate requirements team member to allow proper time for responses to be prepared.

The requirements review meeting begins with a brief introduction by the chairperson. All participants are introduced, review materials are listed, and the procedure for conducting the review is presented. A presentation is then given summarizing the problem that led to the requirements and the procedure that was used to define these requirements. At this time, the user representative inquires about the requirement concerning the use of a particular database as stated in the requirements document. The project technical lead responds to this question. The user representative accepts this response, which is so noted by the recorder in the official minutes of the meeting.

The meeting continues with an analysis of the requirements and a description of the contractor's planned approach for developing a solution to the problem. At this time, the questions from the client representative and the outside computing organization are discussed. The project manager responds to questions concerning the use of a subcontractor on the project. Certain suggestions have been made which require the approval of the subcontractor. These suggestions are placed on the action list. The technical lead acknowledges the problems that the independent computing organization has pointed out. He notes that certain system vendors must be contacted to resolve the problem. This item is also placed on the action list. A general discussion among all review team members follows.

At the end of the review, the chairperson seeks a decision from the reviewers about the acceptability of the requirements document. They agree to give their approval, providing that the suggestions noted on the action list are thoroughly investigated. All participants agree to this decision and the meeting is adjourned.

The chairperson distributes a copy of the minutes of the meeting, including action items, to all participants. The project manager informs the subcontractor of the suggestions made at the meeting. The subcontractor subsequently agrees with the suggestions. The project technical leader contacts the system vendor from which the current operating system was purchased and learns that the latest version can be easily installed before it is needed for this project. He notifies the project manager of this, who subsequently approves its purchase. The requirements document is appropriately revised to reflect the completion of these action items. The chairperson verifies that all action items have been completed. The project manager submits a Management Report to management, summarizing the review.

Effectiveness

Since the cost to correct an error increases rapidly as the development process progresses, detection of errors by the use of formal reviews is an attractive prospect.

Software Validation, Verification, Testing, and Documentation

Some of the qualitative benefits attributable to the use of formal reviews are given below:

Highly visible systems development

Early detection of design and analysis errors

More reliable estimating and scheduling

Increased product reliability, maintainability

Increased education and experience of all individuals involved in the process

Increased adherence to standards

Increased user satisfaction

Little data is available which identifies the quantitative benefits attributable to the use of formal reviews.

Experience with this technique indicates that it is most effective on large projects. The costs involved in performing formal reviews on small projects, however, may be sufficiently large enough to consider lessening the formality of the reviews or even eliminating or combining some of them.

Applicability
Formal reviews are applicable to large or small projects following all development phases and are not limited by project type or complexity.

Learning
This technique does not require any special training. However, the success or failure of a formal review is dependent on the people who attend. They must be intelligent, skilled, knowledgeable in a specific problem area, and be able to interact effectively with other team members. The experience and expertise of the individual responsible for directing the review is also critical to the success of the effort.

Costs
The method requires no special tools or equipment. The main cost involved is that of human resources. If formal reviews are conducted in accordance with the resource guidelines expressed in most references, the cost of reviews for average programs are not high. However, the cost of reviewing major programs can be significant. Most references suggest that formal review meetings should not require more than 1 to 2 hours. Preparation time can amount to as little as ½ hour and should not require longer than ½ day per review.

References
1. FREEDMAN, D.P., and WEINBERG, G.M., "Ethno—Technical Review Handbook," 1977 Ethnotech, Inc.
2. WEINBERG, G.M., "Programming as a Social Activity," *The Psychology of Computer Programming*, Van Nostrand, Reinhold, 1971.
3. MYERS, G., "Reliable Software Through Composite Design," Petrocelli/Charter, 1975.

4. SHNEIDERMAN, BEN, "Software Psychology—Human Factors in Computer and Information Systems," Winthrop Publishing, 1980.
5. GLASS, R., "Software Reliability Guidebook," Prentice-Hall, Englewood Cliffs, N.J., 1979.

Formal Verification

Basic features

The purpose of formal verification is to apply the formality and rigor of mathematics to the task of proving the consistency between an algorithmic solution and a rigorous, complete specification of the intent of the solution.

Information input

The two inputs which are required are the solution specification and the intent specification. The solution specification is in algorithmic form, often but not always, executable code. The intent specification is descriptive in form, invariably consisting of assertions, usually expressed in Predicate Calculus.

Additional inputs may be required depending upon the rigor and specific mechanisms to be employed in the consistency proof. For example, the semantics of the language used to express the solution specification are required and must be supplied to a degree of rigor consistent with the rigor of the proof being attempted. Similarly, simplification rules and rules of inference may be required as input if the proof process is to be completely rigorous.

Information output

The proof process may terminate with a successfully completed proof of consistency, or a demonstration of inconsistency, or it may terminate inconclusively. In the former two cases, the proofs themselves and the proven conclusion are the outputs. In the latter case, any fragmentary chains of successfully proven reasoning are the only meaningful output. Their significance is, as expected, highly variable.

Outline of method

The usual method used in carrying out formal verification is Floyd's Method of Inductive Assertions or a variant thereof. This method entails the partitioning of the solution specification into algorithmically straightline fragments by means of strategically placed assertions. This partitioning reduces the proof of consistency to the proof of a set of smaller, generally much more manageable lemmas.

Floyd's Method dictates that the intent of the solution specification be captured by two assertions. The first assertion is the input assertion which describes the assumptions about the input. The second assertion is the output assertion which describes the transformation of the input, which is intended to be the result of the

245

Software Validation, Verification, Testing, and Documentation

execution, of the specified solution. In addition, intermediate assertions must be fashioned and placed within the body of the solution specification in such a way that every loop in the solution specification contains at least one intermediate assertion. Each such intermediate assertion must express completely the transformations which are intended to occur or are occurring at the point of placement of the assertion.

The purpose of placing the assertions as just described is to assure that every possible program execution is decomposable into a sequence of straightline algorithmic specifications, each of which is bounded on either end by an assertion. If it is known that each terminating assertion is necessarily implied by executing the specified algorithm under the conditions of the initial assertion, then, by induction, it can be shown that the entire execution behaves as specified by the input/output assertions, and hence as intended. For the user to be assured of this, Floyd's Method directs that a set of lemmas be proven. This set consists of one lemma for each pair of assertions which is separated by a straightline algorithmic specification and no other intervening assertion. For such an assertion pair, the lemma states that, under the assumed conditions of the initial assertion, execution of the algorithm specified by the intervening code necessarily implied the conditions of the terminating assertion. Proving all such lemmas establishes what is known as "partial correctness." Partial correctness establishes that whenever the specified solution process terminates, it has behaved as intended. In addition, total correctness is established by proving that the specified solution process must always terminate. This is clearly an undecidable question, being equivalent to the Halting Problem, and hence its resolution is invariably approached through the application of heuristics.

In the above procedure, the pivotal capability is clearly the ability to prove the various specified lemmas. This can be done to varying degrees of rigor, resulting in proofs of corresponding varied degrees of reliability and trustworthiness. For the greatest degree of trustworthiness, solution specification, intent specification, and rules of reasoning must all be specified with complete rigor and precision. The principal difficulty here lies in specifying the solution with complete rigor and precision. This entails specifying the semantics of the specification language, and the functioning of any actual execution environment with complete rigor and precision. Such complete details are often difficult or impossible to adduce. They are, moreover, when available, generally quite voluminous, thereby occasioning the need to prove lemmas which are long and intricate.

Example

As an example of what is entailed in a rigorous formal verification activity, consider the specification of a bubble sort procedure. (The details of this can be found in Reference 3 for this technique.) The intent of the bubble sort must first be captured by an input/output assertion pair. Next, observing that the bubble solution algorithm contains two nested loops, leads to the conclusion that two additional intermediate assertions might be fashioned, or perhaps one particularly well placed assertion might suffice. In the former case, up to eight lemmas would then need to be established; one corresponding to each of the (possible two) paths from the initial to each intermediate assertion, one corresponding to each of the two paths from an intermediate assertion back to itself, one for each of the (possibly two) paths from one intermediate assertion to the other, and finally one for each of the (possibly two) paths from intermediate to terminating assertion. Each lemma would have to be established through rigorous mathematical logic (see Reference 3). Finally, a proof of necessary termination would need to be fashioned (see Reference 3).

Effectiveness
The effectiveness of formal verification has been attacked on several grounds. First and most fundamentally, formal verification can only establish consistency between intent and solution specification. Hence, inconsistency can indicate error in either or both. The same can be said for most other verification techniques, however. What makes this particularly damaging for formal verification is that complete rigor and detail in the intent specification are important, and this requirement for great detail invites error.

The amount of detail also occasions the need for large, complex lemmas. These, especially when proven using complex, detailed rules of inference, produce very large, intricate proofs which are highly prone to error.

Finally, formal verification of actual programs is further complicated by the necessity to express rigorously the execution behavior of the actual computing environment for the program. As a consequence of this, the execution environment is generally modeled incompletely and imperfectly, thereby restricting the validity of the proofs in ways which are difficult to determine.

Despite these difficulties, a correctly proven set of lemmas establishing consistency between a complete specification and a solution specification whose semantics are accurately known and expressed conveys the greatest assurances of correctness obtainable. This ideal of assurance seems best attainable by applying automated theorem provers to design specifications, rather than code.

Applicability
Formal verification is a technique which can be applied to determine the consistency between any algorithmic solution specification and any intent specification. As elaborated upon earlier, however, the trustworthiness of the results is highly variable depending primarily upon the rigor with which the specifications are expressed and the proofs are carried out. Formal verification is best employed on critical code where errors have severe consequences.

Learning
As noted, the essence of this technique is mathematical. Thus, the more mathematical sophistication and expertise which practitioners possess, the better. In particular, a considerable amount of mathematical training and expertise is necessary for the results of applying this technique to be significantly reliable and trustworthy.

Software Validation, Verification, Testing, and Documentation

Costs

This technique, when seriously applied, must be expected to consume very significant amounts of the time and effort of highly trained mathematically proficient personnel. Hence, considerable human-labor expense must be expected.

As noted earlier, human effectiveness can be considerably improved through the use of automated tools such as theorem provers. It is important to observe, however, that such tools can be prodigious consumers of computer resources. Hence, their operational costs are also quite large.

References

1. FLOYD, R.W., "Assigning Meanings to Programs," in *Mathematical Aspects of Computer Science*, 19, SCHWARTZ, J.T. (ed.), American Mathematical Society, Providence, R.I., pp. 19–32, 1967.
2. ELSPAS, B., et al., "An Assessment of Techniques for Proving Program Correctness," *ACM Computing Surveys*, 4, pp. 97–147, June, 1972.
3. GOOD, D.I., LONDON, R.L., and BLEDSOE, W.W., "An Interactive Program Verification System," *Proceedings 1975 International Conference on Reliable Software*, IEEE Catalog 75CH0940-7CSR, pp. 482–492.
4. HOARE, C.A.R., "An Axiomatic Basis for Computer Programming," *CACM*, 12, October 1969, pp. 576–583.

Global Roundoff Analysis of Algebraic Processes

Basic features

The technique involves the use of computer software to locate numerical instabilities in algorithms consisting of algebraic processes. Global roundoff analysis is the determination of how rounding error propagates in a given numerical method for many or all permissible sets of data. This technique has two areas of application: Case I—to decide whether an algorithm is as accurate as can be expected given the fundamental limitation of finite precision arithmetic; and Case II—to decide which of two competing algorithms is "more stable," i.e., less susceptible to rounding errors.

Information input

a. Case I—Analysis of a single algorithm
- algorithm described in a simple programming language
- data set for algorithm
- choice and type of rounding error measures
- stopping value for maximizer

b. Case II—Comparison of two algorithms
- each algorithm described in a simple programming language
- data set for algorithms

- choice of rounding error measure and mode of comparison
- stopping value for maximizer

Information output

a. Case I—Analysis of a single algorithm
- output computed for the initial data set
- list of values found by the maximizer
- final set of data
- if instability diagnosed, then all arithmetic operations at the final set of data are listed
b. Case II—Comparison of two algorithms
- output computed for the initial algorithms
- list of values found by the maximizer
- final set of data

Outline of method

For an algorithm and a data set, d, then:

(a) A function $w(\bar{d})$, called a Wilkinson number, has been defined which measures the effects of rounding errors. Large values for w is the sign of an unstable algorithm.

(b) Wilkinson number has been shown to be a "smooth" function of d, i.e. as the original data set values are altered in small increments, the values of w are correspondingly altered in small increments.

(c) An approximation to Wilkinson numbers has been developed which is straight forward to compute.

(d) The representation of the algorithm is analyzed.

(e) Using the initial data set as a starting point, the global analysis program uses numerical maximization techniques to modify the data set. The search is directed toward finding a data set with a disastrously large value of $w(\bar{d})$.

Example

Triangular Matrix Inversion (4). The better matrix inversion algorithms are known from experience to almost invariably produce satisfactory results. However, the question remains whether there is a guarantee that the results are *always* good. The question can be reformulated as: Is the traditional back substitution algorithm for inverting an upper triangular matrix numerically stable in the sense that there is a modest bound, depending on the matrix size, for w? To apply the technique, the algorithm is represented as a program in figure 23.9. Note that the statement "TEST (N = 4)" indicates that the search for numerical stability will be conducted in the domain of 4x4 matrices. An approximation to w, W_4, will be calculated.

Software Validation, Verification, Testing, and Documentation

Figure 23.9
Triangular Matrix Inversion

```
      TEST (N = 4)
C     COMPUTE S = (T INVERSE), WHERE T IS A NONSINGULAR, UPPER
C     TRIANGULAR MATRIX.
      DIMENSION (S(N,N),T(N,N))
C     INPUT T.
C     INPUT T.
C        FOR J =  i to N BY 1
               FOR I = J to 1 BY  -1
                   INPUT (T(I,J))
                   END (I)
               END(J)
C
C     COMPUTE S.
          FOR K = 1 TO N BY 1
              S(K,K) = 1.0/T(K,K)
              FOR I = K - 1 TO 1 By  -1
                  S(I,K) = -SUMMATION(T(I,J)*S(J,K),J = I + 1 TO K)/T(I,I)
                  END (I)
              END(K)
C
C     OUTPUT S.
          FOR J = 1 TO N BY 1
              FOR I = J TO 1 BY  -1
                  OUTPUT(S(I,J))
                  END (I)
              END(J)
          STOP
```

The compiler portion of the package checks the program for errors, then translates them into a form suitable for analysis.

The initial data set for the search for numerical instability was:

$$T_0 = \begin{pmatrix} 1 & 0 & 0 & 0 \\ & 2 & 0 & 0 \\ & & 3 & 0 \\ & & & 4 \end{pmatrix}$$

The roundoff analysis program was told to seek a value of W in excess of 10,000. The maximizer located the following matrix:

$$T_\infty \approx \begin{pmatrix} -0.001 & 5.096 & 5.101 & 1.853 \\ & 3.737 & 3.740 & 3.392 \\ & & 0.0006 & 5.254 \\ & & & 4.567 \end{pmatrix}$$

with $W_4(T_\infty) > 10,000$ in 6 seconds CPU time on a IBM 370/168.

The fact that W_4 can be large for data like T seems implicit in known results, e.g., (6), verifying the ill behavior of triangular matrices with diagonal entries approaching zero.

Effectiveness

Failure of the maximizer to find large values of w does not guarantee that none exist (2). Thus, the technique tends to be optimistic; unstable methods may appear stable. However, experience indicates that this method is surprisingly reliable. At least, the failure of the maximizer to find large values of w can be interpreted as providing evidence for stability equivalent to a large amount of practical experience with low order matrices.

Applicability

The technique is intended for noniterative methods from numerical linear algebra.

Learning

Most algorithms should be able to be analyzed in 2 to 8 hours of training and preparation assuming the software is available.

Costs

The performance of the technique is related to the performance of the algorithm being checked.

References

1. MILLER, W., "Software for Roundoff Analysis," *ACM Transactions on Mathematical Software*, 1, 2, June 1975, 10 pp. 8–128.
2. MILLER, W., "Computer Search for Numerical Instability," *Journal of the ACM*, 4, October 1975, pp. 512–521.
3. MILLER, W., "Roundoff Analysis by Direct Comparision of Two Algorithms," *SIAM Journal of Numerical Analysis*, 13, 1976, pp. 382–392.
4. MILLER, W. and SPOONER, D., "Software for Roundoff Analysis, II," *ACM Transactions on Mathematical Software* 4, 4, 1978, pp. 369–387.
5. MILLER, W. and SPOONER, D., "Algorithm 532 Software for Roundoff Analysis 2," *ACM Transactions on Mathematical Software*, 4, 4, 1978, pp. 388–390.
6. ANDERSON, A. and KARASALO, I., "On Computing Bounds for the Least Singular Value of a Triangular Matrix," *BIT*, 1975, pp. 1–4.

Inspection

Basic Features

Informal reviews constitute a thorough inspection mechanism used to detect errors in system components and documentation. Several inspections are generally con-

Software Validation, Verification, Testing, and Documentation

ducted for each item as it progresses through the lifecycle. The most commonly recognized inspections are conducted during the design and programming stages and are referred to as design inspections and code inspections. However, the inspection concept may be applied to any functionally complete part of a system during any or all phases of the lifecycle and are typified by utilization of checklists and summary reports. Another unique feature of an inspection is the use of data from past inspections to stimulate future detection of categories of errors.

Information Input

The input required for each inspection falls into three main categories: relevant project documents, backup documentation, and inspection checklists.

Project Documents   These are documents produced by the development team to describe the system. The specific documents required are dependent upon the lifecycle phase currently in progress. For example: an inspection conducted during the design phase would necessitate availability of Functional Specifications or System/Subsystem Specifications.

Backup Documentation   This type of input is documentation which is not usually contractually required, yet preparation of which is necessary to support systems development or otherwise record project progress. Specific types of backup documentation vary by the phase in which the inspection is conducted. Data dictionaries and cross-reference tables are examples of backup documentation utilized during a design inspection. Program listings are an example of code inspection backup documentation.

Checklists   Each member of the inspection team uses a checklist for review preparation and during the course of the inspection itself. The checklist content may vary based upon the particular application being inspected and is updated from feedback of other recent inspections. For example, a checklist to be employed during a code inspection of a COBOL probram component would contain items like:

Are specialized printer controls used to enhance component readability (e.g., use of EJECT or SKIP commands)?

Does each procedure have only one exit and entry?

Are IF-THEN-ELSE statements indented in a logical fashion?

Are file, record and data names representative of the information they contain and do they conform to established naming conventions?

Are comments explicit and accurate?

.

.

.

etc.

Introduction to Technique and Tool Descriptions

Information Output

The information output associated with an inspection is either related to inspection planning and scheduling or inspection results.

Inspection Schedule Memo   The memo is produced upon notification from management that an inspection should be forthcoming. The memo defines the roles and responsibilities of each inspection team member, estimated time required for each inspection task, and a summary of the status of the item being reviewed (including any previous inspections conducted).

Problem Definition Sheet/Error Description Summary   This form is used to record information about each detected error. It describes the location, nature, and classification of the errors.

Summary Report   A Summary Report is used to document correction of all errors reported during an inspection. Data recorded on the report is tabulated and becomes part of cumulative error statistics which can be used to improve the development and inspection process.

Management Reports   These reports are the means by which management is informed about the types of errors being detected and the amount of resources being expended to correct them. The information from these reports highlights frequent sources of errors, providing input to management for future updates to the inspection checklist.

Outline of Method

Roles and Responsibilities   The group of people responsible for the inspection results are usually called an inspection team and are given responsibilities based upon their contribution to the item being inspected. The leader of the group is responsible for all process planning, moderating, reporting, and follow-up activities. The designer implementer (person responsible for building the item) and the tester of the item being inspected are also members of the inspection team. Management does not normally participate in an inspection.

The Process   There are five basic steps involved in every inspection: planning, preparation, inspection meeting, rework and follow-up. The first inspection for a particular item contains another step: overview presentation. These steps are summarized below.

While these steps should not vary functionally for inspections conducted at different development phases, the responsibilities of the individuals on the inspection team will necessarily vary slightly. This occurs because the primary responsibility for the item shifts as the lifecycle progresses. For example, during a design inspection, the designer is the focal point. However, during a code inspection or document inspection, the implementation is the focal point.

- *Planning.* Set up inspection schedule and assemble inspection team.
- *Overview Presentation.* (Conducted only for the first inspection of the item during the development process.) Distribute applicable Product and Backup Documentation and present a high level summary of the item to be inspected.
- *Preparation.* Team members read and review documentation and list any questions.
- *Inspection Meeting.* Conduct detailed description of the item, noting all errors detected. Use checklists to ensure inspection completeness and Problem Definition Report to summarize errors.
- *Rework.* Estimate time to correct errors and implement the corrections.
- *Follow-up.* Verify that all errors have been corrected using Problem Definition Sheet as a checklist. Complete Summary and Management Reports.

Example

The following is an example of a design inspection of a software component or item which defines the roles and responsibilities of the inspection team members. Upon decision of management to conduct a design inspection, the selected leader initiates process planning by identifying team members and their roles and responsibilities. If this is the first inspection for this item (i.e., there has been no requirements inspection), the leader next schedules an overview presentation. The project and backup documentation (i.e., Functions Specification, system flow charts, etc.) are distributed and the item designer leads the team through a high level description of the item.

After the presentation each team member reads and reviews the distributed documentation and lists any questions. This list of prepared questions is often given to the leader and/or designer prior to the inspection meeting.

At the designer inspection meeting the implementer leads the team through a detailed description of the design of the item being inspected. Backup documentation facilitates the description and clarifies points which may be brought up. The checklist is used by each team member to help identify errors and enforce standards. The problem definition sheet is prepared by the team leader at the end of the inspection. The item design will either be approved as-is, approved with modifications, or rejected. In the last two cases, the problem definition sheet is given to the designer and the correction process begins.

At the start of this rework process an estimate is made by the leader and designer specifying time required for correction. This estimate is entered on the Problem Definition Sheet and is provided to management. Management can then make a judgment as to whether their project schedule will be affected. Necessary changes to the item are made and the item is either reinspected or submitted to follow-up procedures.

During follow-up, the Problem Definition Sheet is used as a checklist for the leader and designer to verify that all errors have been analyzed and corrected. The reader then fills out the Summary and Management Reports and submits them to management.

Effectiveness

Since the cost to correct an error increases rapidly as the development process progresses, detection of errors by early use of inspections is an attractive prospect.

Studies have been carried out which indicate that inspections are an effective method of increasing product quality (reliability, usability and maintainability). Experience with the technique indicates that it is effective on projects of all sizes. The best results are generally achieved when the inspection leader is experienced in the inspection process.

Some of the best quantitative results of the use of inspections have come from IBM, which has been studying the use of the technique for a number of years. One study, detailing and comparing the benefits of inspections and structured walkthroughs, indicated 23% higher programmer productivity with inspections than with walkthroughs. No data was available documenting the amount of increased programmer productivity attributable to inspections alone. The study also reported 38% fewer errors in the running code than if solely applying walkthroughs as an error detection mechanism.

The qualitative benefits attributable to the use of inspections are substantative. The following list is illustrative of some of these positive effects:

- Programs which are less complex
- Subprograms which are written in a consistent style, complying with established standards
- Highly visible systems development
- More reliable estimating and scheduling
- Increased education and experience of all individuals involved in the inspection process
- Increased user satisfaction
- Improved documentation
- Less dependence on key personnel for critical skills

Applicability

While most commonly used inspections are for design and code, the technique is not limited to these phases and can be applied during all phases, for most types of applications (i.e., business, scientific, etc.) on large or small projects.

255

Software Validation, Verification, Testing, and Documentation

Learning

The experience of the inspection leader is essential to the success of the effort. A correct attitude about the process is essential to all involved, including the appropriate managers. Many excellent texts about inspections (and other types of reviews) are in existence which should supply the required level of detail as well as discuss some team psychology issues pertinent to inspection conduct.

Costs

The method requires no special tools or equipment. The main cost involved is that of human resources. If inspections are conducted in accordance with the resource guidelines expressed in most references, the costs of inspections are negligible compared with the expected returns. It should be kept in mind that follow-up inspections to correct previously detected errors can increase the original cost estimation. Most references suggest that inspection meetings should last no longer than 2 hours, and can reasonably be kept to 15 minutes. Preparation time can amount to as little as ½ hour and should not require longer than ½ day per inspection.

References

(1) "Code Reading: Structured Walkthroughs and Inspections," IBM, IPTO Support Group, World Trade Center, Postbus 60, Zoetenmeer, Netherlands, March 1976.

(2) FAGEN, M.E., "Design and Code Inspections to reduce errors in Program Development," *IBM Systems Journal*, No. 3,1976.

(3) FREEDMAN, D.P. and WEINBERG, G.M., "Ethno—Technical Review Handbook," Ethnotech, Inc., 1977.

(4) "Systematic Software Development and Maintenance (SSDM)," BCS Document #10155, February 1977.

Interactive Test Aids

Basic Features

Interactive test aids, debuggers, are tools used to control and/or analyze the dynamics of a program during execution. The capabilities provided by these tools are used to assist in identifying and isolating program errors. These capabilities allow the user to:

suspend program execution at any point to examine program status,

interactively dump the values of selected variables and memory locations,

modify the computation state of an executing program,

trace the control flow of an executing program.

Information Input

Interactive test aids require as input the source code that is to be executed and the commands that indicate which testing operations are to be performed by the tool during execution. Included in the commands are indications of which program statements are to be affected by the tool's operation. Commands can be inserted in the source code and/or entered interactively by the user during program execution at preselected break points.

Information Output
The information output by an interactive test aid is a display of requested information during the execution of a program. This information may include the contents of selected storage cells at specific execution points or a display of control flow during execution.

Outline of Method
The functions performed by an interactive test aid are determined by the commands input to it. Some common commands are described below.

BREAK: Suspend program execution when a particular statement is executed or a particular variable is altered.

DUMP: Display the contents of specific storage cells, e.g., variables, internal registers, other memory locations.

TRACE: Display control flow during program execution through printed traces of:

statement executions (using statement labels or line numbers),

subroutine calls, or

alterations of a specified variable.

SET: Set the value of a specified variable.

CONTENTS: Display the contents of certain variables at the execution of a specific statement.

SAVE: Save the present state of execution.

RESTORE: Restore execution to a previously SAVEd state.

CALL: Invoke a subroutine.

EXECUTE: Resume program execution at a BREAK point.

EXIT: Terminate processing.

These commands allow complete user control over the computation state of an executing program. It allows the tester to inspect or change the value of any variable at any point during execution.

The capabilities of special interactive testing aids can also be found in many implementations of interpreters and compilers for such languages as BASIC, FORTRAN, COBOL, and PL/I.

Example
A critical section of code within a routine is to be tested. The code computes the values of three variables, X, Y, and Z, which later serve as inputs to other routines. To

ensure that the values assigned to X, Y, and Z have been correctly computed in this section of code, an interactive testing aid is used to test the code.

Two BREAK commands are initially inserted into the code. A BREAK command is inserted immediately before the first statement and immediately after the last statement of the section of code being tested. To display the value of X, Y, and Z, a CONTENTS command is placed before the second BREAK command. The program containing the above mentioned code is executed. When the first BREAK command is encountered, execution is halted and a prompt is issued to the user requesting that a command be entered. A SAVE command is typed by the user in order to save the present state of execution. Then SET command is entered to set the values of two variables, A and B, which are used to compute the values of X, Y, and Z. The EXECUTE command is then issued to resume program execution.

At the end of execution of the relevant section of code the preinserted CONTENTS command displays the computed values of X, Y, and Z. The second BREAK command allows time for these values to be examined and gives the user the opportunity to enter new commands. At this time, a RESTORE command is entered that will restore the computation state to the state that was previously saved by the SAVE command. For this example, the computation state returns to that which followed the first BREAK command, allowing the code under analysis to be tested with different input values. Different values for A and B are entered and the contents of X, Y, and Z are observed as before. This process is repeated several times using carefully selected values for A and B and the corresponding values of X, Y, and Z are closely examined each time. If results of several computations look suspicious, their input and output values are noted and the code is more thoroughly examined. The program is finally terminated by entering the EXIT command at one of the two possible break points.

Effectiveness
To be an effective testing tool, an interactive test aid should be used with a disciplined strategy to guide the testing process. The tools can be easily misused if no testing methodology is combined with their use.

Applicability
Interactive test aids can be applied to any type of source code. Most existing tools, however, are language dependent (i.e., will operate correctly only for specified languages).

Learning
A minimal amount of learning is required to use these tools. It is comparable to the learning required in using a text editor. However, if the tool is to be used most efficiently, some learning is required in utilizing the tool with an effective testing strategy.

Costs

Programs executing under an interactive test aid will require more computing resources (e.g., execution time, memory for diagnostic tables) than if executed under normal operation. The cost is dependent on the implementation of the tool. For example, those based on interpretive execution will involve costs different from those driven by monitor calls.

References

(1) MYERS, Glenford, "The Art of Software Testing," Wiley-Interscience, New York, 1975.

(2) "Sperry Univac Series 1100 FORTRAN (ASCII) Programmer Reference," Sperry Rand Corporation, 1979.

(3) TAYLOR, R.N., MERILATT, R.L., and OSTERWEIL, L.J., "Integrated Testing and Verification System for Research Flight Software—Design Document," NASA CR 159095, July 31, 1979.

Interface Checker

Basic Features

Interface checkers analyze the consistency and completeness of the information and control flow between components, modules or procedures of a system.

Information Input

Information needed by interface checkers consists of either:

    a. a formal representation of system requirements, or

    b. a formal representation of system design, or

    c. a program coded in a high-level language.

Information Output

Module interface inconsistencies and errors are revealed. The information can be provided as error messages included with a source listing or as a separate report.

Outline of Method

Interface checkers are fully automated tools which analyze a computer processable form of a software system requirements specification, design specification or code. The method for each of the three representations—requirements, design, and code— will be illustrated below by examining the interface checking capabilities of three existing tools.

PSL/PSA (Problem Statement Language/Problem Statement Analyzer) (1) is an automated requirements specification tool. Basically, PSL/PSA describes system requirements as a system of inputs, processes and outputs. Both information and control flow are represented within PSL. Interface checking performed by PSA consists of ensuring that all data items are used and generated by some process and that all processes use data. Incomplete requirements specifications are, therefore, easily detected.

The Design Assertion Consistency Checker (DACC) (2) is a tool which analyzes module interfaces based on a design which contains information describing, for each module, the nature of the inputs and outputs. This information is specified using assertions to indicate the number and order of inputs, data types, units (e.g., feet or radians), acceptable ranges, and so on. DACC checks module calls against the assertions in the called module for consistency. This produces a consistency report indicating which assertions have been violated.

PFORT (3) is a static analysis tool which is primarily used for checking Fortran programs for adherence to a portable subset of the Fortran language but it also performs subprogram interface checking. PFORT matches actual with dummy arguments and checks for unsafe references, such as constraints being passed as arguments.

Interface checking capabilities can also be included within a particular language's compiler as well. For example, Ada (4) provides a parameter passing mechanism whereby parameters are identified to be input or output or input/output. Moreover, data type and constraints (e.g., range and precision) must match between the actual arguments and the formal parameters (in non-generic subprograms).

In summary, interface checking tools will generally check for:

modules which are used but not defined,

modules which are defined but not used,

incorrect number of arguments,

data type mismatches between actual and formal parameters,

data constraint mismatches between actual and formal parameters,

data usage anomalies.

Example

Application   A statistical analysis package written in Fortran utilizes a file access system to retrieve records containing data used in the analysis.

Error   The primary record retrieval subroutine is always passed a statement number in the calling program which is to receive control in case an abnormal file processing error occurs. This is the last argument in the argument list of the subroutine call. One program, however, fails to supply the needed argument. The compiler is not able to detect the error. Moreover, the particular Fortran implementation is such that no execution time error occurs until a return to the unspecified statement number is attempted, at which time the system crashes.

Error Discovery   This error can easily be detected by using an interface checker at either the design (e.g., DACC) or coding phase (e.g., PFORT) of the software development activity. Both DACC and PFORT can detect incorrect numbers of arguments.

Effectiveness
Interface checkers are very effective at detecting a class of errors which can be difficult to isolate if left to testing. They are generally more cost effective if provided as a capability within another tool such as a compiler, data flow analyzer or a requirements/design specification tool.

Applicability
The method is generally applicable.

Learning
The use of interface checkers requires only a very minimal learning effort.

Costs
Interface checkers are quite inexpensive to use, usually much less than the cost of a compilation.

References
(1) TEICHROW, D. and HERSHEY III, E.A., "PSL/PSA: A Computer-Aided Technique for Structured Documentation and Analysis of Information Processing Systems," *IEEE Transactions on Software Engineering*, SE-3, 1977 (41-48).

(2) BOEHM, B., McLEAN, R. and URFRIG, D., "Some Experience with Automated Aides to the Design of Large-scale Reliable Software," *IEEE Transactions on Software Engineering*, SE-1, 1975 (125-133).

(3) RYDER, B.G. and HALL, A.D., "The PFORT Verifier," *Computing Science Technical Report* #12, Bell Labs, March 1975.

(4) "Preliminary Ada Reference Manual," *SIGPLAN Notices*, Vol. 14, No. 6, part A, (June, 1979).

Mutation Analysis

Basic Features
Mutation analysis is a technique for detecting errors in a program and for determining the thoroughness with which the program has been tested. It entails studying the behavior of a large collection of programs which have been systematically derived from the original program.

Information Inputs
The basic input required by mutation analysis is the original source program and a collection of test data sets on which the program operates correctly, and which the user considers to adequately and thoroughly test the program.

Information Outputs

The ultimate output of mutation analysis is a collection of test data sets and good assurance that the collection is in fact adequate to thoroughly test the program. It is important to understand that the mutation analysis process may very well have arrived at this final state only after having exposed program errors and inadequacies in the original test data set collection. Hence, it is not unreasonable to consider errors detected, new program understanding, and additional test data sets to also be information outputs of the mutation analysis process.

Outline of Method

The essential approach taken in the mutation analysis of a program is to produce from the program a large set of versions, each derived from a trivial transformation of the original, and to subject each version to testing by the given collection of test data sets. Because of the nature of the transformations, it is expected that the derived versions will be essentially different programs from the original. Thus, the testing regimen should demonstrate that each is in fact different. Failure to to so invites suspicion that the collection of test data sets is inadequate. This usually leads to greater understanding of the program and either the detection of errors or an improved collection of test data sets, or both.

A central feature of mutation analysis is the mechanism for creating the program mutations—the derived versions of the original program. The set of mutations which is generated and tested is the set of all programs which differ from the original only in a small number (generally 1 or 2) of textual details, such as a change in an operator, variable or constant. Research appears to indicate that larger numbers of changes contribute little or no aditional diagnostic power.

The basis for this procedure is the "Competent Programmer" assumptions which state that program errors are not random phenomena, but rather result from lapses of human memory or concentration. Thus, an erroneous program should be expected to differ from the correct one only in a small number of details. Hence, if the original program is incorrect, then the set of all programs created by making a small number of the small textual changes just described should include the correct program. A thorough collection of test data sets would reveal behavioral differences between the original, incorrect program and the derived correct one.

Hence, mutation analysis entails determining whether each mutant behaves differently from the original. If so, the mutant is considered incorrect. If not, the mutant must be studied carefully. It is entirely possible that the mutant is in fact functionally equivalent to the original program. If so, its identical behaior is clearly benign. If not, the mutant is highly significant, as it certainly indicates an inadequacy in the collection of test data sets. It may, furthermore, indicate an error in the original program which previously went undetected because of inadequate testing. Mutation analysis facilitates the detection of such errors by automatically raising the probability of each such error and then demanding justification for concluding that each has not in fact been committed. Most mutations quickly manifest different behavior under exposure to any reasonable test data set collection, and thereby demonstrate the absence of the error corresponding to the mutation by which they were created. This forces detailed attention on those mutants which behave identically to the original and thus forces attention on any actual errors.

If all mutations of the original program reveal different execution behavior, then the program is considered to be adequately tested and correct within the limits of the "Competent Programmer" assumption.

Example

Consider the Fortran program, figure 23.10, which counts the number of negative and non-negative numbers in array A:

```
SUBROUTINE COUNT (A, NEG, NONNEG)
DIMENSION A(5)
NEG = 0
NONNEG = 0
DO 10 I = 1,5

IF (A(I).GT.0) NONNEG = NONNEG + 1
IF (A(I).LT.0) NEG = NEG + 1

10   CONTINUE
RETURN
END
```

Figure 23.10 Subroutine Count

and the collection of test data sets produced by initializing A in turn to:

I	II	III
1	1	−1
−2	2	−2
3	3	−3
−4	4	−4
5	5	−5

Mutants might be produced based upon the following alterations:

a. Change an occurrence of any variable to any other variable, e.g.,

A to I
NONNEG to NEG
I to NEG
.
.
.

b. Change an occurrence of a constant to another constant which is close in value:

263

e.g.,

1 to 0

0 to 1

0 to − 1

1 to 2

c. Change an occurrence of an operator to another operator:

e.g.,

NEG + 1 to NEG*1

NEG + 1 to NEG − 1

A(I).GT.0 to A(I).GE.0

A(I).LT.0 to A(I).NE.0

Thus, the set of all "single alteration" mutants would consist of all programs containing exactly one of the above changes. The set of all "double alteration" mutants would consist of all programs containing a pair of the above changes.

Clearly many such mutations are radically different and would quickly manifest obviously different behavior. For example, in changing variable I to A (or vice versa) the program is rendered uncompilable by most compilers. Similarly changing "NEG = 0" to "NEG = 1" causes a different outcome for test case I.

Significantly, changing A(I)GT.0 to A(I).GE.0 or A(I).LT.0 to A(I).LE.0 produces no difference in run-time behavior on any of the three test data sets. This rivets attention on these mutants, and subsequently on the issue of how to count zero entries. One rapidly realizes that the collection of test data sets was inadequate in that it did not include any zero input values. Had it included one, it would have indicated that:

IF (A(I).GT.0) NONNEG = NONNEG + 1 should have been

IF (A(I).GE.0) NONNEG = NONNEG + 1.

Thus, mutation analysis has pointed out both this error and this weakness in the collection of test data sets. After changing the program and collection, all mutants will behave differently strongly raising our confidence in the correctness of the program.

Effectiveness

Mutation analysis can be an effective technique for detecting errors, but it must be understood that it requires combining an insightful human with good automated tools. Even then it must be understood that it is a reliable technique for demonstrating the absence only if all possible mutation errors (i.e., those involving alteration, interchanging, or omission of operators, variables, etc.) are examined.

The need for good tools is easily understood when one realizes that any program has an enormous number of mutations, each of which must be generated, exercised by the test data sets, and evaluated. On the surface, this would appear to entail thousands of edit runs, compilations and executions. Clever tools have been built, however, which operate off a special internal representation of the original program. This representation is readily and efficiently transformed into the various mutations, and also serves as the basis for very rapid simulation of the mutants' executions, thereby avoiding the need for compilation and loading of each mutant.

This tool set still does not bypass the need for humans, however. Humans must still carry out the job of scrutinizing mutants which behave identically to the original program in order to determine whether the mutant is equivalent or whether the collection of test data sets is inadequate.

At the end of a successful mutation analysis, many errors may have been uncovered, and the collection of test data sets has certainly been made very thorough. Whether the absence of errors has been established, however, must be considered relative to the "Competent Programmer" assumption. Under this assumption, clearly all errors of mutation are detectable by mutation analysis; thus, the absence of diagnostic messages or findings indicates the absence of these errors. Mutation analysis cannot, however, assure the absence of errors which cannot be modeled as mutations.

Applicability

Mutation analysis is apparently applicable to any algorithmic solution specification. As previously indicated, it can only be considered effective when supported by a body of sophisticated tools. Tools enabling analysis of Fortran and COBOL source text exist. There is, furthermore, no reason why tools for other coding languages, as well as algorithmic design languages, could not be built.

Learning

This technique requires the potential mutation analyst to become familiar with the philosophy and goals of this novel approach. In addition it appears that the more familiar the analyst is with the subject algorithmic solution specifications, the more effective the analyst will be. This is because the analyst may well have to analyze a collection of test data sets to determine how to augment it, and may have to analyze two programs to determine whether they are equivalent.

Costs

In view of the previous discussion, it is important to recognize that significant amounts of human analyst time are likely to be necessary to do mutation analysis. The computer time required is not likely to be excessive if the sophisticated tools described earlier are available. The interested reader is urged to consult the following references for explanation of this.

References

(1) DEMILLO, R.A., LIPTON, R.J. and SAYWARD, F.G., "Program Mutation: A New Approach to Program Testing," *Infotech State-of-the-Art Report on Software Testing*, V.2, INFOTECH/SRA, 1979, pp. 107-127.

(2) LIPTON, R.J. and SAYWARD, F.G., "The Status of Research on Program Mutation," *Digest of the Workshop on Software Testing and Test Documentation*, Fort Lauderdale, Fla. 1978, pp. 355-373.

Software Validation, Verification, Testing, and Documentation

Peer Review

Basic Features

A peer review is a process by which project personnel perform a detailed study and evaluation of code, documentation, or specification. The term peer review refers to product evaluations which are conducted by individuals of equal rank, responsibility, or of similar experience and skill. There are a number of review techniques which fall into the overall category of a peer review. Code reading, round-robin reviews, walkthroughs and inspections are examples of peer reviews which differ in formality, participant roles and responsibilities, output produced and input required.

Information Input

The input to a particular peer review will vary slightly depending on which form of peer review is being conducted. In general, each of the forms of peer review require that some sort of review package is assembled and distributed. This package commonly contains a summary of the requirement(s) which are the basis for the product being reviewed. Other common imputs are differentiated by the stage of the life-cycle currently in process. For example, input to a peer review during the coding phase would consist of program listings, design specifications, programming standards and a summary of results from the design peer review previously held on the same product. Common input to particular forms of peer review are described below. (A summary of the methodology for each of these reviews appears in Section 5.)

   a. Code-Reading Review
       Component requirements
       Design specifications
       Program listings
       Programming standards
   b. Round-Robin Reviews
       Component requirements
       Design or code specifications
       Program listings (if during coding phase)
   c. Walkthrough
       Component requirements
       Design or code specifications
       Program listings (if coding phase walkthrough)
       Product standards
       Back-up documentation (i.e., flowcharts, HIPO charts, data dictionaries, etc.)
       Question list (derived by participants prior to review)

d. Inspections

> Component requirements
> Design or code specifications
> Program listings (if during coding phase)
> Product standards
> Back-up documentation
> Checklist (containing descriptions of particular features to be evaluated)

Information Output

The output from a peer review varies by form of review. One output common to each form of a peer review is a decision or consensus about the product under review. This is usually in the form of a group approval of the product as is, an approval with recommended modifications, or a rejection (and rescheduled review date).

Specific output from peer reviews described in Section 5 are as follows:

a. Code Reading Review and Round-Robin Review

> Informal documentation of detected problems
> Recommendation to accept or reject reviewed product
> Discrepancy List

b. Walkthrough

> Action List (formal documentation of problems)
> Walkthrough Form (containing review summary and group decision)

c. Inspection

> Inspection Schedule and Memo (defining individual roles, responsibilities, agenda and schedule)
> Problem Definition Set
> Summary report (documenting error correction status and related statistics on the errors)
> Management report (describing errors, problems and component status)

Outline of Method

The peer review methodology and participant responsibilities vary by form of review. Summaries of these methodologies are provided in the later part of this section. However, there are a few features common to each methodology.

For example, most peer reviews are not attended by management. (An exception is made in circumstances where the project manager is also a designer, coder or tester—usually on very small projects.) The presence of management tends to inhibit participants, since they feel that they are personally being evaluated. This would be contrary to the intent of peer reviews—that of studying the product itself.

Another common feature is the assembly and distribution of project review materials prior to the conduct of the peer review. This allows participants to spend some amount of time reviewing the data to become better prepared for the review.

At the end of most peer reviews the group arrives at a decision about the status of the review product. This decision is usually communicated to management.

Most reviews are conducted in a group organization as opposed to individually by participants or by the project team itself. While this may seem an obvious feature, it bears some discussion. Most organizations doing software development and/or maintenance employ some variation of a team approach. Some team organizations are described below.

> Conventional Team—A senior programmer directs the efforts of one or more less experienced programmers.

> Egoless Team—Programmers who are of about equal experience share product responsibilities.

> Chief Programmer Team—A highly qualified senior programmer leads the efforts of other team members for which specific roles and responsibilities have been assigned (i.e., back-up programmer, secretary, librarian, etc.).

The group which participates in the peer review is not necessarily the same as the team organized to manage and complete the software product. The review group is likely to be composed of a subset of the project team plus other individuals as required by the form of review being held and the stage of the lifecycle in process. The benefits of peer reviews are unlikely to be attained if the group acts separately, without some designated responsibilities. Some roles commonly used in review groups are described below. These roles are not *all* employed in any one review but represent a list.

> Group/Review leader—the individual designated by management with planning, detecting, organizing and coordinating responsibilities. Usually has responsibilities after the review to ensure that recommendations are implemented.

> Designer—the individual responsible for the specification of the product and a plan for its implementation.

> Implementer—the individual responsible for developing the product according to the plan detailed by the designer.

> Tester—the individual responsible for testing the product as developed by the implementer.

> Coordinator—the individual designated with planning, directing, organizing and coordinating responsiblities.

> Producer—the individual whose product is under review.

> Recorder—the individual responsible for documenting the review activities during the review.

> User Representative—the individual responsible for ensuring that the user's requirements are addressed.

Standards Representative—the individual responsible for ensuring that product standards are conformed to.

Maintenance Representative—the individual who will be responsible for updates or corrections to the installed product.

Others—individuals with specialized skills or responsiblities which contribute during the peer review.

While the forms of peer reviews have some similarities and generally involve designation of participant roles and responsibilities, they are different in application. The remainder of this section will summarize the application methods associated with the forms of peer reviews previously introduced.

Code Reading Review   Code reading is line-by-line study and evaluation of program source code. It is generally performed on source code which has been compiled and is free of syntax errors. However, some organizations practice code reading on uncompiled source listings or hand written code on coding sheets in order to remove syntax and logic errors prior to code entry. Code reading is commonly practiced on top-down, structured code and becomes cost ineffective when performed on unstructured code.

The optimum size of the code reading review team is three to four. The producer sets up the review and is responsible for team leadership. Two or three programmer/analysts are selected by the producer based upon their experience, responsibilities with interfacing programs, or other specialized skill.

The producer distributes the review input about two days in advance. During the review the producer and the reviewers go through each line of code checking for features which will make the program more readable, usable, reliable and maintainable. Two types of code reading may be performed: reading for understanding and reading for verification. Reading for understanding is performed when the reader desires an overall appreciation of how the program module works, its structure, what functions it performs, and whether it follows established standards. Assuming that figure 23.11 depicts the structure of a program component, a reviewer reading for understanding would review the modules in the the following order: 1.0, 2.0, 2.1, 2.2, 3.0, 3.1, 3.2, 3.3.

In contrast to this top-to-bottom approach, reading for verification implies a bottom-up review of the code. The component depicted above would be perused in the following order: 3.3, 3.2, 3.1, 3.0, 2.2, 2.1, 2.0, 1.0. In this manner it is possible to produce a dependency list detailing parameters, control switches, table pointers, and internal and external variables used by the component. The list can then be used to ensure hiearchical consistency, data availability, variable initiation, etc. Reviewers point out any problems or errors detected while reading for understanding or verification during the review.

The team then makes an informal decision about the acceptability of the code product and may recommend changes. The producer notes suggested modifications

Software Validation, Verification, Testing, and Documentation

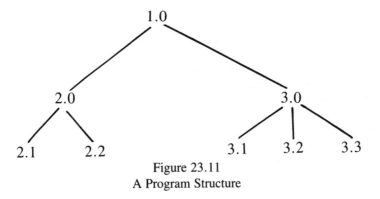

Figure 23.11
A Program Structure

and is responsible for all changes to the source code. Suggested changes are evaluated by the producer and need not be implemented if the producer determines that they are invalid.

There is no mechanism to ensure that change is implemented or to follow up on the review.

Round-Robin Review   A round-robin review is a peer review where each participant is given an equal and similar share of the product being reviewed to study, present, and lead in its evaluation.

A round-robin review can be given during any phase of the product lifecycle and is also useful for documentation review. In addition, there are variations of the round-robin review which incorporate some of the best features from other peer review forms but continue to use the alternating review leader approach. For example, during a round-robin inspection, each item on the inspection checklist is made the responsibility of alternating participants.

The common number of people involved in this type of peer review is four to six. The meeting is scheduled by the producer, who also distributes some high level documentation. The producer will either be the first review leader or will assign this responsibility to another participant. The temporary leader will guide the other participants (who may be implementers, designers, testers, users, maintenance representatives, etc.) through the first unit of work. This unit may be a module, paragraph, line of code, inspection item, or other unit of manageable size. All participants (including the leader) have the opportunity to comment on the unit before the next leader begins the evaluation of the next unit. The leaders are responsible for noting major comments raised about their piece of work. At the end of the review all the major comments are summarized and the group decides whether or not to approve the product. No formal mechanism for review follow up is used.

Walkthroughs   This type of peer review is more formal than the code reading review or round-robin review. Distinct roles and responsibilities are assigned prior to review. Prereview preparation is greater, and a more formal approach to problem documentation is stressed. Another key feature of this review is that it is presented by the producer. The most common walkthroughs are those held during design and code, yet recently they are being applied to specifications documentation and test results.

The producer schedules the review and assembles and distributes input. In most cases the producer selects the walkthrough participants (although sometimes this is done by management) and notifies them of their roles and responsibilities. The walkthrough is usually conducted with less than seven participants and lasts not more than 2 hours. If more time is needed a break must be given or the product should be reduced in size. Roles usually included in a walkthrough are producer, coordinator, recorder, and representatives of user, maintenance and standards organizations.

The review is opened by the coordinator, yet the producer is responsible for leading the group through the product. In the case of design and code walkthrough, the producer simulates the operation of the component, allowing each participant to comment based upon his area of specialization. A list of problems is kept and at the end of the review each participant signs the list or other walkthrough form indicating whether the product is accepted as-is, accepted with recommended changes, or rejected. Suggested changes are made at the discretion of the producer. There is no formal means of follow up on the review comments. However, if the walkthrough review is used for products as they evolve during the lifecycle (i.e., specification, design, code and test walkthrough), comments from past reviews can be discussed at the start of the next review.

Inspections Inspections are the most formal, commonly used form of peer review. The key feature of an inspection is that it is driven by the use of checklists to facilitate error detection. These checklists are updated as statistics indicate that certain types of error are occurring more or less frequently than in the past. The most commonly held types of inspections are conducted on the product design and code, although inspections may be used during any lifecycle phase. Inspections should be short since they are often quite intensive. This means that the product component to be reviewed must be of small size. Specifications or design which will result in 50-100 lines of code are normally manageable. This translates into an inspection of 15 minutes to 1 hour, although complex components may require as much as 2 hours. In any event, inspections of more than 2 hours are generally less effective and should be avoided. Two or three days prior to the inspection the producer assembles input and gives it to the coordinator for distribution. Participants are expected to study and make comments on the materials prior to the review.

The review is lead by a participant other than the producer. Generally, the individual who will have the greatest involvement in the next phase of the product lifecycle is designated as reader. For example, a requirements inspection would likely be lead by a designer, a design review by an implementer, and so forth. The exception to this occurs for a code inspection which is lead by the designer. The inspection is organized and coordinated by an individual designated as the group leader or coordinator.

The reader goes through the product component, using the checklist as a means to identify common types of errors as well as standards violations. A primary goal of an inspection is to identify items which can be modified to make the component more understandable, maintainable, or usable. Participants (identified earlier in this section) discuss any issues which they identified in preinspection study.

At the end of the inspection an accept/reject decision is made by the group and the coordinator summarizes all the errors and problems detected and provides this list to all participants. The individual whose work was under review (designer, implementer, tester, etc.) uses the list to make revisions to the component. When revisions are implemented, the coordinator and producer go through a minireview using the problem list as a checklist.

The coordinator then completes Management and Summary Reports. The Summary report is used to update checklists for subsequent inspections.

Example

The following is an example describing a code reading review.

Three days prior to estimated completion of coding, the producer of a program component begins preparation for a code reading review. The component is composed of 90 lines of FORTRAN code and associated comments. The producer obtains copies of the source listing, and requirements and design specifications for the component and distributes them to three peers, notifying them of the review date and place.

Each reviewer reads the code for general understanding, reviewing a major function and its supporting functions prior to reviewing the next major function.

One reviewer notes an exception to the programming standards. Another thinks that the data names are not meaningful. The third has found several comments which inaccurately represent the function they describe. Each reviewer makes a note of these points as well as any comments about the structure of the component. Next, the requirements are studied to ensure that each requirement is addressed by the component. It appears that the requirements have all been met.

The code reading review is led by the producer. After a brief description of the component and its interfaces, the producer leads the reviewers through the code. Rather than progressing through the component from top to bottom, the decision is made to perform code-reading from the bottom up. This form of code-reading is used to verify the component's correctness (see section 5).

As the code is being perused, one of the reviewers is made responsible for keeping a dependency list. As each variable is defined, referenced, or modified, a notation is made on the list.

The verification code reading uncovers the use of a variable prior to its definition. This error is documented on a error list by the producer. In addition, each of the problems detected earlier during the code reading (as performed by each individual) is discussed and documented.

At the end of the review, the error list is summarized to the group by the producer. Since none of the problems are major, the participants agree to accept the code with the agreed to minor modifications. The producer then uses the error/problem list for reference when making modifications to the component.

Effectiveness
Studies have been conducted which identify the following qualitative benefits of the forms of peer reviews.

higher status visibility,

decreased debugging time,

early detection of design and analysis errors which would be much more costly to correct in later development phases,

identification of design or code inefficiencies,

ensuring adherence to standards,

increased program readability,

increased user satisfaction,

communication of new ideas or technology,

increased maintainability.

Little data is available which identifies the quantitative benefits attributable to the use of a particular form of peer review. However, one source estimates that the number of errors in production programs was reduced by a factor of ten by utilizing walkthroughs. Another source estimates that a project employing inspections achieved 23% higher programmer productivity than with walkthroughs. No data was available indicating the amount of increased programmer productivity attributable to the inspections alone.

Applicability
Peer reviews are applicable to large or small projects during all development phases and are not limited by project type or complexity.

Learning
None of the peer reviews discussed require extensive training to implement. They do require familiarity with the concept and methodology involved. Experience has shown that peer reviews are most successful when the individual with responsibility for directing the review is knowledgable about the process and its intended results.

Costs
The reviews require no special tools or equipment. The main cost involved is that of human resources. If the reviews are conducted in accordance with the resource guidelines expressed in most references, the cost depends upon the number of re-

views required. Most references suggest that peer reviews should be no longer than 2 hours, preferrably ½ to 1 hour. Preparation time can amount to as little as ½ hour and should not require longer than ½ day per review.

References

(1) "Code Reading Structured Walk-Throughs and Inspections," IBM IPTO Support Group, World Trade System Center, Postbus 60, Zoetenmeer, Netherlands, March 1976.

(2) FAGEN, M.E., "Design and Code Inspections to Reduce Errors in Program Development," *IBM Systems Journal*, No.3,1976.

(3) YOURDON, E., "Structured Walkthroughs," Yourdon Inc., 1977.

(4) FREEDMAN, D.P. and WEINBERG, G.M., "Ethno—Technical Review Handbook," 1977, Ethnotech, Inc.

(5) DALY, E.B., "Management of Software Development," *IEEE Transactions on Software Engineering*, May 1977.

(6) SHNEIDERMAN, Ben, "Software Psychology—Human Factors in Computer and Information Systems," Winthrop Publishing, 1980.

Physical Units Checking

Basic Features

Many (scientific, engineering, and control) programs perform computations whose results are interpreted in terms of physical units, such as feet, meters, watts, and joules. Physical units checking enables specification and checking of units in program computations, in a manner similar to dimensional analysis. Operations between variables which are not commensurate, such as adding gallons and feet, are detected.

Information Input

Units checking requires three things to be specified within a program: 1) the set of elementary units used (such as feet, inches, acres), 2) relationships between the elementary units (such as feet = 12 inches, acre = 43,560 square feet), and 3) the association of units with program variables. The programing language used must support such specifications, or the program must be preprocessed by a units checker.

Information Output

The information output depends upon the specific capabilities of the language processor or preprocessor. At a minimum, all operations involving variables which are not commensurate are detected and reported. If variables are commensurate, but not identical (i.e., they are the same type of quantity, such as units of length, but one requires application of a scaler multiplier to place it in the same units as the other), the system may insert the required multiplication into the code, or may only report what factor must be applied by the programmer.

Introduction to Technique and Tool Descriptions

Outline of Method

The specification of the input items is the extent of the actions required by the user. Some systems may allow the association of a units expression with an expression within the actual program. Thus, one may write LOTSIZE (LENGTH * WIDTH * square feet) as a boolean expression, where the product of LENGTH and WIDTH must be in units of square feet. The process of ensuring that LENGTH * WIDTH is in square feet is the responsibility of the processing system.

Example

A short program in Pascal-like notation is shown for computing the volume and total surface area of a right circular cylinder. The program requires as input the radius of the circular base and the height of the cylinder. Because of peculiarities in the usage environment of the program, the radius is specified in inches, the height in feet; volume is required in cubic feet, and the surface area in acres. Several errors are present in the program, all of which would be detected by the units checker.

In the following, comments are made explaining the program, the errors it contains, and how they would be detected. The comments are keyed by line number to the program.

Line Number	Comment
2	All variables in the program which are quantities will be expressed in terms of these basic units.
3	These are the relationships between the units known to the units checker.
5–10	Variable radius is in units of inches, height is in units of feet, and so forth.
12	Input values are read into variables radius and height.
13	Lateral surface must be expressed in square feet. (RADIUS/12) is in feet, and can be so verified by the checker.
15	Lateral-surface and top-surface are both expressed in square feet, thus their sum is in square feet, also. Area is expressed in acres, however, and the checker will issue a message to the effect that though the two sides are commensurate the conversion factor of 43,560 was omitted from the right side of the assignment.
16	The checker will detect that the two sides of the assignment are not commensurate. The right side is in units of feet quadrupled, the left is in feet cubed.

```
(1)    program cylinder (input, output);
(2)    elementary units inches, feet, acre;
```

275

```
(3)      units relationships feet = 12 inches; acre = 43,560 feet**2;
(4)      constant pi = 3.1415927
(5)      var radius (inches),
(6)          height (feet),
(7)          volume (feet**3),
(8)          area (acre),
(9)          lateral-surface (feet**2),
(10)         top-surface (feet**2): real;
(11)     begin
(12)         read (radius, height);
(13)         lateral-surface : = 2*PI*(radius/12)*height;
(14)         top-surface : = PI* (radius/12)**2
(15)         area : = lateral-surface + 2* top-surface;
(16)         volume : = PI *((radius**3)*height);
(17)         write (area, volume);
(18)     end;
```

Effectiveness

The effectiveness of units checking is limited only by the capabilities of the units processor.

Simple units checkers may only be able to verify that two variables are commensurate, but not determine if proper conversion factors have been applied. That is, a relationship such as 12 inches = feet may not be fully used in checking the computations in a statement, such as line 13 of the example. There we asserted that (radius/12) would be interpreted as converting inches to feet. The checker may not support this kind of analysis, however, to avoid ambiguities with expressions such as "one-twelfth of the radius."

Applicability

Certain application areas, such as engineering and scientific, often deal with physical units. In others, however, it may be difficult to find analogies to physical units. In particular, if a program deals only in one type of quantity, such as dollars, the technique would not be useful.

Units checking can be performed during all stages of software development, beginning with requirements specifications.

Learning

Dimensional analysis is commonly taught in first year college physics on statics; conversion from English to metric units is common throughout society. Direct application of these principles in programming, using a units checker, should require no additional training beyond understanding the capabilities of the specific units checker and the means for specifying units-related information.

Cost

If the units checking capabilities are incorporated directly in a compiler its usage cost should be negligible. If a preprocessor is used, such systems are typically much slower than a compiler (perhaps operating at 1/10 compilation speed), but only a single analysis of the program is required. The analysis is only repeated when the program is changed.

References

(1) KARR, Michael and LOVEMAN III, David B., "Incorporation of Units into Programming Languages," *CACM*, Vol. 21, No.5, pp. 385-391, May 1978.

Regression Testing

Basic Features

Regression testing is a technique whereby spurious errors caused by system modifications or corrections may be detected.

Information Input

Regression testing requires that a set of system test cases be maintained and available throughout the entire life of the system. The test cases should be complete enough so that all of the system's functional capabilities are thouroughly tested. If available, acceptance tests should be used to form the base set of tests.

In addition to the individual test cases themselves, detailed descriptions or samples of the actual expected output produced by each test case must also be supplied and maintained.

Information Output

The output from regression testing is simply the output produced by the system from the execution of each of the individual test cases. When the output from previous acceptance tests has been kept, additional output from regression testing should be a comparison of the before and after executions.

Outline of Method

Regression testing is the process of retesting the system in order to detect errors which may have been caused by program changes. The tecnique requires the utilization of a set of test cases which have been developed (ideally, using functional testing) to test all of the system's functional capabilities. If an absolute determination of portions of the system which can potentially be affected by a given change can be made, then only those portions need to be tested. Associated with each test case is a description or sample of the correct output for that test case. When the tests have been executed, the actual output is compared with the expected output for correctness. As errors are detected during the actual operation of the system which were not detected by regression testing, a test case which could have uncovered the error should be constructed and included with the existing test cases.

Although not required, tools can be used to aid in performing regression testing. Automatic test harnesses can be used to assist the managing of test cases and in controlling the test execution. File comparators can often be useful in verifying actual output with expected output. Assertion processors are also useful in verifying the correctness of the output for a given test.

Example

Application   A transaction processing system contains a dynamic data field editor which provides a variety of input/output field editing capabilities. Each transaction is comprised of data fields as specified by a data element dictionary entry. The input and output edit routine used by each data field is specified by a fixed identifier contained in a data field descriptor in the dictionary entry. When a transaction is input, each field is edited by the appropriate input editor routine as specified in the dictionary entry. Output editing consists of utilizing output editor routines to format the output.

Error   An input edit routine to edit numeric data fields was modified to perform a fairly restrictive range check needed by a particular transaction program. Current system documentation indicated that this particular edit routine was only being used by that single transaction program. However, the documentation was not up-to-date in that another, highly critical, transaction program also used the routine, often with data falling outside of the range check needed by the other program.

Error Discovery   Regression testing would uncover the error given that a sufficient set of functional tests were used for performing the testing. If only the transaction program for which the modification was made were tested, the error would not have been discovered until actual operation.

Effectiveness
The effectiveness of the technique depends upon the quality of the data used for performing the regression testing. If functional testing, i.e., tests based on the functional requirements, is used to create the test data, the effectiveness is highly effective. The burden and expense associated with the technique, particularly for small changes, can appear to be prohibitive. It is, however, often quite straightforward to determine which functions can be potentialy affected by a given change. In such cases, the extent of the testing can be reduced to a more tractable size.

278

Applicability
This method is generally applicable.

Learning
No special training is required in order to apply the technique. If tools are used in support of regression testing, however, knowledge of their use will be required. Moreover, successful application of the technique will require establishment of procedures and the management control necessary to ensure adherence to those procedures.

Costs
Since testing is required as a result of system modifications anyway, no additional burden need result because of the method (assuming that only the necesary functional capabilities are retested). The use of tools, however, to support it could increase the cost but it would also increase its effectiveness.

References
(1) PANZL, David J., "Automatic Software Test Drivers," *Computer*, April 1978.
(2) FISHER, K.F., "A Test Case Selection Method for the Validation of Software Maintenance Modification," *IEEE COMPSAC*, 1977.
(3) FISHER, K.F., RAJI, F., and CHRUSCICK, A., "A Methodology for Re-testing Modified Software," *National Telecommunications Conference*, New Orleans, LA., Nov. 1981.

Requirements Analyzer

Basic Features
The requirements for a system will normally be specified using some formal language which may be graphical and/or textual in nature. A requirements analyzer can check for syntactical errors in the requirements specifications and then produce a useful analysis of the relationships between system inputs, outputs, processes, and data. Logical inconsistencies or ambiguities in the specifications can also be identified by the requirements analyzer.

Information Input
The form and content of the input will vary greatly for different requirements languages. Generally, there will be requirements regarding what the system must produce (outputs) and what types of inputs it must accept. There will usually be specifications describing the types of processes or functions which the system must apply to the inputs in order to produce the outputs. Additional requirements may concern timing and volume of inputs, outputs, and processes as well as performance mea-

sures regarding such things as response time and reliability of operations. The form of the inputs to the requiements analyzer is specified by the requirements specification language and varies considerably for different languages. In some cases all inputs are textual, whereas some languages utilize all graphical inputs from a display terminal (e.g., boxes might represent processes and arrows between the boxes might represent information flow).

Information Output

Nearly all analyzers produce error reports showing syntactical errors or inconsistencies in the specifications. For example, the syntax may require that the outputs from a process at one level of system decomposition must include all outputs from a decomposition of that process at a more detailed level. Similarly, for each system output there should be a process which produces that output. Any deviations from these rules would result in error diagnostics.

Each requirements analyzer produces a representation of the system which indicates static relationships among system inputs, outputs, processes, and data. Some analyzers also represent dynamic relationships and provide an analysis of them. This may be a precedence relationship, e.g., process A must execute before process B. It may also include information regarding how often a given process must execute in order to produce the volume of output required. Some analyzers produce a detailed representation of relationships between different data items. This output can sometimes be used for developing a data base for the system. A few requirements analyzers go even further and provide a mechanism for simulating the requirements using the generated system representation including the performance and timing requirements.

Outline of Method

The user must provide the requirements specifications as input for the analyzer. The analyzer carries out the analysis in an automated manner and provides it to the user who must then interpret the results. Often the user can request selected types of outputs, e.g., an alphabetical list of all the processes or a list of all the data items of a given type. Some analyzers can be used either interactively or in a batch mode. Once the requirements specifications are considered acceptable, a few analyzers provide the capability for simulating the requirements. It is necessary that the data structure and data values generated from the requirements specifications be used as input to the simulation, otherwise the simulation may not truly represent the requirements.

Example

Suppose that a process called PROCESS B produces two files named H2 and H3 from an input file name M2. (The purposes of the files are irrelevant to the discussion.) Suppose also that PROCESS D accepts Files H2 and H3 as input and produces Files J3 and J6 output. In addition, PROCESS G is a subprocess of PRO-

CESS D and it accepts File H3 as input and produces File J6. Then the pseudo specification statements, figure 23.12, might be used to describe the requirements. (Note that these requirements are close to design, but this is often the case.)

```
                 PROCESS B
                   .
                   .
                   .
                 USES FILE M2
                 PRODUCES FILES H2, H3

                 PROCESS D
                   .
                   .
                   .
                 USES FILES H2, H3
                 PRODUCES FILES J3, J6

                 PROCESS G
                   .
                   .
                   .
                 SUBPROCESS OF PROCESS D
                 USES FILE H3
                 PRODUCES FILE J6
```

Figure 23.12
Requirements Specification Statements

The requirements specifications imply a certain precedence of operations, e.g., PROCESS D cannot execute until PROCESS B has produced files H2 and H3. Detailed descriptions of what each process does would normally be included, but are omitted for brevity. The requirements analyzer would probably generate a diagnostic since the statement for PROCESS D fails to indicate that it includes the subprocess G. A diagnostic would also be generated unless there are other statements which specify that file M2, needed by PROCESS B, is available as an existing file or else is produced by some other process. Similarly, other processes must be specified which use files J3 and J6 as input unless they are specified as files to be output from the system. Otherwise, additional diagnostics would be generated. It can be seen that some of the checks are similar to data flow analysis for a computer program. However, for large systems the analysis of requirements becomes very complex if requirements for timing and performance are included, and if timing and volume analysis are to be carried out. (Volume analysis is concerned with such things as how often various processes must execute if the system is to accept and/or produce a specified volume of data in a single given period of time.)

Effectiveness

Some requirements analyzers are very effective for maintaining accurate requirements specifications. For large systems with a large number of requirements they are essential. On the other hand, most existing requirements analyzers are rather expensive to obtain and use, and they may not be cost effective for development of small systems.

Applicability

Requirements analyzers are applicable for use in developing most systems. They are particularly useful for analysis of requirements for large and complex systems.

Learning

Most requirements analyzers require a considerable amount of training of personnel.

Cost

Most requirements analyzers are expensive to obtain and use. They generally require a large amount of storage within a computer and so can only be used on large computers.

References

(1) ALFORD, Mack W., "A Requirements Engineering Methodology for Real-Time Processing Requirements," *TRW Software Series*, TRW-SS-76-07, Systems Engineering and Integration Division, September 1976.
(2) TEICHROEW, Daniel, "A Survey of Languages for Stating Requirements for Computer-Based Information Systems," *The University of Michigan, Proceedings of the Fall Joint Computer Conference*, 1972, pp. 1203-1224.

Requirements Tracing

Basic Features

Requirements tracing provides a means of verifying that the software of a system addresses each requirement of that system and that the testing of the software produces adequate and appropriate responses to those requirements.

Information Input

The information needed to perform requirements tracing consists of a set of system requirements and the software which embodies the capability to satisfy the requirements.

Introduction to Technique and Tool Descriptions

Information Output
The information output by requirements tracers is the correspondence found between the requirements of a system and the software that is intended to realize these requirements.

Outline of Method
Requirements tracing generally serves two major purposes. The first is to ensure that each specified requirement of a system is addressed by an identifiable element of the system software. The second is to ensure that the testing of that software produces results which are adequate responses in satisfying each of these requirements.

A common technique used to assist in making these assurances is the use of test evaluation matrices. These matrices represent a visual scheme of identifying which requirements of a system have been adequately and appropriately addressed and which have not. There are two basic forms of test evaluation matrices. The first form identifies a mapping that exists between the requirement specifications of a system and the modules of that system. This matrix determines whether each requirement is realized by some module in the system, and, conversely, whether each module is direcly associated with a specific system requirement. If the matrix reveals that a requirement is not addressed by any module, then that requirement has probably been overlooked in the software design activity. If a module does not correspond to any requirement of the system, then that module is superfluous to the system. In either case, the design of the software must be further scrutinized, and the system must be modified accordingly to effect an acceptable requirements-design mapping.

The second form of a test evaluation matrix provides a similar mapping, except the mapping exists between the modules of a system and the set of test cases performed on the system. This matrix determines which modules are invoked by each test case. Used with the previous matrix, it also determines which requirements will be demonstrated to be satisfied by the execution of a particular test case in the test plan. During actual code development, it can be used to determine which requirement specifications will relate to a particular module. In this way, it is possible to have each module print out a message during execution of a test indicating which requirement is referenced by the execution of this module. The code module itself may also contain comments about the applicable requirements.

If these matrices are to be used most effectively in a requirements tracing activity, the two matrices should be used together. The second matrix is built prior to software development. After the software has been developed and the test cases have been designed (based upon this matrix), it is necessary to determine whether the execution of the test plan will actually demonstrate satisfaction of the requirements of the software system. By analyzing the results of each test case, the first matrix can be constructed to determine the relationship that exists between the requirements and software reality.

Software Validation, Verification, Testing, and Documentation

The first matrix is mainly useful for analyzing the functional requirements of a system. However, the second matrix is also useful in analyzing the performance, interface, and design requirements of the system, in addition to the functional requirements. Both are often used in support of a more general requirements tracing activity, that of preliminary and critical design reviews. This is a procedure used to ensure verification of the traceability of all the above mentioned requirements to the design of the system. In addition to the use of test evaluation matrices, these design reviews may include the tracing of individual subdivisions in the software design document back to applicable specifications made in the requirements document. This is a constructive technique used to ensure verification of requirements traceability.

Example

Application   A new payroll system is to be tested. Among the requirements of this system is the specification that all employees of age 65 or older:
1. receive semi-retirement benefits, and
2. have their social security tax rate readjusted.

To ensure that these particular requirements are appropriately addressed in the system software, test evaluation matrices have been constructed and filled out for the system.

Error   An omission in the software causes the social security tax rate of individuals of age 65 or older to remain unchanged.

Error Discovery   The test evaluation matrices reveal that the requirement that employees of age 65 or older have their social security tax rate adjusted has not been addressed by the payroll program. No module in the system had been designed to respond to this specification. The software is revised accordingly to accommodate this requirement, and a test evaluation matrix is used to ensure that the added module is tested in the set of test cases for the system.

Effectiveness
Requirements tracing is a highly effective technique in discovering errors during the design and coding phases of software development. This technique has proven to be a valuable aid in verifying the completeness, consistency, and testability of software. If a system requirement is modified, it also provides much assistance in retesting software by clearly indicating which modules must be rewritten and retested. Requirements tracing can be a very effective technique in detecting errors early in the software development cycle which could otherwise prove to be very expensive if discovered later.

Introduction to Technique and Tool Descriptions

Applicability

This technique is generally applicable in large or small system testing and for all types of computing applications. However, if the system requirements themselves are not clearly specified and documented, proper requirements tracing can be very difficult to accomplish in any application.

Learning

Knowledge and a clear understanding of the requirements of the system is essential. More complex systems will result in a corresponding increase in required learning.

Costs

No special tools or equipment are needed to carry out this technique if done manually. The major cost in requirements tracing is that associated with human labor expended. Requirements tracing is often a feature of requirements analyzers which are expensive to obtain and use.

References

(1) "THREADS: A Functional Approach to Project Control," *Computer Sciences Corp.*, El Segundo, California, 1975.
(2) HETZEL, W.C., "An Experimental Analysis of Program Verification Methods," *Ph.D. Thesis*, University of North Carolina, 1976.

Software Monitors

Basic Features

These tools monitor the execution of a program in order to locate and identify possible areas of inefficiency in the program. Execution data is obtained while the program executes in its normal environment. At the end of execution, reports are generated by the monitor summarizing the resource usage of the program.

Information Input

Software monitors require as input the program source code to be executed and any data necessary for the program to run. Certain commands must also be provided by the user in specifying the information to be extracted by the monitor and in specifying the format of the generated output reports. These commands may specify:

what is to be measured (e.g., execution times, I/O usage, core usage, paging activity, program waits),

the specific modules to be monitored,

the frequency that data is to be extracted during program execution (sampling interval),

285

the titles, headings, content of each output report,

the units used to construct graphs,

whether the graphs are to be displayed as plots or histograms.

Information Output

The output of a software monitor is a set of one or more reports describing the execution characteristics of the program. Information that may be contained in these reports is given below.

A summary of all the sample counts made during data extraction, e.g., the number of samples taken where the program was executing instructions, waiting for the completion of an I/O event, or otherwise blocked from execution.

A summary of the activity of each load module.

An instruction location graph that gives the percentage of time spent for each group of instructions partitioned in memory.

A program timeline that traces the path of control through time.

A control passing summary that gives the number of times control is passed from one module to another.

A wait profile showing the number of waits encountered for each group of instructions.

A paging activity profile that displays pages-in and pages-out for each group of instructions.

This information is often represented in histograms and/or plotted graphs.

Outline of Method

Software monitors typically consist of two processing units. The first unit runs the program being monitored and collects data concerning the execution characteristics of the program. The second unit reads the collected data and generates reports from it.

A software monitor monitors a program by determining its status at periodic intervals. The period between samples is usually controlled through an elapsed interval timing facility of the operating system. Samples are taken from the entire address range addressable by the executing task. Each sample may contain an indication of the status of the program, the load module in which the activity was detected, and the absolute location of the instruction being executed. Small sample intervals increase sampling accuracy but result in a corresponding increase in the overhead required by the CPU.

The statistics gathered by the data extraction unit are collected and summarized in reports generated by the data analysis unit. References to program locations in these reports will be in terms of absolute addresses. However, in order to relate the absolute locations to source statements in the program, the reports also provide a means to locate in a compiler listing the source statement that corresponds to that instruction. In this way, sources of waits and program locations that use significant amounts of CPU time can be identified directly in the source code; any performance improvements to the program will occur at these identified statements.

Software monitors are similar to another tool used to monitor program execution, test coverage analyzers. Test coverage analyzers keep track of and report on the number of times that certain elementary program constructs in a program have been traversed during a sequence of tests. During the monitoring of a program, both tools count the frequency that certain events occur. After program execution, both generate reports summarizing the data collected. However, because these tools serve different functions, they are different in their techniques of gathering information and in the type of information each collects. Test coverage analyzers are used to measure the completeness of a set of program tests, while software monitors measure the resource usage of a program as a means of evaluating program efficiency. As an evaluation of program efficiency requires consideration of execution time expenditure, software monitors utilize a strict timing mechanism during the collection of data. This is absent in monitors such as test coverage analyzers which are not used to evaluate program performance.

Example

Application   A program that solves a set of simultaneous equations is constructed. The program first generates a set of coefficients and a right hand side for the system being solved. It then proceeds to solve the system and output the solution.

Error   In the set of calculations required to solve the system, a row of coefficients is divided by a constant and then subtracted from another row of coefficients. The divisions are performed within a nested DO-loop but should be moved outside the innermost loop, as the dividend and divisors within the loop do not change.

Error disovery   The performance of the program is evaluated through the use of a software monitor. Examination of the output reveals that the program spends almost 85% of its time in a particular address range. Further analysis shows that 16.65% of all CPU time is used by a single instruction. A compiler listing of the program is used to locate the source statement that generated this instruction, which is found to be the statement containing the division instruction. Once the location of the inefficiency is discovered, it is left to the programmer to determine whether and how the code can be optimized.

Effectiveness
Software monitors are valuable tools in identifying performance problems in a program. Their overall effectiveness, however, is dependent upon the quality of their use.

287

Software Validation, Verification, Testing, and Documentation

Applicability
Software monitors can be applied to any kind of program in any programming language.

Learning
There are no special learning requirements for the use of software monitors. In order to use the tools effectively, however, the input parameters to the monitor must be carefully selected in determining the most relevant reports to be generated. Once the areas of a program which are most inefficient have been identified, it requires skill to modify the program to improve its performance.

Costs
The largest cost in using a software monitor is that incurred by the CPU to extract the data during execution. In one implementation, extraction of data resulted in an increase of user program CPU time by 1% to 50%. Storage requirements also increase in order to provide memory for diagnostic tables and the necessary program modules of the tool.

References
(1) "Problem Program Evaluator (PPE) User Guide," Boole and Babbage, Inc., Sunnyvale, California, March, 1978.
(2) RAMAMOORTHY, C.V. and KIM, K.H., "Software Monitors Aiding Systematic Testing and Their Optional Placement," *Proceedings of the First National Conference on Software Engineering*, IEEE Catalog No. 75CH0992-8C, September, 1975.

Specification-Based Functional Testing

Basic Features
Functional testing can be used to generate system test data from the information in requirements and design specifications. It is used to test both the overall functional capabilities of a system and functions which originate during system design.

Information Input

Data Information   The technique requires the availability of detailed requirements and design specifications and, in particular, detailed descriptions of input data, files and data bases. Both the concrete and algebraic abstract properties of all data must be described. Concrete properties include type, value ranges and bounds, record structures, and bounds on file data structure and data base dimensions. Abstract properties include subclasses of data that correspond to different functional capabili-

288

ties in the system and subcomponents of compound data items that correspond to separate subfunctional activities in the system.

Function Information   The requirements and design specifications must also describe the different functions implemented in the system.

Requirements functions correspond to the overall functional capabilities of a system or to subfunctions which are visible at the requirements stage and are necessary to implement overall capabilities. Different overall functional capabilities correspond to conceptually distinct classes of operations that can be carried out using the system. Different kinds of subfunctions can also be identified. Process descriptions in structured specifications, for example, describe data transformations which are visible at requirements time and which correspond to requirements subfunctions. Requirements subfunctions also occur implicitly in data base schemata. Data base functions are used to reference, update and create data bases and files.

The designer of a system will have to invent both general and detailed functional constructs in order to implement the functions in requirements specifications. Structured design techniques are particularly useful for identifying and documenting design functions. Designs are represented as an abstract hiearchy of functions. The functions at the top of the hiearchy denote the overall functional capabilities of a program or system and may correspond to requirements functions. Functions at lower levels correspond to the functional capabilities required to implement the higher level functions. General design functions often correspond to modules or parts of programs which are identified as separate functions by comments. Detailed design functions may be invented during the programming stage of system development and may correspond to single lines of code.

Information Output

The output to be examined depends on the nature of the tested function. If it is a straight input/output function, then output values are examined. The testing of other classes of functions may involve the examination of the state of a data base or file.

Outline of Method

The basic idea in functional testing is to identify "functionally important" classes of data. The two most important classes of data are *extremal values* and *special values*. Different kinds of sets of data have different kinds of extremal values and different classes of special values must be used to test different kinds of functions.

Extremal Values   The simplest kinds of extremal values are associated with elementary data items. If a variable is constrained to take on values which lie in the range (a,b), then the extremal values are a and b. If a variable is constrained to take on values from a small set of discrete values then each of those values can be thought of as an extremal case.

Software Validation, Verification, Testing, and Documentation

The construction of extremal cases for data structures (e.g., group data items) can be more complicated. It is necessary to construct extremal values of both the component elementary parts of the data structure as well as its dimensions. The data structure can be treated as a single quantity. In this case, when it takes on an extremal value all of its elements take on that value. It is also possible to consider its components as a set of values in which one, more, or all of the components have extremal values. The construction of extremal values for files and data bases is similar to that for data structures. Files with extremal dimensions contain the smallest possible and largest possible number of records. If the records are variable sized they contain records of the smallest and largest dimensions.

Special Values There appear to be two kinds of special values that are important for data processing programs. The first is useful for testing functional capabilities in which data is moved around from one location to another, as in a transaction-update program. Functions of this type should be tested over distinct sets of data (i.e., values in different files, records, variables or data structure elements should be different) in order to detect the transfer of the incorrect data from the wrong source or into the wrong destination. The second kind of special data is useful for testing logical functional capabilities that carry out different operations on the basis of relationships between different data items. It is important to test functional capabilities of this type over special values such as those in which sets of data that enter into the comparison are all the same.

Additional kinds of special values are important for scientific programs or programs which do arithmetic calculations. They include zero, positive and negative values "close" to zero, and large negative and positive values.

Functional testing requires that tests be constructed in which the input data is extremal, non-extremal and special as well as tests that result in program output that is extremal, non-extremal or special.

Examples
Example 1: Testing of requirements functions

Application A computerized dating system was built in which a sequential file of potential dates was maintained. Each client for the service offered would submit a completed questionnaire which was used to find the five most compatible dates. Certain criteria had to be satisfied before any potential data was selected and it is possible that no date could be found for a client or less than five dates found.

Error An error in the file processing logic causes the program to select the last potential date in the sequential file whenever there is no potential date for a client.

Error Discovery The number of dates which are found for each client is a dimension of the output data and has extremal values 0 and 5. If the "find-a-date" functional capability of the system is tested over data for a client for which no date should exist then the presence of the error will be revealed.

Example 2: Testing of detailed design functions

Application The designer of the computerized dating system in Example 1 decided to process the file of potential dates for a client by reading in the records in sets of 50 records each. A simple function was designed to compute the number of record subsets.

Error The number of subsets function returns the value 2 when there are less than 50 records in the file.

Error Discovery The error will be discovered if the design function is tested over the extremal case for which it should generate the minimal output value 1. Note that this error is not revealed (except by chance) when the program is tested at the requirements specifications level. It will also not necessarily be revealed unless the code implementing the design function is tested independently and not in combination with the rest of the system.

Effectiveness
Studies have been carried out which indicate functional testing to be highly effective. Its use depends on specific descriptions of system input and output data and a complete list of all functional capabilities. The method is essentially manual and somewhat informal. If a formal language could be designed for describing all input and output data sets then a tool could be used to check the completeness of these descriptions. Automated generation of extremal, non-extremal and special cases might be difficult since no rigorous procedure has been developed for this purpose.

For many errors it is necessary to consider combinations of extremal, non-extremal and special values for "functionally related" input data variables. In order to avoid combinatorial explosions, combinations must be restricted to a small number of variables. Attempts have been made to identify important combinations (see references) but there are no absolute rules, only suggestions and guidelines.

Applicability
This method is generally applicable.

Learning
It is necessary to develop some expertise with the identification of extremal and special cases and to avoid the combinatorial explosions that may occur when combinations of extremal and special values for different data items are considered. It is also necessary to become skilled in the identification of specifications functions although this process is simplified if a systematic approach is followed for the representation of requirements and design.

Costs

The method requires no special tools or equipment and contains no hidden excessive tests.

References

(1) HOWDEN, William E., "Functional Program Testing," *IEEE Transactions on Software Engineering*, SE-7, March, 1980.

(2) HOWDEN, William E., "Functional Testing and Design Abstractions," *Journal of Systems and Software*, Vol. 1, 307-313, 1980.

(3) MYERS, Glenford, "The Art of Software Testing," Wiley-Interscience, New York, 1975.

Symbolic Execution

Basic Features

Symbolic execution is applied to paths through programs. It can be used to generate expressions which describe the cumulative effect of the computations which occur in a program path. It can also be used to generate a system of predicates describing the subset of the input domain which causes a specified path to be traversed. The user is expected to verify the correctness of the output which is generated by symbolic execution in the same way that output is verified which has been generated by executing a program over actual values. It is used as a basis for data flow analysis and proof of correctness.

Information Input

Source Code   The method requires the availability of the program source code.

Program Paths   The path or paths through the program which are to be symbolically evaluated must be specified. The paths may be specified directly by the user or, in some symbolic evaluation systems, selected automatically.

Input Values   Symbolic values must be assigned to each of the "input" variables for the path or paths which are to be symbolically evaluated. The user may be responsible for selecting these values or the symbolic evaluation system which is used may select them automatically.

Information Output

Values of Variables   The variables whose final symbolic values are of interest must be specified. Symbolic execution will result in the generation of expressions which describe the values of these variables in terms of the dummy symbolic values assigned to input variables.

System of Predicates   Each of the branch-predicates which occur along a program path constrains the input which causes that path to be followed. The symbolically evaluated system of predicates for a path describes the subset of the input domain that causes that path to be followed.

Outline of Method

Symbolic Execution   Symbolic values are symbols standing for sets of values rather than actual values. The symbolic execution of a path is carried out symbolically executing the sequence of assignment statements occurring in the path. Assignment statements are symbolically executed by symbolically evaluating the expressions on the right hand side of the assignment. The resulting symbolic value becomes the new symbolic value of the variable on the left hand side. An arithmetic or logical expression is symbolically executed by substituting the symbolic values of the variables in the expression for the variables.

The branch conditions or branch predicates which occur in conditional branching statements can be symbolically executed to form symbolic predicates. The symbolic system of predicates for a path can be constructed by symbolically executing both assignment statements and branch predicates during the symbolic execution of the path. The symbolic system of predicates consists of the sequences of symbolic predicates that are generated by the execution of the branch predicates.

Symbolic Execution Systems   All symbolic execution systems must contain facilities for: selecting program paths to be symbolically executed, symbolically executing paths, and generating the required symbolic output.

Three types of path selection techniques have been used: interactive, static and automatic. In the interactive approach, the symbolic execution system is constructed so that control returns to the user each time it is necessary to make a decision as to which branch to take during the symbolic execution of a program. In the static approach, the user specifies the paths he wants executed in advance. In the automatic approach, the symbolic execution system attempts to execute all those program paths having consistent symbolic system of predicates. A system of predicates is consistent if it has a solution.

The details of symbolic execution algorithms in different systems are largely technical. Symbolic execution systems may differ in other than technical details in the types of symbolic output they generate. Some systems contain, for example, facilities for solving systems of branch predicates. Such systems are capable of automatically generating test data for selected program paths (i.e., program input data which will cause the path to be followed when the program is executed over that data).

Software Validation, Verification, Testing, and Documentation

Example

Application A FORTRAN program called SIN was written to compute the sine function using the McLaurin series.

PREDICATES:

(X**3/6).GE.E
(X**5/120).GE.E
(X**7/5040).LT.E

SIN = ?SUM − (X**3/6) − (X**5/120)
Symbolic output for SIN

Figure 23.13
Symbolic Execution Example

Errors The program contained three errors, including an uninitialized variable, the use of the expression $-1**(I/2)$ instead of $(-1)**(I/2)$, and the failure to add the last term computed in the series on to the final computed sum.

Different paths through SIN correspond to different numbers of iterations of the loop in the program that is used to compute terms in the series. The symbolic output in figure 4.27.6-1 was generated by symbolically evaluating the path that involves exactly three iterations of the loop.

Error Discovery The errors in the program are discovered by comparing the symbolic output with the standard formula for the McLaurin series. The symbolic evaluator that was used to generate the output represents the values of variables that have been uninitialized with a question mark at the name of the variable. The error involving the expression $(-1)**(I/2)$ results in the generation of the same rather than alternating signs in the series sum. The failure to use the last computed term can be detected by comparing the predicates for the symbolically evaluated path with the symbolic output value for SIN.

Effectiveness

Studies have been carried out which indicate that symbolic evaluation is useful for discovering a variety of errors but that, except in a small number of cases, it is not more effective than the combined use of other methods such as dynamic and static analysis (1).

One of the primary uses of symbolic evaluation is in raising the confidence level of a user in a program. Correct symbolic output expressions confirm to the user that the code carries out the desired computations. It is especially useful for nonprogrammer users.

Introduction to Technique and Tool Descriptions

Applicability

The method is primarily useful for programs written in languages which involve operations that can be represented in a concise formal way. Most of the symbolic evaluation systems that have been built are for use with algebraic programming languages such as FORTRAN and PL-1. Algebraic programs involve computations that can be easily represented using arithmetic expressions. It is difficult to generate symbolic output from programs which involve complex operations with "wordy" representations such as the REPLACE and MOVE CORRESPONDING operations in COBOL.

Learning

It takes a certain amount of practice to choose paths and parts of paths for symbolic evaluation. The user must avoid the selection of long paths or parts of paths that result in the generation of expressions that are so large that they are unreadable. If the symbolic evaluation system being used gives the user control over the types of expression simplification that are carried out, then he must learn to use this in a way that results in the generation of the most revealing expressions.

Costs

Storage and execution time costs for symbolic evaluation have been calculated in terms of program size, path length, number of program variables and the cost of interpreting (rather than compiling and executing) a program path.

The storage required for symbolically evaluating a path of length P in a program with S statements containing N variables is estimated to be on the order of $10(P + S + V)$ (2). Let C1 be the cost of preprocessing a program for interpretation, C2 the cost of interpreting a program path, Cons is the cost of checking the consistency (i.e., solvability) of a system of symbolic predicates and Cond is the cost of evaluating a condition in a conditional statement. Cons and Cond are expressed in units of the cost of interpreting a statement in a program. The cost (in execution time) of symbolically executing a program path is estimated to be on the order of $C1 + C2 (1 + E + Cons/10 + Cond/100)$ (2).

References

(1) HOWDEN, William E., "An Evaluation of the Effectiveness of Symbolic Testing," *Software—Practice and Experience*, 8, 1978.

(2) HOWDEN, William E., "Symbolic Testing—Design Techniques, Costs and Effectiveness," *U.S. Department of Commerce*, NTIS PB-268, 517, Springfield, Virginia.

(3) HOWDEN, William E., "Symbolic Testing and the DISSECT Symbolic Evaluation System," *IEEE Transactions on Software Engineering*, SE-3, 1977.

(4) KING, J.C., "Symbolic Execution and Program Testing," *CACM*, 19, 1976.

(5) CLARKE, L.A., "A System to Generate Test Data and Symbolically Execute Programs," *IEEE Transactions on Software Engineering*, SE-2, 1976.

Software Validation, Verification, Testing, and Documentation

Test Coverage Analyzers

Basic Features

Test coverage analyzers monitor the execution of a program during program testing in order to measure the completeness of a set of program tests. Completeness is measured in terms of the branches, statements or other elementary program constructs which are used during the execution of the program over the tests.

Information Input

Test coverage analyzers use the program source code and a set of program tests to generate test coverage reports. Sophisticated coverage analyzers may also involve input parameters that describe which of several alternative coverage measures are to be used.

Information Output

Typical output consists of a report which describes the relevant feature of the program which has been "exercised" over a sequence of tests. Branch coverage analyzers keep track of and report on the number of times that each branch in a program has been traversed during a sequence of tests (1). A program branch is any transfer of control from one program statement to another, either through execution of a control transfer instruction or through normal sequential flow of control from one statement to the next.

Different kinds of coverage analyzers will report different kinds of information. Analyzers which measure coverage in terms of pairs of branches, loop iteration patterns or elementary program functions have been proposed but branch coverage analyzers are the most widely used. In addition to coverage information, analyzers may also record and print variable range and subroutine call information. The minimum and maximum values assumed by each variable in a program, the minimum and maximum number of times that loops are iterated during the executions of a loop and a record of each subroutine call may be reported.

Outline of Method

Branch Analyzers Branch coverage analyzers typically consist of two parts, a preprocessor and a postprocessor. The preprocessor inserts "probes" into the program for which test coverage analysis is required.

The probes call subroutines or update matrices that record the execution of the part of the program containing the probe. Theoretical studies have been carried out to determine the minimum number of probes required to determine which branches are executed during a program execution. The probes may also record information for determining minimal and maximal variable values, loop iteration counts and subroutine calls.

The information which is generated by program probes has to be processed before test coverage reports can be generated. If a sequence of tests has been carried out, the information from the different tests has to be merged. The processing of the information generated by probes during program testing is processed and reports are generated by the coverage analyzer postprocessor.

Function Analyzers Function analyzers are based on the idea that each program construct implements one or more elementary functions. Loop constructs, for example, involve functions which determine if a loop is to be entered, when it is to be exited, how many times it is to be iterated, the initial value of the loop index variable (if present) and subsequent values of the loop index. It is possible to define complete sets of tests for these functions which will cause the function to act incorrectly on at least one test if the function contains one of a predefined set of possible functional errors (2). Test coverage analyzers can be built which keep track of the data over which constructs are executed and which report on the functional completeness of the data used in the execution of the constructs. Function coverage analyzers can be constructed using the preprocessor probe insertion and postprocessor report generation approach used for branch coverage analyzers.

Example

Application A quicksort program was constructed which contains a branch to a separate part of the program code that carries out an insertion sort. The quicksort part of the code branches to the insertion sort. The quicksort part of the code branches to the insertion sort whenever the size of the original list to be sorted or a section of the original list is below some threshold value. Insertion sorts are more effective than quicksorts for small lists and sections of lists because of the smaller constants in their execution time formulae.

Error The correct threshold value is 11. Due to a typographical error, the branch to the insertion sort is made whenever the length of the original list, or the section of the list currently being processed, is less than or equal to one.

Error Discovery Parts of the insertion sort code are not executed unless the list or list section being sorted is of length greater than one. Examination of the output from a branch coverage analyzer will reveal that parts of the program are never executed, regardless of the program tests which are used. This will alert and draw the attention of the programmer to the presence of the error.

It is interesting to note that the error is not discoverable by the examination of test output data alone since the program will still correctly sort lists.

Effectiveness

Research results confirm that test coverage analyzers are a necessary and important tool for software validation. Previously assumed "complete" test sets for production software have been found to test less than 50% of the branches in a program (1). The use of test coverage analyzers reveals the inadequacy of such test sets.

Studies indicate that although test coverage of all parts of a program is important, it is not enough to simply test all branches, or even all program paths. A large percentage of errors are only detectable when a program is tested over extremal cases or special values that are closely related to the functions performed in the program. There appear to be three situations in which branch coverage is effective in finding errors. The first is that in which an error in part of a program is so destructive that any test that causes that part of the program to be executed will result in incorrect output. The second is that in which parts of a program are never used during any program execution, and the third that in which unexpected parts of a program are used during some test. Other kinds of errors require additional test selection techniques, such as functional testing.

Applicability
Test coverage analysis can be applied to any kind of program in any programming language.

Learning
There are no special learning requirements for the use of test coverage analyzers. Once a set of tests has been found to be inadequate it requires skill to generate data that will cause the unexercised features of the program to be used during program execution.

Costs
Test coverage analyzers can be inexpensive to use. The major expense is the capital cost for the tool. It is estimated that the construction of a test coverage tool requires a level of effort which is more than that required for a parser but less than twice that effort. The major part of test coverage analyzer consists of the parser that is used to determine probe insertion points for a program.

References

(1) STUCKI, Leon G., "Automatic Generation of Self-metric Software," *Proc. 1973 IEEE Symposium on Computer Software Reliability*, 94 (1973).

(2) HOWDEN, William E., "Completeness Criteria for Testing Elementary Program Functions," *University of Victoria, Dept. of Mathemetics*, DM-212-IR, May 1980.

(3) GANNON, Carolyn,"Error Detection Using Path Testing and Static Analysis," *Computer*, August 1979.

Test Data Generators

Basic Features
Test data generators are tools which generate test data to exercise a target program. They may generate data through analysis of the program itself or through analysis of

the expected input to the program in its normal operating environment. Test data generators may use numerical integrators and random number generators to create data.

Information Input
Test data generators require as input:
- a. the program for which data is to be generated, or
- b. a quantifiable description of the domain of possible inputs to the program from which the test data generator is to produce representative values.

Information Output
The output produced by test data generators is a set of data that can be used effectively to detect execution-time errors in a program. It is generally intended that such test data cause the program to be thoroughly exercised when executed. It is also desirable to have this input data be representative of the actual data used in real program operation in order to properly evaluate results obtained from program execution.

Outline of Method
Test data generators generate test data for a program in a systematic, deterministic manner. There are two major methods currently used to generate test data. Both methods can be implemented as fully automated tools.

One method of test data generation analyzes the structure of a program and, based upon this analysis, generates a set of test data which will drive execution along a comprehensive set of program paths. This method attempts to maximize the structural coverage achieved during execution with the derived data. Though this approach requires a detailed, rigorous structural analysis of a program (which is often quite difficult, if not impossible), tools have been developed which aid in the automation of this analysis. There are tools which can analyze a program and identify certain structural elements in that program. Data is then automatically generated that will drive execution through each of these program elements.

If it is desirable to increase the coverage achieved by the test data, there also exist tools which use automated program analysis to aid in accomplishing this. After monitoring program execution with the generated data, it may be possible to increase the current structural coverage achieved by using automated tools which assist in determining how to alter the current set of test data as necessary to cause different branching conditions to occur. Test data generators that create test data based upon the amount of structural coverage that the data will achieve are generally very sophisticated tools. Much research and development work is currently being done in this area.

A second approach to generating test data is based upon analysis of the possible inputs to a program under real, operational usage. This technique requires more knowledge of the software for which input data is to be generated than the previous technique. However, in this approach the output generated from program execution provides more meaningful results to the user during testing. One such tool that utilizes this technique examines the domain of all possible input values to a program under normal program operation and partitions this domain into mutually exclusive subdomains. For each subdomain there is an associated probability that a sequence of actual input values will belong to that partition. Data is then generated by sampling from each subdomain with the distribution of sampling determined by the subdomain's associated probability. Automated tools have been built to assist in computing these probabilities and in sampling from the appropriate partitions.

This technique attempts to mirror the intended operation of a program by generating test data which is representative of its operational input. This mode of program testing can be very useful during a preliminary period of software operational use. Using this technique, reasonably accurate predictions can be made on the software's performance in real operation.

Other test data generators exist which use less sophisticated techniques than those described above. Many of them generate data based upon commands given by the user and/or from data descriptions in a program, such as in a COBOL program's data definition section. This is mainly a COBOL oriented technique in which the test data is intended to simulate transaction inputs in a database management situation. This technique, however, can be adapted to other environments.

Example

Test data is required for a new payroll program. A test data generator is used to generate data normally contained in the payroll records of each employee on the payroll. The data fields in these records consists of:

Employee identification number

Employee name

Indication of hourly or salaried employee

Salary rate (if salaried)

Hourly rate (if hourly)

Number of hours worked during last pay period

Number of tax exemptions declared

Federal withholding tax rate

Social security tax rate

Marital status

A file of records containing this information is created by the test data generator. For each field in a record, a value with the appropriate data type is randomly generated (e.g., alphanumeric for Employee Name, integer for Employee Identification Number, real for Federal Withholding Tax Rate). The file is then reformatted in an organization that is acceptable to the payroll system as input. The generated test data will then be fed to the payroll program to be tested.

Introduction to Technique and Tool Descriptions

Effectiveness

The overall effectiveness of automated test data generators in use today is generally poor. Though these tools permit the generation of more test data than any human tester could create (thereby devising more test cases), a burden is created on the human tester to evaluate all the test results obtained from program execution with the generated data. Unfortunately, test data generators themselves do not have a facility by which to verify these test results. In addition, most of the test data generators in use today create data in a manner which is totally insensitive to the functional peculiarities of a program. The data may often be meaningless in content. It may focus testing upon an unimportant portion of the program and totally ignore critical portions. A human tester, however, often has a certain intuition about which program areas need to be more thoroughly tested than others and so creates his test data accordingly. The overall ignorance of test data generators in determining which data items would offer the most potential in discovering errors is the major factor behind their current ineffectiveness in program testing.

Applicability

Test data generators are generally applicable for any system requiring input data for operation.

Learning

For those test data generators which only require as input the source program for which test data is desired, very little learning is required to use these tools. The user interface with the tool will always be the same, and the user Manual for the tool should provide sufficient information for its operation. For those data generators which create data based upon the domain of expected inputs to the program, much more learning is required. It is necessary to acquire some knowledge about the application environment and operational usage of the software so that representative input data can be generated.

Costs

Automated test data generators are generally quite expensive. This is primarily due to the relatively infrequent use of these tools in actual testing environments. The initial costs in building test data generators have very rarely been offset by benefits obtained in using them. As yet, the derived utilization of the more sophisticated tools that exist have not justified their cost. Accordingly, test data generators are among the most costly testing tools that exist today.

References

(1) CLARKE, L.A., "A System to Generate Test Data and Symbolically Execute Programs," *IEEE Transactions on Software Engineering*, SE-2, September, 1976.

(2) HOWDEN, W.E., "Methodology for Generation of Program Test Data," *IEEE Transactions on Computers*, TC-24, May, 1975.

(3) MILLER, E.F. and MELTON, R.A., "Automated Generation of Testcase Datasets," *1975 International Conference on Reliability*, Los Angeles, April, 1975.

(4) NAFTALY, S.M. and COHEN, M.C., "Test Data Generators and Debugging Systems . . . ," Workable Quality Control, Part I and II, *Data Processing Digest*, Vol. 18, 2 and 3, February and March, 1972.

Test Support Facilities

Basic Features

An environment simulation, or test bed, is a test site used to test a component of software. This test site simulates the environment under which the software will normally operate. A test bed permits full control of inputs and computer characteristics, allows processing of intermediate outputs without destroying simulated execution time, and allows full test repeatability and diagnostics. To be effective, the controlled circumstances of the test bed must truly represent the behavior of the system of which the software is a part.

Information Input

The information input to a test bed is the software for which a testing environment is to be simulated and which will later be installed in a real system.

Information Output

The information output by a test bed are the results observed through execution of the software installed in the test bed. This information is used as a preliminary means of determining whether the software will operate as intended in its real environment.

Outline of Method

Test beds provide an environment in which to monitor the operation of software prior to installation in a real system. To be of value, this environment must realistically reflect those properties of the system which will affect or be affected by the operation of the software. However, the test bed should simulate only those components in the system which the software requires as a minimum interface with the system. This will permit testing to focus only on the software component for which the test bed is built.

Test beds are built through the consideration of, and proper balance between, three major factors:

the amount of realism required by the test bed to properly reflect the operation of system properties,

resources available to build the test bed, and

the ability of the test bed to focus only on the software being tested.

Introduction to Technique and Tool Descriptions

Test beds come in many forms, depending on the level of testing desired. For single module testing, a test bed may consist merely of test data and a test driver. A test driver is a program which feeds input data to the program module being tested, causes the module to be executed, and collects the output generated during the program execution. If a completed, but non-final version of software is to be tested, the test bed may also include stubs. A stub is a dummy routine that simulates the operation of a module that is invoked within a test. Stubs can be as simple as routines that automatically return on a call, or they can be more complicated and return simulated results. The final version of the software may be linked with other software subsystems in a larger total system. The test bed for one component in the system may consist of those system components which directly interface with the component being tested.

As illustrated in the above examples, test beds permit the testing of a component of a system without requiring the availability of the full, complete system. They merely supply the inputs required by the software component to be executed and provide a repository for outputs to be placed for analysis. In addition, test beds may contain monitoring devices which collect and display intermediate outputs during program execution. In this way, test beds provide the means of observing the operation of software as a component of a system without requiring the availability of other system components, which may be unreliable.

Example

The federal government has just distributed to all American corporations new tax rates to be imposed on the earnings of all employees beginning at the start of next year. Due to these new tax rates, Company XYZ has had to revise its current payroll program so that it will accommodate the new federal regulations by January 1.

In order to test this new program, a test bed is being constructed to simulate the operation of the payroll system. To simulate the inputs to this system, a test file of data containing all the information necessary for the system to operate is created. The file consists of a record of information for each employee in the company. Each record contains the following data:

Employee identification number

Employee name

Indication of hourly or salaried employee

Salary rate (if salaried)

Hourly rate (if hourly)

Number of hours worked during last pay period

Number of tax exemptions declared

Federal witholding tax rate

Social security tax rate

Marital status

A test driver controls the execution of the payroll program. It feeds the above data to the program in the proper format. At the end of program execution, the driver simulates the check-writing facility of the payroll system in the following manner. It directs the output of the payroll program to an output file. The output consists of a record of data for each company employee. Each record contains the following information:

Employee name

Employee social security number

Check date

Total employee earnings less deductions

The test driver then dumps this information from the output file onto a hardcopy device so that the output can be analyzed and verified for correctness.

Effectiveness

The use of test beds has proven to be a highly effective and widely used technique to test the operation of software. The use of test drivers, in particular, is one of the most widely used testing techniques.

Applicability

This method is generally applicable, from single module to large system testing and for all types of computing applications.

Learning

In order to build an effective test bed, it is necessary to develop a solid understanding of the software and its dynamic operation in a system. This understanding should aid in determining what parts of the test bed deserve the most attention during its construction. In addition, knowledge of the dynamic nature of a program in a system is required in gathering useful intermediate outputs during program execution and in properly examining these results.

Cost

The amount of realism desired in a test bed will be the largest factor affecting cost. Building a realistic test bed may require the purchasing of new hardware and the development of additional software in order to properly simulate an entire system. In addition, these added resources may be so specialized that they may seldom, if ever, be used again in other applications. In this way, very sophisticated test beds may not prove to be highly cost-effective.

References
(1) HARTWICK, R.D., "The Advanced Targeting Study," *SAMSO-TR-71-124*, Volume 1, June 1971.

(2) PANZL, D.J., "Automatic Software Test Drivers," *IEEE Computer*, April 1978.

Walkthroughs

Basic Features

Walkthroughs (WT) constitute a structured series of peer reviews of a system component used to enforce standards, detect errors, and improve development visibility and system quality. They may be conducted during any of the lifecycle phases and may also be applied to documentation. An identifying feature of a WT is that it is generally presented by the creator or producer of the material being reviewed rather than an independent or third party. In addition, because of the presenter's advance preparation and his familiarity with the material, less preparation by other members is required.

Information Input

Walkthrough Package This set of materials includes all necessary backup documentation for the WT. Examples of materials made available include (but are not limited to) module flow charts, system flow charts, HIPO charts (or other high-level representation schemes), and module listings. Other important materials may include sections of the Functional Specification, System/Subsystem Specification and Database Specification (as applicable) which pertain to the component under review. Often, copies of applicable standards are also part of the WT input.

Questions List Some organizations which practice a more formal version of a WT require reviewers to submit the component to the presenter prior to the WT. This enables the presentor to be better prepared to respond to the questions at the WT.

Information Output

Action List During the WT, a list of problems and questions is recorded. This action list is distributed to all participants and is used by the producer (reviewee) as the basis for subsequent changes to the component.

Walkthroughs Form During the course of the WT, this form is completed by an individual with recording responsibilities. The form identifies participants and their responsibilities, the agenda for the WT, the decision of the WT (accept as-is, revise, revise and schedule another WT), and is signed by all participants at the end of the WT.

Outline of Method

Roles and Responsibilities The group of individuals participating in a WT are usually referred to as reviewers. The leader of the WT is called the coordinator. The coordinator is responsible for WT planning, organization, and distribution of materials. The WT is called to order, moderated, and summarized by the coordinator.

The producer (or reviewee) is that individual whose module or component is to be reviewed during the WT. In most cases, the producer is generally responsible for selecting the coordinator and review team (in most situations; sometimes management may perform this function) and providing the WT package materials to the coordinator. During the WT the producer initially provides a general description of the module, then leads the reviewers through a detailed, step-by-step description of the module. After the WT the producer should objectively consider every item on the action list and make changes to his product as he deems appropriate.

The reviewers are composed of individuals from varying backgrounds and fulfill responsibilities based upon their area of specialization. Some roles which are fulfilled are those of recorder and representatives of the user, standards and maintenance groups. In general, these participants are responsible for being familiar with the material being presented, submitting comments prior to the review, and listening and contributing during the WT. At the end of the review each must cast a vote indicating whether the module is acceptable, needs revision, or is rejected.

Because of the organization which each is representing, some specific responsibilities are associated with each reviewer. In addition to contributing to the WT, the recorder must make written note of the participants assembled and the action items which result from the review.

The user representative is often involved during early WT's of a module (i.e., during requirements analysis and design). His responsibility is to ensure that the proposed solution is usable and does, in fact, meet the needs of his organization.

The standards representative, referred to by some sources as a "standards bearer," is responsible for checking that the product being reviewed adheres to organization standards. In some cases, he may be asked to provide input to a request to deviate from a standard.

The maintenance representative, referred to by some sources as the "maintenance oracle," must view the product from the standpoint of the group who will be required to maintain the product. Items which may be of prime concern to this individual are documentation and program comments, program functionality or modularity, naming conventions, and data decomposition.

The Process   Many organizations practice walk-throughs which differ radically in formality. The process described in the following paragraphs falls at the midpoint between these extremes. There are four basic steps in the process:

Scheduling.   When the work item module is very near completion (including documentation), the producer notifies management and selects the WT participants. The WT date is agreed upon and facilities are scheduled. The WT should not exceed 2 hours and is best kept to less than 1 hour. This implies that the work item is of manageable size. Sources suggest the following guidelines for work package size:

- 5–10 pages of specifications for a requirements WT,
- 1–5 structure charts (or HIPO diagrams) for a preliminary or detailed design WT,
- 50–100 lines of code for a code or test WT.

Preparation. The producer collects appropriate information for use at the WT and gives it to the coordinator for distribution. Each reviewer studies the materials, making a note of questions or comments. Most sources estimate that a maximum of 1 hour preparation by reviewers is necessary.

Walkthrough Meeting. After the coordinator opens the review, the producer uses test data to simulate the operation of the component. Each specification, design phrase, or line of code is reviewed. The recorder documents comments or questions using the action list. Each reviewer signs the Walkthrough, documenting the decision of the meeting (accept product as-is, accept with modification, or reject). The recorder provides a copy of action list to all participants and supplies a copy of the Walkthrough Form to management.

Re-Work. The producer reviews each action item, making product changes as he feels necessary. He may decide to implement all, part or none of the suggested changes. No follow-up is held to ensure that suggestions are incorporated; it is assumed that the producer is in the best positon to make implementation decisions. Major items on the action list may be summarized at the next WT for the module.

Example

One week prior to completion of coding of a module of 75-100 lines, the producer notifies his line manager of the need for a WT. Upon management approval the producer selects a coordinator (one of the lead analysts from the development shop), a standards representative (from the Quality Assurance group), a maintenance representative (from the Production Program organization), and a user representative (from the group requesting the system). Three days prior to the inspection he notifies the coordinator of the planned WT and suggested participants. At this time he gives the coordinator copies of the program listing (including comments), a systems-level flowchart depicting how it interfaces with other modules, a data dictionary, a set of test data items, and a section from the Functional Specification detailing the user requirement associated with the module.

The coordinator notifies the selected participants, receives their commitment to attend and distributes to each a copy of the materials furnished by the producer.

Each participant reviews the materials. The standards representative finds two instances of deviations from published standards and notifies the coordinator (who in turn notifies the producer). The user representative verifies that the code addresses each designed aspect by reviewing the proceedings of the previous design WT. He is satisfied that each requirement had been addressed and notifies the coordinator that he finds no errors and feels that his presence is not required for the code walkthrough. The maintenance representative finds no immediate concerns with the code but makes a note to inquire about the structure of the data files.

The WT begins with a brief introduction by the coordinator, who then turns the review over to the producer. He uses the system flowchart to give a summary of the functions of the module and proceeds to go line-by-line through the code using the selected test data. Upon reaching the lines of concern to the standards representative, a brief discussion occurs to explain the reasons for the deviations from standard. In this instance, the reviewers are satisfied that the deviations are justified. The recorder so notes on the action list and the meeting proceeds. The maintenance representative points out one line of highly complex code and suggests that it be broken up into two less complex steps. Agreement cannot be immediately reached, so the suggestion is added to the action list.

At the end of the module review the coordinator seeks a decision from the reviewers about the module. They agree to give their approval, providing that the suggested changes are made and that the producer will further investigate the effect of breaking up the complex line of code. Each signs the Walkthrough form and the meeting is adjourned.

The recorder distributes a copy of the action to all participants. The producer makes the changes he feels are necessary. He runs a benchmark of the module with the complex code and again with the code broken down. Since no significant loss of efficiency resulted, he modifies the code. The module is now ready for unit test which may be followed by another WT.

Effectiveness. Studies have been conducted which identify the following qualitative benefits of Walkthroughs:

higher status visibility

decreased debugging time

early detection of design and analysis errors which would be much more costly to correct in later development phases

identification of design or code inefficiencies

ensuring adherence to standards

increased program readability

increased user satisfaction

communication of new ideas or technology

increased maintainability

Little data is available which identifies the quantitative benefits attributable to the use of Walkthroughs. However, one source estimates that the number of errors in production programs was reduced by a factor of ten.

Applicability. The Walkthrough is applicable to large or small projects during all development phases and is not limited by project type or complexity.

Introduction to Technique and Tool Descriptions

Learning. The Walkthrough does not require special training to implement. However, experience has shown that the effectiveness of the Walkthrough increases as the WT experience of the reviewers increases.

Costs. The WT requires no special tools or equipment to implement. The direct costs are equal to the expense associated with the human resources involved.

References

(1) "Code Reading: Structured Walkthroughs and Inspections," IBM IPTO Support Group, World Trade System Center, Postbus 60, Zoetenmeer, Netherlands, March 1976.

(2) FAGAN, M.E., "Design and Code Inspections to Reduce Errors in Program Development," *IBM Systems Journal*, No. 3, 1976.

(3) FREEDMAN, D.P., and WEINBERG, G.M., "Ethno—Technical Review Handbook," Ethnotech, Inc., 1977.

(4) DALY, E.B., "Management of Software Development," *IEEE Transactions on Software Engineering*, May 1977.

(5) SHNEIDERMAN, Ben, "Software Psychology—Human Factors in Computer and Information Systems," Winthrop Publishing, 1980.

Glossary

BLACK BOX TESTING *see* FUNCTIONAL TESTING

BOUNDARY VALUE ANALYSIS a selection technique in which test data is chosen to lie along "boundaries" or extremes of input domain (or output range) classes, data structures, procedure parameters, etc. Choices often include maximum, minimum, and trivial values or parameters. This technique is often called stress testing.

BRANCH TESTING a test method satisfying coverage criteria that require, for each decision point, each possible branch be executed at least once.

CAUSE-EFFECT GRAPHING test data selection technique. The inputs and ouputs of the program are determined through analysis of the requirements. A minimal set of inputs is chosen avoiding the testing of multiple inputs which cause identical output.

COMPLETENESS the property that all necessary parts of the entity in question are included. Completeness of a product is often used to express the fact that all requirements have been met by the product.

CONSISTENCY the property of logical coherency among constituent parts. Consistency may also be expressed as adherence to a given set of rules.

CORRECTNESS the extent to which software is free from design and coding defects, i.e. fault free. It is also the extent to which software meets its specified requirements and user objectives. (IEEE Software Engineering Terminology)

DEBUGGING the process of correcting syntactic and logical errors detected during coding. With the primary goal of obtaining an executing piece of code, debugging shares with testing certain techniques and strategies but differs in its usual ad hoc application and local scope.

DESIGN-BASED FUNCTIONAL TESTING the application of test data derived through functional analysis (see FUNCTIONAL TESTING) extended to include design functions as well as requirement functions.

DRIVER code which sets up an environment and calls a module for test.

DYNAMIC ANALYSIS involves execution or simulation of a development phase product. It detects errors by analyzing the response of a product to sets of input data.

EXTREMAL TEST DATA test data that is at the extremes, or boundaries, of the domain of an input variable or which produces results at the boundaries of an output domain.

310

Introduction to Technique and Tool Descriptions

FORMAL ANALYSIS   uses rigorous mathematical techniques to analyze the algorithms of a solution. The algorithms may be analyzed for numerical properties, efficiency, and/or correctness.

FUNCTIONAL TESTING   application of test data derived from the specified functional requirements without regard to the final program structure.

INSPECTION   a manual analysis technique in which the program (requirements, design, or code) is examined in a very formal and disciplined manner to discover errors.

INSTRUMENTATION   the insertion of additional code into the program in order to collect information about program behavior during program execution.

INVALID INPUT   (test data for invalid input domain)   test data that lies outside the domain of the program's function.

PATH TESTING   a test method satisfying coverage criteria that each logical path through the program be tested. Often paths through the program are grouped into a finite set of classes; one path from each class is then tested.

PROOF OF CORRECTNESS   the use of techniques of mathematical logic to infer that a relation between program variables assumed true at program entry implies that another relation between program variables holds at program exit.

REGRESSION TESTING   testing of a previously validated program which has been modified for extension or correction.

SIMULATION   use of an executable model to represent the behavior of an object. During testing the computational hardware, the external environment, and even code segments may be simulated.

SPECIAL TEST DATA   test data based on input values that are likely to require special handling by the program.

STATEMENT TESTING   a test method satisfying the criterion that each statement in a program be executed at least once during program testing.

STATIC ANALYSIS   direct analysis of the form and structure of a product without executing the product. It may be applied to the requirements, design or code.

STRESS TESTING   see BOUNDARY VALUE ANALYSIS.

STUB   special code segments that when invoked by a code segment under test will simulate the behavior of designed and specified modules not yet constructed.

SYMBOLIC EXECUTION   an analysis technique that derives a symbolic expression for each program path.

TEST DATA SET   set of input elements used in the testing process.

TEST DRIVER   a program which directs the execution of another program against a collection of test data sets. Usually, the test driver records and organizes the output generated as the tests are run.

TEST HARNESS   see TEST DRIVER.

TESTING   examination of the behavior of a program by executing the program on sample data sets.

VALID INPUT   (test data for a valid input domain)   test data that lies within the domain of the function represented by the program.

311

Software Validation, Verification, Testing, and Documentation

VALIDATION   determination of the correctness of the final program or software produced from a development project with respect to the user needs and requirements.

VERIFICATION   in general, the demonstration of consistency, completeness, and correctness of the software at each stage and between each stage of the development lifecycle.

WALKTHROUGH   a manual analysis technique in which the module author describes the module's structure and logic to an audience of colleagues.

NOTE: Most of the definitions above from:

ANDRION, W.R., BRANSTAD, M.A., AND CHERNIAVSKY, J.C., "Validation, Verification, and Testing," NBS Special Publication 500–75.

Book Five
Management Guide for
Software Documentation

Abstract

This guide is to assist managers in the establishment of policies and procedures for effective preparation, distribution, control, and maintenance of documentation which will aid in re-use, transfer, conversion, correction and enhancement of computer programs. Such documentation, together with the computer programs themselves, will provide software product packages which can be transferred and used by people other than the originators of the programs. "Software" and "documentation" are defined, some documentation problems are discussed, and policies, procedures, and applicable standards are outlined. Appendices provide checklists in support of documentation policies and procedures, and references to relevant guidelines, standards, and the literature. A glossary of terms is included.

Key words: documentation; guidelines; life-cycle; software; specifications; standards.

314

Introduction

Much has been written during the past years about improved methods of software development, top-down design, stepwise refinement, hierarchical decomposition, and other related subjects. Most of these methodologies use and produce software documentation as an integral part of the methods. However, relatively little useful information has been written on the process of software documentation. On the other hand, many complaints have been recorded about lack of documentation, poor documentation, outdated documentation, or too much documentation. Two major thrusts could provide solutions to these complaints: improved documentation methods and improved management techniques which facilitate the production, distribution, and maintenance of software documentation. The documentation methodology appears to be progressing: various authors, committees, and working groups have developed standards and guidelines applicable to these problems [See Appendices 5 and 6]. What appears to be lacking is a clear understanding of the management support, resources, and facilities required for useful application and tailoring of these techniques.

The following chapters are intended to provide some basic information for managers which will help them to identify documentation problems, structure documentation tasks, and direct projects towards production of useful documentation.

The purpose of Book Five thus is twofold. First, it provides a general overview of the field of software documentation. It is written to provide managers with an overview of the software development process and software documentation issues in order to assist the managers in assessing their own documentation requirements.

Secondly, it provides references to relevant material such as standards, guidelines, articles in the literature, and books which can be used to develop in-house standards, guidelines, and procedures at any desired level. This is important, since effective software documentation requires tailoring of that documentation to the needs of each individual project, based on project size, type, duration, organization, and many other factors.

Software Validation, Verification, Testing, and Documentation

The following chapters discuss different views of software documentation, document types, and documentation quality, cite some common problems associated with documentation, and outline solutions dealing with matters of policy, planning, procedures, standards, and resources.

24. What is Software Documentation?

The term "software documentation" means different things to different people. A few common definitions [5-1] (numbers in square brackets refer to the appropriate appendix at the end of Book 5 and the serial number of the reference, e.g. appendix 5, reference 1), illustrate the point:

"Software" is defined as "computer programs, procedures, rules, and possibly associated documentation and data concerned with the operation of a data processing system."

"Documentation" is defined as "the management of documents which may include the actions of identifying, acquiring, processing, storing, and disseminating them," or alternately "a collection of documents on a given subject."

"Document" is defined as "a data medium and the data recorded on it, that generally has permanence and can be read by man or machine."

"Computer program" is defined as "a series of instructions or statements in a form acceptable to a computer."

Collectively these definitions cover such a broad area that it is important for the term "software documentation" to be defined in the context in which it is to be used. Managers should insure that definitions to be used for a specific project are clearly understood. Key issues are that:

1. The concept of "software" may or may not include "documentation" or "data." In large military computer systems the term software is synonymous with computer programs and excludes data and documentation. They are specified separately, and are treated as items separate from the computer programs. In the commercial sector documentation and data usually are included in software. It is important to specify precisely what is meant when the term software is used.

2. Documentation may mean the process of documenting, or a collection of documents, and again the term needs further explanation and definition if it is used in a context where misunderstandings may arise.

3. Computer programs are primarily machine-oriented but must contain human readable information for operation and maintenance.

317

Software Validation, Verification, Testing, and Documentation

4. Documentation serves primarily the human reader, but automated means do assist in preparation, coordination, and maintenance of documents.

In the context of this paper we deal primarily with documents which are necessary for the development and use of computer programs. The main purposes of documents are to serve human communications and to improve human-machine interaction. Documents augment computer programs, which are for the use of machines only. Programs and associated documentation are necessary parts of software packages, which in turn are essential parts of computer systems. Two major areas of documentation can be distinguished: development documentation and product documentation. They will be discussed in the following paragraphs.

Development Documentation

The notion of development documentation is closely related to the software life cycle. The term "life cycle" refers to the period of time between the formulation of the idea about a software product and the time the use of the software product ends. It covers the total "life" of the product. Most systems undergo such a development "life cycle." The establishment of a life cycle is primarily a management tool. It divides the time of development into manageable parts and provides a framework of milestones, which help managers monitor progress and make decisions about direction and control of the project. These parts, or "life cycle phases," cover different activities such as initiation, requirements analysis, design, programming, testing, operation and maintenance. The development of large systems is often based on a "life cycle methodology," providing for well-defined phases and procedures for document preparation.

FIPS PUB 38 [5-5] uses three major phases: the initiation, development, and operational phases. The development phase is subdivided into definition, design, programming, and test stages. In other environments the initiation phase or parts of it are also known as conceptual, validation, concept formulation, contract definition, or demonstration and validation phases. Similarly the phase called development in FIPS 38 is also known as full scale development, acquisition, or full scale engineering development. The operations phase similarly is called deployment, or production and deployment phase, or operations and maintenance phase.

What is of critical importance is that development cycle phases are specified, and that appropriate documentation is defined which permits systematic software development. Based on specified phases and stages, documentation is then required at fixed points in the life cycle. The names of the different phases and the number of phases depend on the project characteristics. The more phases and stages are specified, the more documentation may be required. Rigid application of the phased approach may lead to "overspecification" of the life cycle and to resultant "over-documentation."

Documents needed during development of computer programs describe and specify *what* the user needs, i.e. the user requirements, and *what* the computer programs do. Documents also deal with the specification of *how* programs should be constructed and *how* their performance should be tested.

Typical document types needed here are requirements and functional specifications (emphasizing "what the system does"), as well as design specifications, development, and test plans (emphasizing "how the system does it").

Development documentation is most useful during systems analysis, software design, programming and testing. It is the communications vehicle during the development process, recording technical details and key decisions for each stage of the process. It primarily serves analysts, designers, programmers, testers, maintainers, and managers.

Product Documentation

Product documentation is a critical element for the use, operation, maintenance, and conversion of software systems. A "program product" or "product" refers to a well-tested computer program which is fully documented and supported by a responsible organization, and which is capable of wide distribution. It may be commercially available or it may be produced by a non-commercial source, but it must be capable of wide application and use. A program product differs from an experimental program or a one-shot temporary program, which may lack basic documentation and may have been only casually tested.

Product documentation is prepared for the end-user to have available during normal operation, or for maintenance programmers who correct errors, or who may enhance programs by adding new features based on changed user requirements. The end-user of a computer program needs to know how the program functions, how the computer or related devices are to be operated, and what should be done if there should be a malfunction in hardware or software.

Additional information is required by maintenance personnel. Needed are details on the system environment such as relationships and interactions with computer installation support facilities, and other manual or automated data systems. This kind of information is especially useful if programs are to be transferred from one location to another.

Document types included in product documentation are computer program abstracts, user manuals, maintenance manuals, and operator manuals as well as product specifications.

Product documentation primarily serves the end-user. It also serves people who change, transfer, enhance, or maintain computer programs. Additionally, it provides information to managers at several levels, who are responsible for development, maintenance, operation, or enhancement.

The distinction between development documentation and product documentation is however not a precise one. Product documentation is primarily instructional. Some product documentation is started during development such as a user manual or maintenance manual, and some development documentation is of interest during

319

operation or maintenance. Essentially they represent two types of documentation prepared for different audiences: in the first case all those persons concerned with development of a product, and in the second case all those concerned with use and application of the software product.

Functional View of Documentation

To further clarify the concept of documentation, we may look at the functions which documentation serves. Four major groupings can be discerned: inter-task communication, instructional reference, quality assurance support, and historical reference.

Intertask Communication

Most software development projects are subdivided into tasks, which often are carried out by different types of people. Analysts formulate system requirements, designers develop overall program designs, and programmers provide detailed code. In addition, quality assurance specialists are concerned with methods for quality software development and overall system testing, auditors monitor overall system integrity, and maintainers improve operations or provide enhancements and extensions. Intertask communications are established usually in a formalized way to provide requirements to designers, designs to coders, and system specifications to auditors and maintenance people. Inter-task communication between teams of different specialists is carried out by means of functional, design, test, or system specifications.

Instructional Reference

Users who usually are not computer specialists need to be trained in system operation. They need readily available reference material. Similarly, special documentation must be available to persons concerned with maintaining software. This includes not only correction of software errors which may show up after a system has become operational, but also system improvements based on changed user requirements or a changed system environment. This documentation is provided in training, user, maintenance, and operators' manuals.

Quality Assurance Support

System documentation tells three basic things: what a system does, how it does it, and how well it performs. The third question is answered by testing and evaluating computer systems and software. Requirements documents, design specifications, quality assurance plans, test plans and test procedures need to be provided, and results need to be reported; these documents need to be provided to all persons concerned with system performance and quality.

Historical Reference

Many computer systems and programs provide new services to users. In a rapidly changing technology it has been found useful to record capabilities, system features, and operational details in a form that will be of value to others. This will facilitate re-use of well-proven ideas and assist in transfer and conversion of programs to new system environments. In may also save time and energy and permit concentration on other efforts with higher priority. Finally, it may prevent false starts by illustrating problem solutions that have been proven ineffective. System specifications, a variety of manuals, and test reports may all serve this important purpose.

User's View

A completely different viewpoint regarding software documentation may be summarized as the "user's view." This refers particularly to the operational end-user, who may be a bank teller, an air reservation clerk, a postal clerk, a chemist, a factory worker, a librarian, a manager, or some other person without a background in computers. The end-user is not interested in the intricacies of the development cycle. A manager, for instance, might want to know whether a particular new application is of interest and useful to the organization. Some other end-user may like to learn with a minimum of effort what a system is doing, how one operates it, and how one obtains useful results.

"User documentation" includes material found in product documentation such as a computer program abstract, a product specification, user, training, and maintenance manuals. It should be up-to-date and readily available. User documentation must be prepared in a language most familiar to the specific user group for which it is intended. It should be designed for easy comprehension and use. Since there are often hundreds, or even thousands of end users who operate computer systems, design of product documentation which accommodates the "user viewpoint" will do much to enhance productivity and prevent wasted hours spent looking for operational information.

Preparation of user documentation should be started early in the development cycle, and users should participate in development and documentation reviews throughout the life of the project.

Documentation Coverage

Documentation is required during all phases of the development and operation of a computer program. Documentation preparation should be viewed as a continuous effort covering the total life cycle. It evolves from preliminary drafts during project initiation through various reviews and changes into development. It then continues past computer program and documentation delivery, to changes caused by user feedback, changed user requirements, and changed system environment.

This documentation process requires a determination of what documents need to be produced, i.e. a choice of document types. It involves planning, i.e. decisions on when various document types are to be produced and reviewed, and what their contents should be. It also involves decisions on who should produce the various documents, and how documents should be controlled.

321

Documentation Types

The same information may be packaged in one or several different document types. The number of document types produced for any one project varies and depends on the size of the project, the audiences addressed, the number of phases identified for management control, and other factors. Important considerations are also the economics of the paperwork: the cost of paper, printing, storage and distribution, and the frequency of revisions affect the number of document types. Management decisions about required number and document types must be made early during a project. FIPS 38 [5-5] and FIPS 64 [5-8] present a framework by outlining 13 document types.

In-Line Documentation

Computer programs primarily serve to provide processing instructions to computers. In order to maintain programs, their structure and content must also be understood by people. Large programs in particular are sometimes difficult to read. Methods have been developed to assist in better understanding of programs. This is done by including "comments" in the computer program listing. These comments are not processed by the machine but serve only to inform program users about details pertaining to its functioning. "User" here is used in a generic sense—i.e. any person who uses the program for whatever reason. This means programmers or computer-oriented people who have access to the program. This practice is called "in-line documentation" or sometimes "program documentation."

Any well-written program will contain a sufficient number of comments to permit people to read it. These comments should be prepared while programs are being written, and should be updated as programs are developed, tested, and modified. In an ideal case, documentation is prepared in-line describing what the program is to do. This later is expanded to include how the program is to do it. Finally the programmer writes the program, inserting the code in the documentation. Guidance pertaining to the use of comments often appears in "programming standards" since details and format conventions vary with programming languages. Especially in smaller programs, in-line documentation often is a large part of the documentation needed or provided.

Documentation Quality

It is not sufficient merely to produce documentation because regulations or procedures require it, or because it is required in the contract. Depending on available resources, size, risk of project, and other factors, conscientious management decisions have to be made regarding the intended quality of documentation and quality control. This includes factors such as extent, level of detail, and formality of documentation. Quality may range from handwritten notes filed in a development folder or project notebook to formal specifications which are subject to formal review procedures. Similarly, a user's manual may consist of a set of typewritten pages stapled together, or it may be a well-designed booklet using distinct typography and extensive tables and graphics, all created to improve readability and understanding.

The quality of documentation needs to be planned for each document type. To assist in specification of documentation quality, four levels of documentation can be identified [5-5]. These levels are characterized by increasing detail of documentation.

Minimal Level (Level 1)   It is appropriate for single use, one-shot programs, requiring less than one person-month. This would include the program listing, development notes, test data, and a program abstract.

Internal Level (Level 2)   This may apply to special-purpose programs which, after careful consideration of the possible interest to others, appear to have no sharing potential. Here documentation requirements may be satisfied, in addition to information given in level 1, by the liberal use of comments in the program listing which would aid the user in program setup and use. Formal documentation effort would be minimal.

Working Document Level (Level 3)   This level applies to programs to be used by several people in the same organization, or to programs which may be used in other organizations. Documents will be typewritten, but minimum review or editing will be required beyond that required for a "working paper."

Formal Publication Level (Level 4)   This level applies to programs which are to be formally announced for general use. It also is desirable for programs which are to be referenced by a scientific publication. It is required by critical programs or by programs dealing with repeated management applications, such as payroll. The format of documentation will conform to formal editorial conventions and standards required by the developing organization.

Reference [5-5] also provides guidance on how to establish these levels.

Documentation quality considerations apply to both the structure and the content of documentation. Contents may be judged by their accuracy, completeness, and clarity. Structure is determined by the order of parts and the simplicity of the overall arrangement. The four levels provide increasingly greater constraints on the documentation process to achieve quality documentation.

Continuity of Content

System documentation occurs over a period of time and is an ongoing process. Early in the development process requirements are stated: "what the system is expected to do." These requirements appear initially in broad general terms in a feasibility study. They are later detailed and restated in a requirements document. The

Software Validation, Verification, Testing, and Documentation

requirements are translated into designs, and eventually are translated into computer programs. It is essential from a management viewpoint that throughout the development there is a capability to identify processing details, and that these details be related back to design documents and finally to requirements statements. Only then can system tests verify that user requirements are being satisfied by the system. This "traceability" is achieved by appropriate structuring and identifying of paragraphs, sections, and chapters of text which are clearly referenced to previous documents. Some automated verification systems have mechanized some of these functions.

25. Documentation Problems and Causes

Managers concerned with documentation for computer-based projects face problems in several areas. They have to determine what types of documents are required at what times. They also have to determine how much documentation should be prepared, and of what quality that documentation should be. They then have to ensure that documentation is maintained in a timely fashion as systems change. Such changes are caused either by program errors or by changed user requirements. Lack of observance of these factors will lead to what commonly is called "documentation problems." The following section illustrates some of these problems.

Some Documentation Problems

Reports dealing with problems related to computer systems show recurring concerns: lack of documentation, incomplete documentation, and inaccurate documentation.

One Government study identified problems associated with lack of documentation. In one case a programmer inherited a program which had been modified by three other programmers. Without adequate documentation of the original program and the subsequent modifications, it was impossible to continue work and the program had to be completely rewritten. In another case about 6 man-months were lost when a system had to be redesigned, because adequate documentation was not available. Additionally, auditors were unable to evaluate internal controls, and management could not adequately review the project. In another case it took over a year to determine how the various programs in a complex system operated.

A Federal agency contracted for maintenance of accounting and administrative records of one of its functions. The system specifications were only 80 percent complete when the contract was let and were never completed by anyone. This and other factors caused "expenditures of over $1 million for systems analysis and arbitration support from outside consultants."

Poorly prepared documentation often is a contributing factor to faulty software. A common problem is poor requirements definition. In one case involving a $150 million project, the report noted that "the specifications received by the programming staff were often so poorly written that the staff could not understand them." "Clarification often resulted in amended specifications which again had to be clarified." To cite an example: "one task was amended 11 times, including reversing much of the original task, adding requirements, changing the logic, correcting requirements, and cancelling the eighth change." Almost 1000 out of 4000 programmer-hours expended on the project resulted from errors in user specifications.

Causes of Problems

Several general causes can be identified in connection with most documentation problems: low priority assignment for documentation, insufficient funding and personnel assigned, lack of planning for documentation, failure to specify needed documentation, and some personal attitudes regarding documentation.

Low Priority for Documentation

The importance of documentation is often not considered when large projects are initiated. In one case a Federal agency had set up a comprehensive management information system. A detailed formal review, 8 years after its conception, and after expenditure of $15 million, showed weaknesses in system documentation [8-5]. The agency "management has not encouraged the systems analysts to maintain and update systems documentation, feeling it would divert their limited resources from program maintenance and other more important functions [8-8]."

Lack of Resources

Low priority for documentation efforts often leads to inadequate resources to perform necessary documentation tasks. This, in turn, leads to diversion to other tasks of people who should prepare required documentation. The final result is erroneous, incomplete, or otherwise deficient project documentation.

Lack of Planning

Insufficient planning at the beginning of a project usually has severe consequences. A study of problems associated with computerized models attributed 70 percent of the problems to inadequate management planning. Specifically, "management did not clarify documentation requirements for the model. As a result, only the developer understood how it worked and the relationship maintained by the various variables incorporated into it."

Failure to Specify

In a similar vein, systems are still being developed without initial requirements specifications. One agency contracted for a centralized accounting system at a fixed cost of about a million dollars over a time period of 2 ½ years. After 30 months, the system was only about one-fourth complete, and the agency cancelled the contract.

Documentation Problems and Causes

Among several problems which contributed to the failure of the project was a lack of specification of precise system requirements.

Personal Attitudes

The causes cited so far can be viewed as impersonal factors contributing to documentation problems. There are also some factors which appear to be closely related to the people who are doing the documentation work. These may be grouped under the heading "personal attitudes." Experience has shown that programmers often have little interest in documentation. This is partly due to the nature of the programming activity; daily pressures of a project often override some perceived uncertain future needs for documentation. High writing standards for documentation are not recognized as a necessary skill, and they certainly are not being rewarded. Few people like to document. It appears unproductive and not particularly creative. Documentation is not visible; as long as a project can move along, documentation "is not needed" and priorities easily shift to more visible objectives. If documentation is not really needed, why then make the extra effort? Such inhibiting attitudes should be recognized and overcome.

These examples are typical, and similarities exist in many projects. The following section offers some guidance on how to overcome documentation problems.

26. Solutions to Problems

As stated in the introduction, there are both technical and managerial solutions to documentation problems. Because of their fundamental importance, this document stresses management solutions. These solutions can be addressed in several ways.

There must be management and staff commitment to documentation. These groups must realize that a certain amount of formal or informal documentation is important and should be produced, distributed and maintained.

This commitment should be backed up by management support, in terms of appropriate guidance and positive incentives for the staff to develop documentation, of designated staff assigned to do the work, and of resources made available.

Visible evidence of this commitment should be produced:

Policies must be established, recorded, and published with regard to system and software documentation.

Documentation effort needs to be planned as an integral part of overall systems and software development.

Project managers must establish, record, and publish procedures facilitating documentation development and maintenance.

Additional procedures should be established dealing with documentation quality and quality measures, and providing means to achieve and audit the desired quality.

Standards and guidelines need to be identified or prepared dealing with all aspects of documentation.

Organizational climate must be conducive to documentation work, and managers must recognize its need, and must support integration of the documentation effort into the overall systems development work.

Finally, a continuous review process must be established to ensure compliance with policy and procedures, as well as observance of standards and guidelines.

The remainder of this report addresses these issues.

Documentation Policy

Policies are prepared by the highest echelon in an organization and provide guidance to decision makers at all lower levels about matters pertaining to the organization as a whole. Policy provides broad direction to decision makers. It does not provide detailed prescriptions on what to do, or how to do something. Policy may be informal, unwritten, and undeclared, but formal, written, well publicized policy clearly establishes the sense of discipline required for high quality software documentation.

Software documentation does play a vital role during planning, development, and operation of systems, and is necessary when systems are upgraded, maintained, converted, or transferred. Some formal statements regarding software documentation policy should be prepared, and all persons affected by it should be informed of it.

Policies should support the basic elements of documentation:

Documentation efforts should cover the whole software life cycle—i.e. documentation is required during the early phases of a project, it must be maintained, and it must be available until a development project is terminated. After that it must be available for use, maintenance, and enhancement of computer programs during the life of the programs.

Documentation should be managed—i.e. a detailed plan should be prepared outlining documentation products, time schedules, responsible persons, and resources. Direction and control are required to maintain documentation.

Documentation should be of a specified quality, up-to-date, and accurate. It must accurately reflect the status and quality of the computer programs it specifies. Updating procedures must be planned for, and resources must be made available for this.

Documentation should be prepared for a variety of users. Users may be managers, analysts, professionals with no computer expertise, maintenance programmers, or clerical personnel. Depending on tasks performed, they require various degrees of detail and different presentation of material. A documentation professional should be charged with responsibility for proper design of different types of documentation destined for different users.

The documentation effort should be integrated into the overall systems development process, and such a process must be defined.

Support tools should be specified which help to develop and maintain software products throughout the system life cycle; They should be used wherever economically feasible.

Existing standards should be specified and used or alternately a set of standards should be developed, consistent with the scope and magnitude of the project.

The checklist in Appendix 2 helps to develop a policy statement, or to assess usefulness of existing policy statements.

Documentation Planning

Planning is a necessary ingredient of any project, large or small. Plans should be prepared in written form to serve as a reminder to an individual or as a communications medium among many people. A documentation plan may be part of an overall project plan or a stand-alone document. It may be prepared very informally as a one-page document, or it may be a comprehensive formal document, produced under rigid documentation standards and control.

Documentation Plan

Planning should start early during a project, and the plan should be reviewed throughout the project's existence. Any plan indicates intended future activities and is subject to change as a project progresses. Provisions need to be made for regular review of plans by all concerned, and for appropriate changes. The plan should be kept up to date, as the situation requires, and should be available to all persons affected by the plan.

A documentation plan should state *what* is to be done, *how* it is to be done, *when* it is to be done and by *whom*, *what* the available resources are, and what *external factors* have to be taken into account to achieve the desired results. Distribution of the plan should be specified and all responsibilities should be clearly delineated.

Document types and content   What document types are to be produced, and what the document content should be needs to be decided and recorded. The list in Appendix 1 shows document types and gives references to sources which provide guidance for the contents of these documents. Appendices 5, 6, and 7 contain lists of FIPS and related standards and guidelines.

Document format and identification   Standardized document formats are essential for maintenance and quality control. They usually are designed to enhance readability and clarity and thus help to improve system quality. Similarly, identification standards, such as document numbers, revision numbers, date, author, responsible organization etc. are essential for maintaining up-to-date documentation. Most organizations have developed their own agency-wide standards in this area. These standards usually are followed. If no standards exist or if they are inadequate, some format and identification standards will be required. Some relevant standards are listed in Appendix 7.

Schedule   A detailed schedule should be prepared, listing various documentation products, milestones, and persons responsible for delivery of the various items. Often a flow chart outlines the necessary activities—e.g.:

  prepare drafts,

  review drafts,

  prepare graphics,

  edit,

  approve,

  print, and

  distribute.

Solutions to Problems

Project Librarian

On larger projects a project librarian should be designated to collect project development data, maintain a basic set of documentation, and maintain an index of project documentation. Depending on the size of the organization, this may be a part-time assignment for an appropriate staff member, or a fulltime job supported by additional personnel. Typical items to be collected for future project planning are:

A brief chronology of significant events,

monthly estimates of machine-time estimates,

monthly estimates of staff-time estimates,

a list of changes to these estimates, and

a summary of actual times expended.

Storage of Vital Documentation

Development documentation represents a vital asset to any organization and an investment of human energy, time, and money. A backup facility in a physically different location should be set up to store vital documentation. This applies to hard copy and on-line storage. In case of damage or destruction by natural or man-made causes, backup card decks, tapes, disks, listings, and flowcharts or system diagrams can be used to reconstruct systems. One person should be charged with the responsibility for regularly updating and maintaining the facility. Size of the backup facility depends on size of the project, its criticality, and on other related factors.

Document Reviews

In large development projects formal reviews take place at various points during the life cycle as part of a formal "development methodology." The documentation process and the overall methodology must be closely integrated. Major events in this process are the requirements review and several design reviews.

Requirements Reviews The purpose of the requirements review is to confirm that the developers and designers understand what the ultimate system user needs, and that the system user understands the limitations and constraints placed upon the developers of the system. An approved functional requirements document is the result of this effort. Based on common understanding between users and developers of "what the system is to do," detailed development and design can be undertaken. It is essential that user representatives participate actively in this review.

Design Reviews Three major reviews often are scheduled: a system design review, preliminary design review, and critical design review. The number and formality of these reviews depend on the needs of the project.

- During the system design review the overall system structure is reviewed with respect to the requirements. Results are a system specification.

- In a preliminary design review the basic design approach and test plans for each system component are reviewed.

331

Software Validation, Verification, Testing, and Documentation

- Next, a critical design review permits analysis of detailed computer program designs and initial test procedures for each program component.

Results of design reviews are final documents which specify "how" systems or programs are to be designed, developed, and tested to meet the requirements stated by the ultimate system user.

Formal minutes should provide a record of all meetings. Regardless of size of project and formality of project management, requirements should be clearly understood, agreed on, and documented to serve users, developers, and all others concerned. Similarly, details of development and design need to be determined, agreed on, and documented to permit translation of requirements into detailed computer programs and program components.

The checklist in Appendix 3 helps in planning documentation activities.

Procedures

Procedures supporting the policies outlined above will cover both preparation and use of documentation throughout the life of a project. Guidance is needed for document preparation, logical sequence of preparation of documents, and procedures for review, approval, quality assurance, distribution, and control of documentation. Once preparation is complete, documents need to be maintained, stored, and updated. The revision process should be outlined. The checklist in Appendix 4 will help in developing appropriate procedures, or in assessing usefulness of existing procedures.

Standards and Guidelines

Many standards and guidelines are available which can be used in support of software documentation. A few are discussed in the next paragraphs; others are cited in Appendices 5 and 6.

Availability

Guidance is available for preparing adequate documentation in support of software systems. Appendix 5 lists Federal standards and guidelines published as part of the Federal Information Processing Standards Publications Series (FIPS-PUB's) by the National Bureau of Standards. Appendix 6 lists standards and guidelines prepared by the American National Standards Institute (ANSI) or by professional societies. Appendix 7 lists books which contain standards and guidelines of interest in this connection.

Use of Guidelines and Standards

Most guidelines provide broad guidance that is applicable to many different situations. Judgment is required to specify what document types are required, how much documentation should be provided, what should be contained in the documents, what documentation quality is desired, and at what times during a project documents are to be produced.

To be most useful, guidelines should be interpreted in terms of individual project requirements. The guidelines are not to be interpreted as rigid specifications which must be followed precisely. Such interpretation could easily lead to "over-documentation" i.e., production of too much paper.

In contracting for software it is important not only to specify that documentation is desired based on agency standards or based on FIPS PUB 38, but also to specify types of documents desired, documentation level and quality, and other desired detail. Most guidelines and standards do not rigidly specify document types and level of documentation; they rather offer choices and ranges of detail. Based on the type of project, the guidelines listed in Appendices 5 through 7 can be used to specify what is desired.

Development Documentation

Two documents in the FIPS PUB series—FIPS PUB 38 [5-5] and FIPS PUB [5-8]—define 13 document types and provide detailed content guides for these documents. They cover documents required for project initiation such as a project request, feasibility study, or cost-benefit analysis. Also covered are documents detailing functional and data requirements, system, subsystem, program and data base specifications, test plan and test analysis report, and manuals for users, operators, and maintenance programmers. While FIPS 38 and FIPS 64 are tied to the concept of a typical development life cycle, which is representative of medium and large size projects, other guidelines are not linked to a life cycle concept.

Product Documentation

FIPS PUB 30 [5-4] defines a software summary, which is a form (Standard Form 185). The General Services Administration uses it to describe and announce computer programs in the Federal Software Exchange Program to enter data into a central registry of selected Government computer programs which are available for Government-wide shared use. Agencies having requirements for software that they plan to acquire from commercial sources are required to review the Federal Software Exchange Catalog to meet their requirements.

Similarly, the American National Standard for Computer Program Abstracts provides content guidance for a series of narrative paragraphs, outlining purpose, operation, and other details of computer programs [6-4]. The American National Standard Guidelines for the Documentation of Digital Computer Programs [6-1] describe scientific computer programs. They combine some of the contents of FIPS PUB 30 and FIPS PUB 38 and give a description of computer program products intended for wide dissemination.

A similar set of guidelines for documentation of computer models has recently been published by NBS [6-2]. These guidelines are also product-oriented and include model descriptions for four types of users: managers, analysts, programmers, and users.

27. Required Resources

In order to develop quality software and corresponding quality documentation, resources must be allocated, planned for, and provided. This requires people, money, and facilities.

People

Documentation is prepared for people and addresses a variety of audiences. This must be taken into consideration in the planning and preparation of documentation. For instance, the amount of technical detail needed by a manager is quite different from that needed by a maintenance programmer.

Development documentation usually is prepared by the programmer. On the other hand, it has proven useful to have product documentation prepared by technical writing specialists. If this is not possible, care should be taken to assign documentation authorship to persons who are trained for, interested in, and motivated to do this work. Early interaction and communication is desirable between persons preparing the documentation and the persons preparing the computer programs. Writers should have an opportunity to meet with analysts, designers, programmers, testers, and users early during the course of a development project. Such interaction permits writers to gain familiarity with the intent and purpose of the project, and the many other details essential for their work.

Computer program development is managed by people. Standards and guidelines will be useless unless they are used properly. Proper use requires both competent direction and competent application of the standards.

Competent direction requires a manager who appreciates the importance of documentation and who can judge the balance between the documentation required on a project and the overall requirements of the project. This guideline should help in establishing this balance by outlining documentation planning and review processes, and by references to detail about levels of documentation, document content, and procedures [5-5].

Competent application of standards and guidelines requires a motivated and experienced staff, who follow available guidance in the overall framework of system development. General guidance needs to be translated into specific project-unique detail which requires experience and judgment. This guideline should assist in this effort as well, by providing references to details of document content, to levels of documentation, and to document types [5-5, 5-8].

Technical work and managing are critically dependent on people. No guidelines or standards can substitute for good people. Some training in technical writing and documentation techniques may be appropriate and useful. The prime requirement, however, remains the employment and retention of good personnel both for computer program development and for documentation.

Facilities

Certain automated software tools have been used successfully in the preparation of computer-related documentation. Flowchart generators are programs that can automatically prepare flowcharts from computer code. Other computer programs can provide indexes, lists of data elements, cross references, and word processing functions. These capabilities avoid tedious retyping of draft material, and permit automatic reprinting of updated documents. Computer techniques have also been developed to check documents for consistency and to provide correlation between requirements and design documents, or between design documents and computer code. Computer programs also have been used to assist in managing, preparing, and maintaining documentation. Such automated aids have proven most effective in medium and large size projects. Application of automated documentation aids requires knowledgeable people to analyze requirements, to determine which applications are useful, and to introduce these techniques. They should be used if their cost and additional resources can be justified in terms of the overall project resources.

Funding

Although documentation costs are rarely identified as unique budget items, they are a significant part of the development costs.

Funds need to be allocated for document preparation, printing, storage and distribution, and maintenance. Time and effort are required for document reviews and updating. This should be reflected in the project budget and in schedules. Services of documentation specialists or other persons familiar with the field should be solicited while planning a software project to assist in the establishment of reasonable budgets. Some commercial firms specialize in the production of documentation and provide a viable alternative to in-house efforts. They often provide needed special capabilities on a limited time basis, and they help to identify the cost of documentation for a given project.

Conclusions

The chapters in Book Five identified software documentation as a critical element in software development and software engineering.

The concept of software documentation is a broad one. It covers the whole development life cycle, and is a necessary part of a user-oriented software product package. Managing the documentation portion of a software development requires resources for the needed documentation. It is desirable to produce documentation to accommodate the needs of development phases, and to provide timely, accurate, and complete documentation for users and maintenance staff. Decisions must be made on the extent, amount, types, and quality of documentation. Assignment of appropriate priorities, provision of adequate resources, proper planning, and specification of needed detail will help in providing the documentation required for a software development project. The general guidance provided in this report, the appended checklists, and lists of references provide enough information to permit adequate specification of all documentation requirements, and to review policies and procedures as well as standards and guidelines to ensure adequacy of planning and development efforts.

Glossary

This glossary lists some of the terms which occur frequently in the software documentation field. Some of the terms were taken from reference [5-1]. Other terms are based on, or adapted from, draft 7 of the Software Engineering Terminology developed by the Terminology Task Group, Subcommittee on Software Engineering Standards, IEEE Computer Society. The terms and definitions listed here should be considered as examples; in many cases major concepts may need additional definition.

AS BUILT Pertaining to an actual configuration of software code resulting from a software development project.

BASELINE A specification or product that has been formally reviewed and agreed upon, that serves as the basis for further development, and that can be changed only through formal change control procedures.

BLOCK DIAGRAM A diagram of a system, instrument or computer, in which the principal parts are represented by suitably annotated geometrical figures to show both the basic functions of the parts and the functional relationships between them.

BUILD TO Pertaining to a baseline specification from which a computer program will be coded.

COMPUTER PROGRAM ABSTRACT A brief description of a computer program, providing sufficient information for potential users to determine the appropriateness of the computer program to their needs and resources.

DESIGN SPECIFICATION A specification that documents how a system is to be built. It typically includes topics such as system or component structure, algorithms, control logic, data structures, data set use information, input-output formats, interface descriptions, etc. Contrast with: Requirements specification.

DEVELOPMENT SPECIFICATION Sometimes a synonym for requirements specification. Contrast with: Design specification.

DOCUMENT A data medium and the data recorded on it that generally has permanence and is human or machine readable.

DOCUMENTATION 1) A collection of documents on a given subject. 2) The process of generating a document.

DOCUMENTATION PLAN A management document describing the approach that will be taken for a documentation effort. The plan typically describes what documentation types

337

Software Validation, Verification, Testing, and Documentation

are to be prepared, what their contents are to be, when this is to be done and by whom, how it is to be done, and what the available resources and external factors affecting the desired results are.

FLOWCHART   A graphical representation of the definition, analysis, or method of solution of a problem, in which symbols are used to represent operations, data, flow, equipment, etc.

FORMAL SPECIFICATION   1) A specification written and approved in accordance with established standards. 2) A specification expressed in a requirements specification language.

FUNCTIONAL SPECIFICATION   A specification that documents the functional requirements for a system or system component. It describes what a system is to do rather than how it is to be built.

FUNCTIONAL REQUIREMENTS DOCUMENT   See: FUNCTIONAL SPECIFICATION

INTERFACE SPECIFICATION   A specification that documents the interface requirements for a system or system component.

LEVEL OF DOCUMENTATION   A description of required documentation indicating its scope, content, format, and quality. Selection of the level may be based on project, cost, intended usage, extent of effort, or other factors.

LIFE CYCLE   See: SOFTWARE LIFE CYCLE.

MAINTENANCE PLAN   A document that identifies the management and technical approach that will be used to maintain software products. It typically includes topics such as tools, resources, facilities, and schedules.

PERFORMANCE SPECIFICATION   1) A specification that sets forth the performance requirements for a system or system component. 2)Syn. for: Requirements specification.

PROGRAMMING SPECIFICATION   See: DESIGN SPECIFICATION.

PROJECT NOTEBOOK   A central repository of written material such as memos, plans, technical reports, etc. pertaining to a project.

PROJECT PLAN   A management document describing the approach that will be taken for a project. The plan typically describes the work to be done, the resources required, the methods to be used, the configuration management and quality assurance procedures to be followed, the schedules to be met, the project organization, etc. "Project" here is a generic term. Some projects may also need integration plans, security plans, quality assurance plans, etc. See also: Documentation plan, Software development plan, Test plan.

QUALITY ASSURANCE   A planned and systematic pattern of all actions necessary to provide adequate confidence that the item or product conforms to established requirements.

REQUIREMENTS SPECIFICATION   A specification that documents the requirements of a system or system component. It typically includes functional requirements, performance requirements, interface requirements, design requirements, development standards, etc. See also: SYSTEM SPECIFICATION, DESIGN SPECIFICATION.

SOFTWARE   Computer programs, procedures, rules and possibly associated documentation and data concerned with operation of a data processing system.

SOFTWARE DEVELOPMENT NOTEBOOK   A collection of material pertinent to the development of a given software module. Contents typically include the requirements, design,

338

Glossary

technical reports, code listings, test plans, test results, problem reports, schedules, notes, etc. for the module.

SOFTWARE DEVELOPMENT PLAN   The project plan for the development of a software product.

SOFTWARE DOCUMENTATION   Technical data or information, including computer listings and printouts, in human readable form, which describe or specify the design or details, explain the capabilities, or provide operating instructions for using the software to obtain desired results from a software system.

SOFTWARE LIFE CYCLE   The period of time that starts when a software product is initiated and ends when a product is no longer available for use.

SOFTWARE PRODUCT   Software that has been developed, tested, and documented to a level suitable for delivery to a customer.

SOFTWARE QUALITY ASSURANCE   A planned and systematic pattern of all actions necessary to provide adequate confidence that software conforms to established requirements and standards, and that it achieves satisfactory performance.

SPECIFICATION   1) A document that defines requirements, details a design, or describes a product. A specification usually is the basis for contracts, awards, and agreements to "build" a product. 2) The process of developing a specification. The process includes determining and obtaining the necessary information and producing the document.

SYSTEM DOCUMENTATION   Documentation conveying the requirements, design philosophy, design details, capabilities, limitations, and other characteristics of a system.

SYSTEM LIFE CYCLE   That period of time which starts when a system product is initiated and ends when the product is withdrawn from use. A software life cycle typically includes phases denoting activities such as initiation, requirements analysis, design, implementation, test, installation and checkout, operation and maintenance.

TEST PLAN   A document describing the testing that is to be performed to verify that a system or system component satisfies the specified requirements, the test personnel, and the test methods. See also: PROJECT PLAN.

TEST PROCEDURE   A formal document developed from a test plan that presents detailed instructions for the setup, operation, and evaluation of results for each defined test.

TEST REPORT   A document describing the results of the testing carried out for a system or system component.

USER   1) An individual applying the software to the solution of a problem, e.g. test or operation. 2) Any entity applying the software to the solution of a problem, e.g. a personnel department, another computer program, a network, an operator.

USER DOCUMENTATION   Documentation conveying to the end-user of a system instructions for using the system to obtain desired results—e.g. a user's manual.

Appendix 1:

Document Types

The following document types are outlined in the referenced documents. The references provide detailed outlines of document content. Some guidelines also indicate how to tailor contents to suit individual project constraints. (FIGS PUB 38 and FIPS PUG 64).

Analysts Manual (Computer Models)	NBS SP 500-73
Computer Program Abstract	ANSI X3.88-1980
(See also: Software Summary)	FIPS PUB 30
Cost Benefit Analysis	FIPS 64
Data Base Specification	FIPS 38
Data Requirements Document	FIPS 38
Feasibility Study	FIPS 64
Functional Requirements Document	FIPS 38
Maintenance Manual	FIPS 38
Maintenance Manual (Computer Models)	NBS SP 500-73
Operator's Manual	FIPS 38
Operator's Manual (Computer Models)	NBS SP 500-73
Program Specification	FIPS 38
Project Request	FIPS 64
Quality Assurance Plan	ANSI/IEEE 730
Software Summary	FIPS 30
(See also: Computer Program Abstracts)	ANSI X3.88-1980
Test Plan	FIPS 38
Test Report	FIPS 38
User's Manual	FIPS 38
User's Manual (Computer Models)	NBS SP-500-73

Appendix 2:

Policy Checklist

Has a decision been made to provide adequate documentation?

Has a policy statement dealing with documentation been published?

Has a person or organization been charged with responsibility for the preparation of documentation, development documentation, product documentation?

Have resources been made available for documentation?

Has a person or organization been charged with responsibility for documentation quality?

Have relationships been established between various levels of management, and functional organizational elements such as software engineering, hardware engineering, systems engineering, quality assurance, and documentation to identify required responsibilities, activities, and communications channels dealing with preparation, distribution, and maintenance of documentation?

Have all documentation requirements been integrated with the overall project development schedule?

Have appropriate documentation standards been identified?

Has a position been taken with regard to support tools and automated documentation support?

Appendix 3:

Planning Checklist

Has a documentation plan been prepared?

Have the required document types been defined?

Have required contents been outlined and described?

Have documentation standards been identified?

Have documentation standards been developed?

Have responsibilities been assigned for:
    document preparation?
    project librarian?
    alternate document storage?
    documentation review?
Have quality criteria been established?

Have schedules been established for deliverables:
    draft outline?
    first draft, other drafts?
    special graphics, diagrams?
Have review dates been specified?

Has an approval cycle been established?

Appendix 4:

Procedures Checklist

Has a review procedure been established?

Has participation of analysts, developers, programmers, maintenance persons, auditors, users, and managers been considered?

Has an approval cycle been set up?

Has a distribution list been established?

Has a method been established for keeping documentation up to date?

Has a feedback mechanism been established to obtain user comments and reactions to documentation?

Have maintenance procedures been established for storage and distribution?

Have procedures been set up for document identification and document control?

Has a facility been set up for vital document storage?

Appendix 5:

FIPS Standards and Guidelines

This appendix lists Federal Information Processing Standards and Guidelines which have been issued by the National Bureau of Standards. Copies of these publications are available from the National Technical Information Service, U.S. Department of Commerce, Springfield, VA 22161. Information concerning prices and related standards or guidelines may be obtained from the Standards Administration Office, Institute for Computer Sciences and Technology, NBS, Washington DC 20234.

1. FIPS PUB 11-1
Dictionary for Information Processing
1977 September 30
   An alphabetic listing of over 4000 terms and their definitions. It was prepared by ANSI Technical Committee X3K5 and also contains terms approved by the International Organization for Standardization. A revised edition is in preparation.

2. FIPS PUB 20
Guidelines for Describing Information Interchange Formats.
1972 March 1
   Characteristics of formatted information, which must be considered for interchange of such information, are identified and described. The objective is to clarify and improve documentation for formatted information transfer. The guidelines describe physical and logical characteristics. A glossary of terms is also attached.

3. FIPS PUB 24
Flowchart Symbols and their Usage in Information Processing.
1973 June 30
   Standard flowchart symbols and their use are specified. The standard is also known as ANSI X3.5-1970.

4. FIPS PUB 30
Software Summary for Describing Computer Programs and Automated Data Systems.

Appendix 5

1974 June 30

A standard software summary form is defined (SF-185), together with instructions for describing computer programs for identification, reference, and dissemination. The form is used to record summaries of programs developed or acquired by Federal agencies, and by GSA to register selected Government software.

Appendix 6:

Other Standards and Guidelines

This appendix lists Standards and Guidelines published by the American National Standards Institute and by professional organizations. Information on availability and costs can be obtained from the publishers.

1. American National Standard Guidelines for the Documentation of Digital Computer Programs
ANSI N413-1974,
American Nuclear Society,
555 North Kensington Avenue,
La Grange Park, IL 60525

2. Guide for Technical Documentation of Computer Projects
ANSI X3K1
Technical Report No. 3

3. American National Standard for Computer Program Abstracts
ANSI X3K7
X3.88-1980

4. IEEE Standard for Software Quality Assurance Plans
ANSI/IEEE Std 730
The Institute of Electrical and Electronic Engineers, Inc.
345 East 47th Street,
New York, NY 10017
September 1981

Book Six
Computer Model
Documentation Guide

Abstract

Book Six provides guidelines for preparing documentation for computer models. Recommended structures for four types of manuals providing model information for four different classes of audiences (managers, users, analysts, and programmers) is presented. This document specifies the content of sections and subsections for each type of manual. Manuals prepared using these guidelines will enable persons interested in a model to understand the capabilities and limitations of that model.

Key words: documentation; manuals; models; simulation.

28. Introduction

Book Six provides guidelines for preparing documentation for computer models, as well as complete submodels delivered separately. The primary goal of model documentation is to communicate effectively the details of model design and operation to persons with varying interests in a model. Since a model's developers are frequently not the model's ultimate users, complete, concise documentation is essential for effective model use. Documentation should inform analysts familiar with the phenomena being modeled, or the modeling techniques employed, of the essential features and assumptions of a new model. Throughout its life cycle, a model may be used and modified by various people, making accurate and current documentation of the underlying computer program essential for proper, correct use and maintenance of the model. Ultimately, model results may be used in a decision-making environment by individuals who are unfamiliar with the details of modeling and the associated benefits, risks, and costs. In such situations, model documentation should describe, in non-technical terms, the environment in which a model can be useful, limitations on its use, and the manpower, time, and dollar costs required by its use. These guidelines recommend structures and some conventions for preparing model documentation in the form of manuals for users, analysts, programmers, and managers. Each type of manual should provide clear, concise documentation that is directed toward an audience with a particular interest in a model.

These guidelines devote a chapter to each type of manual, i.e., The Manager's Manual, The User's Manual, The Programmer's Manual, The Analyst's Manual. Each Chapter begins with a table of contents that lists recommended topics of interest to users of that manual. Items may be added to or deleted from this table of contents, however, according to individual requirements. The discussion for each manual enlarges upon the items required in each of the sections and subsections, as recommended in the table of contents for that manual. Terms used in each manual should be those directed toward that manual's audience.

These guidelines are for models that are used chiefly in a decision-making environment. Thus, the main goal of a Manager's Manual is to assist managers to make decisions. To accomplish this, the Manual must describe the model and its ap-

349

plication to managers (including the management that sponsored the model) who may be interested in using a developed capability. The Manual should provide managers with sufficient information to permit them to accurately assess model input requirements (including time, money, and other resources), available outputs, and the accuracy and precision of the results. Managers can use this Manual in justifying the employment of the model and in evaluating subsequent results.

A user is assumed to be interested mainly in deriving results from a model for specific applications. The guidelines recommend that the User's Manual be organized into a section for the user and a section for the data technicians who will set-up and run the model. To use the model intelligently, a user must be aware of its logical structure, the general simulation approach, and any assumptions and limitations affecting the model's applicability. A user need not be interested in details of programming or analysis beyond the preparation of input and the interpretation of model results.

Programmers are interested primarily in maintaining and modifying a model. A programmer must correct any errors discovered during model usage that are not attributable to user-entered data. Programmers, especially those required to convert a model to another computer system, need to understand features of a model that are installation unique. Thus, the Programmer's Manual must provide all the details necessary to understand the operation of a model: to debug it, to maintain and modify it, and to convert the model to other computer systems.

These guidelines assume an analyst to be interested primarily in the analytical techniques and algorithms used in a model. An analyst is concerned with the equations used in a model and the methods used for model verification and validation. An analyst does not need to know user details such as input and output formats, or programming details involving language syntax.

Decisions about which of these manuals are actually required, whether or not they should be prepared in separate volumes, etc., should be made on a case-by-case basis. Also, a plan should be developed for documentation updates and maintenance, so that these manuals remain current. Such issues as these should be dealt with early during the model planning and development phases, so that documentation requirements actually become part of the development plan, rather than an afterthought. Further, applicable documentation produced using programming conventions should be used in conjunction with these guidelines.

Other guidelines prepared specifically to support computer software documentation are available which may be used in conjunction with this guideline. These documents are:

- FIPS PUB 30, Software Summary for Describing Computer Programs and Automated Data Systems. It is used to announce computer programs which are transferable, and have broad applicability. A standard software summary form is defined (SF-185), which permits description of the program for identification, reference and dissemination. This form is used by the General Services Administration for registry of programs and for publication of program abstracts in the Federal Software Exchange Catalog.

- FIPS PUB 38, Guidelines for Documentation of Computer Programs and Automated Data Systems. It provides guidance to documentation content for the development phase, including requirements documentation, system specifications, user, operations and maintenance manuals, and test documentation.
- FIPS PUB 64, Guidelines for Documentation of Computer Programs and Automated Data Systems for the Initiation Phase. This document provides guidance for project requests, feasibility studies, and cost benefit analyses.

29. Guidelines for Preparing a Manager's Manual

This chapter provides a recommended structure for the Manager's Manual and describes the contents of each section and subsection. A manual prepared using these guidelines will provide descriptions of model capabilities and requirements such that model strengths and limitations will be communicated to decision makers and potential users. The Manager's Manual will provide managers with sufficient information to permit them to accurately assess model input requirements (including time, money, and other resources), available outputs, and the accuracy and precision of the results. Managers can use the Manager's Manual in justifying the employment of the model and in evaluating subsequent results. Figure 29.1 is a recommended table of contents for preparing a Manager's Manual. The sections and subsections included in that figure list suggested topics that are of interest to managers. Items may be added to or deleted from this table of contents, however, according to individual requirements.

Introduction

The introduction should identify the sponsoring organization, provide the background of the project, state the purpose of the model, and present an overview of the remaining sections in the manual. A common introduction used for other manuals prepared for a model may be used only if that introduction is void of specialized terms. The specific purpose of the Manager's Manual should be included in the introduction in a statement of the form:

"The purpose of this manual is to communicate to management the capabilities and limitations of (model name)."

Model Description

This section should provide a summary of model capabilities and limitations. Use high-level block diagrams to clarify the narrative, as needed.

Guidelines for Preparing a Manager's Manual

```
1.   Introduction

2.   Model Description

2.1   Capabilities
2.2   Input/Output Classes
2.3   Assumptions and Limitations

3.   Model Development and Experimentation

3.1   Development History
3.2   Verification and Validation
3.3   Model Experiments
3.4   Costs and Resource Requirements

4.   Current and Additional Applications

4.1   Current Use
4.2   Additional Applications

APPENDICES

    A.   Project Documentation

    B.   Bibliography
```

Figure 29.1
Recommended Table of Contents for a
Management Summary Manual

Capabilities

This subsection should briefly summarize the capabilities of the model. Include highlights of mathematical and engineering concepts (but not equations) used as the basis of the model. Include a statement of the model's primary purpose. For example, "the model can be used to determine the daily number of machines in a job shop required to process the daily orders." Provide an overview of functional details that explains how the model accomplishes its stated purpose. Discuss the general areas of the model's applicability, including the decision making environments. For example, describe the types of systems and situations that can be simulated by the model (possibly with minor changes), including the number and kinds of subsystems that can be simulated. For example, if a job shop model includes order processing, machine repair, or distribution subsystems, then their descriptions should be provided. Also include the relationship of this model to any other models (i.e., another model may prepare input data for this model).

Input/Output Classes
Provide a short discussion on the different classes of input data required to drive the model and of output data generated by the model. For example, a job shop model might require entering the number of production centers, the number of machines per production center, the service rates of the machines, and the routing of the jobs (orders). Examples of model output include statistics that show the utilizations (percent busy time) of the production centers and the job turnaround (total processing) times. Identify any special preprocessing required for input data, as well as all postprocessing required on model results.

Assumptions and Limitations
List assumptions and limitations concerning the applicability of the model. Identify any restrictions on model usage caused by accuracy limitations of input data and output quantities. Provide comments on levels of detail in the model that affect the model's applicability. For example, an analytical representation rather than a detailed simulation of a system component could affect model application. Also describe any use of random parameters that may affect the accuracy and use of model output.

Model Development and Experimentation
This section should describe significant model experiments already run and should provide details on model verification and validation procedures used. Include information on the model's development history resource costs and requirements, and use.

Development History
This subsection should provide pertinent details of the history of model development. Include comments on any alternative methods to computer simulation that were considered. Provide information on any "lessons learned" during model development, such as cost overruns, model development delays, user dissatisfaction with model results, insufficient workload data to support current and future model applications, inadequate model documentation, poorly defined problems, etc.

Verification/Validation
This subsection should describe any verification and validation procedures performed on the model. Include any analyses performed on the sensitivity of model output data to variations in model input data.

Model Experiments

Describe significant model experiments performed and their results. Briefly describe the purpose of each experiment and the extent to which each experiment's goals were realized. Discuss the management decisions affected by each experiment. Discussion of major model experiments may be included in separate subsections.

Costs and Resource Requirements

This section should provide details on the costs and resource requirements of the model. Include the cost (in time and money) of collecting and validating input data. For example, long and costly data collection efforts may be necessary. Provide comments on model maintenance and experiment costs. Discuss job turnaround times (including typical run times) and peculiar model requirements such as abnormally large core requirements or long run times. Include comments on model portability and security requirements, as needed.

Current and Additional Applications

This section should summarize benefits already derived from the model and recommend other applications for the model.

Current Use

This subsection should briefly describe how the model has been used by management in its decision-making process. Provide details of recommendations and conclusions derived using the model.

Additional Applications

This subsection should provide details of any additional applications and uses of the model beyond the current usage. Discuss in general terms any extensions and enhancements to the model which are feasible and could improve its utility. Identify any extensions which have been scheduled or planned.

Appendices

Two appendices should be provided as required. Appendix A should reference all other project documentation (including the User's Manual, Analyst's Manual, and Programmer's Manual), including references to the organization and person responsible for maintaining the document. Include references to any documentation of experiments performed using the model. Appendix B should list all applicable documents (excluding project documentation previously included in Appendix A), including cited and uncited references.

30. Guidelines for Preparing a User's Manual

This Chapter presents a recommended User's Manual organizational structure and discusses the contents of sections and subsections to be included therein. A User's Manual prepared using these guidelines will enable a nonprogramming model user to understand the model's logical structure, the input data requirements, the results produced by the model, and the use of model results. Figure 30.1 presents a recommended table of contents for a User's Manual. The sections and subsections contained in the figure cover the general needs of a user interested in a model. In documenting a particular model, however, sections and subsections may be added to improve clarity, and some subsections may be omitted for simple models. Note that there is a certain amount of redundance among the various sections of a User's Manual prepared according to these guidelines. Nevertheless, the progressively increasing level of detail dictated by this structure is desirable to satisfy different levels of user interest in the manual.

Introduction

The User's Manual introduction should contain the background of the project, the purpose of the model, and an overview of the remaining sections in the manual. A common introduction may be used for all the manuals prepared for a model, but the specific purpose of the User's Manual should be included in a statement of the form:

"The purpose of this manual is to provide nonprogramming users of (model name) with the information necessary to use the model effectively."

Description of the Model

This section should contain a well-structured presentation of the logical details of the model. The material here should be descriptive and include block diagrams and tables and charts where needed; it should not give details needed by a data technician to run the model.

Software Validation, Verification, Testing, and Documentation

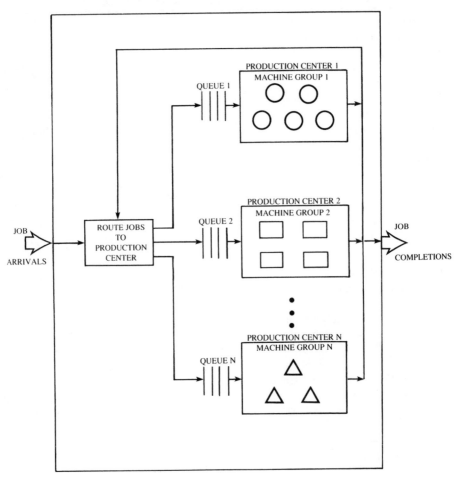

Figure 30.2
Physical System Highlights Example

Overview

This subsection should provide sufficient general information about the model to assist a user in determining the applicability of the model for specific needs.

Model Identification   The identification should contain the name of the physical system being simulated, name of the model (acronym and expansion), programming language(s) used to implement the model, computer(s) on which the model may be run, and relationships, if any, to other models.

Physical System Highlights   Include a block diagram that shows the physical system or phenomenon being simulated. Discuss, at a macro level, the major system

358

elements shown in the diagram, their relation to each other, and the flow of control, information, data, and activity between them, as appropriate. In the case of complex models, provide in this subsection a first-level block diagram that shows the major subsystems and their interactions, and postpone the details of each of the subsystems until Subsection Model Identification Figure 30.2 is an example of physical system highlights depicting the operations of a typical shop model.

Model Applicability   Discuss the general magnitude of model applicability. The types of systems or situations that can be simulated by the model (possibly with minor changes) and the number of subsystems (e.g., production centers and machines per production center in a job shop simulation) that can be handled are examples of material to be included in this subsection.

Input and Output   Provide a general statement of the different kinds of input data needed to drive the model, the output data generated by the model, and uses of model output. For example, a job shop model might require entering the number of production centers, the number of machines per production center, the service rates of the machines, and the routing of the jobs (orders). Examples of model output include statistics that show the utilizations (percent busy time) of the production centers and the job turnaround (total processing) times. The principal model use could be to determine the number of machines in a job shop required to process the daily orders.

Highlight any special data collection procedures (e.g., run other models or computer programs, extact data from documents or listings, conduct sampling experiments) required to produce model input data. List any unique data sources or other organizations that might have to be contacted to gather data. Figure 30.3 is an example of an input/output schematic.

Methodology
This subsection should provide the user with a detailed understanding of how the model works.

Physical System Details   The operations that take place in each of the blocks in the Physical System Block Diagram should be discussed in detail. Detailed block diagrams of subsystems should be provided for a complex model. The level of detail used in the simulation (e.g., the smallest meaningful time increment for event-type models, the way in which complex system interactions are simplified in the model) should be clearly indicated.

Model Logic and Data Flow   This subsection should describe the logical flow of data through the model, from the entry of input data to the generation of output data. Include a schematic that indicates the major model software elements, the data flow between model elements, and model inputs and outputs. Figures 30.4 and 30.5 are

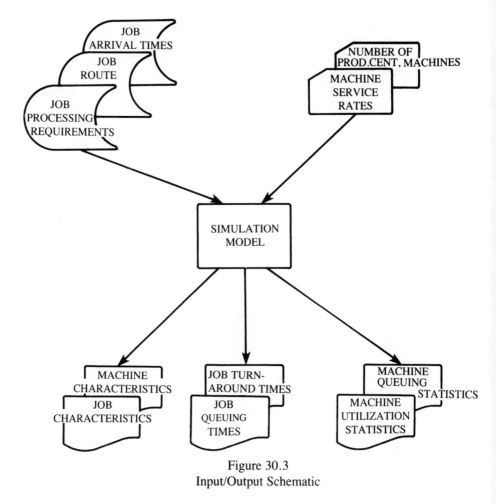

Figure 30.3
Input/Output Schematic

two types of schematics for the same model. Either of these two types, or any other type of schematic that clearly depicts model logic and data flow, may be used. Accompanying discussion should relate model elements and data flow to physical system elements and data flow. For complex models, include a table that relates physical system names to the program segments that simulate them.

Assumptions and Limitations

All the system-related assumptions, assumptions on model parameters (e.g., hard-coded values), limitations on output accuracy, and any restrictions on the use of the model should be discussed in detail.

System-Related Assumptions and Limitations   List any assumptions that limit or describe the kinds of systems or phenomena that are treated in the model. For exam-

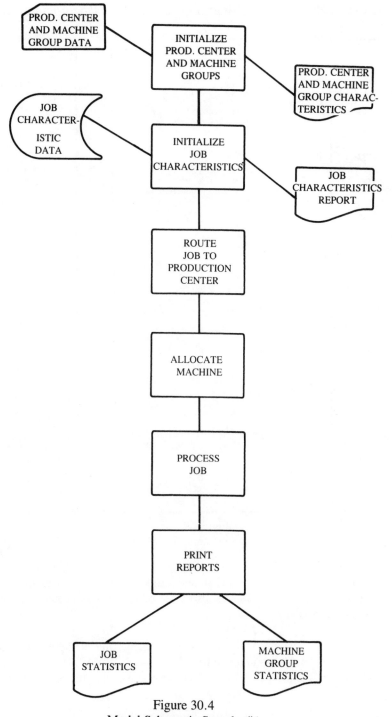

Figure 30.4
Model Schematic Sample #1

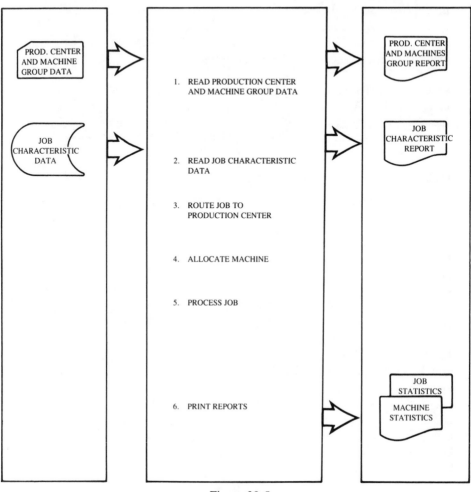

Figure 30.5
Model Schematic Sample #2

ple, a description of a job shop model should define the model's boundaries (i.e., the subsystems that the model includes), the kinds of activities simulated (e.g., machine failures and repairs), etc.

Model Parameters   List the valid ranges for principal model input parameters (e.g., the maximum and minimum number of subsystems). Also list values for any parameters that are included in the model software and cannot be modified by the user.

362

Output Limitations   List any limitations on output usage caused by inaccuracy of the output data. For example, all digits in an output data field may not be significant because the input data are estimates, and high precision in the output data is either unobtainable or inappropriate.

Restrictions on Model Use   Enumerate all restrictions on model usage. For example, a job shop model restriction might be that only first-in, first-out queuing disciplines are modeled for the production centers.

Model Input Data

This section should describe in detail all the input data needed to run the model. The material in this and the four subsequent sections should serve as a reference for both the user and the data technician who runs the model.

General Description

This subsection should describe the overall input data structure and the data media (tape, cards, disk data sets, etc.). Include a table that shows input data set names, their media, and any general data limitations. Also, describe the interdependence, if any, of input data sets. (Detailed descriptions of individual data items within the input data sets should be left for the subsection on detailed descriptions.)

Detailed Descriptions

Input data items are normally organized in related groups, such as machine performance characteristics, job processing requirements, etc., or as the data items that are entered on one punch card. These related groups of data establish and define a data set and should be described together. The input data sets and the items within each data set should be discussed in the order of their appearance in the run stream. For each input data set, provide the following information (each data set description should begin on a new page).

Data Set Name   In this subsection, give an overview of the data set's contents and its purpose.

Number of Inputs.   Indicate the number of data sets of this type and the maximum number of data items in the data set that may (or must) be used in the simulation. Discuss any factors that influence the total number of inputs from this data set.

Other Related Data Sets.   List any data sets whose contents depend on or dictate the input values for this data set. Discuss the relationships between data items in the data sets.

Description of Data Items.   In this subsection, provide general comments on the format of the data items (e.g., free form, integer in card columns 8–11,

NAMELIST) followed by the description of each of the data items. For each item, the following should be given: name, type, format (if fixed), permissible range or fixed value, unit of measurement, default value (value assumed by the program when the item is omitted), definition of the item describing how it is used in the model, relationship to other data items. Tables should be used where appropriate.

Sample Input. A format layout should be provided for the data set to provide the user with a visual reference for preparing the input data.

Data Collection and Maintenance
An important part of model application is data collection. Therefore, it is necessary to include appropriate instructions on data collection and maintenance. Specific responsibilities need to be assigned to analysts and users for these functions.

Data Sources Discuss the data sources for each input data set. The discussion should identify the form in which raw data are available, other organizational elements from which the data must be collected, if appropriate, and the time required to collect the data.

Collection Procedures Describe any special statistical techniques or experiments for obtaining the data. Identify any other computer programs or models that must be used to collect or process data, and list or reference instructions for their use. Where appropriate, include a flowchart that illustrates the major data collection steps and their sequence. Figure 30.6 is an example of special procedures to be used in obtaining data for a model. In this example, the type and frequency of orders are analyzed along with production center performance data to produce a statistical data base. This data base is then used as input to a model of the order handling process. The order model produces data that profiles the arrival patterns, routing distributions, and processing requirements of the jobs. These data are, in turn, used as input to the job shop model.

Updating Procedures Give step-by-step procedures for maintaining the data sets and preparing them for new experiments. Identify any other computer programs that must be used to update the data sets, and list or reference instructions for their use. Where appropriate, include a flowchart that illustrates the major update procedures and their sequence.

Model Output Data
This section should describe in detail all the output data produced by the model and should indicate their meanings and uses.

General Description
Discuss the overall output structure in this section. Indicate the number and types of output data sets, output media, correlation between outputs, quantity of output (op-

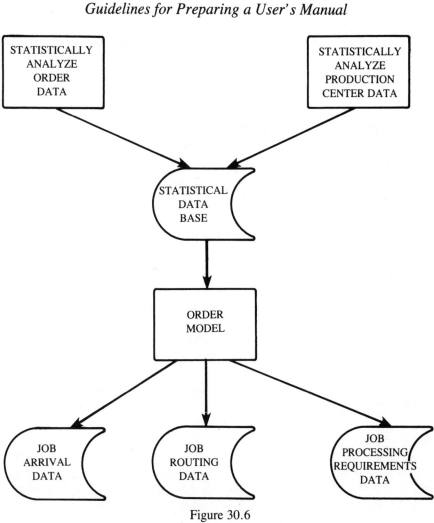

Figure 30.6
Special Procedures Example

tional and mandatory), and postprocessing, if any, that should be performed on the output data.

Detailed Description

For each output data set (or major group of logically connected data items), provide the following information (each output data set should begin on a new page).

Data Set Name   Give the full name or acronym of the output data set or group of data under this subheading. Give an overview of the data set's contents, its purpose, and its relation to other model results.

Description of Items. Each output item should be included in a table that shows its name, a brief description, and gives information to use in validity checking, if appropriate. Accompanying discussion should expand on each item's description and should show how the items are derived or calculated. Include mathematical formulae where appropriate.

Interpretation. Explain how the data items can be used, and describe actions to be taken for any subsequent runs based on the output.

Sample Output. Include a sample of the output data set. A sample format is satisfactory where it is not practical to provide an actual sample.

Run Preparation Instructions

This section of the User's Manual should describe procedures for organizing the input data to submit computer runs as discussed in the Model Input Data section, above.

Run-Stream Description

This subsection should give a pictorial (or tabular) representation of the deck constituting the run-stream that shows all the control cards and the data cards in proper sequence. Mandatory and optional cards should be discussed. If the model is interactive, include comments on any special techniques used for interactive submission of jobs.

Resource Requirements

This subsection should describe the computer resources required by the model. These include main memory, mass storage, number of tape units, execution time, numbers of punched cards, and printed lines expected as output. If the computer resources vary depending on input data, provide aids to estimate them.

Restart/Recovery Procedures

For models that require large amounts of computer resources it is important to recover from abnormal terminations and to restart the job. If any such provisions are made in the model design, they should be discussed in this subsection.

Sample Model Run

Include a sample run that illustrates the complete input scenario and the resulting output to assist a beginning user in making a test run and verifying correctness of procedures.

Trouble-Shooting Guide

Tabulate user input error-messages produced by the model software, and describe the required corrective action. Since other errors should be handled by programmers, those errors should be discussed in the programmer's manual.

Appendices

Three appendices should be provided as required. Appendix A should provide an alphabetical listing of all abbreviations and acronyms used in the User's Manual. Appendix B should list all specialized User's Manual terms and their definitions. All applicable documents, including cited and uncited references, should be provided in Appendix C.

31. Guidelines for Preparing a Programmer's Manual

This chapter provides a recommended organization for a Programmer's Manual and describes the contents of each section and subsection proposed for that manual. A Programmer's Manual written using these guidelines will enable a programmer to maintain and modify a model. The guidelines will provide all the details necessary for a programmer to understand the operation of the model and to trace through it for debugging, for making modifications, and for determining if and how the model can be converted to other computer systems. Figure 31.1 is a recommended table of contents for a Programmer's Manual. The sections and subsections included in the figure cover the general needs of a programmer interested in a model. In documenting a particular model, however, sections and subsections may be added to improve clarity, and some subsections may be omitted for simple models. Any appropriate documentation produced using a program documentation language could be used to satisfy the guidelines contained herein.

Introduction

The introduction to the Programmer's Manual should contain the background of the project, the purpose of the model, and an overview of the remaining sections in the manual. A common introduction may be used for all the manuals prepared for a model, but the specific purpose of a Programmer's Manual should be included in a statement of the form:

"The purpose of this manual is to provide programmer personnel of (model name) with the information necessary to effectively maintain and modify the model."

Model Specifications

This section should provide a summary of the model's specifications, including capabilities (i.e., problems addressed and methods of solution), a description of the host computer system, and the processing requirements (i.e., memory, peripherals,

Guidelines for Preparing a Programmer's Manual

Figure 31.1
Recommended Table of Contents for a Programmer's Manual

languages) placed by the model on that host system. The details should be presented in tabular form (supplemented by narrative description, as appropriate), whereby one table describes the complete modeling system and additional tables describe major submodels or programs as needed for clarity.

Model Description

This section should contain a well-structured presentation with emphasis on the operational details of the model. The discussion should be written in an easy-to-understand manner that cross-references special model language terms with modeled system features whenever possible. This section should be divided into four subsections.

Processing

This subsection should provide details on model operations for programmers who need to understand the processing techniques used in the model. The discussion should be at the Macro level, with a discussion of internal routine details postponed until later. Details on I/O formats and default input data values should be reserved for the User's Manual. Block diagrams should be used as necessary to supplement the narrative.

Overview   This subsection should present, in modeled system terminology, an overview of the problem solved by the model. Include a discussion of the basic tasks modeled. Figure 31.2 is an example of a block diagram that could supplement a narrative description in this subsection.

Major Components   This subsection should describe the flow of data or control information through the model at the major routine, or routine group, level. Include detailed block diagrams that depict paths among the modeled tasks, highlighting major decision points in the logic flow. This subsection may contain as many levels of discussion as are necessary to clearly describe model operation.

Model Initialization and Wrap-Up   This subsection should note any differences in the performance of model tasks accomplished during model initialization and wrap-up and those same tasks when performed during normal processing.

Data Structures

This subsection should provide information on all data structures internal to the model. Include descriptions of local and global variables, arrays, and data sets, as well as any special data structures, such as the set-entity relationships in SIMSCRIPT. If required for understanding, separate descriptions of each array index should be provided.

370

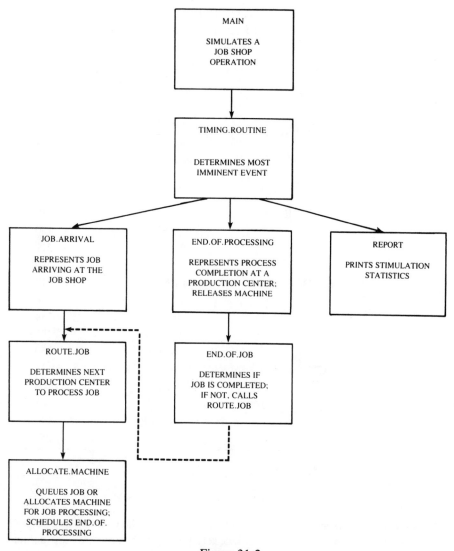

Figure 31.2
Example of a Model Overview Block Diagram

Local Data Structures This subsection should contain the meaning and purpose of all local variables, arrays, and data sets (local data structures have their values defined only within particular routines). To improve clarity, local data structures should be associated with the routines in which they appear.

Table 31.1
Cross-Referenced Data Structure List Sample

	Name		Source Code
Number	Item	Routine	Line Number
1	AMGO (V)[1]	MAIN	15
2	AOPOS (A)[2]	FASTER	52
3	BVBC (V)	MAIN	12
		TFBAI	163
		PRNTREP	210
			212
			290
4	CMCODE (V)	MAIN	10
		ACSUMT	150
		PRNTREP	211
			286
5	LEVDAT (DS)[3]	MAIN	13
		AUXSUM	120
		THBAB	184
		THBAI	195
		PRNTREP	250
6	TCTV (V)	MAIN	14
		ABFSTR	106
			108
		PRNTREP	210
			253

[1]Item is a variable.
[2]Item is an array.
[3]Item is a data set.

Global Data Structures This subsection should contain the meaning and purpose of all global variables, arrays, and data sets (global data structures are defined throughout the model). Include an alphabetized list of global data structures (including special data structures), cross-referenced by the routines in which they appear, and the source code line numbers (Table 31.1). Source code line numbers can be obtained from the source listing as described later. Examples of global data structures that should be included in this subsection are the COMMON blocks of FORTRAN.

Special Data Structures Any special data structures, both local and global, should be listed and described in this subsection. For example, a job shop model implemented in SIMSCRIPT might represent the jobs with temporary entities, the job processing requirements with entity attributes, and the sequence of production centers required to process the job with a set (owned by the job with production centers as numbers). A GPSS implementation, however, might represent the jobs with transactions, the processing requirements with transaction parameters, and the route with a row in a matrix save value (the columns contain the sequence of production centers).

Overlays

If the model is overlayed, this subsection should provide details of the overlay design decisions that determined the overlay strategy. Included should be a narrative and a block diagram description of the control flow of the overlays and their interactions. Figure 31.3 contains a sample overlay structure with a main program, four primary overlay segments, and five secondary overlay segments. Routines residing in each overlay, and their memory requirements, should be listed (Table 31.2). References should be made to the discussion of model processing in this manual to reinforce or clarify the overlay discussion.

Model Modifications

This subsection should include information concerning changes in model software and data bases. Include a description of any programming conventions used in the model (e.g., all variables referencing one data base may begin with a specific character). In addition, this subsection should provide procedures needed by programmers during the model compilation, recompilation, and execution stages. Include a sample control card setup that illustrates each of those states, including mandatory and optional cards. If the model is interactive, include comments on interactive procedures.

Planned Maintenance This subsection should identify all planned periodic maintenance on the model and its data bases (e.g., periodic data base updates).

Other Changes This subsection should identify procedures for making all modifications to the model other than planned periodic maintenance. Provide details for making changes necessitated by programming errors discovered during model usage, as well as changes to the model required by changes in the host modeling language. Include directions for implementing software changes to produce a new version of the model (e.g., changes in model applicability).

Description of Routines

This section should provide a detailed description of principal model routines. Include a discussion of all types of routines that comprise the model (i.e., event, subroutine, function, etc). Provide an alphabetized listing of all routine names along

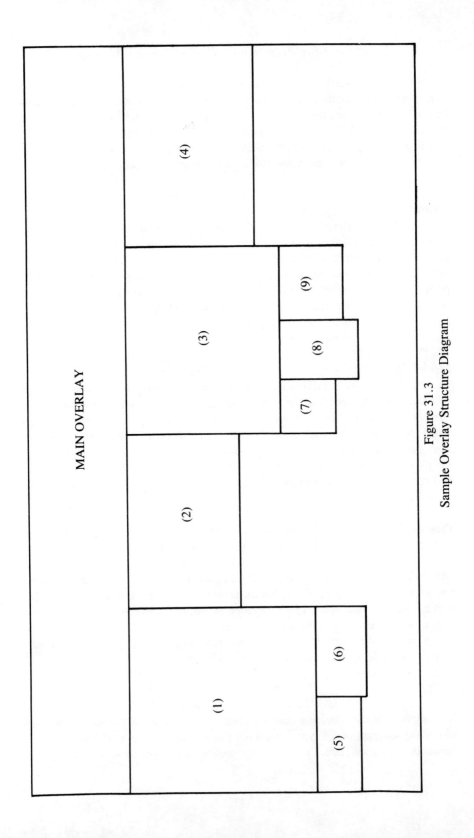

MAIN OVERLAY

(1)
(2)
(3)
(4)
(5)
(6)
(7)
(8)
(9)

Figure 31.3
Sample Overlay Structure Diagram

Table 31.2
Sample List of Routines by Overlay Segment

Overlay Segment Number	Routine Name	Memory Requirements (KBYTES)
1	MAIN	50
	ROUT1	10
	ROUT2	20
	ROUT3	20
2	PROC1	100
	PROC2	25
	PROC3	25
3	COMP1	75
	COMP2	50
4	SOLV1	75
	SOLV2	50
5	LSIGN1	100
	LSIGN2	20
	LSIGN3	15
6	COMP10	140
7	FIND1	70
	FIND2	48
8	SUM10	140
9	WRITER	137
10	REPORT	128

with calling routines and called routines (Table 31.3) or a block diagram showing routine linkages, as needed. Each routine should be described in a separate subsection. For each routine, provide the following information.

Routine Name (First Routine)

Purpose Briefly state the purpose of the routine (e.g., routine ALLOCATE computes the time a job is scheduled to complete its processing at a production center).

Type Specify the type of routine (i.e., function, subroutine). A description of all routine types in the model should be contained in the introductory comments of this section.

Calling Sequence List all variables, arrays, pointers in the routine calling sequence.

Table 31.3
Cross-Referenced Routine List Example

Number	Calling Routine	Called Routine
1	ABFSTR	NONE
2	ACSUMT	TFBAI
		THBAB
3	AUXSUM	ACSUMT
4	FASTER	ABFSTR
		AUXSUM
5	MAIN	FASTER
6	PRNTREP	NONE
7	TFBAI	PRNTREP
8	THBAB	THBAI
9	THBAI	PRNTREP

Argument Definition   Define all routine arguments.

Calling Routines   List all routines that call this routine.

Called Routines   List all routines called by this routine.

Files   List all files this routine creates or uses.

Error Messages   Itemize all error messages which can originate in this routine.

Narrative   Include a narrative description as necessary, to amplify and highlight subtleties included in the code. As a minimum, include any equations and formulae referenced from the Analyst's Manual.

Block Diagrams   Use block diagrams or other documentation aids (such as program documentation languages), as required, to clearly depict operation of the routine.

Sample Test Run   Provide the results of test runs, along with values of input data, for each complex routine to assist in verifying changes to those routines.

Data Base Description
This section should discuss all mass storage files used or created by the model. Each file should be described in a separate subsection and should contain the following information (each file description should begin on a new page).

File Name (First File)
Provide the full name or acronym of all the model files.

Purpose Briefly state the purpose of the file (e.g., contains preprocessed destination data).

Format Explain the format of the file (i.e., block, size, record size, data item identification, and field sizes).

Routines Identify all routines that use or create the file.

Updating Include instructions for file maintenance and updating as appropriate.

Source Listing
This section should contain the source code of the model. If the source listing is large, it should be bound separately and made available upon request. Also, source listings with line numbers can be referenced as a cross-reference for model variables.

Error Messages
All program-generated error messages, the names of the routines in which they are generated, and suggested corrective actions should be listed in this section. Each error message may be described in a separate subsection.

Appendices
Four appendices to this manual should be provided as required. Appendix A should define all terms in the Programmer's Manual not defined elsewhere in the document. A list of applicable documents, including cited and uncited references, should be provided in Appendix B. Appendix C should provide an alphabetized index that gives the page on which each subject contained in the Programmer's Manual may be found. If the Programmer's Manual is divided into more than one volume, the index in the first volume should be the index of the volumes. The index in each of the remaining volumes should reference only those subjects within that volume. Appendix D should provide a listing of model test results along with values entered into the model that produced those results. Include any interim model outputs necessary to understand the final outputs. Provide analyses of model results as necessary.

32. Guidelines for Preparing an Analyst's Manual

This chapter presents a recommended organization for an Analyst's Manual and describes the contents of each section and subsection to be included in that manual. An Analyst's Manual prepared using these guidelines will enable an analyst to understand a model's functional structure, the algorithms used in the model, and techniques employed for model verification and validation. Figure 32.1 contains a recommended table of contents for an Analyst's Manual. The sections and subsections included cover the general needs of an analyst interested in a model. In documenting a particular model, however, sections and subsections may be added to improve clarity, and some subsections may be omitted for simple models.

Introduction

The introduction to the Analyst's Manual should contain the background of the project, the purpose of the model, and an overview of the remaining sections in the manual. A common introduction may be used for all the manuals prepared for a model, but the specific purpose of the Analyst's Manual should be included in a statement of the form:

> "The purpose of this manual is to provide nonprogramming analysts of (model name) with the details of the algorithms used in the model and the techniques employed for model verification and validation."

Functional Description of the Model

This section should contain a well-structured presentation with emphasis on the functional details of the model. The discussion should be written in an easy-to-understand manner that, whenever possible, avoids the use of highly specialized terms. The section should be divided into four subsections.

Overview

This subsection should provide a functional description of the model in sufficient detail for an analyst to understand the salient system features that were modeled.

```
1.  Introduction

2.  Functional Description of the Model

2.1  Overview

2.2  Detailed Methodology

2.3  Assumptions and Limitations
     2.3.1   Stochastic Assumptions
     2.3.2   Magnitude Limitations
     2.3.3   Critical Values

2.4  Model Flexibility

3.  Model Input and Output Data

3.1  Input Data
3.2  Output Data

4.  Model Verification and Validation

4.1  Verification Techniques
4.2  Validation Considerations

APPENDICES

     A.  Glossary

     B.  Bibliography
```

Figure 32.1
Recommended Table
of Contents for an
Analyst's Manual

Functional flow charts and other graphics should be used to enhance the narrative. Include a statement of the kind of model (i.e., discrete-event model that stimulates jobs entering a job shop at arbitrary points in time, being routed through a predetermined sequence of production centers, and being processed at the production centers) and the degree to which the model portrays the real world system. Figure 32.2 is an example of modeled system highlights. Included should be the set of model responses (output) produced by a given set of model input data. Figure 32.3 provides

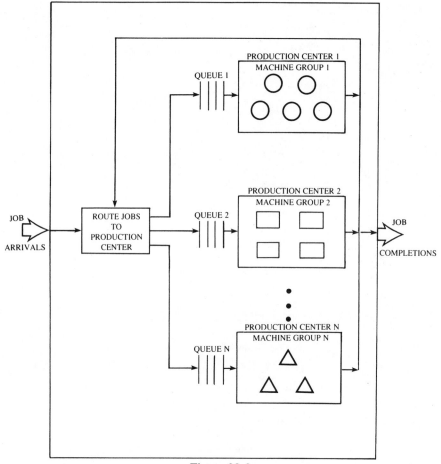

Figure 32.2
Modeled System Highlights Example

an example of the types of model input and output. For additional details on model description, the analyst should be directed to the appropriate section of the User's Manual for this model.

Detailed Methodology

This subsection should provide the functional details for analysts to understand the algorithms and equations used in the model. Well-known mathematical equations (and formulae) should be clearly identified and references should be cited for their derivation. For example, in a job shop model the queuing discipline simulated for each production center should be stated. Include the derivation for extensions of known results or for the development of new analytical techniques. Special compli-

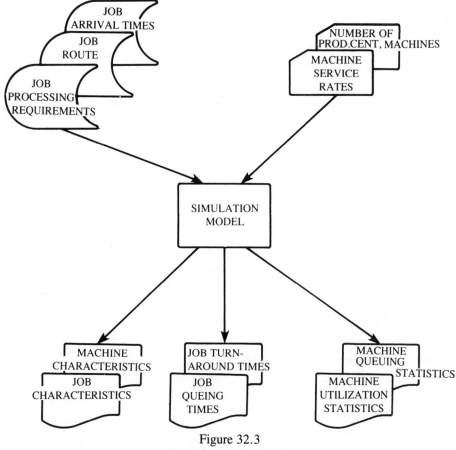

Figure 32.3
Input/Output Schematic

cating details, such as the use of precalculated data for job arrival times should be stated. The description must be detailed enough to demonstrate how the model uses the input data to calculate output information. Functional flow charts and graphs should be used to enhance the narrative descriptions of each algorithm. Figure 32.4 is an example of a model functional flow chart. This section should include a subsection for each major algorithm or set of equations.

Assumptions and Limitations
This subsection should list all model assumptions and all factors that affect or limit model output use. The following items should be included as appropriate.

Stochastic Assumptions In this subsection, itemize all stochastic assumptions that affect model output accuracy. For example, the treatment of certain random vari-

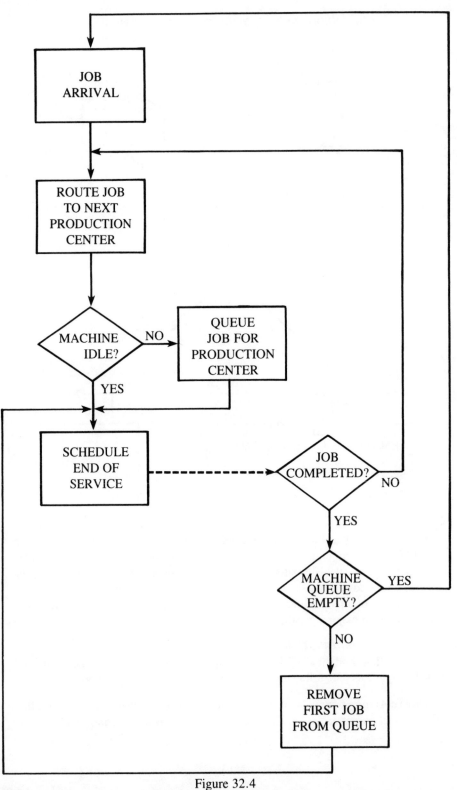

Figure 32.4
Model Functional Flow Example

ables in a simplistic manner, by using only their mean values and not sampling from a statistical distribution, should be described in this subsection. Each stochastic item should be described in a separate subsection.

Magnitude Limitations   This subsection should include all limitations on the size of the problems the model can address. For example, the current dimensions of certain arrays in a model may limit the number of activities that can be represented in that model. Each limitation should be described in a separate subsection.

Critical Values   This subsection should identify critical input data values to which model outputs are sensitive. Many elements that have a range of values will have one value that is particularly significant to the analyst. This may be a breakpoint, a minimum stock level, or a critical job rate, etc. Each critical value should be described in a separate subsection.

Model Flexibility

This subsection should address the capability of adapting the model to changing requirements, such as anticipated physical system operational changes, interacting with new or improved models, and planned periodic changes. An example of a flexible design is one that facilitates the addition of a machine failure and repair subsystem to a job shop model. Model components and procedures designed to be flexible shall be clearly identified. Factors that affect model flexibility are the familiarity of the analyst with the model, the model's size, its complexity, and its data structures. Subsections should be used as required.

Model Input and Output Data

This section should discuss the categories of input data and the accuracy of model output data. The material contained in the next two subsections will enable the analyst to assure the existence of the data necessary to execute the model and to ascertain the accuracy of the data generated by the model.

Input Data

Identify all categories of input data and any special analytical techniques required to obtain those data. If the sources of input data include output from other models, provide sufficient details to enable an analyst to assess the appropriateness of those data in solving his problem. For example, if the arrival rate of jobs is provided by a separate model of the order handling process, the analyst needs to determine that the simulated ordering process corresponds to the one existing in his job shop. Details on input data types and formats should be reserved for the User's Manual.

Output Data

This subsection should provide the analyst with a methodology for assessing the accuracy of model output data. Since the accuracy of the output values will be judged

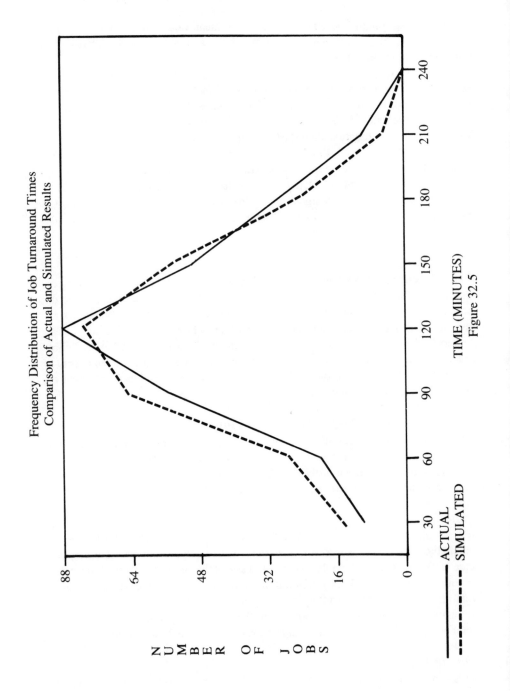

Frequency Distribution of Job Turnaround Times
Comparison of Actual and Simulated Results

TIME (MINUTES)
Figure 32.5

ACTUAL
SIMULATED

in relating to the method used to derive them, a review of the algorithms used to compute those output values may be necessary at this point. Describe in detail any corrective actions to be taken by an analyst in case of inaccurate output values, (i.e., Should the analyst contact a programmer for a program change or have a user modify the input data deck to correct the problem?). Subsections may be used as required.

Model Verification and Validation

This section of the Analyst's Manual should describe the methodology used to verify and validate the model. Model verification (sometimes referred to as software validation) is concerned with the compatibility of the model's programmed structure to the analyst's design and with model debugging. Model validation provides the analyst, and user, with the confidence that the model provides a good representation of the modeled system.

Verification Techniques

This section should provide an analyst with concise procedures by which the model was verified. Each equation included in the Analyst's Manual should be verified and cross-referenced to the Programmer's Manual for this model. Include all other verification techniques used.

Validation Considerations

This section should provide an analyst with the description of any procedures that were used to ensure that the model is an "accurate" abstraction of the real system. Any methodology used to determine how well the model represents the real system should be presented in this section. While complete confidence in a model may be impossible, a good validation procedure can increase the amount of confidence an analyst has in a model. Figure 32.5 is an example of a graph that could be used in a model validation procedure.

Appendices

Two appendices to this manual should be provided as required. Appendix A should define all terms in the Analyst's Manual not defined elsewhere in the document. Appendix B should provide a list of applicable documents and a bibliography designed for use by system analysts.

33. Model Summary

It is suggested that documentation for each model include the information outlined below, as part of the model documentation package. This information provides general information about the model and facilitates its possible use by others.

A. Basic Description

1. Name or title of Model.
2. Developer(s).
3. Agency or company.
4. Sponsor; purpose or objective of sponsor.
5. When developed?
6. Where developed?
7. Development time and cost?
8. Developed separately or as part of larger study?

B. Subject Matter of Model.

1. Major purpose of model.
2. Scope of model.
3. State basic description or theory underlying the model.
4. State specific discipline(s) required for model use, if required.
5. How does model differ from other similar models?

C. Modeling Technique.

1. Describe type of model.
2. Does model use any standard packages (e.g. linear programming, statistical, etc.)?

3. Was the model developed from another model? If yes, describe process.
4. Is its structure clear? Its variables?
5. Describe data requirements of model.
6. Does model receive any data from other models?
7. What constraints are affecting the model?

D. Computer Aspects of Model.

1. In what computer language is the model written?
2. What machine(s) is it programmed for?
3. How much time does it take to run?
4. Size of model (lines of code, core to run etc.).
5. How many parameters does model require?

E. Validation of Model.

1. Has model been validated? How?
2. Has model been documented? How well?
3. Has model been critiqued or appraised? By whom? At what point?
4. Has there been a sensitivity analysis performed on the model? By whom?
5. Can the model by used from current documentation? Has it been used?

F. Model Use.

1. If asked, how would you demonstrate the utility of the model? Have you demonstrated it?
2. With whom should one get in touch to discuss use of the model?
3. How much would it cost to transfer the model?
4. Are the model relationships or parameters easy to use for the user?
5. Have there been any papers given or written on the model? Cite references.
6. Is the output of the model special or is it designed for a general audience?

Bibliography

1. Balen, N.E. "An Air Force Guide to Contracting for Software Acquisition," Bedford, MA: Mitre Corporation, January 1976 (NTIS No. AD-A020-444).

2. Comptroller General of the United States. "Ways to Improve Management of Federally Funded Computerized Models," Washington, DC: National Bureau of Standards, Department of Commerce, General Services Administration, August 23, 1976 (LCD-75-111).

3. Connally, J.T. "Software Acquisition Management Guidebook: Regulations, Specifications and Standards," Bedford, MA: Mitre Corporation, October 1975 (NTIS No. AD-A016-401).

4. Control Analysis Corporation. "Draft Report TAC Warrior Analysts Manual," Palo Alto, CA: Control Analysis Corporation, 1978.

5. Cooley, B. "Documenting Simulation Models for Management Use," Winter Simulation Conference, Gaithersburg, MD: National Bureau of Standards, December 1977.

6. Gass, Saul I. "Computer Model Documentation," Winter Simulation Conference, Gaithersburg, MD: National Bureau of Standards, December 1978.

7. Gass, Saul I. "Computer Science and Technology: Computer Model Documentation: A Review and an Approach," Washington, DC: National Bureau of Standards, Department of Commerce, February 1979 (NBS Pub. No. 500-39).

8. Hagan, S.R., et al. "An Air Force Guide for Monitoring and Reporting Software Development Status," Bedford, MA: Mitre Corporation, September 1975 (NTIS No. AD-A016-488).

9. Jet Propulsion Laboratory. "Software Design and Documentation Language," Pasadena, CA: National Aeronautics and Space Administration, July 1977.

10. Katzan, Harry, Jr., "Systems Design and Documentation, An Introduction to the HIPO Method," New York, NY: Van Nostrand Company, 1976.

11. Mihran, G. Arthur, "Simulation Statistical Foundations and Methodology," New York, NY: Academic Press, 1973.

12. ————, "Study for Assessing Ways to Improve the Utility of Large-Scale Models," Palo Alto, CA: Control Analysis Corporation, 1977.

13. Mulford, James O. and Jarze, Lyle R. "Critique of the TAC Turner and TAC Warrior Documentation," Washington, DC: FEDSIM, April 1978.

14. Nance, Richard E. "The Feasibility of and Methodology for Developing Federal Documentation Standards for Simulation Models," Blacksburg, VA: Virginia Polytechnic Institute, June 1977.

15. Newton, Otis L. and Weatherbee, James E. "Guidelines for Documenting Computer Simulation Models," Washington, DC: FEDSIM, October 1979.

16. ————. "Update 2 to Computer Program Documentation Guidelines," Washington, DC: FEDSIM, March 1979.

17. ————. "Update 3 to Computer Program Documentation Guidelines," Washington, DC: FEDSIM, June 1979.

Bibliography

18. _____. "Update 4 to Computer Program Documentation Guidelines," Washington, DC: FEDSIM, June 1979.

19. Ramapriyan, H.K., Mulford, James O., and Jarze, Lyle R. "Evaluation of Computer Program Documentation Guidelines," Washington, DC: FEDSIM, June 1978.

20. Ramapriyan, H.K., Weatherbee, James E., and Newton, Otis L. "Update 1 to Computer Program Documentation Guidelines," Washington, DC: FEDSIM, January 1979.

21. Schoeffel, W.L. "An Air Force Guide to Software Documentation Requirements," Bedford, MA: Mitre Corporation, June 1976 (NTIS NO. AD-A027-051).